Applying Communication Theory for Professional Life

Fifth Edition

Sara Miller McCune founded SAGE Publishing in 1965 to support the dissemination of usable knowledge and educate a global community. SAGE publishes more than 1000 journals and over 600 new books each year, spanning a wide range of subject areas. Our growing selection of library products includes archives, data, case studies and video. SAGE remains majority owned by our founder and after her lifetime will become owned by a charitable trust that secures the company's continued independence.

Los Angeles | London | New Delhi | Singapore | Washington DC | Melbourne

Applying Communication Theory for Professional Life

A Practical Introduction

Fifth Edition

Marianne Dainton

La Salle University

Elaine D. Zelley

La Salle University

Los Angeles | London | New Delhi
Singapore | Washington DC | Melbourne

BRIEF CONTENTS

DETAILED CONTENTS

PREFACE

This book is designed to serve as a communication theory textbook for upper-level undergraduate and master's degree students. Although it is intended for upper-level students, we make no presumption that the students have previous knowledge or background in communication or communication theory. Rather, the text is meant to serve as a practical introduction to the topic for students pursuing (or currently working in) careers in communication-related industries.

We have found that the primary challenge of instructors teaching communication theory to career-oriented students is the abstract nature of the topic; many students have difficulty seeing the relevance of communication theory in their professional lives. Our goal for writing this book is to make communication theory tangible to students by explaining the theories in practical ways and by assisting students in seeing how theory can be used in professional life. The response to previous editions of this book has been overwhelmingly favorable, and we are grateful to have achieved our goal.

This fifth edition is a major revision of the textbook. We have eliminated the chapter on individual and social approaches to communication (although not necessarily the theories from that chapter) and included a new chapter on strategic communication theories. Also, the chapter on mediated communication is substantially revised. In total we have included eight new theories and brought back a theory from the second edition of the book. We have also modified seven of the case studies based on reviewers' feedback and the changes made in the chapter in which the case appears.

As relevant, modifications or changes to theories have been included, and new research that uses those theories has been incorporated. Popular culture references have been updated as well. Given the increasingly divergent political rhetoric in the United States, we have sought to provide appropriate and balanced political examples. Finally, thanks to feedback from the faculty who have adopted this text as well as the reviewers, we have adjusted the learning objectives for each chapter, we have added a box summarizing the main points of each theory at the beginning of the chapter, and we have included discussion questions.

As a reminder to instructors and students, this textbook is not meant to provide a comprehensive survey of all communication theory, nor is it meant to focus only on particular contexts of communication. Instead, we have selected representative theories that have clear applicability to communication practitioners. To illustrate that there are many more theories for each context, we also have included a box in each chapter highlighting some additional theories for that context. Finally, we have not limited ourselves only to theories developed in the communication discipline because we believe all theories that address communication—whether developed within the field or not—are important tools for communication professionals.

1 INTRODUCTION TO COMMUNICATION THEORY

LEARNING OBJECTIVES

After reading this chapter, you will be able to do the following:

1. Analyze a definition of communication, articulating the definition's level of observation, intentionality, and normative judgment

2. Identify the various contexts in which communication takes place

3. Describe the nature of communication competence

4. Discriminate between commonsense, working, and scholarly theories

5. Use the criteria for evaluating theory to determine the relative usefulness of a communication theory

If you Google© the phrase "communication is easy," you will find over 6 million pages, with over 600,000 video hits for the same phrase. Of course, if mastering the communication process really only required viewing a 4-minute video, we would all be maestros of getting our messages understood. Unfortunately, much of popular culture tends to minimize the challenges associated with the communication process. Yes, in the 21st century, we believe communication skill is important—you need only to peruse the content of talk shows, dating apps, advice columns, and organizational performance reviews to recognize that communication skills can make or break an individual's personal and professional life. Companies want to hire and promote people with excellent communication skills (Beaton, 2017). Divorces occur because spouses believe they "no longer communicate" (Dutihl, 2012). Communication is perceived as a magical elixir, one that can ensure a happy long-term relationship and guarantee organizational success. Yet, despite lauding communication as the *sine qua non* of contemporary success, the secret to that success is treated superficially at best in our modern information environment. Clearly, popular culture holds paradoxical views about communication: It is easy to do yet powerful in its effects, simultaneously simple and magical.

We believe the communication process is complex. "Good" communication means different things to different people in different situations. Accordingly, simply adopting a set of particular skills is not going to guarantee success. Genuinely good communicators are those who understand the underlying principles behind communication and are able to enact, appropriately and effectively, particular communication skills as the situation warrants. This book seeks to provide the foundation for those sorts of decisions. We focus on communication theories that can be applied in your personal and professional lives. Understanding these theories—including their underlying assumptions and the predictions they make—can make you a more competent communicator.

WHAT IS COMMUNICATION?

This text is concerned with communication theory, so it is important to be clear about the term **communication**. The everyday view of communication is quite different from the view of communication taken by communication scholars. In the business world, for example, a popular view is that communication is synonymous with information. Thus, the communication process is the flow of information from one person to another (Axley, 1984). Communication is viewed as simply one activity among many others, such as planning, controlling, and managing (Deetz, 1994). It is *what* we do in organizations.

Communication scholars, on the other hand, recognize communication as more than just the flow of information. In a simplified world in which a short YouTube clip could explain to viewers why communication is "easy," we could handily provide you with a one-sentence definition of the term *communication*. Based on that simple definition, we would all understand the meaning of the term, and we would all use the term in exactly the same way. However, scholars disagree as to the scope of the process, whether a source or receiver orientation should be taken, and whether message exchange needs to be successful to count as communication. Back in 1976, Dance and Larson reported 126 published definitions of the term *communication*. The variations in the definitions were profound. Table 1.1 highlights the ways the definitions varied.

In looking at the multitude of definitions of communication, Dance (1970) identified three variations. First, Dance argued that definitions varied based on the **level of observation**, which he described as the scope of what is included in the definition. For example, Dance (1967, as reported in Dance & Larson, 1976, Appendix A) defined communication as "eliciting a response through verbal symbols." This definition limits what is considered communication in two ways. First, it limits communication to only that which elicits a response. Consider an example where

TABLE 1.1 ■ Ways Definitions Vary		
Differences in Definitions	**Stance**	**Taken**
Level of observation: *Are there limitations on what counts as communication?*	**Narrow**	**Broad**
	Yes	No
Intentionality: *Do only messages sent consciously and on purpose count?*	**Source**	**Receiver**
	Yes	No
Normative judgment: *Does the message have to be successfully received to count as communication?*	**Evaluative**	**Nonevaluative**
	Yes	No

you instruct a coworker to fill out a particular form. If that coworker doesn't respond in any way, by this definition, communication hasn't occurred. The second way this definition limits communication is in saying communication is only verbal. So, if your coworker gives you the "okay" gesture when you've asked her to fill out the report, her response to your request would not be considered communication, as it was purely nonverbal. Definitions that make such limitations are said to have a relatively narrow level of observation; only specific types of message exchanges "count" as communication. These types of definitions might suggest messages that don't meet the requirements to be considered communication are *informative* rather than *communicative*.

Other definitions, however, try to be very inclusive about behaviors that might be considered communication. To illustrate, another definition identified by Dance and Larson (1976) says communication is "all of the procedures by which one mind can affect another" (Weaver, 1949, as cited in Dance & Larson, Appendix A). Notice that this definition does not give any indication of whether the mind is of a human, an animal, or even an alien (if there are such things). More importantly, it suggests *all* behavior can count as communication. Such definitions are considered to have a broad level of observation. As such, the first way to differentiate between theories is to consider what "counts" as communication.

A second distinction made by Dance (1970) is the stance the definition takes on **intentionality**. Some definitions explicitly indicate that for communication to occur, the exchange of messages has to be on purpose. For example, Miller (1966) defined communication as "those situations in which a source transmits a message to a receiver with conscious intent to affect the latter's behaviors" (as cited in Dance & Larson, 1976, Appendix A). Definitions such as this are said to take a **source orientation**. So, for example, if your boss were to yawn while you gave a presentation, this definition would not consider the yawn as communication if your boss did not yawn on purpose (i.e., if she yawned as a physiological response to tiredness rather than to suggest you were boring her).

However, other definitions take a **receiver orientation** to communication. Such definitions buy into the notion that "you cannot not communicate"; anything you say or do is potentially communicative, regardless of whether you intended to send a message or not (see Watzlawick et al., 1967). For example, Ruesch and Bateson (1961, as cited in Dance & Larson, 1976, Appendix A) say that "communication does not refer to verbal, explicit, and intentional transmission of messages alone. . . . The concept of communication would include all those processes by which people influence one another." In this case, if you (as the receiver) were to interpret your boss's yawn as a message of boredom, it should be considered communication, regardless of whether the boss intended to send that message or not.

The final way Dance (1970) argues that definitions of communication vary is **normative judgment**, which is a focus on whether the definition requires an indication of success or accuracy. Some definitions would suggest that even if people misunderstand each other, communication has still occurred. Berelson and Steiner (1964), for example, say communication is "the transmission of information, ideas, emotions, skills, etc., by the use of—symbols—words, pictures, figures, graphs, etc. It is the act or process of transmission that is called communication" (as cited in Dance & Larson, 1976, Appendix A). In this case, it is the transmission that is important, not the understanding. So, if a student has no idea what a teacher is talking about, by this definition, communication has still occurred, it just may not have been very effective communication. Definitions like this are said to be nonevaluative.

Other definitions limit communication to only those situations where the receiver and the source share the same understanding after the communicative effort. These definitions, identified as being evaluative, require shared meaning in order to be considered communication; unsuccessful messages are not considered to be communication. To illustrate, Gode (1959, as cited in Dance & Larson, 1976, Appendix A) defines communication as "a process that makes common to two or several what was the monopoly of one or some." This definition suggests that if the message has not resulted in a common understanding, communication has not occurred. In the example of student–teacher interaction described earlier, if the student doesn't understand the teacher, then by this definition the teacher has not communicated. They may have lectured, cajoled, or presented, but they have not communicated.

By now you understand some of the complexities of the nature of communication. Throughout the book, different theorists likely use different definitions of communication. Sometimes these variations in definition will be obvious, sometimes they will be less so. For example, the systems interactional perspective (see Chapter 8) spends a great deal of time articulating the nature of communication. In so doing, it becomes clear that this theory takes a broad level of observation, a receiver orientation, and is nonevaluative. Alternatively, Aristotle's theory of rhetoric (Chapter 6) focuses specifically on persuasive speaking and provides techniques for persuasion. As such, this theory has a narrow level of observation (focusing primarily on oral, persuasive communication), the focus is on intentional acts (a source orientation), and its focus on ethical versus unethical communication makes it evaluative in nature.

CONTEXTS OF COMMUNICATION

Although we hesitate to provide a single definition of communication, we can identify some specific contexts of communication. In fact, we have organized this book around these specific contexts. The first context that requires consideration is the cognitive context, by which we mean the influence our thoughts have on the way we communicate. Second is the interpersonal context, which refers to the interactions between two individuals, who most often have a relationship with each other. Third is the intercultural context, which focuses on interpersonal communication when two people are from different cultures. The fourth context is not specifically focused on a setting for communication but on a particular type of communication: the persuasive context. Readers should know that persuasion actually takes place in a variety of settings, ranging from inside one person's mind to the mass media. In fact, many communication professions focus on persuasion, which is why the fifth context is aligned with strategic communications: the creation of messages to achieve organizational goals. The sixth and seventh contexts also are closely aligned with the world of work: the group context and the organizational context. Then, the eighth context is the mediated context, which is concerned with how technology influences our interpersonal, group, and organizational communication. Finally, the ninth and final context is the mass communication context, which focuses on the influence of mass-mediated messages. Table 1.2 provides an overview of these contexts and the theories covered in this text that are associated with each context.

TABLE 1.2 ■ Contexts of Communication	
Context	**Theories**
Cognitive	<ul><li>Message Design Logics</li><li>Uncertainty Reduction Theory</li><li>Expectancy Violations Theory</li><li>Planning Theory</li></ul>
Interpersonal	<ul><li>Politeness Theory</li><li>Social Exchange Theory</li><li>Dialectical Perspective</li><li>Privacy Management Theory</li></ul>
Intercultural	<ul><li>Hofstede's cultural dimensions</li><li>Communication accommodation theory</li><li>Co-Cultural Theory</li><li>Social Role Theory of Gender</li></ul>
Persuasion	<ul><li>Aristotle's Theory of Rhetoric</li><li>Narrative Paradigm</li><li>Social Judgment Theory</li><li>Elaboration Likelihood Model</li></ul>
Strategic Communication	<ul><li>Theory of Planned Behavior</li><li>Extended Parallel Processing Theory</li><li>Inoculation Theory</li><li>Situational Crisis Communication Theory</li></ul>
Group	<ul><li>Systems Interactional Perspective</li><li>Functional Group Decision-making</li><li>Groupthink</li><li>Symbolic Convergence Theory</li></ul>
Organizational	<ul><li>Organizational Culture</li><li>Organizational Assimilation</li><li>Organizational Identification and Control</li><li>Organizing Theory</li></ul>

(Continued)

TABLE 1.2 ■ Contexts of Communication (continued)	
Context	**Theories**
Mediated	• Channel Expansion Theory • Social Information Processing Theory • Uses and Gratifications Theory • Spiral of Silence
Mass Communication	• Agenda-Setting Theory • Cultivation Theory • Social Cognitive Theory • Encoding/Decoding Theory

COMMUNICATION COMPETENCE

Because we believe one of the goals of studying communication theory is to make you a better communicator, we should articulate more clearly the nature of **communication competence**. Research indicates that communication competence is most often understood as achieving a successful balance between effectiveness and appropriateness (Spitzberg & Cupach, 1989). *Effectiveness* is the extent to which you achieve your goals in an interaction. Consider the many different goals an individual might have in their personal and professional lives. Personally, you might have the goal of initiating a new relationship, or persuading your boss to give you a raise. Professionally, you might have a goal of increasing social media engagement with your company or boosting rates of vaccinations among a target demographic. If you achieve these goals, you have been effective. *Appropriateness* refers to fulfilling social expectations for a particular situation. Did you assertively ask for the raise, or was it a meek inquiry? Were you ethical in your campaign to boost vaccinations, or did you engage in some less-than-above-board behavior? Many times, a person is effective without being appropriate; consider a job applicant who lies on a resume to get a job for which they are unqualified. That person might be very effective in getting the job, but is such deceit appropriate? On the other hand, many times people are appropriate to the point of failing to achieve their goals. For example, a person who doesn't wish to take on an additional task at work but says nothing because they fear causing conflict might be sacrificing effectiveness for appropriateness. The key is that when faced with communicative decisions, the competent communicator considers how to be both effective *and* appropriate. We believe the theories described in this book will help you achieve your communication goals by providing an indication of both what should be done as well as how you should do it.

THE NATURE OF THEORY

The term **theory** is often intimidating to students. We hope by the time you finish reading this book you will find working with theory to be less daunting than you might have expected. The reality is that you have been working with theories of communication all of your life, even if they haven't been labelled as such. Theories simply provide an abstract understanding of the communication process (Miller, 2002). As an abstract understanding, they move beyond describing a single event by providing a means by which all such events can be understood. To illustrate, a theory of customer service can help you understand the poor customer service you received from your cable company this morning. Likewise, the same theory can also help you understand a good customer service encounter you had last week at a favorite restaurant. In a professional context, the theory can assist your organization in training and developing customer service personnel.

At their most basic level, theories provide us with a lens by which to view the world. Think of theories as a pair of glasses. Corrective lenses allow wearers to observe more clearly, but they also affect vision in unforeseen ways. For example, they can limit the span of what you see, especially when you try to look peripherally outside the range of the frames. Similarly, lenses can also distort the things you see, making objects appear larger or smaller than they really are. You can also try on lots of pairs of glasses until you finally pick a pair that works best for your lifestyle. Theories operate in a similar fashion. A theory can illuminate an aspect of your communication so you understand the process much more clearly; theory also can hide things from your understanding or distort the relative importance of things.

We consider a **communication theory** to be any systematic summary about the nature of the communication process. Certainly, theories can do more than summarize. Other functions of theories are to focus attention on particular concepts, clarify observations, predict communication behavior, and generate personal and social change (Littlejohn, 1989). We do not believe, however, that all of these functions are necessary for a systematic summary of communication processes to be considered a theory.

Although similar to at least two other terms, we want to be careful to differentiate theories from other abstract notions. First, a **concept** refers to an agreed-upon aspect of reality. For example, *time* is a concept, as is *love*, the color *orange*, and a *bitter* taste. All of these notions are abstract, meaning they can be applied to a variety of individual experiences or objects and can be understood in different ways. That is, you might love your cat in a different way than you love your mother; you might think time drags when in a class you don't much like but that it speeds up over the weekend; and you might hate the color orange and love the bitterness of certain foods. However, in and of themselves these concepts are not theories; they represent an effort to define or classify something, but they do not provide insights into how or why we experience them in a particular way. Typically, theories provide a way to predict or understand one or more concepts. So, a definition of communication described earlier is a concept, but how that definition is used to explain the communication process is a theory.

A second term you might confuse with theory is a **model**. Part of the confusion you might experience is because the term *model* is used in at least four ways (Gabrenya, 2003; Goldfarb & Ratner, 2008): as a synonym to the term *theory*, as a precursor to a theory (a model is developed and eventually becomes a theory), as a physical representation of a theory (i.e., a diagram such as the one that appears for expectancy violations theory in Chapter 3), or as a specific—often mathematical—application of predication (e.g., a researcher might develop a mathematical model to predict which job categories are going to be in high demand in upcoming years). Because of these varying ways of understanding a model, we believe the term *theory* is preferable when talking about systematic summaries of the communication process.

Of central interest is the importance of theory for people in communication, business, and other professions. Our definition of theory suggests that any time you say a communication strategy *usually* works this way at your workplace, or that a specific approach is *generally* effective with your boss, or that certain types of communication are *typical* for particular media organizations, you are in essence providing a theoretical explanation. Most of us make these types of summary statements on a regular basis. The difference between this sort of theorizing and the theories provided in this book centers on the term *systematic* in the definition. Table 1.3 presents an overview of three types of theory.

The first summary statements in the table describe what is known as **commonsense theory**, or theory-in-use. This type of theory is often created by an individual's own personal experiences or developed from helpful hints passed on from family members, friends, or colleagues. Commonsense theories are useful because they are often the basis for our decisions about how to communicate. Sometimes, however, our common sense backfires. For example, think about common knowledge regarding deception. Most people believe that liars don't look the person they are deceiving in the eyes, yet research indicates this is not the case (DePaulo et al., 1985). Let's face it: If we engage in deception, we will work very hard at maintaining eye contact simply *because* we believe liars don't make eye contact! In this case, commonsense theory is not supported by research into the phenomenon.

TABLE 1.3 ■ Three Types of Theory	
Type of Theory	**Example**
Commonsense theory	Never date someone you work with—it will always end badly.
	The squeaky wheel gets the grease.
	The more incompetent you are, the higher you get promoted.
Working theory	Audience analysis should be done prior to presenting a speech.
	To get a press release published, it should be newsworthy and written in journalistic style.
Scholarly theory	Effects of violations of expectations depend on the reward value of the violator (expectancy violations theory).
	The media do not tell us what to think but what to think about (agenda-setting theory).

A second type of theory is known as **working theory**. These are generalizations made in particular professions about the best techniques for doing something. Journalists work using the "inverted pyramid" of story construction (most important information to least important information). Filmmakers operate using specific camera shots to evoke particular emotions in the audience, so close-ups are used when a filmmaker wants the audience to place particular emphasis on the object in the shot. Giannetti (1982), for example, describes a scene in Hitchcock's *Notorious* in which the heroine realizes she is being poisoned by her coffee, and the audience "sees" this realization through a close-up of the coffee cup. Working theories are more systematic than commonsense theories because they represent agreed-on ways of doing things for a particular profession. In fact, these working theories may very well be based on scholarly theories. However, working theories more closely represent guidelines for behavior rather than systematic representations. These types of theories are typically taught in content-specific courses (such as public relations, media production, or public speaking).

The type of theory we focus on in this book is known as **scholarly theory**. Students often assume (incorrectly!) that because a theory is labeled as *scholarly* it is not useful for people in business and the professions. Instead, the term *scholarly* indicates that the theory has undergone systematic research. Accordingly, scholarly theories provide more thorough, accurate, and abstract explanations for communication than do commonsense or working theories. The downside is that scholarly theories are typically more complex and difficult to understand than commonsense or working theories. If you are genuinely committed to improving your understanding of the communication process, however, scholarly theory will provide a strong foundation for doing so.

EVALUATING THEORY

Earlier we suggested that all theories have strengths and weaknesses; they reveal certain aspects of reality and conceal others. An important task students and scholars face is to evaluate the theories available to them. We are not talking about evaluation in terms of "good" versus "bad" but evaluating the *usefulness* of the theory. Each of you is likely to find some of the theories presented in this text more useful than others. Such a determination is likely due at least in part to your own background and experiences, as well as your profession. We would like to challenge you to broaden your scope and consider not just the usefulness of each theory to you personally but the usefulness of the theory for people's personal and professional lives in general.

A number of published standards can be used to evaluate theories (e.g., Griffin et al., 2015; West & Turner, 2017). All are appropriate and effective tools for comparing the relative usefulness of a given theory. Because this text is geared toward working professionals, however (or those who wish to soon be working in the profession of their choice), we believe the following five criteria outlined in Table 1.4 best capture the way to assess the relative usefulness of communication theories in the communication, business, and related professions. Note that we are talking about the *relative* usefulness of the theory. We are not talking about either/or, good or bad, weak, or strong. Instead, we hope you look at these distinctions as continua that range from very useful at one end to not particularly useful at the other end.

TABLE 1.4 ■ Criteria for Evaluating Theory	
Area of Evaluation	**What to Look For**
Accuracy	Has research supported that the theory works the way it says it does?
Practicality	Have real-world applications been found for the theory?
Succinctness	Has the theory been formulated with the appropriate number (fewest possible) of concepts or steps?
Consistency	Does the theory demonstrate coherence within its own premises and with other theories?
Acuity	To what extent does the theory make clear an otherwise complex experience?

The first area of focus is **accuracy**. Simply put, the best theories correctly summarize the way communication actually works. Recall, however, that we are referring to scholarly theories. As such, we do not mean accuracy in terms of whether the theory accurately reflects your own personal experience (although we would hope that it does!). Instead, when we use the term *accuracy*, we are suggesting that systematic research supports the explanations provided by the theory. Thus, in assessing this quality, you should look at research studies that have used the theory to see whether the research supports or fails to support it.

A second way to evaluate theories is **practicality**. The best theories can be used to address real-world communication problems; in fact, Lewin (1951) said, "There is nothing so practical as a good theory" (p. 169). Clearly, some profound theories have changed the way we understand the world even though they aren't actually *used* by most people on a daily basis (Einstein's theory of relativity or Darwin's theory of evolution, for example). In terms of communication theories, however, theories that are accurate but can't be used in everyday life are not as good as theories that have great practical utility. For example, a theory that can help a person make better communicative decisions in their interactions with coworkers is better than a theory so abstract that it cannot be used by an individual in daily communication. Thus, a theory with more applications is better than a theory without practical uses. In assessing this criterion, you should look not only for how the theory has been used in the research literature but also whether the theory has made the leap to professional practice.

Succinctness is the third way to evaluate a good business or professional communication theory. *Succinctness* refers to whether or not a theory's explanation or description is sufficiently concise. Importantly, succinctness does not mean the theory is necessarily easy to understand or has only a few short steps; because the world is complex, theories trying to explain it are often fairly complex as well. Instead, what we mean by succinctness is whether the theory is formulated using as few steps as possible. The "three bears" analogy works here. Theories that have extra steps or include variables that don't help us understand real-world experiences would be considered overly complex. Theories that do not have enough steps, that don't delve beneath the surface, or that don't have enough variables to understand real-world problems are too simple. Theories that include no more and no less than necessary to understand a phenomenon thoroughly are considered just right; they are appropriately succinct. The best way to think of succinctness is to compare how much of the communication situation is explained by the theory in proportion to how many concepts are being used to explain it. The larger the situation and the smaller the number of necessary steps or concepts, the more succinct the theory.

The fourth way to evaluate a theory is to consider its **consistency**. The most useful theories have both internal and external consistency. By **internal consistency**, we mean the ideas of the theory are logically built on one another. A theory that proposes at one point that cooperation among team members guarantees success and at a different point proposes that competition is more effective than cooperation has a logical flaw. Similarly, theories that "skip" steps do not have much internal consistency. A theory predicting that age is related to the experience of jealousy and that one's expression of jealousy affects the future of the relationship, but then fails to tell us how the experience of jealousy is related to the expression of jealousy, has a logical gap. As such, it does not have strong internal consistency.

External consistency, on the other hand, refers to the theory's coherence with other widely held theories. If we presume that widely held theories are true, then the theory under evaluation that disagrees with those believed supported theories also presents a logical problem. As such, the notion of consistency, whether internal or external, is concerned with the logic of the theory. The most useful theories are those that have a strong logical structure.

The final area for evaluation is **acuity**. *Acuity* refers to the ability of a theory to provide insight into an otherwise intricate issue. Earlier we said theories evaluated as "succinct" are not necessarily easy to understand because the real world is often complicated. A theory that explains an intricate problem, however, is of greater value than a theory that explains something less complex. Think of acuity as the "wow" factor. If, after understanding the theory, you think "wow, I never considered that!" the theory has acuity. If, on the other hand, you think "no duh," the theory does not demonstrate acuity. To illustrate, a theory that explains a complex problem, such as how organizational cultures can influence employee retention, is a more useful theory than a theory that explains a relatively straightforward problem, such as how to gain attention in a speech. Those theories that explain difficult problems show acuity; those that focus on fairly obvious problems demonstrate superficiality.

CHAPTER SUMMARY

In this chapter, we discussed the popular perception of communication, which suggests that the communication process is paradoxically simple yet powerful. We identified three ways our understanding of communication can vary: the level of observation (what is included or not included in the definition), the role of intentionality (whether speaker intent is required), and normative judgment (whether success is required in order for an interaction to be considered communication). We then turned our attention to communication competence, indicating that competent communicators are those who can balance effectiveness and appropriateness. Next, we discussed the nature of theory. We differentiated between concepts, models, and theories. We also discussed the distinctions between commonsense theories, working theories, and scholarly theories. Finally, we provided a means by which scholarly theories of communication can be evaluated, namely accuracy, practicality, succinctness, consistency, and acuity.

DISCUSSION QUESTIONS

1.   Why do you think people assume that "communication is easy?" Conversely, why do you think people put so much focus on communication for personal and professional success? How do you make sense of this paradox?

2.   Think about your own view of communication. Do you tend to take a broad or narrow level of observation? Do you tend to focus more on the source's intentions or the receiver's interpretations? Do you think that there must be some indicator of success for message exchange to be considered communication?

3.   Review the contexts for communication we have listed. Do you think communication in some contexts is easier/more complex than other communication contexts? Why?

4.   We defined communication competence as both effectiveness and appropriateness. Can you come up with any situations in which you don't need one or the other? That is, can you ever be a competent communicator with just effectiveness and not appropriateness, or vice versa?

5.   We suggested that people use theories all of the time, they are just not necessarily scholarly theories. Come up with some examples of commonsense or working theories that you think people use.

KEY TERMS

Accuracy (p. 10)

Acuity (p. 11)

Commonsense theory (p. 8)

Communication (p. 2)

Communication competence (p. 6)

Communication theory (p. 7)

Concept (p. 7)

Consistency (p. 11)

External consistency (p. 11)

Intentionality (p. 3)

Internal consistency (p. 11)

Level of observation (p. 2)

Model (p. 8)

Normative judgment (p. 3)

Practicality (p. 10)

Receiver orientation (p. 3)

Scholarly theory (p. 9)

Source orientation (p. 3)

Succinctness (p. 10)

Theory (p. 7)

Working theory (p. 9)

CASE STUDY 1
Attribution Theory

Attribution theory was developed by social psychologists to explain how we answer the question "why?" as regards our own and other's behavior. According to attribution theorists, human beings often work like detectives, continually trying to make sense of what inspired various events, mannerisms, and behavior. Just as a crime scene investigator pieces together clues in an effort to determine a suspect's motive, the theory says that you, too, go through life picking up clues and making judgments about what you believe influenced your own and other's communication. These judgments and conclusions provide reasons for behavior that are called attributions.

The foundations of the theory can be traced to 1958, when Heider focused his attention on the process of drawing inferences—the assumptions individuals make regarding the causes of behavior as well as the judgments made about who is responsible for that behavior. Specifically, Heider proposed that individuals try to determine whether a behavior in question was caused by dispositional or situational factors. Dispositional factors refer to internal or personal features, such as one's personality, character, or biological traits. These factors are relatively stable and unique to each individual. Conversely, situational factors refer to external dynamics that are relatively uncontrollable and are determined by the environment or circumstance at hand, such as the weather, noise, or even traffic. Heider (1958) created a clear set of propositions to explain this process (Spitzberg & Manusov, 2015).

Attribution theory has been widely studied, with thousands of studies focused on establishing the validity of its claims. Although originally designed to be a universal theory of human behavior, results of these studies indicate that the attribution process is not as global as originally conceived; attribution seems to only take place in certain contexts, and in certain cultures (Spitzberg & Manusov, 2015). Moreover, despite its strong propositional logic, scholars have criticized the theory for failing to articulate the reasons behind the motivations; it's great to know what happens once the attribution process has started, but what prompts the attribution process itself (Malle, 2011)? Nevertheless, the theory has served as a foundation to understand numerous communication experiences, including crisis communication (Coombs, 2007), effective customer service (Leung et al., 2020), and coworker satisfaction (Jia et al., 2021). Because "most of the dimensions and principles of attribution theories are recognizable immediately in everyday interactions," the theory holds great promise for understanding the communication process (Spitzberg & Manusov, 2015, p. 44).

Questions for Consideration

1. Attribution theory does not specifically define communication. However, review the description of the theory carefully. What do you think might be the level of observation for the theory's view of communication? Do you think it takes a source orientation or a receiver orientation? What about normative judgment?

2. Provide an example for how attribution theory can be used for each communication context. Are there any contexts that you think attribution theory would not work? Why?

3. Consider communication competence. How might the attributions that someone makes provide evidence of effectiveness and appropriateness?

4. What are the concepts associated with attribution theory? Why are these concepts rather than theories or models?

5. Use the five criteria for evaluating a theory to evaluate attribution theory. What conclusions can you draw about how useful the theory is for understanding communication?

2 THEORY DEVELOPMENT

In Chapter 1, we defined theory as "any systematic summary about the nature of the communication process." We further introduced the topic of scholarly theory, which is different from other forms of theory because it has been carefully researched. The focus of this chapter is on the methods by which scholarly theories are created, developed, and modified. Our first concern is the nature of how theory and research are related.

THEORY–RESEARCH LINK

As much as we would like to provide a simple answer to how theory and research are linked, we can't easily articulate the connection because of debate about the theory–research relationship akin to the classic question, "Which came first, the chicken or the egg?" In this case, scholars disagree as to what starts the process: theory or research.

Some scholars argue that research comes before theory. This approach is known as **inductive theory**. Scholars using inductive theory, also known as grounded theory, believe the best theories emerge from the results of systematic study (Glaser & Strauss, 1967). That is, these scholars observe or examine a particular topic, and, based on patterns that emerge over time, they develop a theory; the research comes *before* the theory. If someone wanted to develop a theory about how management style affects employee performance, then that person would study management style and employee performance in great depth before proposing a theory. Preliminary theories may be proposed, but the data continue to be collected and analyzed until adding new data brings little to the researcher's understanding of the phenomenon or situation.

On the other hand, some scholars believe in **deductive theory**. Deductive theory is generally associated with the scientific method (Reynolds, 1971). The deductive approach requires that a hypothesis, or working theory, be developed before any research is conducted. Once the theory has been developed, the theorist then collects data to test or refine the theory (i.e., to support or reject the hypothesis). What follows is a constant set of adjustments to the theory with additional research conducted until evidence in support of the theory is overwhelming. The resulting theory is known as a law (Reynolds, 1971). In short, deductive theory development starts with the theory and then looks at data. As an example, a researcher might start with the idea that supportive management styles lead to increased employee performances. The researcher would then seek to confirm his or her theory by collecting data about those variables.

As indicated earlier, these two approaches represent different starting points to what is in essence a "chicken or the egg" argument. But neither approach advocates a single cycle of theorizing or research. Instead, both approaches suggest theories are dynamic—they are modified as the data suggest, and data are reviewed to adjust the theory. Consider the model depicted in Figure 2.1. We believe this is the most accurate illustration of the link between theory and research. In this model, the starting points are different, but the reality of a repetitive loop between theory and research is identified.

FIGURE 2.1 ■ The Theory–Research Link

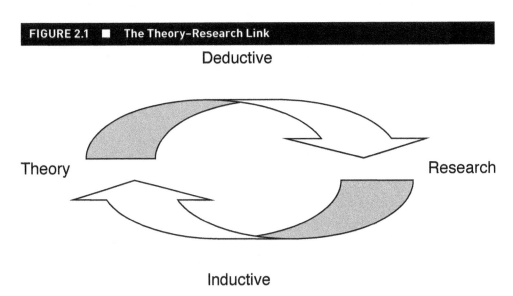

WHAT IS RESEARCH?

Because research is a fundamental part of theory development, we must turn our attention to the question of what counts as research. Frey et al. (2002) described research as "disciplined inquiry that involves studying something in a planned manner and reporting it so that other inquirers can potentially replicate the process if they choose" (p. 13). Accordingly, we do not mean informal types of research, such as reflections on personal experience, off-the-cuff interviews with acquaintances, or casual viewing of communication media. When we refer to research, we mean the methodical gathering of data as well as the careful reporting of the results of the data analysis.

Note that *how* the research is reported differentiates two categories of research. **Primary research** is reported by the person who conducted it. It is typically published in peer-reviewed academic journals. **Secondary research** is reported by someone other than the person who conducted it. This is research reported in newspapers, popular or trade magazines, handbooks and textbooks, and the Internet. Certainly, there is value to the dissemination of research through these media. Textbooks, for example, can summarize hundreds of pages of research in a compact and understandable fashion. The Internet can reach billions of people. Trade magazines can pinpoint the readers who may benefit most from the results of the research. Regardless of whether the source is popular or academic, however, primary research is typically valued more than secondary research as a source of information. With secondary research, readers risk the chance that the writers have misunderstood or inadvertently distorted the results of the research. Similar to the childhood game of "whisper down the lane," the message typically becomes more vague and less accurate as it gets passed from person to person—or website to website.

RESEARCH METHODS IN COMMUNICATION

Every 60 seconds over 15 million texts are sent, 210 million emails are sent, almost 700,000 videos are viewed on TikTok, and there are over 4 million Google© searches (Chaffey, 2021). Those figures are for *every* minute of *every* day. According to the American Academy of Child and Adolescent Psychiatry (2020), teens spent approximately 9 hours a day looking at a screen *before* the COVID-19 pandemic. During the pandemic, this number likely rose significantly. These are astonishing numbers. It is clear that we are inundated with information. But what value does this information have? The proliferation of verifiably fake news (i.e., flagrant untruths), as well as hyperpartisan stories intended to pander to readers' preexisting beliefs, makes information literacy more important than ever. Even if you never conduct a research study in your life, knowing which information has been methodically collected and reported accurately will undoubtedly help you make more informed personal and professional decisions. This section focuses on the four research methods commonly used in the development of scholarly communication theory. When reading about these methods, pay particular attention to the types of information revealed and concealed by each method. This approach will allow you to be a better consumer of research.

Experiments

When people think of experiments, they often have flashbacks to high school chemistry classes. People are often surprised that communication scholars also use experiments, even though there isn't a Bunsen burner or beaker in sight. What makes something an experiment has nothing to do with the specific equipment or instruments involved; rather, experimentation is ultimately concerned with control. It is important to emphasize that an **experiment** is the *only* research method that allows researchers to conclude that one thing causes another. For example, if you are interested in determining whether friendly customer service causes greater customer satisfaction, whether advertisers' use of bright colors produces higher sales, or whether sexuality in film leads to a more promiscuous society, the only way to determine these things is through experimental research.

Experimental research allows researchers to determine potential causes and effects because experiments are so controlled. In experimental research, the researcher is concerned with two variables. A **variable** is simply any concept that has two or more values (Frey et al., 2002). Sex is a variable because we have men and women. Note that just looking at maleness is not a variable because there is only one value associated with it; it doesn't *vary*, so it isn't a *variable*. Masculinity is considered a variable, however, because you can be highly masculine, moderately masculine, nonmasculine, and so on.

Returning to our discussion of experimental research, then, the research is concerned with two variables. One of the variables is the presumed cause. This is known as the **independent variable**. The other is the presumed effect. This is known as the **dependent variable**. If you are interested in knowing whether bright colors in advertisements cause increased sales, your independent variable is the color (bright versus dull), and the dependent variable is the amount of sales dollars (more, the same, or less). The way the researcher determines causality is by carefully controlling the study participants' exposure to the independent variable. This control is known as **manipulation**, a term that commonly conjures negative connotations but in the research world is imperative to establishing causality. In the study of advertisements just described, the researcher would expose some people to an advertisement that used bright colors and other people to an advertisement that used dull colors, and then they would observe the effects on sales based on these manipulations.

Experiments take place in two settings. A **laboratory experiment** takes place in a controlled setting so the researcher might better control efforts at manipulation. In the communication field, laboratories often simulate living rooms or conference rooms. Typically, however, they have two-way mirrors and cameras mounted on the walls to record what happens. For example, John Gottman has a mini "apartment" at the University of Washington. He has married couples "move in" to the apartment during the course of a weekend, and he observes all of their interaction during that weekend.

Some experiments don't take place in the laboratory but in participants' natural surroundings; these are called **field experiments**. These experiments often take place in public places, such as shopping malls, libraries, or schools, but they might take place in private areas as well. In all cases, participants must agree to be a part of the experiment to comply with ethical standards set by educational and research institutions.

Surveys

The most common means of studying communication is through the use of surveys. Market research, audience analysis, and organizational audits all make use of surveys. Unlike experiments, the use of surveys does not allow researchers to claim one thing causes another. The strength of **survey research** is that it is the *only* way to find out how someone thinks, feels, or intends to behave. In other words, surveys capture people's perception. If you want to know what people think about your organization, how they feel about a social issue, or whether they intend to buy a product after viewing an advertising spot you created, you need to conduct a survey.

In general, there are two types of survey research. An **interview** asks participants to respond orally. It might take place face-to-face or over the phone. One special type of interview is a **focus group**, which is when the interviewer (called a facilitator) leads a small group of people in a discussion about a specific product or program (Frey et al., 2002). A **questionnaire** asks participants to respond in writing. It can be distributed by mail, via the Internet, or administered with the researcher present. Some research is more suited for interviews than questionnaires. Interviews allow the researcher to ask more complex questions because they can clarify misunderstandings through probing questions. Questionnaires, however, might be more appropriate for the collection of sensitive information because they provide more anonymity to the respondent (Salant & Dillman, 1994).

The key concepts associated with any type of survey research are questioning and sampling. First, the purpose of a survey is quite simple: to ask questions of a group of people to understand their thoughts, feelings, and behaviors. Questions might take two forms. **Open-ended questions** allow respondents to answer in their own words, giving as much (or as little) information as they would like. For example, a market researcher might ask study participants to describe what they like about a particular product. Or an interviewer might ask someone to respond to a hypothetical situation. **Closed-ended questions** require respondents to use set answers. In this case, a market researcher might say something like "Respond to the following statement: Product X is a useful product. Would you say you strongly agree, agree, neither agree nor disagree, disagree, or strongly disagree?" Neither method is better than the other; the two types of questions simply provide different kinds of data that are analyzed using different means.

The second key concept associated with survey research is **sampling**. Researchers are typically concerned with large groups of people when they conduct surveys. These groups are known as a **population**, which means all people who possess a particular characteristic (Frey et al., 2002). For example, marketing firms want to study all possible consumers of a product. Newspaper publishers want to gather information from all readers. Pharmaceutical industries want to study everyone with a particular ailment. The size of these groups makes it difficult to study everyone of interest. Even if every member of the population could be identified, which isn't always the case, studying all of them can be extremely expensive.

Instead, survey researchers study a sample, or a small number of people in the population of interest. According to a basic premise in statistics known as the law of large numbers (LLN), if a sample is well selected and of sufficient size, the survey's results are likely also to hold true for the entire group. A **random sample**, in which every member of the target group has an equal chance of being selected, is better than a **nonrandom sample**, such as volunteers, a convenience sample (college students), or a purposive sample (people who meet a particular requirement, such as age, sex, or race). Essentially, a random sample of consumers is more likely to give representative information about brand preferences than a convenience sample, such as stopping people at the mall on a particular day to answer a few questions.

Textual Analysis

The third method used frequently by communication scholars is textual analysis. A text is any written or recorded message (Frey et al., 2002). Comments on a social media post, a transcript of a medical encounter, and an employee newsletter can all be considered texts. **Textual analysis** is used to uncover the content, nature, or structure of messages. It can also be used to evaluate messages, focusing on their strengths, weaknesses, effectiveness, or even ethicality. So textual analysis can be used to study the amount of violence on television, how power dynamics play out during doctor–patient intake evaluations, or how an organization responds to negative social media posts about their products or services.

There are three distinct forms textual analyses take in the communication discipline. **Rhetorical criticism** refers to "a systematic method for describing, analyzing, interpreting, and evaluating the persuasive force of messages" (Frey et al., 2002, p. 229). There are numerous types of rhetorical criticism, including historical criticism (how history shapes messages), genre criticism (evaluating particular types of messages, such as political speeches or corporate image restoration practices), and feminist criticism (how beliefs about gender are produced and reproduced in messages).

Content analysis seeks to identify, classify, and analyze the occurrence of particular types of messages (Frey et al., 2002). It was developed primarily to study mass-mediated messages, although it is also used in numerous other areas of the discipline. For example, public relations professionals often seek to assess the type of coverage given to a client. Typically, content analysis involves four steps: the selection of a particular text (e.g., newspaper articles), the development of content categories (e.g., "favorable organizational coverage," "neutral organizational coverage," "negative organizational coverage"), placing the content into categories, and an analysis of the results. In our example, the results of this study would be able to identify whether a particular newspaper has a pronounced slant when covering the organization. One modern derivation of this type of research is **text mining**, also known as **data mining**. Data mining is the use of advanced "data analysis tools to discover previously unknown, valid patterns and relationships in large data sets" (Seifert, 2007, p. 2). Given the immense amount of information available on the Internet, organizations can use complex programs to sift through enormous amounts of data to uncover the frequency and uses of particular words or ideas. In addition, communication professionals also tend to use **data analytics**, which are "all activities related to gathering relevant social media data, analyzing the gathered data, and disseminating findings as appropriate to support business activities such as intelligence gathering, insight generation, sense making, problem recognition/opportunity detection, problem solution/opportunity exploitation, and/or decision making" (Holsapple et al., 2014, p. 4).

The third type of textual analysis typically conducted by communication scholars is **interaction analysis** (also known as **conversation analysis**). These approaches typically focus on interpersonal or group communication interactions that have been recorded, with a specific emphasis on the nature or structure of interaction. The strength of this type of research is that it captures the natural give-and-take that is part of most communication experiences. The weakness of rhetorical criticism, content analysis, and interaction analysis is that *actual* effects on the audience can't be determined solely by focusing on texts.

Ethnography

Ethnography is the final research method used by scholars of communication. First used by anthropologists, **ethnography** typically involves the researcher immersing himself or herself into a particular culture or context to understand communication rules and meanings for that culture or context. For example, an ethnographer might study an organizational culture, such as Johnson & Johnson's corporate culture, or a particular context, such as communication in hospital emergency rooms. The key to this type of research is that it is naturalistic and emergent, which means it must take place in the natural environment for the group under study and the particular methods used adjusted on the basis of what is occurring in that environment.

Typically, those conducting ethnographies need to decide on the role they will play in the research. A **complete participant** is fully involved in the social setting, and the participants do not know the researcher is studying them (Frey et al., 2002). This approach, of course, requires the researcher to know enough about the environment to be able to fit in. Moreover, there are numerous ethical hurdles the researcher must overcome. Combined, these two challenges prevent much research from being conducted in this fashion. Instead, **participant–observer** roles are more frequently chosen. In this case, the researcher becomes fully involved with the culture or context, but they have admitted their research agenda before entering the environment. In this way, knowledge is gained firsthand by the researcher, but extensive knowledge about the culture is not necessarily a prerequisite (Frey et al., 2002). Researchers choosing this strategy may also elect which to emphasize more: participation or observation. Finally, a researcher may choose to be a **complete observer**. Complete observers do not interact with the members of the culture or context, which means they do not interview any of the members of the group under study. As such, this method allows for the greatest objectivity in recording data, while simultaneously limiting insight into participants' own meanings of the observed communication.

In short, Communication scholars use four primary research methods: experiments, which focus on causation and control; surveys, which focus on questioning and sampling; textual analysis, which focuses on the content, nature, or structure of messages; and ethnography, which focuses on the communication rules and meanings in a particular culture or context. A summary of the strengths and weaknesses of each of the four methods is summarized in Table 2.1.

Because this textbook is oriented toward students who are likely to use theory and research in the professional realm, we wish to make clear that people who work in the professions also

TABLE 2.1 ■ Four Methods of Communication Research

Research Method	What It Reveals	What It Conceals
Experiments	Cause and effect	Whether the cause–effect relationship holds true in less controlled environments
Surveys	Respondents' thoughts, feelings, and intentions	Cannot establish causality; cannot determine what people actually do
Textual analysis	The content, nature, and structure of messages	The effect of the message on receivers
Ethnography	Rules and meanings of communication in a culture or context	May provide a highly subjective (and therefore biased) view of the culture or context

use research, although that research is not used to develop scholarly theory (although it might be used to develop or refine a working theory). Marketing and public relations professionals, human resources executives, and managers in many industries conduct research as part of the creation and assessment of campaigns, for strategic planning, and for decision-making. Like academics, professionals also use experiments (typically for product testing), surveys (especially focus groups), textual analysis (especially media monitoring), and ethnographies of a sort (typically observations of how customers use a product).

SOCIAL SCIENCE AND THE HUMANITIES

Thus far, we have talked about the central role research plays in the development of theories and how research comes either before creating the theory (in the case of inductive theory development) or after (in the case of deductive theory development). The reason for these differing approaches can be traced back to philosophical divisions within the field of communication. Communication has been described as both an art and a science (Dervin, 1993). On one hand, we respect the power of a beautifully crafted and creatively designed advertisement. On the other hand, we look to hard numbers to support decisions about the campaign featuring that advertisement. Although art and science are integrally related in the everyday practice of communication, in the more abstract realm of theory the two are often considered distinct pursuits. This concept can be traced to distinctions between the academic traditions of the humanities (which includes the arts) and the social sciences.

You might have some ideas about the terms *humanistic* and *social scientific* because most college students are required to take some courses in each of these areas. The distinctions between the humanities and social science are based on more than just tradition; however, they are based on very different philosophical beliefs. The interpretation of meaning is of central concern in the humanities (Littlejohn, 2002). Meaning is presumed to be subjective and unique to the individual, even though meaning is likely influenced by social processes. For individuals trained in the **humanistic approach**, **subjectivity** is a hallmark; one's own **interpretation** is of interest. Think about the study of English literature, a discipline at the heart of the humanities. English scholars study the interpretation of texts in an effort to understand the meaning of the object of study.

On the other hand, **objectivity** is a central feature of social science. Social scientists believe that through careful standardization (i.e., objectivity), researchers can observe patterns of communication that can hold true for all (or most) people, all (or most) of the time. These patterns that hold true across groups, time, and place are known as **generalizations**. To illustrate, psychology is a discipline rooted in the social sciences. As such, psychology scholars seek to explain general principles of how the human mind functions. These principles are intended to explain all people, all over the world, throughout history.

Because the humanities and social sciences have different areas of interest, they treat theory and research differently. Table 2.2 seeks to identify some of those distinctions. The first area of difference is the philosophical commitment to understanding the nature of human beings and the extent of their free will. Certainly, no one believes human beings are mere puppets who have no choice in how they behave. Communication theorists vary, however, in the extent to which they believe people *act* versus *react* to communication. For example, social scientists tend to follow **determinism**, which means they believe past experience, personality predispositions, and a number of other antecedent conditions *cause* people to behave in certain ways. Accordingly, deterministic approaches to human interaction propose that people in general tend to react to situations. Social scientists tend to look at the causes and effects of communication, such as what causes a public health message to fail or the effects of a particular marketing campaign.

Conversely, most humanists believe people have control over their behavior and make conscious choices to communicate to meet their goals. Theorists taking this stance are called pragmatists because they believe people are practical and plan their behavior. **Pragmatism** believes human beings are not passive reactors to situations but dynamic actors. Humanists, then, tend to focus on the choices people (or organizations) make, such as the CDC's inconsistent and confusing messages about mask wearing during the COVID-19 pandemic.

TABLE 2.2 ■ Differences Between Social Scientific and Humanistic Approaches to Communication

Issue	Social Science	Humanities
Belief about human nature	Determinism	Pragmatism
Goal of theory	Understand and predict	Understand only
Process of theory development	Deductive	Inductive
Focus of research	Particularism	Holism
Research methods	Experiments, quantitative survey, and textual analysis	Ethnography, qualitative survey, and textual analysis

A second way to differentiate between humanistic and social scientific scholarship is through a focus on *why* theories are developed. For example, the goal of social scientific theory is to both understand and predict communication processes. Because social science is interested in generalizations, the ability to predict is paramount. If a theorist understands the general pattern at the heart of a social scientific theory, they should be able to predict how any one individual might communicate. Those in the humanities, however, believe interpretations are always subjective; they are unique to the individual. Accordingly, humanists believe theorists can never actually predict how a person will behave; all that can be done is to try to understand human communication.

Although not directly related to the distinction between social science and the humanities, we note that some theories strive to do more than simply predict or understand. A special group of theories, called critical approaches, seeks to improve the world through social change. The goal of critical theory is to empower people in their professional and personal lives. For more information on critical communication theory, see Craig (1999).

The third difference between social science and the humanities is the process of theory development. Recall our discussion of the theory–research link discussed earlier in the chapter. Deductive theory is based on the scientific method, so it should be no surprise that the **social scientific approach** to theory development is *deductive*. Those in the humanities, however, tend to start with data and subsequently develop theory. For example, scholars of English literature would start with reading Shakespeare's plays before developing a theory about them. Thus, those in the humanities tend to use inductive theory development.

Finally, the focus and methods of research also vary in the social scientific and humanistic approaches. The focus of research for the social scientific method is on standardization and control. Because of these objectives, social scientists incrementally study narrowly defined areas at a time, believing the whole picture will be uncovered eventually. This approach is known as **particularism**. Humanists, on the other hand, believe in looking at the big picture; they propose that all pieces of the puzzle contribute to an understanding of the problem. Accordingly, they use holism, looking at the situation in its entirety, as the focal point of research.

Given the different areas of focus, it's not a surprise that the final difference between social scientists and humanists is the research methods they use. Earlier in this chapter, we discussed the four research methods used by communication scholars. Of the four, one is clearly social scientific, and one is clearly humanistic. Experimental methods, with their concern for causation and control, are uniquely suited for the social sciences. Remember that social science seeks to make predictions, and the best way to do that is to have research that supports particular causes and effects. Similarly, ethnography is uniquely suited for humanistic research. Ethnography leans to the understanding of communication in contexts and cultures, which is appropriate for theory that uses holism in its quest for interpretation of communicative events.

The uses of survey research and textual analysis cannot be easily classified. Instead of the methods themselves being associated with either social science or the humanities, the specific way data are analyzed determines whether the method is social scientific or humanistic. The two methods of data analysis are quantitative and qualitative. Quantitative methods are adapted from those used in the hard sciences, such as chemistry and biology. Accordingly, quantitative methods are associated with social science. Qualitative methods are those that have historically been used by the humanities.

Quantitative methods typically rely on numbers or statistics as the data source (Reinard, 1998). These data and statistics are generally explanatory and comprehensive; they seek to predict what will happen for large groups of people. To accomplish this, researchers control the study by identifying the variables of interest before data collection takes place and trying to prevent extraneous influences from affecting the data. As described earlier, these commitments allow social scientists to make generalizations.

Qualitative methods reject the limitations on individual interpretation that control requires. Moreover, qualitative research eschews the use of numbers and uses verbal descriptions of communicative phenomena. Typically, the data are in the form of extended quotes or transcripts of communication. Finally, qualitative research typically centers on a description or critique of communication rather than on generalizations (Reinard, 1998).

Social scientists tend to use quantitative surveys or textual analyses. For example, they'll collect data about how many people prefer a new formulation of a product versus a previous formulation of a product or how frequently a manager uses a particular communication strategy in interaction. Humanists tend to use qualitative surveys and textual analyses. They ask participants to respond at length to questions in their own words about a particular product, or they identify various communication themes evident in a corporate brochure.

A final note should be made about the distinctions between social science and the humanities. The purpose of talking about these two academic traditions is because communication is *both* social scientific and humanistic. As such, you shouldn't view these distinctions as dichotomies but as continua. Individual theories may be more or less social scientific or humanistic (not either/or), with elements borrowed from both traditions.

HOW THEORIES CHANGE AND GROW

Our final concern in this chapter is to be clear that once developed, theories continue to change and grow. As we indicated in Figure 2.1, whether a researcher starts with the theory or starts with research, theory development continues the loop between research and theory, refining, modifying, and extending the theory. Specifically, Kaplan (1964) argues that theories can change by extension or by intension. Growth by **extension** means the theory adds more concepts and builds on what was already established. For example, in 1959, Thibaut and Kelley created interdependence theory, which is described in Chapter 4. One central aspect of the theory is the prediction that relationship dependence (otherwise known as commitment) can be determined by examining an individual's satisfaction with the relationship, as well as his or her perception of the availability and quality of alternatives to the relationship. Caryl Rusbult (1980), a student of John Thibaut, continued working on the theory and presented an expanded version of the theory, which she called the investment model. Her model argues that looking at satisfaction and alternatives is not enough to predict commitment; one also has to examine how much an individual has invested in the relationship. That is, people who are unhappy in their relationship, and who believe they can find a better partner, might stay in the relationship because they have invested a great deal of time, money, or even love, and they don't want to "lose" their investment. Thus, we can conclude that interdependence theory has grown through extension because a new concept—investment—was added to the theory to make its predictions more robust.

Conversely, growth by **intension** means scholars gain a deeper and more nuanced understanding of the original concepts presented in the theory. For example, communication accommodation theory, which is described in Chapter 5, was originally called speech accommodation theory, as the focus was purely on how our dialects and word choice varied based on to whom an individual was speaking. However, researchers quickly realized that accommodation occurs in other areas of verbal and nonverbal communication, such as speaking rate, politeness, and listening (see Gallois et al., 2005, for a review). The theory has grown by intension; the same principles of accommodation are still acknowledged by the theory, and no new concepts were added. Instead, additional research has allowed scholars to understand more fully the complex ways accommodation occurs, adding to the scope of the theory.

CHAPTER SUMMARY

In this chapter, we looked at how theories are developed and changed. We looked at two ways to create theory: inductive and deductive theory development. We discussed the links between theory and research, and we differentiated between primary and secondary research. We also identified the four primary research methods used by communication scholars: experiments, surveys, textual analysis, and ethnography. In addition to describing the key elements of each of these methods, the chapter focused on what each reveals and conceals about communication. Next, we turned our attention to the differences between social scientific and humanistic approaches to theory and research, centering our discussion on beliefs about human nature, the goal of theory, the development of theory, the focus of research, and the research methods used. Finally, we talked about how theories change through the processes of extension and intension.

DISCUSSION QUESTIONS

1. Identify a research study that has been reported in either television news or in a newspaper. Then identify what the original researchers actually found. Discuss what this means in terms of primary versus secondary research.

2. Imagine that you want to study phubbing behavior (ignoring the people around you and focusing on your phone). Develop four different studies using each of the four research methods. What would you learn about phubbing from each of these approaches, and how would they differ from each other?

3. One of the essential differences between humanistic and social scientific scholarship has to do with determinism vs. pragmatism. What are your own views about human nature? Do you tend to focus more on the causes for people's communication or more on the choices that people make?

4. One way to think about the difference between holism and particularism is to imagine putting together a jigsaw puzzle. How would holism help you in putting together the puzzle, and how would particularism help you in doing so?

5. Refer back to one of the commonsense theories you identified in Chapter 1. Has this theory changed in any way? If so, was it through extension or intension? If not, why do you think it hasn't changed?

KEY TERMS

Closed-ended questions (p. 19)

Complete observer (p. 21)

Complete participant (p. 21)

Content analysis (p. 20)

Data analytics (p. 20)

Data mining (p. 20)

Deductive theory (p. 16)

Dependent variable (p. 18)

Determinism (p. 23)

Ethnography (p. 21)

Experiment (p. 18)

Extension (p. 25)

Field experiments (p. 18)

Focus group (p. 19)

Generalizations (p. 23)

Humanistic approach (p. 23)

Independent variable (p. 18)

Inductive theory (p. 15)

Intension (p. 26)

Interaction analysis/conversation analysis (p. 21)

Interpretation (p. 23)

Interview (p. 19)

Laboratory experiment (p. 18)

Manipulation (p. 18)

Nonrandom sample (p. 20)

Objectivity (p. 23)

Open-ended questions (p. 19)

Participant-observer (p. 21)

Particularism (p. 24)

Population (p. 19)

Pragmatism (p. 23)

Primary research (p. 17)

Qualitative (p. 25)

Quantitative (p. 25)

Questionnaire (p. 19)

Random sample (p. 20)

Rhetorical criticism (p. 20)

Sampling (p. 19)

Secondary research (p. 17)

Social scientific approach (p. 24)

Subjectivity (p. 23)

Survey research (p. 19)

Text/data mining (p. 20)

Textual analysis (p. 20)

Variable (p. 18)

CASE STUDY 2
Attribution Theory Reconsidered

In Chapter 1 we provided a brief overview of Attribution Theory, which centers on the process of determining the motivations behind behavior. In short, the theory predicts that our attributions for why someone behaves the way they do influence our interpretations of the behavior. Although Fritz Heider is considered the creator of the theory, his work emerged from the classic philosophical problem of the connections between what happens in the real world and what happens in the human mind (Malle, 2011). Heider (1958) developed his theory to provide an answer to that problem. His work was largely theoretical, with little research conducted as a part of the development of the theory. He did conduct an experiment that provided support for one part of his theory; however, the study found that attributions do influence the interpretations of behavior (Heider, & Simmel, 1944).

Expanding on Heider's work, Jones and Davis (1965) focused specifically on the intentionality of dispositional (internally driven) behavior. Jones and Davis argued that we can make "correspondent inferences," or assumptions about the type of person someone is, by looking at the intentionality of their actions, whether the actions are socially desirable, and whether the actions have noncommon effects (the actions are unexpected). For instance, if one of your coworkers knows that a presentation to the board is important to the entire team, but fails to get his or her part of the presentation to the rest of the team members by the deadline, you are likely to perceive it as intentional, socially undesirable, and unexpected. As such, you will probably make the correspondent inference that this coworker is lazy (at best) or is maliciously sabotaging the team (at worst).

Continuing the study of attributions, Kelley's (1967, 1973) covariation model explains the causal nature of the complete attribution process. Specifically, this model has a greater scope than does Jones and Davis's correspondent inference theory because Kelley seeks to explain attributions overall, whereas Jones and Davis focused only on the intentionality of dispositional inferences. According to Kelley (1967, 1973), individuals judge the causality of another's behavior by examining four factors: consensus, consistency, distinctiveness, and controllability. When the first three of these features are combined (i.e., consensus, consistency, distinctiveness), a perceiver can judge whether the actions were internally controlled (i.e., disposition) or externally controlled (i.e., situational). That is, you assign meaning based on perceived controllability—how much command an individual had over the behavior.

To date, there have been over 15,000 published research studies that utilize Attribution Theory. Given that the theory makes predications about the types of attributions people are likely to make in particular situations, it should come as no surprise that much of this research is experimental in nature. However, some scholars have incorporated a broader range of research methods when using the theory. Cowan (2013), for example, interviewed Human Resources professionals about their attributions for the causes of workplace bullying. She then did a thematic analysis of these interviews, finding that HR professionals believe that workplace bullying happens as a result of aggressive management styles, deficient communication skills, the organizational culture, contemporary issues, and personality clashes.

Questions for Consideration

1. Based on what you read in Chapter 1 and the additional information just provided, was Attribution Theory developed using an inductive or a deductive theory development process? Why?

2. Which research method(s) have been used to test the theory? Is this the best method? Why, or why not?

3. How has the choice of research methods influenced what we know about attributions? That is, what have the methods revealed, and what have they concealed?

4. Do you believe that Attribution Theory is social scientific or humanistic? Provide details from the information in Chapter 1 and this chapter to support your case.

5. In what ways has Attribution Theory changed or grown? Is this intension, extension, or both?

3 COGNITION AND INTRAPERSONAL COMMUNICATION

LEARNING OBJECTIVES

After reading this chapter, you will be able to do the following:

1. Define behaviorism and cognition

2. Explain patterns of miscommunication between the three message design logics

3. Identify types of, conditions for, and communicative strategies for reducing uncertainty

4. Use the concepts of expectancy, violation valence, and communicator reward valence to predict whether someone will reciprocate or compensate a violation

5. Explain the principles of planning theory

Regardless of whether you take a source or receiver orientation to communication, messages have no meaning without an individual's interpretation. Everyone has to process every message internally while considering how best to make sense of these messages. In other words, meaning is derived only after an individual perceives a message and gives it meaning; meaning resides in ou *interpretations* of words or actions, not in the words or behaviors themselves. Consequently, communication is also an intrapersonal process.

DEFINING COGNITION

The roots of communication as an intrapersonal process can be traced to one of the major debates in psychology in the 20th century. At the beginning of the 1900s, American psychology was dominated by a focus on **behaviorism** (Runes, 1984). Most of us are familiar with Pavlov and his studies of salivary production in dogs. By associating the ringing of a bell with food, Pavlov was able to experimentally cause dogs to salivate when hearing a bell, even if the food was not present. Such is a description of a behavioral approach—a focus on external cause and behavioral effect. Major psychological figures such as J. B. Watson and B. F. Skinner argued that because we cannot observe mental processes, we should focus only on these causes and effects (Runes, 1984).

However, in the middle part of the 1900s, psychologists began arguing for a **cognitive** approach to understanding human behavior. Rather than focusing solely on external causes (or stimuli) and behavioral effects, these scholars argued we should be concerned with the mental processes used to process stimuli and generate particular effects (Runes, 1984). A major proponent of this approach was Noam Chomsky, who spearheaded a significant critique of behaviorism. **Cognition**, then, includes the processes of reducing, elaborating, transforming, and storing stimuli (Neisser, 1967). It refers to what happens in the mind that causes us to behave in particular ways.

In this chapter, we explain four theories that examine the cognitive and intrapersonal aspects of communication. First, we introduce message design logics, which proposes that variations in beliefs about communication explain problematic communication encounters. The second theory presented in this chapter, uncertainty reduction theory, strives to explain and predict initial encounters with people. In other words, what drives you to initiate communication, and how do you go about reducing your uncertainty in a new situation? Third, expectancy violations theory (EVT) seeks to predict and explain people's behavior when their expectations about what will happen are breached. The fourth theory presented, planning theory, explains the process by which communicators can achieve their goals.

Altogether these theories emphasize the internal processes that serve as antecedents to the highly personalized creation of meaning, and each perspective applies to numerous communication contexts. From making judgments about a coworker based on their communication style (i.e., message design logics) to determining how best to reduce one's uncertainty during a job transfer (i.e., URT), each of the theories presented illustrates the internally driven process necessary to bring individual meaning to various messages. Table 3.1 provides an overview of these four theories.

TABLE 3.1 ■ Overview of Intrapersonal Communication Theories	
Theory	**Main Idea**
Message Design Logics	Because people have different beliefs about the nature of communication, their messages are constructed differently.
Uncertainty Reduction Theory	People find the experience of uncertainty uncomfortable, so they use communication to reduce it.
Expectancy Violations Theory	The violation of someone's expectations can lead to either positive or negative results depending on the valence of the violation and the reward value of the individual who has violated expectations.
Planning Theory	Communication competence is increased when an individual engages in planning to meet their goals.

MESSAGE DESIGN LOGICS

Everyone has been faced with the challenge of having to confront a coworker or subordinate who isn't pulling their weight. The dilemmas communicators confront when dealing with these sorts of situations can be understood by the theory of message design logics. According to O'Keefe (1988, 1997), because people think about communication differently, they also construct very different types of messages. A **message design logic** (MDL), then, is your belief about communication that, in turn, links thoughts to the construction of messages. Stated differently, people's views about the nature and function of communication affect their messages. Variation in message type is particularly evident when a person is faced with communication challenges such as trying to influence someone's behavior or dealing with a difficult coworker. According to O'Keefe (1997), there are three types of design logics from which people operate.

Three Message Design Logics

Building upon her previous work looking at impression management in persuasive interaction (O'Keefe & Delia, 1982) and ways in which individuals negotiate multiple goals in persuasive interaction (O'Keefe & Shepherd, 1987), O'Keefe (1988, 1997) developed her theory. Using an inductive approach, she analyzed the techniques people used to try to influence others. Despite a plethora of strategies that might be used, she found that individuals tended to rely on uniform techniques. Specifically, O'Keefe identified three distinct MDLs: expressive, conventional, and rhetorical. Each MDL emphasizes a different goal or combination of goals for communication.

The **expressive logic** is a sender-focused pattern (O'Keefe, 1988). That is, a person who relies on this pattern primarily values self-expression. The goal of communication is to convey the sender's thoughts and feelings. People who use the expressive MDL have a very difficult time holding back their thoughts; if it's in their heads, it's out their mouths. They appreciate openness, honesty, and clarity in communication and mistrust those who seem overly strategic in their communication. Such communicators pay little attention to context or what may be considered appropriate behavior. They feel a genuine obligation to say what is on their minds right there and then. When the situation calls for them to protect someone else's face or self-esteem, they typically accomplish this in a relatively simple fashion by editing their comments (e.g., replacing profanity with a euphemism) rather than through genuine efforts at politeness (see Chapter 4 for a discussion of politeness theory). For example, when faced with a colleague or employee who isn't pulling their weight, a person using an expressive MDL might respond in this way: "You are a real screwup. You have been given many chances to mend your ways, but you just don't seem to care. You come in late, you never work as hard as the rest of us. . . . You aren't going to get away with this. You're fired." (O'Keefe, 1988, p. 100).

Note that the content of this message is focused entirely on what the sender is feeling at the time. The sender might have tried to temper their anger by editing their language, but other than that, little effort is made to modify the expression of thoughts and feelings or to understand the other person's viewpoint.

Second, a person relying on **conventional logic** views communication as a rule-based game played cooperatively (O'Keefe, 1988). As such, those using a conventional MDL are primarily concerned with appropriateness; these individuals view communication contexts, roles, and relationships as having particular guidelines for behavior (O'Keefe, 1997). They are concerned about saying and doing the "right" thing in any given situation. To do the right thing, they follow the rules of politeness (see Chapter 4 for more on politeness theory). Keeping our example of dealing with a difficult employee, a person using a conventional MDL might respond like this: "You continue to be late returning from lunch. When you took this job all the rules and regulations were explained to you, and since then I've mentioned to you twice that we take our hours seriously in this office. In the future, please return from lunch promptly" (O'Keefe, 1988, p. 102). In this case, the message sender makes several allusions to communication rules; not only do they point out that this behavior violates the office's "rules and regulations," but the speaker also throws in "please" as an attempt at politeness.

The third MDL is **rhetorical**. Individuals using a rhetorical MDL view communication as a powerful tool used to create situations and negotiate multiple goals (O'Keefe, 1988). Instead of emphasizing self-expression (expressive logic) or social appropriateness (conventional logic), "those acting on the basis of a rhetorical design logic focus on the effect of messages on the recipient" (Bonito & Wolski, 2002, p. 256). This approach is noted for flexibility, as well as for its sophistication and depth of communication skill. Those using a rhetorical MDL pay close attention to other people's communication in an effort to figure out others' points of view. They try to anticipate and prevent problems by redefining situations to benefit all parties involved in the interaction. Unlike the expressive MDL, which is reactive and self-focused, the rhetorical MDL is proactive, flexible, and recognizes that words have relational consequences, now and in the future (O'Keefe, 1988). An example of a rhetorical MDL is as follows:

> I understand that you have been making it a habit to return late from lunch. People have started to notice your behavior and comment on it. Since it is causing a lot of problems in the office, I think it would be better if you start coming back on time. If you need to be late and can tell me in advance, I'm sure we can work things out for you occasionally. (p. 103)

In this case, the manager seeks to balance their own goal (stopping the employee's lateness) with the employee's goal (maintaining face and protecting oneself against embarrassment). At the same time, the sender strives to maintain a good working relationship with the subordinate in the future. This is accomplished by redefining the situation from one of personal incompetence to that of off-setting office gossip. As well, the sender acknowledges their own flexibility by stating that occasional lateness for a good reason is okay. The sender attempts to show understanding for the other person's situation and lateness. By reframing the message, the rhetorical communicator has found "a common drama in which to play" (O'Keefe, 1988, p. 88).

Message Design Logics Preferences

Reading the three examples presented might give you insight into the MDL under which you tend to operate. More than likely, one of those messages is similar to something you might say in a situation you perceive as harassing, and the other message types might reflect something you would never say in a million years. Indeed, one of the challenges highlighted by this theory is the difficulty individuals have when dealing with others who use a different MDL. O'Keefe et al. (1997) argued that when two people use the same MDL, these individuals recognize that the problems are communication problems. When two parties use different MDLs, however, these individuals often do not realize they have communication problems; instead, they blame the difficulties on perceived bad intentions, mistaken beliefs, or undesirable personality characteristics. For example, a person who uses an expressive MDL tends to view those using a rhetorical MDL as dishonest because they "manipulate" their perception of the situation. Table 3.2 presents some forms of miscommunication due to differing MDLs.

Although individuals tend to prefer using one MDL to another, O'Keefe and colleagues have cautioned that MDLs are not the same as personality traits; instead, they can change and develop over an individual's life span. In fact, O'Keefe and Delia (1988) found that the three MDLs reflect a developmental process, with the expressive MDL the least developed and the rhetorical MDL the most developed pattern. However, O'Keefe et al. (1997) warned that this developmental trajectory should not imply that the rhetorical strategy is superior to others: "Every design logic provides a logically consistent and potentially satisfactory way for an individual to use language" (p. 49). They believe all communicators should recognize and accommodate diversity in MDLs. Knowing the variation is half the battle.

Again, O'Keefe's (1988, 1997) theory suggests that individuals tend to rely on one of the three MDLs, particularly when faced with conflict or attempts to influence. Users of expressive

TABLE 3.2 ■ **Forms of Miscommunication Based on Message Design Logics**

Message Producer	Message Recipient		
	Expressive MDL	**Conventional MDL**	**Rhetorical MDL**
Expressive MDL	Genuine differences in opinion prevent communicators from achieving any connection.	Expressive remarks perceived as embarrassing or crude due to inappropriateness.	Expressive person perceived as inconsiderate and uncooperative.
Conventional MDL	Ritualistic messages are taken literally by the expressive person (such as "Let's get together soon").	Differing views of appropriateness of the situation lead to perceived inappropriate behavior.	Conformity to appropriateness viewed as rigidity, overly conservative approach to interaction.
Rhetorical MDL	Messages viewed as unnecessarily elaborate and indirect; sender viewed as dishonest.	Failure to see coherence of complex messages because of focus on "correct" context.	Incompatible assumptions about goals can lead to misunderstanding of others' intent.

Source: O'Keefe, B. J., Lambert, B. L., & Lambert, C. A. (1997). Conflict and communication in a research and development unit. In B. D. Sypher (Ed.), Case studies in organizational communication 2, p. 42. Guilford Press.

MDLs view communication primarily as a means of sharing their unique feelings, beliefs, and ideas. Those who rely on conventional MDLs perceive communication as a rules-based game; to play the "game" one must operate using social conventions for appropriateness. Last, a rhetorical MDL emphasizes a highly flexible approach to communication in which the speaker adapts to the situation, using self-expression or relying on social conventions as appropriate.

UNCERTAINTY REDUCTION THEORY

The second intrapersonal theory discussed here is uncertainty reduction theory (URT). Berger and Calabrese's (1975) URT holds that social life is filled with ambiguities. Not knowing what to wear on the first day at a new job (Should I wear a suit or go with business casual?), uncertainty as to how to greet a new boss (Should I call her Megan? Ms. Smith? Mrs. Smith? Dr. Smith?), and wondering whether you will get along with the new office mate who just transferred from another location (Will they bother me with questions? Will they gossip about team members?) are just a few typical concerns during an average workday. Guided by several assumptions and **axioms** of human behavior, URT seeks to explain and predict when, why, and how individuals use communication to minimize their doubts when interacting with others.

Three assumptions guide the uncertainty reduction framework. First, Berger and Calabrese (1975) maintained that the primary goal of communication is to minimize uncertainties humans have about the world and the people therein. Second, they proposed that individuals experience uncertainty on a regular basis and that the experience of uncertainty is an unpleasant one. Third, Berger and Calabrese assumed that communication is the primary vehicle for reducing uncertainty. Importantly, with so many uncertainties presented to you within a given 24-hour period, Berger (1979) admitted individuals couldn't possibly reduce uncertainty about all of these new people or situations. Instead, he argued there are three possible preceding conditions that influence whether people have the motivation necessary to reduce their uncertainty.

Berger (1979) argued that individuals are motivated to reduce uncertainty only under one of three specific antecedent conditions. First, anticipation of future interaction suggests you are more motivated to reduce uncertainty about someone you are likely to see again. Thus, you are more inclined to use uncertainty reduction behaviors when a new office mate joins the team because you know you will be working with this person on a daily basis. The second condition, **incentive** value, includes the notion that you are prompted to learn more about someone when the individual in question has the potential to provide you with rewards or even punishments. In other words, what can this person do for you or to you? The third antecedent condition is **deviance**. If a person is odd, eccentric, bizarre, or unusual in some way that counters your expectations, URT suggests individuals will be more likely to reduce their uncertainty about the individual.

Types of Uncertainty

Beyond the antecedent conditions that prompt people to want to reduce uncertainty, Berger and Bradac (1982) argued there are two distinct variations, or types, of uncertainty. The first type, **behavioral uncertainty**, takes into account your insecurity about which actions are appropriate in a given situation. For example, when starting a job at a new company, there is often some ambiguity about the hours "required." Do employees of my position begin promptly at 9:00 a.m. and leave right at 5:00 p.m.? Or am I expected to arrive early and stay late? Should I work through lunch, eating at my desk, or do colleagues expect me to go out to lunch with them and socialize? These are all examples of typical behavioral uncertainty for a new employee not yet sure how to act within the new organization.

The second type of uncertainty is **cognitive uncertainty**. Whereas individuals experiencing behavioral uncertainty question how they should act in a given situation, those who experience cognitive uncertainty are unsure as to what to think about someone or something. In other words, cognitive uncertainty emphasizes the doubts in your ability to pinpoint the attitudes and beliefs of others. When a colleague makes a comment about how "comfortable" you look on a casual Friday, you may wonder, was this a compliment? Or was the remark a subtle hint that you may be dressed in a manner that is too casual for the office? Should you even care what the person thinks of your attire? All of these questions emphasize cognitive uncertainty.

Axioms Explaining the Uncertainty Reduction Process

URT seeks to explain and predict the ways in which individuals use communication to reduce ambiguity. Specifically, the process of reducing uncertainty is predicated on eight axioms, or self-evident truths, established and supported in previous research (Berger & Calabrese, 1975). These axioms are summarized in Table 3.3.

As you can see, these axioms make sense; they are, after all, "self-evident truths." Unlike a commonsense theory, however, URT's axioms have been classified, paired together to create theorems, and tested systematically over time, thereby providing URT with scholarly credence. Moreover, the axioms presented in Table 3.3 supply only the backbone of the theory. In other words, to say that using friendly nonverbal behaviors reduces uncertainty is not enough to warrant a scholarly theory. Discussed next, communication strategies to reduce uncertainty provide additional substance to URT's axioms.

Uncertainty Reduction Strategies

When examining communication strategies for reducing uncertainty, it is important to remember Berger and Calabrese's (1975) original premise: Uncertainty reduction is central to all social relations. However, there are multiple ways an individual can go about reducing their uncertainty. Berger and Calabrese identified three overarching strategies that typify most uncertainty-reduction communication: passive, active, and interactive.

Indicative of the **passive strategy**, individuals observe their surroundings and surreptitiously gather clues about which behaviors are appropriate as well as which attitudes and beliefs others hold. The passive approach is much like playing detective. The **active strategy** to uncertainty reduction involves seeking information from a third party. Rather than playing detective yourself, you go to someone else who may know more about the person or situation in question.

TABLE 3.3 ■ Axioms of Uncertainty Reduction Theory	
Axiom 1	As your verbal communication with a communication partner increases, your level of uncertainty about that person decreases; as a result, verbal communication continues to increase.
Axiom 2	As welcoming nonverbal expressions increase, uncertainty decreases and vice versa.
Axiom 3	The greater your uncertainty, the more information-seeking behaviors you use. Conversely, as your uncertainty lessens, you seek less information.
Axiom 4	When uncertainty in a relationship is high, the intimacy level of communication content will be low. On the other hand, the reduction of uncertainty leads to greater intimacy.
Axiom 5	The more uncertain you are, the more you will use reciprocal communication strategies and vice versa.
Axiom 6	The more similarities you perceive to share with the target person(s), the more your uncertainty is reduced. Alternatively, perceiving dissimilarities leads to increased uncertainty.
Axiom 7	As uncertainty decreases, liking increases. Conversely, if your uncertainty rises, your liking of the person will decrease.
Axiom 8	Shared communication networks, or shared ties, lessen your uncertainty. On the other hand, if you share no common relations, your uncertainty intensifies.

Source: Axioms 1 through 7 are adapted from Berger and Calabrese (1975). Axiom 8 is adapted from Parks and Adelman (1983).

Last, the **interactive strategy** is when you go straight to the source in question and ask for as much information as possible.

For example, imagine yourself in a new position at a new company. As the December holiday season approaches, you begin to wonder whether you should give a gift to your boss. You could wait to see if others give gifts (passive strategy), you could ask several peers what they do for their supervisors (active strategy), or you could directly ask your boss what the company culture is like and what they expect (interactive strategy). Clearly, there are many possible goals that would influence which plan to enact. If the overarching goal is to appear appropriate, effective, and appreciative, the active strategy is probably the best choice. By asking others in your position what they do, you can get a good sense of what your supervisor expects without offending or embarrassing them.

Beyond Initial Interactions

URT was originally concerned with explaining and predicting the ambiguity associated with initial interactions (Berger, 1979; Berger & Calabrese, 1975). That is, research using URT emphasized when, why, and how individuals minimize doubt when in new situations or when meeting new people. Berger (1997) has since expanded his position on URT, however, noting that uncertainty exists in new and developing relationships as well as in long-term, ongoing relationships. For example, when Allen is suddenly laid off, Dan and Davida become (under-standably) uncertain about their own job security. Even in the face of positive change, uncertainty is inevitable. Imagine you are promoted and will now manage some of your closest friends at work. This change in power—from peer to superior—will likely increase your uncertainty. All relationships are characterized by change and growth—both of which promote the rise of uncertainty. Furthermore, as discussed in Chapter 4, some researchers believe a little bit of uncertainty is actually necessary for maintaining a healthy relationship.

To review, URT focuses on when and why individuals use communication to reduce uncertainty about others. Uncertainty predictably decreases when nonverbal immediacy, verbal messages, self-disclosure, shared similarities, and shared social networks increase. People routinely use passive, active, and interactive information-seeking strategies to reduce their uncertainty when encountering others.

EXPECTANCY VIOLATIONS THEORY

Developed by Judee Burgoon (1978, 1994), expectancy violations theory (EVT) explains the meanings people attribute to the violation, or infringement, of their personal space. Importantly, whereas much of Burgoon's work emphasizes nonverbal violations of physical space (known as the study of proxemics), personal space can also refer to psychological or emotional space. Similar to URT, EVT is derived from a series of assumptions and axioms.

EVT builds on a number of communication axioms; most central to the understanding of EVT, however, is the assumption that humans have competing needs for personal space and for affiliation (Burgoon, 1978). Specifically, humans all need a certain amount of personal space, also thought of as distance or privacy; people also desire a certain amount of closeness with others, or affiliation. When you perceive that one of your needs has been compromised, EVT predicts you will try to do something about it. Thus, Burgoon's initial work focused on the realm of physical space—what happens when someone violates your expectations for appropriate physical distance or closeness.

Beyond explaining individuals' physical space and privacy needs, EVT also makes specific predictions as to how individuals will react to a given violation. Will you **reciprocate**, or return, someone's unexpected behavior, perhaps moving closer or turning toward the individual? Or will you **compensate**, or counteract, by doing the opposite of your partner's behavior? Before making a prediction about reciprocation or compensation, however, you must evaluate EVT's three core concepts: expectancy, violation valence, and communicator reward valence.

Core Concepts of Expectancy Violations Theory

First, **expectancy** refers to what an individual anticipates will happen in a given situation. Expectancy is similar to the idea of social norms and is based on three primary factors. The first factor associated with expectancy emphasizes the *context* of the behavior. In a formal business meeting, for example, hugging a colleague to show support may be inappropriate and may raise some eyebrows. If, however, you hug the same colleague while attending their mother's funeral, the gesture may be perfectly acceptable. A second factor, the *relationship* one has with the person in question, must be examined. If attending the funeral of your boss's mother, a hug may still be perceived as inappropriate, whereas if the funeral is for the mother of a colleague who is also a personal friend, a hug would likely be more suitable. The third factor, *communicator charac-teristics*, also fuels your expectations; you have beliefs about the way people of both sexes and of certain ages, ethnicities, socioeconomic status, and the like will communicate.

By examining the context, relationship, and communicator's characteristics, individuals arrive at a certain expectation for how a given person will likely behave. Changing even one of these expectancy variables might lead to a different expectation. Once you have determined, however, that someone's behavior was, in fact, a breach of expectation, you then judge the behavior in question. This breach is known as the **violation valence**—the positive or negative evaluation you make about a behavior you did not anticipate. Importantly, not all violations are evaluated negatively. Very often a person behaves in a way you might not have expected, but this surprising behavior is viewed positively. For example, a normally bad-tempered colleague brings coffee and muffins to the Monday morning staff meeting, or the habitually shy intern actually makes eye contact with you and gives an opinion on a new project.

Notably, others' behavior can be confusing and hard to interpret. Therefore, the third ele-ment that must be addressed before predicting reciprocation or compensation involves assessing the person whose behavior is in question. Similar to the violation valence, the **communicator reward valence** (also called the rewardingness of partner) is an evaluation you make about the person who committed the violation. Specifically, how rewarding or interpersonally attractive do you perceive this person to be? If you view the person engaging in the violation to be like-able, charismatic, nice-looking, and smart, then you will likely believe the person has a positive reward valence. Conversely, if you perceive the violator to be rude, stingy, unattractive, or con-ceited, you will likely judge this person as having a negative reward valence. Importantly, the same behavior can be interpreted positively if committed by someone with a positive commu-nicator reward valence and negatively by someone with a negative reward valence. For example, let's say you make a flawless presentation to a difficult client. Afterward, a respected colleague congratulates you and gives an unexpected pat on the shoulder. You will likely judge this act positively and as a gesture of support. On the other hand, let's say it's a different colleague who gives the unexpected pat on the shoulder, one who is always grandstanding and trying to make the focus of attention all about them. In this second case, you will probably view the pat on the back as negative and patronizing. Thus, assessing the behavior itself is insufficient to make a reasonable prediction of how one will react to the violation. You need to consider your relation-ship and view of the person performing the violation.

Predicting Reactions When Expectations Are Violated

After assessing expectancy, violation valence, and communicator reward valence of a given situ-ation, it becomes possible to make rather specific predictions about whether the individual who perceived the violation will reciprocate or compensate for the behavior in question. These pre-dictions are described in Figure 3.1.

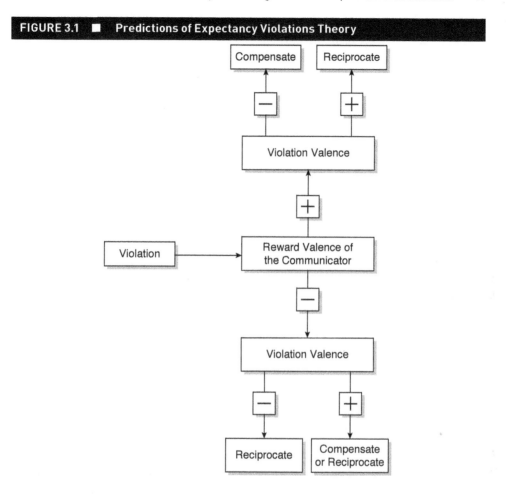

FIGURE 3.1   ■   Predictions of Expectancy Violations Theory

Guerrero and Burgoon (1996) and Guerrero et al. (2000) noticed that predictable patterns develop when considering reward valence and violation valence together. Specifically, if the violation valence is perceived as positive, and the communicator reward valence is also perceived as positive, the theory predicts you will reciprocate the positive behavior. For example, your boss gives you a big smile after you've given a presentation. Guerrero and Burgoon would predict that you smile in return. Similarly, if you perceive the violation valence as negative and perceive the communicator reward valence as negative, the theory again predicts you reciprocate the negative behavior. Thus, if a disliked coworker is grouchy and unpleasant to you, you will likely reciprocate and be unpleasant in return.

Conversely, if you perceive a negative violation valence but view the communicator reward valence as positive, it is likely you will compensate for your partner's negative behavior. For example, one day your boss appears sullen and throws a stack of papers in front of you. Rather than grunt back, EVT predicts you will compensate for your boss's negativity, perhaps by asking if everything is okay (Guerrero & Burgoon, 1996). More difficult to predict, however, is the situation in which someone you view as having a negative reward valence violates your expectations with a positive behavior. In this situation, you may reciprocate, giving the person the "benefit of the doubt." Alternatively, you may view the communicator as having suspicious motives, thereby compensating. For example, if the disliked coworker comes in one day and is very pleasant, you might be pleasant in return, but you also might treat the person with suspicion.

As evidenced, EVT focuses broadly on the infringement of one's expectations for "normal" behavior. Burgoon's research has chiefly emphasized the violation of nonverbal space; however, other expectations, such as behavioral norms, can also be violated. Notably, violations are not necessarily negative. One must evaluate the anticipated behavior, the communicator's characteristics, and the violation itself.

PLANNING THEORY

Author Antoine de Saint-Exupéry famously said "A goal without a plan is just a wish." The final theory we will discuss in this chapter focuses on both goals and plans. Specifically, planning theory describes the cognitive processes that people use to develop communication plans to achieve their goals (Berger, 2015). Although professional communicators develop strategic plans for their organizations, this theory focuses more on the sorts of plans we use in our everyday interactions, although it certainly can be applied to organizational plans as well. For example, you might have the goal of gaining compliance from someone, or reducing your uncertainty, or obtaining permission for violating an expectation. Each of these activities is more likely to be achieved if you have a plan for how to do so.

Goals, Plans, and Planning

Planning theory differentiates between **goals**, which are desired end states; **plans**, which are cognitive structures that allow us to develop a plan of action; and **planning**, which is a process of assessing a situation, determining the goals to be pursued, retrieving, or creating a plan, and then enacting the plan (Berger, 1997). The theory is grounded in seven propositions, described in Table 3.4.

In short, the theory suggests that although all communication is designed to meet our goals, we are not always aware of what our goals are. How many times have you looked back on your own behavior and thought "why did I say that?" Although you might not have been aware of it at the time, you likely can come up with an explanation for why you said what you said and did what you did. That is because goals often operate at low levels of consciousness.

Further, planning theory suggests that you will be a more competent communicator if you actually engage in planning to achieve your goals. That is, you should carefully determine what you want to achieve and the best way to achieve it. During the planning process you develop a plan, or a sequence of actions. The good news is that once you have developed a plan, it gets stored in your memory so you can use it again without thinking about it too much. It's a bit like riding a bike; learning how to do so is challenging, but once you have mastered it you can ride without spending any cognitive energy thinking about how to do it.

TABLE 3.4 ■	Propositions of Planning Theory
Proposition 1	Humans seek to achieve goals, which results in communication designed to achieve those goals.
Proposition 2	Creating plans to achieve goals promotes more effective and efficient goal satisfaction.
Proposition 3	Communication is used to achieve goals.
Proposition 4	Goals are desired end states, whereas plans are action sequences developed to achieve goals.
Proposition 5	Goals exist in long-term memory, with abstract goals at the top of a hierarchy and subgoals nested underneath them. Achieving subgoals allows people to achieve abstract goals.
Proposition 6	Plans can be consciously formulated to achieve goals, but previously developed plans can be stored in memory and subsequently be performed unconsciously.
Proposition 7	Knowledge of goals and plans helps to understand others' communication.

Plan Complexity

One of the essential aspects of planning theory concerns **plan complexity** (Berger, 2015). There are two ways that plans can be complex. The first is the extent to which the plan includes **contingencies**, which are if/then elements. Imagine you are trying to persuade a coworker to assist you with a major project. Your plan might include something like "If they say they are too busy, I will counter with how important this is to the company." This sort of if/then element increases plan complexity. A second factor that can increase plan complexity is the **specificity** of the plan (Berger, 2015). Returning to the example of asking a coworker to help with a project, a relatively simple plan would be something like "I'm going to ask for assistance." A more complex plan might be something like "I know that Selina is really busy too, so I'm going to wait until Tuesday when she submits the weekly report. Then, I will talk about how much I enjoy working with her, and say that we make a good team. Next, I'll talk about how important this project is, and how worried I am about the details. I will then say how much I appreciate her detail orientation, before asking her if she will work with me on completing the plan." Research indicates that plan complexity increases communication effectiveness (Waldron, 1997).

Because plans do not always go as intended, we often have to adjust our plans. Planning theory suggests that these adjustments follow what is called the **hierarchy principle**, which means that we are likely to make corrections at more specific levels than at more abstract levels (Berger, 1997). Once again, consider your hypothetical efforts to get Selina to assist you with the major project. If Selina immediately rejects your request, a simple and concrete response would be to whine (e.g., "But I really need your help"), or to repeat your previous argument (e.g., "But this is such an important project!"). A more abstract response would be to reconsider both your own and the other person's goals, and to create an entirely new persuasive argument. For example, it takes much more cognitive effort to switch your persuasive strategy from flattery ("you are so good with details") to a reward-based strategy (i.e., "If you help me with this, I will handle that monthly update you hate doing"). For that reason, people generally try to avoid more abstract and high-level plan alterations (Berger, 2015).

Research indicates that having multiple plans can increase plan effectiveness, up until a point. Berger (1997) investigated how the number of plans an individual had affected communicative success. He found that having only one plan and having too many plans both played a negative role in plan success. Instead, individuals who had three alternative plans increased the speed of enacting alternatives when confronted with a failure of the initial plan as compared with those who had no alternatives and too many alternatives (in this case, six). Moreover, the ability to rapidly switch plans is associated with increased credibility (Berger, 2015).

One caution of planning theory is that regardless of how complex a communication plan might be, individuals still have to have the skill to enact the plan. That is to say, even the best plan can fail if the person who is following it is unable to execute it. Consider the common strategy in professional and political situations of having one person write a speech and another person deliver it. Both individuals have to have appropriate skills; the planner has to have the cognitive repertoire to develop a complex plan, and the speaker has to have the ability to recognize when a plan is failing and to move on to contingencies or to switch to an alternative plan (Berger, 2015).

Moreover, communicators have to be careful about reusing plans (Berger, 2015). Situations change and expectations vary, making what has worked in the past ineffective in a current situation. For example, imagine that you have always been successful at writing an academic paper the night before it was due. Then imagine that (a) the paper assignment is more complex than you realized and (b) the paper is a degree-completion assignment that will determine whether or not you receive your degree. Following the same old plan of turning on your computer around 8 the night before might not work out so well for you. In fact, one of the major problems with communication plans is a **success bias**, which is an inflated estimation of the likelihood that a plan will be effective (Berger, 1997). Just because you have devised a plan is no guarantee that the plan will work.

CHAPTER SUMMARY AND RESEARCH APPLICATIONS

This chapter focused on cognition and communication, which refers to the way individuals assess others' behavior, attitudes, and messages to assign meaning. First, message design logics argues that because people have different beliefs about communication they communicate in notably different ways. Margolin and Markowitz (2018) examined Yelp reviews for evidence of different MDLs. Not surprisingly, they found that expressive reviews used "I" more often, and that they involved more emotional evaluations in the review. Rhetorical reviews, on the other hand, tended to be more abstract, and involved more narratives.

Second, URT states that when individuals encounter someone or something new, they experience uncertainty; uncertainty is uncomfortable, so people use communication strategies to reduce it. One application of URT is its usefulness in explaining communication during

TABLE 3.5 ■ Additional Theories of Intrapersonal Communication	
Theory	**Main Idea**
Coordinated Management of Meaning	People interpret the communication of others through the use of rules (Pearce & Cronen, 1980).
Relational Framing Theory	People interpret messages by focusing on either a dominance-submissiveness frame or an affiliation-disaffiliation frame (Dillard & Solomon, 2005).
Theory of Motivated Information Management	Information management is determined by uncertainty discrepancy, outcome expectancy, and efficacy (Affifi & Weiner, 2004).

a crisis such as the COVID-19 pandemic (Grace & Tham, 2021). Organizations that seek to reduce consumers' experiences of uncertainty through increased communication frequency and the availability of interactive messaging through social media managed the crisis more effectively than those who did not.

Next, EVT predicts whether people will reciprocate or compensate when their expectations are violated. Within organizational contexts, EVT has been used to explain the public's responses to corporate social responsibility (CSR) efforts. Park et al. (2021) used corporate credibility rather than communicator reward valence in their study, and found that positive violations (i.e., better than expected CSR) resulted in more favorable evaluations, as expected, and that corporate credibility helps to mitigate the negative effects of negative violations of CSR.

Finally, planning theory focuses on the planning process used to achieve interaction goals. The theory suggests that planning increases the likelihood of meeting our goals, and the more complex a plan is, the better the chances of success. The theory further states that we can spend less cognitive energy by storing previous plans in our memory, but that reliance on existing plans may not always work; planning requires a careful assessment of the situation. Recent research has established that planning improves the quality of emotional support (Ray et al., 2019).

There are many other theories that focus on how cognitions influence communication. Table 3.5 highlights three such theories.

DISCUSSION QUESTIONS

1. Which message design logic do you think you use most often? Provide an example of an interaction that you have had that you think might have been influenced by differences in your MDL versus someone else's MDL.

2. Think of a time when you have experienced a great deal of uncertainty. Did the antecedent conditions identified by URT play a role in your uncertainty? Which strategy(ies) did you use to reduce your uncertainty?

3. EVT makes clear predictions in all cases except when someone with a high reward valence engages in a negative violation valence. What do you think is most likely to happen in those situations? Might your MDL influence your response?

4. Planning theory says that more complex communication plans are most likely to lead to success. Have you ever been in a situation in which you did not engage in sufficient planning? What happened? In retrospect, how might you have adjusted your plans?

KEY TERMS

Active strategy (p. 37)

Axioms (p. 36)

Behavioral uncertainty (p. 37)

Behaviorism (p. 31)

Cognition (p. 32)

Cognitive (p. 32)

Cognitive uncertainty (p. 37)

Communicator reward valence (p. 40)

Compensate (p. 39)

Contingencies (p. 43)

Conventional logic (p. 34)

Deviance (p. 36)

Expectancy (p. 39)

Expressive logic (p. 33)

Goals (p. 42)

Hierarchy principle (p. 43)

Incentive (p. 36)

Interactive strategy (p. 38)

Message design logic (p. 33)

Passive strategy (p. 37)

Plans (p. 42)

Plan complexity (p. 43)

Planning (p. 42)

Reciprocate (p. 39)

Rhetorical (p. 34)

Specificity (p. 43)

Success bias (p. 44)

Violation valence (p. 40)

CASE STUDY 3
You're Fired!

Lisa, Steve, and Chen were feeling triumphant. Just 3 months ago, their company, Ryan Project Systems, had merged with Gierig Strategien AG, a consulting firm headquartered in Germany. At the time, they were optimistic about the merger; the two companies were equivalent in size and mission, and the merger would allow for a stronger global reach. Ryan was already one of the top project management firms in the United States and Asia, and the merger with Gierig added most of Europe to the mix.

However, shortly after the merger, they were a bit less enthusiastic. It seemed that there were a lot of people on the Ryan side that were being let go. Top management assured all employees that these personnel losses were simply a matter of reducing redundant positions—that the personnel changes that happened in the first month had "right-sized" the company and that the organization was now lean, competitive, and ready to become the premier project management organization in the world. Still, in their near daily conference calls, Steve (based in Charlotte, North Carolina) and Chen (based in Taiwan) frequently found time to catch up on the latest gossip of who was on the way out and who was on the way up. In one of their calls, Chen told Steve "Rumor has it Rajesh is being let go."

"Wow! He was one of the people who actually led the integration! Do you think he knew he was actually planning for his . . . uh . . . 'retirement'?," Steve asked.

"Well, Rajesh is pretty smart," Chen mused. "I can't imagine he didn't see this coming. He probably already has an exit plan. You know Rajesh, the next thing we know we'll be getting a LinkedIn notification that he is now a VP at some tech firm."

"I know we're pretty low on the totem pole, but do you think we're safe?" Steve asked.

"No one is safe," Chen snorted. "But we have some pretty strong evidence of our return on investment. Plus, Lisa has all sorts of political connections on both sides of the merger. She'll look out for us. We're a strong team."

Steve wanted to believe this, but his past experience had taught him to be wary. Just 5 years ago he had lost a position at a Fortune 500 company because of political maneuverings. One day he had a performance review that identified him as a high potential contributor, and the next day he was out of a job. He was lucky that he had strong networks, and Lisa created a position for him in her group because she knew what he was capable of.

Fast forward 3 months, and Lisa, Steve, and Chen had just completed a week-long consultation with a company in Barcelona. The Barcelona group was impressed with what the former Ryan employees could deliver, and the meeting concluded with a joint celebration that involved lots of *cava* and seafood. Lisa, Steve, and Chen were already planning their monthly visits as the project was completed, and they enthused that before the merger, their projects were more likely to bring them to boring cities in the American Midwest or polluted and poverty-stricken cities in India than the glittering cities of Europe.

After the trip, Steve returned to North Carolina, Chen returned to Taipei, and Lisa returned to New York. Just 3 days later, Steve received a phone call from Lisa. "We were wrong," Lisa said.

"Uh, I'm not sure what you are talking about," Steve replied.

"The decruitment is not over. More heads are rolling," she said calmly.

"Is it finally some of the folks from the Gierig side?" Steve asked. "Seriously, I don't know how they have such a large market share. So far I am not impressed with their processes."

"Nope, not Gierig," Lisa said. "Me."

Steve was stunned. Their group had just brought in a six-figure contract, and Lisa had negotiated a great deal for the company. "What could they possibly be thinking?" he mused. He didn't realize he had actually said it out loud until Lisa replied.

"They're threatened. We just walked onto their turf and showed them up. They aren't getting away with this," Lisa proclaimed. "I'm seeing a lawyer."

Steve was on the phone with Chen 5 minutes later. Chen was ready to resign right then and there.

"We're next," she intoned morosely.

"Maybe," Steve said, "But maybe not. We need to sit tight and see what happens next."

What happened next was an announcement that their group would now report to Konrad Aulbach, who was the director of corporate Development and a long-term Gierig employee.

In their first conference call, Konrad asked Steve and Chen to create a report detailing their current projects. It seemed reasonable, so they had a quick conference call to plan their attack.

Chen asked, "Do you think he wants a formal report or just a PowerPoint presentation?"

"He said a report, so I guess we should take him on his word," Steve replied.

"How much detail?"

"Well, he's coming from corporate development, so he probably doesn't know much about what we are doing on the ground. I'd rather give too much detail than too little," Steve responded. Chen agreed. The two worked tirelessly on providing a detailed report for each project, specifying their processes and including timelines, budgets, and current status.

They sent their report 3 days later. They were pretty proud that they were able to pull together such a comprehensive report so quickly and also were impressed with all that they were juggling. They felt certain that Konrad would see them for the valuable employees that they were.

They heard nothing for 3 days, and then they received a blistering e-mail from Konrad:

> *I asked you to update me on your projects. I don't have time to wade through all of this crap. I need you to tell me what you are actually working on right now.*

Chen was annoyed, and Steve was frustrated. "If he just wanted an update, why did he ask for a report?" The two of them quickly conferred and sent back a joint e-mail that apologized for any misunderstanding and had bullet points for each of their current projects. Several days later they received another nasty e-mail:

> *I know what projects the company has under contract. What SPECIFICALLY are you doing? I don't see much work coming from either of you.*

"Well, that's because we keep having to write reports for you," Steve thought angrily. But again, he decided to take the high road. He prided himself on being a hard worker who was able to work with anyone. He reached out to Konrad to clarify what he meant by "not seeing much work" coming from them.

"I'm hearing complaints that you aren't delivering on your promises," Konrad told Steve.

Steve was stunned. He knew his clients were enthusiastic supporters of his work, and he had e-mails to prove it. Who could possibly be saying that he wasn't delivering on his promises? As tough as it was, Steve swallowed his pride.

"I'm very surprised to hear that. Can you please let me know who is unhappy so I can reach out to them and rectify the problem?" Steve asked.

"It's not my job to babysit you," Konrad said. "If you can't even tell if your clients are dissatisfied, I'm not certain you have the skills to lead these sorts of projects."

"What the . . . !" Steve silently thought. "This guy has no clue what he is talking about!"

Konrad continued, "Let me spell this out to you. I need you to tell me how you are spending your days so I can determine if our investment in you makes sense."

Steve immediately called Chen after he got off the call with Konrad. He asked her if she had any intel on unhappy clients.

"I have no idea what he is talking about," she concurred. They spent the rest of the phone call discussing each individual client they had worked with in the past 6 months, and could think of no one who could be interpreted as dissatisfied.

"Do you think it might be Marjie Adams?" Steve asked. Marjie had been one of his clients nearly a year before. After the completion of the project, Marjie had a habit of calling Steve and Chen for answers to questions that they had already answered over and over again.

Steve decided that he would comply to Konrad's request by creating a log of billable hours, but he also compiled all of the e-mails he had received from happy clients. He sent an email to Konrad:

I have attached an Excel file of billable hours. If this assists you in keeping track of my activities, I would be glad to continue to do so every week. I also have attached a series of e-mails from previous clients expressing their evaluation of my work. I would be happy to discuss with you any patterns you see that might indicate client dissatisfaction.

For several weeks, there was silence from Konrad, so Steve thought he may have finally put his boss's misperceptions to rest. After all, in the tumultuous environment in which they worked, no news was good news, right? Nearly 2 months later, he received a request for a conference call with Konrad. They hadn't talked since the call in which Konrad had accused him of not meeting client expectations. The call was scheduled for 9 a.m. on a Friday.

Konrad said, "Steve, I want to let you know that human resources is on the phone with us right now. You are being terminated."

Steve was both surprised and not surprised at the same time.

"Might you tell me the cause for my termination?" Steve asked.

Konrad ignored him. "Human resources will inform you about the paperwork for your termination," he said and ended the call.

"What a gutmaggot," Steve thought. "This company is going down the tubes if this is the way they are going to run it."

Questions for Consideration

1. What Message Design Logic does Steve exhibit? What about Konrad?

2. What are the sources of uncertainty in the case? What strategies did Steve use to reduce his uncertainty?

3. Using examples for each of EVT's core components (expectancy, violation valence, and communicator reward valence), how does EVT explain Steve's response to Konrad?

4. To what extent did Steve and Chen engage in planning in order to meet Konrad's demands? How successful were they? What might they have done to improve their communication plan?

5. Which theory alone seems to provide the "best" explanation for the situation? Why do you believe this to be the case? What information might surface that would make a different theory or theories better at explaining the situation? How could you combine several theories to make for an even better explanation of the situation?

4 INTERPERSONAL COMMUNICATION

LEARNING OBJECTIVES

After reading this chapter, you will be able to do the following:

1. Define interpersonal communication

2. Explain the relationship between positive/negative face needs and strategies for engaging in face-threatening acts (FTAs)

3. Make predictions about a relationship's stability and satisfaction using principles of social exchange theory

4. Compare and contrast the central *internal* and *external* dialectics Baxter believes are inherent in close relationships

5. Articulate the complexities associated with information management using Petronio's six principles of privacy management

It's difficult to imagine a profession that doesn't require you to interact with other people. You likely use interpersonal communication (IPC) every day—to handle complaints from a demanding client, to persuade your boss to give you some time off, or to comfort a friend dealing with a difficult relationship. This chapter explains a variety of IPC theories, including those that explain how relationships are initiated and developed, theories of how relationships are maintained over time, and theories that explain why and what to do when people behave in unexpected ways.

DEFINING INTERPERSONAL COMMUNICATION

Interpersonal communication (IPC) has been defined in many ways. Some scholars define IPC based on the situation and number of participants involved (see Miller, 1978). Using Miller's definition, IPC occurs between two individuals when they are in proximity, are able to provide immediate feedback, and use multiple senses. Others define IPC based on the degree of "personalness," or perceived quality, of a given interaction (see Peters, 1974). In Peters' view, IPC

TABLE 4.1 ■ Overview of Interpersonal Communication Theories	
Theory	**Main Idea**
Politeness Theory	Individuals try to promote, protect, or "save face," especially when embarrassing or shameful situations arise unexpectedly.
Social Exchange Theory	We get into and stay in relationships to maximize profits.
Dialectical Perspective	In order to manage our relationships we need to manage contradictory tensions within them.
Communication Privacy Management Theory	People create decision-making rules to help them determine when to reveal and when to conceal private information.

includes communication that is personal and occurring between people who are more than acquaintances. Another view of IPC is a goals approach; that is, IPC includes communication used to define or achieve personal goals through interaction with others (see Canary et al., 2008).

For the purpose of examining IPC theory, we argue that IPC encompasses a number of these definitions. **Interpersonal communication** includes those messages between two interdependent persons, with a particular focus on how IPC messages are offered to initiate, define, maintain, or further a relationship. IPC is more than just saying a polite hello to the salesclerk in your favorite department store and then scurrying away never to be seen again. Instead, it refers both to the *content* and *quality* of messages relayed and the possibility of further relationship development. We present four theories in this chapter critical to current understandings of IPC and the relationships that develop from these communications. First, politeness theory (PT) clarifies the strategies individuals use to maintain their "face," or sense of desired public image. Second, social exchange theory (SET) evaluates relationships on the basis of rewards and costs; this ratio of benefits to drawbacks explains whether a relationship will continue as well as whether partners will feel satisfied. Third, the dialectical perspective describes the contradictions individuals inevitably face within their personal relationships and explains how management of these contradictions can predict a relationship's success or failure. Finally, communication privacy management (CPM) theory builds on these earlier theories and focuses on the decisions we make to reveal or conceal information. Table 4.1 provides an overview of each of these theories.

POLITENESS THEORY

Developed by Brown and Levinson (1978, 1987), politeness theory (PT) explains how and why individuals try to promote, protect, or "save face," especially when embarrassing or shameful situations arise unexpectedly. The theory clarifies how we manage our own and others' identities through interaction, in particular, through the use of politeness strategies. Building on Goffman's (1967) notion of identity and facework, Brown and Levinson (1978, 1987) determined when, why, and how interpersonal interaction is constructed through (or in the absence of) politeness.

Assumptions of Politeness Theory

Three primary assumptions guide PT. First, PT assumes all individuals are concerned with maintaining face (Brown & Levinson, 1978, 1987). Simply put, **face** refers to your desired self-image, the identity you wish to present to others. Erving Goffman (1959) first proposed a dramaturgical approach to understand face, arguing that human interaction is akin to the theater. In different "scenes" and with different "actors," we often wear different "masks" either to highlight or deemphasize different aspects of our personality. Goffman wasn't suggesting we're all narcissistic phonies, but that individuals are selective in revealing different aspects of themselves, in different contexts, and to different audiences. At the law office where she works, for example, Marta might want to project her image as intelligent, competent, and fair. With her young nieces and nephews, however, Marta might want to project the image of a caring and silly aunt who does cartwheels down the sidewalk. And with her new boyfriend, Marta might want to be viewed as caring, trustworthy, and romantic. All of these qualities are part of Marta's identity, but she is thoughtful about what part of her image is highlighted and with whom.

Not only does face refer to the image you want others to have for you, but it also includes the recognition that your interactional partners have face needs of their own. Thus, Marta must recognize that her colleagues, family members, and significant other also each have self-images they want to maintain while at work, at home, and at play. Much like a dance, each party must help the other to uphold their desired image for face to work. If Marta's colleague, Rich, views her attempts to be seen as intelligent as pretentious and unsubstantiated, then Marta hasn't achieved the face she desires.

There are two dimensions to the concept of face: positive face and negative face (Brown & Levinson, 1978, 1987). **Positive face** includes a person's need to be liked, appreciated, and admired by select persons. Thus, maintaining positive face includes using behaviors to ensure these significant others continue to view you in an affirming fashion. **Negative face** assumes a person's desire to act freely, without constraints or imposition from others. It is difficult to achieve positive and negative face simultaneously—that is, acting in a way so that you gain others' approval often interferes with autonomous and unrestricted behavior.

Second, PT assumes human beings are rational and goal oriented, at least with respect to achieving face needs (Brown & Levinson, 1978, 1987). In other words, you have choices and make communicative decisions to achieve your relational and task-oriented goals within the context of maintaining face. Notably, Brown and Levinson (1978, 1987) posited that face management works best when everyone involved helps maintain the face of others. In other words, because "everyone's face depends on everyone else's [face] being maintained" (Brown & Levinson, 1987, p. 61), it is in your own best interest to make decisions that uphold this mutual, and rather vulnerable, construction of face.

The final assumption, despite the understanding of face as mutually constructed and maintained, is that some behaviors are fundamentally face threatening (Brown & Levinson, 1978, 1987). Inevitably, you will threaten someone else's face, just as another person will, at some point, threaten yours. These **face-threatening acts** (FTAs) include common behaviors such as apologies, compliments, criticisms, requests, and threats (Craig et al., 1993).

PT, then, ties together these assumptions to explain and predict how, when, and where FTAs occur, as well as what individuals can do to restore face once endangered. Discussed next, we clarify strategies used to uphold and reclaim one's own face and present strategies that pertain to maintaining or threatening the face of others.

Preserving Face

As stated earlier, face is the self-image individuals desire to present to others as well as the acknowledgment that others have face needs of their own. To create and maintain this desired self-image, individuals must use **facework**—specific messages that thwart or minimize FTAs (Goffman, 1967). There are two categories of facework strategies related to politeness: preventive and corrective. **Preventive facework** includes communications used to help ourselves or others avoid FTAs (Cupach & Metts, 1994). For example, using disclaimers such as hedging or credentialing, avoiding certain topics, changing the subject, or pretending not to notice an FTA are all preventive facework strategies.

Similar to preventive facework, **corrective facework** consists of messages people use to restore their own face or to help others restore face after an FTA (Cupach & Metts, 1994). Corrective facework includes the use of strategies such as avoidance, humor, apologies, accounts or explanations of inappropriate actions, and physical remediation wherein one attempts to repair any physical damage from the FTA.

As noted earlier, your own face needs may conflict with your partner's face needs. How you manage this discrepancy between self and others' needs may instigate your use of an FTA. As you might imagine, behaving so as to gain others' approval (positive face) can obviously interfere with acting so as to appear self-sufficient and unrestricted (negative face). Sometimes, then, individuals need to choose between positive and negative face needs. Especially when your desire to appear unencumbered outweighs your desire to be liked, you may need to engage in an FTA.

According to PT, individuals can choose one of five suprastrategies when communicating in a manner that could potentially threaten the face of another (Brown & Levinson, 1978). Moving from most polite (and least direct) to least polite (and most direct), these suprastrategies include avoidance, going off-record, negative politeness, positive politeness, and bald-on-record. A speaker who uses **avoidance** simply chooses not to communicate in a way that would create embarrassment or a loss of face for another, whereas when a speaker is going **off-record**, they subtly hint of or indirectly mention the face-threatening topic. Hinting or making indirect suggestions leaves the message open to interpretation, thereby minimizing any face threat. For example, Josephine works as a technician in a veterinary hospital where every fourth weekend she is expected to be on call for emergencies and to make daily rounds, checking in on the animals. If something comes up and Josephine wants to switch her weekend shift with a colleague, she can hint that "it really stinks that I have to work this weekend because my friends invited me to go to the beach for one of those last-minute weekend getaway specials." If Josephine's coworker picks up the hint, they may offer to cover her weekend shift. If the colleague doesn't pick up on her subtlety or doesn't want to work the weekend, they can simply take her disclosure at face value—Josephine wishes she were spending the weekend at a beach resort with friends.

A somewhat more direct approach, **negative politeness** occurs when the speaker tries to recognize the other's negative face needs—that is, the receiver's need of freedom and lack of restraint. With negative politeness, you appeal to the receiver's negative face needs through apologies and self-effacement to make yourself appear vulnerable to the other, while also acknowledging that the FTA is impolite and inhibits the other's independence. For example, when Josephine attempts to get a coworker to cover her weekend shift, she might say, "I am so sorry to ask, but I need a huge favor. I know this is last minute, and I really hate to be such a pain, but could you cover my shift this weekend? I know this is really inconvenient, and I wouldn't ask if it weren't really important." By expressing such regret and making oneself appear self-conscious about committing an FTA, the speaker directly acknowledges the other person's discomfort and potential restriction, while still managing to engage in the FTA for which she claims to be so embarrassed.

An even more direct, yet less polite, strategy is that of **positive politeness**. Using positive politeness, the speaker emphasizes the receiver's need for positive face—that is, the need to be liked or appreciated. By ingratiating the receiver with flattery and compliments, you hope to camouflage your face-threatening behavior. For example, Josephine might attempt to "butter up" her colleague with praises before asking him to cover her weekend shift, saying, "Bill, you're the best coworker I've ever had. I feel like we are not only coworkers but friends. As a friend, would you cover my weekend shift?" Finally, the most direct and least polite strategy is **bald-on-record**. Using this strategy, the communicator makes no attempt to protect the other's face and simply commits the FTA. Continuing Josephine's predicament, then, she might simply demand Bill cover for her, saying, "Bill, I need you to cover my shift this weekend."

According to PT, people choose to engage in FTAs rather tactically. Specifically, there are a number of factors people use to decide how polite to be. These factors are described in Table 4.2. For example, when considering how polite to be, communicators determine whether the person

TABLE 4.2 ■ Factors Influencing Politeness Strategies	
Consideration	**Prediction**
Social Power	If someone has more social power than you (for example, someone with an impressive title or a great deal of money), you will be more polite. If someone holds little or no social power over you, you need not be so polite.
Legitimate Power	If someone has legitimate power over you (your boss or even your auto mechanic if your car is not running), you will be more polite. If it is someone with little legitimate power over you, you need not be so polite.
Risk	If what you are going to say has a high chance of hurting someone (you are going to fire them or you are going to report that a spouse is cheating), you will be more polite. If it is not likely to hurt, you need not be so polite.

has more or less **social power** than they do, whether the communicator has **legitimate power** over them at the time, and whether what is going to be said runs the **risk** of hurting the other person (Brown & Levinson, 1987).

Each of the strategies for engaging in an FTA has positive and negative consequences. Going off-record to make a request, for example, leaves much room for ambiguity and a high chance the hint will be ignored. Conversely, using the bald-on-record approach will likely get you what you want but may cost you your own positive face in the process. Furthermore, PT predicts that because humans typically commit FTAs to achieve a desired goal (e.g., to obtain weekend shift coverage), individuals will not use strategies that are more polite than necessary because the cost of ambiguity is too great (Brown & Levinson, 1978).

We should also underscore that the very understanding of face, both positive and negative, varies across cultures, within specific relationships, and even among individuals, to some degree. Thus, a person must carefully weigh each decision to commit an FTA, considering the anticipated payoff in relation to the context, culture, and individual communicator characteristics of a potential FTA target.

In brief, PT emphasizes the notion of face. Particularly in embarrassing or inappropriate situations, individuals typically try to balance their own positive and negative face while also attending to the other's face needs. When deliberately committing an FTA, individuals can save face using a variety of strategies.

SOCIAL EXCHANGE THEORY

Social exchange theory (SET) is a broad approach used to explain and predict relationship maintenance. Developed by Thibaut and Kelley (1959), SET clarifies when and why individuals continue and develop some personal relationships while ending others. Additionally, the theory considers how satisfied you will be with the relationships you choose to maintain.

As the name of the theory suggests, an exchange approach to social relationships is much like an economic method of comparing rewards and costs. Thibaut and Kelley's (1959) theory therefore looks at personal relationships in terms of costs versus benefits. What rewards do you receive from a given relationship, and what does it cost you to obtain those rewards? Before making specific predictions, however, certain assumptions must be understood.

Three assumptions guide SET. First, Thibaut and Kelley (1959) argued that personal relationships are a function of comparing benefits gained versus costs to attain those benefits. Second, and intrinsically tied to the first assumption, people want to make the most of the benefits while lessening the costs. This is known as the **minimax principle**. Last, Thibaut and Kelley maintained that, by nature, humans are selfish. Thus, as a human being, you tend to look out for yourself first and foremost. Although these assumptions are sometimes difficult for students and the general public to accept, they become easier to recognize when explained more clearly within the frame of SET's three core components: outcome value, comparison level (CL), and comparison level of alternatives (CL_{alt}).

Core Components of SET

Three core components make up SET. First, and prefaced in the previous paragraphs, to understand SET, we must acknowledge that social relationships bring both rewards and costs. The outcome of a relationship, therefore, is the ratio of rewards to costs in a given relationship; this can be represented by a simple mathematical equation: Rewards – Costs = Outcome (Thibaut & Kelley, 1959). Relational **rewards** include any benefits you perceive as enjoyable or that help you achieve specific aspirations. For example, rewards between spouses might include companionship, affection, and sharing a joint savings account. Rewards between colleagues might be social support or task-related assistance. Relational **costs** are those drawbacks we perceive as unpleasant or that prevent us from pursuing or achieving an objective. For example, negotiating holiday visits with the in-laws, losing social independence, and having to put grad school on hold because of family obligations all could be potential costs for a married couple. In a professional setting, putting up with a colleague's endless complaining, having to share space with an untidy office mate, or coping with a perpetual text messenger might be viewed as costly.

What an individual perceives as a reward or cost in a given relationship will, of course, vary. The general idea is that people make mental notes of the rewards and costs associated with their relationships. One hopes the rewards outweigh the costs, resulting in a positive **outcome value**. If an individual perceives the relationship to yield more drawbacks than benefits, however, a negative outcome value will result. But the outcome value itself is not enough to predict whether a person will choose to stay in or leave a relationship. Rather, the outcome value becomes a benchmark used to help measure our relational rewards in comparison to our expectations and alternatives. Once the outcome value of a relationship is determined, individuals can begin to determine satisfaction with and stability of that relationship, as well as the likelihood of its continuing.

The second core element of SET is the **comparison level** (CL). The CL represents the rewards a person expects to receive in a particular relationship (Thibaut & Kelley, 1959). Expectations may be based on models for relationships (e.g., parents, friends), one's own experiences with relationships, television and other media representations of relationships, and the like. The importance of understanding what you expect in a relationship is this: SET maintains that individuals compare their current outcome value with their CL. In other words, if you perceive more rewards than costs in your relationship and this matches or exceeds your expectations for the relationship, SET predicts your satisfaction (Outcome > CL). Conversely, if you perceive more rewards than costs in a current relationship but expected to receive even more rewards than you currently have, a sense of dissatisfaction is predicted (CL > Outcome). Thus, predicting one's satisfaction with a relationship is based on a positive outcome value that also meets or exceeds one's expectations (CL).

The third and final component to SET is the **comparison level of alternatives** (CL_{alt}). Thibaut and Kelley (1959) recognized that simply determining one's satisfaction, or dissatisfaction, with a relationship is still not enough to predict whether the relationship will continue or end. Everyone knows a handful of individuals who are dissatisfied with any one of their

FIGURE 4.1 ■ Predictions Made by Social Exchange Theory

Outcome > Comparison Level (CL) = Satisfied

Outcome < CL = Dissatisfied

Outcome > Comparison Level of Alternatives (CL_{alt}) = Stay

Outcome < CL_{alt} = Terminate

personal relationships—whether it is a friendship, marriage, or work partnership—and yet, despite their unhappiness, these individuals remain in that relationship. Why?

SET holds that for any relationship to continue or end, individuals must also examine their CL_{alt} (Thibaut & Kelley, 1959). That is, what are your alternatives to staying in the relationship? Is ending it better or worse than the current situation? Only when you perceive the alternatives to be greater than your outcome and greater than your CL will you end a relationship. Even if satisfied with a current relationship (i.e., Outcome > CL), you may perceive that your alternatives are even better, in which case SET predicts you will terminate the relationship (represented mathematically by CL_{alt} > Outcome > CL).

It should be obvious, then, that many scenarios are possible, depending on the perceptions of *CL_{alt}—Outcome—CL*. Only when individuals have knowledge of all three elements is it possible to make predictions about the state and status of a relationship. An overview of the specific predictions made is shown in Figure 4.1.

To review, SET explains and predicts an individual's decision to maintain or deescalate a particular relationship. Specifically, people evaluate the rewards and costs associated with remaining in their relationships while also considering their expectations and other alternatives.

DIALECTICAL PERSPECTIVE

The dialectical perspective is also useful for explaining and understanding how individuals sustain interpersonal relationships. Specifically, Baxter and Montgomery (1996) and Baxter (1988) argued that relationships are dynamic; these researchers believe it is impossible for a relationship to maintain a certain level of satisfaction or reach a constant status quo. Much like a spiraling trajectory, people continue to develop their relationships by managing a series of opposing, yet necessary, tensions or contradictions.

Assumptions of the Dialectical Perspective

Four primary assumptions guide a dialectical approach to relationship maintenance: praxis, change, contradiction, and totality (Baxter & Montgomery, 1996). First, **praxis** suggests the development of a relationship is neither linear (always moving forward) nor repetitive (cycling through the same things again and again). Instead, a dialectical perspective assumes relationships can become more intimate or less intimate over time (Canary & Zelley, 2000). Thus, relational partners act and react while their relationship's trajectory spirals—moving forward in time and therefore transforming reality.

Change, or motion, is the second assumption (Baxter, 1988; Baxter & Montgomery, 1996). A dialectical approach presumes the only guarantee in a relationship is that it will change. Viewed this way, it is virtually impossible to "maintain" a relationship because maintenance implies a steady state. Instead, Montgomery (1993) argued that relationships are "sustained," not maintained.

Third, a dialectical approach assumes relationships are grounded in interdependent, yet mutually negating, **contradictions** (Baxter, 1988; Baxter & Montgomery, 1996). Stated differently, within every relationship, both partners have essential, yet opposing, needs. Because these needs counteract each other such that you can't achieve both needs at the same time, ongoing tensions result. For example, spouses need to spend time together to sustain their marriage; on the other hand, both partners need to have some time to themselves, away from their partner and relational obligations. Both togetherness and independence are needed, but you can't have both at the same time. The dialectical perspective maintains that relationships are sustained based on partners' communication used to manage these ever-present contradictions.

The fourth and last assumption, **totality**, emphasizes interdependence between relationship partners (Baxter, 1988; Baxter & Montgomery, 1996). Dialectical approaches recognize that without interdependence a relationship cannot exist. Accordingly, a tension you feel will ultimately affect your relationship partner and vice versa, even if that person didn't initially feel the tension.

When these four assumptions are brought together, we reach a rather complex understanding of relationships. To sustain a relationship, therefore, means the relationship will constantly fluctuate, spiraling forward in time, while relational partners experience and try to satisfy **dialectical tensions**, or interdependent, yet opposing, needs.

Central Tensions

Between any two relationship partners (e.g., husband/wife, boss/subordinate, friend/friend, parent/child), three central tensions are thought to exist: autonomy–connection, openness–closedness, and predictability–novelty (Baxter, 1988). These tensions are known as **internal dialectics** because they exist within a dyad. With each pairing of internal tensions, you can see that each individual in a given relationship needs both elements, yet it is impossible to fulfill both needs simultaneously. The **autonomy–connection** dialectic refers to the tension between the desire to feel bonded to one's partner versus the desire to maintain a sense of independence. Similarly, the **openness–closedness** dialectic includes the pull between wanting to open up and self-disclose while also wanting to maintain one's privacy. Finally, the **predictability–novelty** dialectic is the tension between wanting stability or steadiness while also wanting opportunities for spontaneity. According to the dialectical perspective, then, relational partners continually vacillate between each of these three poles.

For example, Will and Vanessa have been married for 8 years. Both have demanding careers and are raising twin boys. To feel satisfied within this marriage while balancing two careers and a family, Will and Vanessa must make time to spend together. This might mean hiring a babysitter and going to dinner occasionally or making a point of staying up after the boys go to bed to discuss their day. In each case, however, the couple is trying to feel connected. At the same time, Will and Vanessa need to maintain a certain amount of independence, some time to pursue their own hobbies or just some quiet time to meditate or read a book.

It should be obvious that it is difficult, if not impossible, to have togetherness and independence simultaneously, hence the dialectical tension. Furthermore, these tensions become magnified when one partner desires connection while the other needs some autonomy. It is this constant struggle and balancing act that propels a relationship forward.

Just as internal tensions exist between two individuals in a relationship (e.g., between husband and wife), three tensions arise externally between the dyad and other people in their lives (e.g., between a couple and their children or their extended families). These tensions, or **external dialects**, mirror the internal dialectical tensions: inclusion–seclusion, revelation–concealment, and conventionality–uniqueness (Baxter, 1988). The key difference between internal and external tensions is that internal dialectics only involve the competing needs of the two people in the relationship. External dialectics appear when the pair interacts with other people in their lives (e.g., coworkers, friends, other family members). Figure 4.2 provides an illustration.

Again, note that it is both necessary and difficult to satisfy both poles of each contradiction simultaneously. The **inclusion–seclusion** dialectic emphasizes the tension partners as a unit experience when they want to spend time with friends, family, or coworkers versus wanting to spend their time alone together as a couple. The **revelation–concealment** dialectic involves the tension between relationship partners who want to disclose aspects of their relationship to the outside world while also wanting to keep some aspects of their relationship private. Last, the dialectic of **conventionality–uniqueness** emphasizes the tension partners feel between wanting to behave in ways considered normative or traditional versus wanting to emphasize their relationship's distinctiveness by doing something differently. Table 4.3 presents an overview of internal and external dialectics.

Returning to Will and Vanessa, they learn they are pregnant with their third child. Elated but also worried about the complications involved in the early stages of pregnancy, they aren't sure whether they should reveal their good news to their family or if they should wait until the first trimester passes. The struggle between deciding whether to disclose their news to friends and family (revelation) or to keep the pregnancy secret (concealment) until the second trimester is difficult, particularly if one partner wants to reveal and the other wants to conceal.

To manage or sustain a relationship, then, these tensions must be managed. Baxter and Montgomery (1996) identified four primary strategies used to handle the internal and external

FIGURE 4.2 ■ Comparison of Internal and External Dialectics

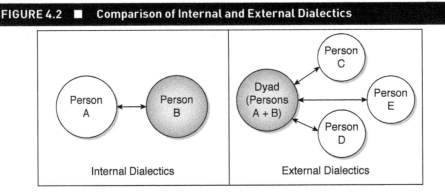

TABLE 4.3 ■ Comparison of Internal and External Dialectics	
Internal Dialectics	**Corresponding External Dialectics**
Autonomy–Connection. Desiring some independence but also desiring a union with your partner	*Inclusion–Seclusion.* Desiring to have strong friendship and family networks but also desiring alone time with your partner
Openness–Closedness. Desiring to be completely open and honest but also desiring to have some private thoughts and feelings	*Revelation–Concealment.* Desiring to tell your family and friends relational information but also desiring to have some private information
Predictability–Novelty. Desiring a stable relationship but also desiring some excitement and spontaneity	*Conventionality–Uniqueness.* Desiring to have a traditional relationship but also desiring a unique relationship

tensions: selection, cyclic or spiraling alteration, segmentation, and integration. The **selection** strategy involves favoring one pole or need at the expense of the other. For example, a couple who dates over long distance may eventually choose autonomy and break up because the tension between living an independent life versus making time to visit the other partner proves too difficult. Much like children playing on a seesaw, partners who use **cyclic alteration** (sometimes referred to as spiraling alteration) fulfill one pole or need now and shift to fulfill the other pole at a later time, creating a back-and-forth, back-and-forth strategy of coping.

The third strategy, **segmentation**, compartmentalizes the relationship such that certain issues coincide with one pole or need, and other issues are appropriate for the opposite pole. For example, if two close friends agree on mostly everything except for their bitter arguments about politics, a segmentation strategy would allow the friends to choose the closedness pole for politics but the openness pole for everything else. The fourth strategy, **integration**, includes several variations and is predicated on incorporating aspects of both poles so as to create a more fulfilling experience. For example, a couple who wants to integrate novelty and predictability might agree that Friday is date night—every Friday (predictability) they will get a babysitter and try a new restaurant (novelty). Obviously a more sophisticated way of managing relational tensions, integration implies relationship partners have an awareness of the tensions and can talk about them so as to find ways to creatively integrate and manage relational tensions.

All told, dialectics presents a rather complicated view of close relationships. This unwieldy depiction is also why it is a "perspective" and not a more precise theory. Nonetheless, dialectics' emphasis of the changing nature of relationships as well as its understanding of the various contradictions and tensions individuals experience makes it a logical approach to which many can easily relate.

COMMUNICATION PRIVACY MANAGEMENT THEORY

In many ways, Petronio's (2002) communication privacy management (CPM) theory builds upon each of the three previous theories. Like PT, CPM is concerned with the dilemma of how and what a communicator should say. Like SET, CPM recognizes the power of maximizing rewards and minimizing costs in making decisions. And, like dialectics, CPM recognizes that managing tensions is the central way relationships are sustained. The basic premise of the theory is that people create decision-making rules to help them determine when to reveal and when to conceal private information.

Sandra Petronio developed the theory after 25 years of researching the process of self-disclosure. Although we discuss this theory in the context of IPC, Petronio views CPM as a macrotheory, as it also can be applied in group and organizational settings. Her theory moves beyond a focus of just self-disclosure to a focus on disclosure in general. Moreover, she argues that disclosure can only be understood in terms of privacy; the two concepts are interdependent.

Principles of CPM

Petronio and Durham (2008) outlined six principles of CPM. The first is the **public–private** dialectical tension. As we just discussed, a dialectical tension refers to competing demands in a relationship. In the case of CPM, the major tension is between revealing and concealing private information. When on a job interview, for example, should you tell the interviewer you had a difficult relationship with your previous supervisor? That might be the honest answer to the question about why you are leaving your present position. But if you reveal the rocky relationship with your boss, will it make the potential employer hesitant to hire you?

The second major principle concerns the nature of **private information** (Petronio & Durham, 2008). Because CPM derives from research into self-disclosure, the theory defines private information as information inaccessible to others. It may be about you, but the information can also be about a team member, a friend, or even about an entire organization. For example, you might have information about a new product under development at your workplace that the company does not want known to competitors. According to Petronio (2002), the central feature of private information is possession. That is, private information is something you own, and because you own it, you have the right to control it. The theory suggests that individuals with private information make decisions about with whom to share information, as well as what they share, when they share it, where they share it, and how they share it.

Next, CPM suggests these decisions about sharing private information are regulated by particular **privacy rules** (Petronio & Durham, 2008). Our decisions about sharing private information are informed by five decision criteria, outlined in Table 4.4. First, privacy rules are developed based on **cultural criteria**. As we discuss in Chapter 5, cultures have varying values, beliefs, and ways of communicating. As such, an individual's culture is likely to influence decisions about what should or should not be revealed. Second, **gender criteria** play a role in privacy rules. Petronio suggests people have been socialized to have differing understandings of disclosure; thus, they may make different decisions when confronted with the tension of whether to share private information. Third, personal variations in **motivational criteria** are used in developing privacy rules. In Chapter 3, we described message design logics (MDLs), which are individual beliefs about the function of communication. Using MDLs as an example, a person with an expressive MDL is likely to be motivated to share more information than would a person with a conventional MDL, simply because of their individual beliefs about the purpose of communication. Of course, **contextual criteria** also influence privacy rules.

TABLE 4.4 ■ Privacy Rule Criteria	
Criteria	**Example**
Cultural	Many African Americans value assertiveness and openness in sharing information.
Gender	In the United States, women are socialized to disclose more than men.
Motivational	Introverts may be less likely to share information than extroverts.
Contextual	Working in a cubicle might make an individual less likely to share information than working in a private office.
Risk–Benefit	Despite gains in LGBTQ+ rights, being ambiguous about your sexual orientation might minimize risks.

Team members attending an off-site retreat at a resort might feel more inclined to share private information than would the same team members at a weekly department meeting. Finally, individuals weigh the **risk–benefit criteria** when considering whether they should disclose private information. Much like what was explained by SET, individuals assess potential rewards and costs of disclosure. For example, knowing that, like yourself, a coworker is also an adult child of an alcoholic, you might decide that sharing your own family history with the coworker might have benefits in terms of cohesion and increased understanding that might overshadow any possible risks.

Much like a fence around your home or even that little plastic bar you use to separate your groceries while in the grocery store checkout lane, the fourth principle focuses on **boundaries** (Petronio & Durham, 2008). The metaphor of a boundary is meant to provide a visual representation of two sides; on one side people keep information to themselves, and on the other side people share private information. Personal boundaries are those that contain individual information (e.g., Bob is the only one who knows he was fired from his last job), and collective boundaries are those that contain shared information (e.g., Bob and Carlos both know Bob was fired from his last job). Once an individual shares information, the ownership of the information changes, as do the decision rules about privacy. The boundary has shifted, and managing the information becomes more complex.

Building on the notion that multiple people might have to maintain a boundary, the fifth principle of CPM is **boundary coordination**, which refers to the ways collective boundaries are maintained (Petronio & Durham, 2008). Petronio (2002) explains that boundary coordination takes place through boundary linkages, boundary ownership, and boundary permeability. First, **boundary linkages** refer to alliances between the owners of the information. Such alliances might be intentional, as when an individual accused of a crime shares incriminating information with a lawyer. That link is easily maintained because of attorney–client privilege. However, boundary linkages might also be unintentional. Imagine that another individual overhears this confession. The person who has overheard the information is now a part of the alliance. In this case, coordination is likely difficult, as the people in the alliance might have competing risk–benefit rules for disclosure.

Boundary ownership refers to the rights and responsibilities borne by the owners of the information (Petronio, 2002). The clearer the privacy rules are to the shared owners of the information, the more likely the information will be managed consonantly. Thus, when an individual intentionally creates a boundary linkage, they are also likely to indicate the rules for disclosure ("Don't tell Harry that I forgot to order the supplies!"). Not surprisingly, the rights and responsibilities are more problematic with unintentional linkages, especially if the individual who shared the information is unaware of the unintended recipient. How many times have you gossiped about someone and realized that someone else may have overheard you? Do you approach the person and say, "please don't repeat this," or do you take the risk that they didn't hear what you said?

Boundary permeability refers to how much information is easily passed through the boundary (Petronio, 2002). Some boundaries are permeable (easy to cross), and others may be impregnable (difficult, if not impossible, to cross). To illustrate, an individual might feel fairly comfortable in disclosing to colleagues what she had for dinner the night before, and other colleagues are likely to reciprocate. This represents a permeable boundary. However, that same individual might be much less comfortable sharing information with colleagues about a disastrous dinner date with another colleague that turned into a romantic fiasco. Of course, when the information is located within a collective boundary, the notion of permeability may be more problematic. This leads to the final principle of CPM.

Petronio (2002) recognized that the management of boundaries is not always a smooth process. Accordingly, she developed the notion of **boundary turbulence**, which occurs when the rules for privacy management are not clear. (Refer to Table 4.4 on privacy rules.) Imagine Lance tells Jamila about a forthcoming merger at work. Lance is a White male who believes information is power, and so his privacy rules dictate keeping this information private. Jamila, on the other hand, is an African American female who believes people have the right to know about issues that might affect them. Her cultural, gender, and individual motivation criteria lead to a privacy rule that would suggest this information should be shared. In this case, differing privacy rules might cause problems with managing the information. Other causes of boundary turbulence are privacy violations, ethical dilemmas, differing expectations, and misconceptions about ownership.

Taken together, these six principles articulate the complexities associated with information management. The theory "allows us to better understand what individuals disclose, what they keep private, and how private information is handled among people" (Petronio & Durham, 2008, p. 320). CPM provides a detailed analysis of a universal problem: What should (or shouldn't) I say?

CHAPTER SUMMARY AND RESEARCH APPLICATIONS

This chapter provided an overview of four theories of IPC. PT explains and predicts strategies individuals use to maintain "face," or sense of desired public image. Useful in personal as well as business and educational contexts, PT has explored how supervisors use humor in order to protect employees' face needs (Chefneux, 2015), how people use politeness when confronting

TABLE 4.5 ■ Additional Theories of Interpersonal Communication

Theory	Main Idea
Communication Theory of Identity	Our four layers of identity—personal, relational, enacted, and communal—are interdependent and performed through interpersonal communication (Hecht, 1993).
Relational Turbulence Model	Relationship uncertainty and partner interference combine to influence our perception that a relationship is fragile or chaotic (Solomon et al., 2016).
Social Penetration Theory	Relationship development occurs through the depth and breadth of communication (Altman & Taylor, 1973).

prejudice (Lewis, & Yoshimura, 2017), and facework strategies for the use of cell phones when you are with a friend (Kelly et al., 2019). SET predicts individuals initiate and maintain relationships so as to maximize personal outcomes; at the same time, however, expectations and alternatives play a role in individuals' ultimate satisfaction and whether they stay in the relationship. Examples of SET include research explaining the various methods employees use to resign from their positions (Klotz & Bolino, 2016) and how cyberloafing is related to abusive supervision in the workplace (Lim et al., 2021). The dialectical perspective suggests that sustaining interpersonal relationships requires communication to manage the necessary but contradictory tensions inherent in all relationships. It has been useful in exploring resilience during times of job instability (Wieland, 2020), as well as strategic decision-making among top management when launching a new venture (Costanzo & Di Domenico, 2015). Finally, CPM articulates a way of understanding the reasons for, and the challenges associated with, the decision to reveal or conceal private information, such as decisions to share religious minority status at work (Charoensap-Kelly et al., 2020) or to share otherwise personal information during workplace training (Thory, 2016). One burgeoning area of research is individuals' decisions to share private information on social networking sites (e.g., Zhang & Fu, 2020).

The four theories we have highlighted are not the only theories of IPC used by scholars. Table 4.5 identifies some other prominent theories of IPC.

DISCUSSION QUESTIONS

1. Think about a time you have had to engage in a face-threatening act. What facework strategy did you use? Did it work? Why or why not?

2. Can you think of any situations when people do not follow the minimax principle? If so, what is the situation, and why do you think the minimax principle is not followed in that situation?

3. The dialectical perspective says that within relationships we have to manage both internal and external tensions. Think about a time when you have faced one of the tensions

identified by the theory. How did you manage it? Was your technique one of the strategies identified by the theory?

4. Have you ever had information that you wanted to share with others, but you have been told not to do so? What did you do? Do any of the privacy rules explain why you did what you did?

KEY TERMS

Autonomy–connection (p. 59)

Avoidance (p. 54)

Bald-on-record (p. 55)

Boundaries (p. 63)

Boundary coordination (p. 63)

Boundary linkages (p. 63)

Boundary ownership (p. 64)

Boundary permeability (p. 64)

Boundary turbulence (p. 64)

Change (p. 59)

Comparison level (p. 57)

Comparison level of alternatives (p. 57)

Contextual criteria (p. 62)

Contradictions (p. 59)

Conventionality-uniqueness (p. 60)

Corrective facework (p. 54)

Costs (p. 57)

Cultural criteria (p. 62)

Cyclic alteration (p. 61)

Dialectical tensions (p. 59)

External dialectics (p. 60)

Face (p. 53)

Face-threatening act (p. 54)

Facework (p. 54)

Gender criteria (p. 62)

Inclusion-seclusion (p. 60)

Integration (p. 61)

Internal dialectics (p. 59)

Interpersonal communication (p. 52)

Legitimate power (p. 56)

Minimax principle (p. 56)

Motivational criteria (p. 62)

Negative face (p. 53)

Negative politeness (p. 55)

Off-record (p. 54)

Openness-closedness (p. 59)

Outcome value (p. 57)

Positive face (p. 53)

Positive politeness (p. 55)

Praxis (p. 58)

Predictability-novelty (p. 59)

Preventive facework (p. 54)

Privacy rules (p. 62)

Private information (p. 62)

Public–private (p. 62)

Revelation-concealment (p. 60)

Rewards (p. 57)

Risk (p. 56)

Risk–benefit criteria (p. 63)

Segmentation (p. 61)

Selection (p. 61)

Social power (p. 56)

Totality (p. 59)

Jason was a man with a plan. Immediately after graduating from college, he created his own cleaning company. He started off cleaning houses doing all of the dirty work by himself, but over time, he grew his company to include commercial and retail cleaning, and he employed almost three dozen employees. The business was lucrative, and by the time he was 32, he sold the company for a hefty profit. He knew he wasn't ready to retire, but it was nice to have a chunk of change that allowed him to be picky about his next career move.

Within 6 months, he heard from one of his old fraternity brothers, Seth. Seth had followed the traditional route after college; he got a job with a small firm and spent his time moving from company to company trying to make it up the corporate ladder. By his early 30s, he was fed up and frustrated with corporate life.

"Bro, I am so done with this crap," Seth told Jason. "It's soul sucking. Seriously, every day I go in and do something pointless, not because it should be done, but because some overpaid drone needs to check a box somewhere."

Jason couldn't help but smirk. "That's why I opted out, man. Be your own boss. Then if you have an idiot for a manager, it's your own damn fault."

Seth groaned. "Woulda, shoulda, coulda. I wouldn't even know where to start. How did you even come up with the idea to create your own business?"

"You know me, dude. I'm a nonconformist. I knew that corporate life wasn't for me, so I started thinking about a business with a built-in demand. One look at our old fraternity house, and it became very clear to me," Jason laughed.

"What are you going to do next," Seth asked.

"I dunno. Maybe travel the world and see what strikes my fancy," Jason replied.

"Why don't you come visit me in Tampa? I'll buy you a beer or two and maybe you can lay some wisdom on me."

"It'll take more than two beers, and I am not laying anything on you, but sure, sounds like fun," Jason responded.

A few weeks later, Jason headed down to Tampa, and he and Seth hung out on the beach and brainstormed about business ideas. Over time, Seth became convinced that starting a cleaning company in Tampa made sense—not only were there plenty of homes, stores, and offices that needed to be cleaned, but the area had plenty of hotels that might magnify the business opportunities. Jason wasn't convinced. First, he had been there and done that with the cleaning industry. Second, he suspected that the area was already saturated with cleaning companies because of its reputation as a vacation destination.

Seth, however, had latched on to the idea and wasn't about to let it go. Rather than starting as a "one man show," as Jason had, Seth wanted to start with a full staff. He had the expertise to develop a website and marketing plan, he had a lot of professional contacts, and he wanted to jump into the market with guns blazing. He also wanted

Jason to stick around and serve as a consultant to help him to bring the business up to speed. Jason was a bit dubious about it all, but he wasn't actually investing any money into the venture, only time and expertise, and he wanted to help out a friend.

It was a rocky start. They had a few contracts for housecleaning, and they got an office in a strip mall in return for cleaning the other tenants' spaces. They hired four employees on that basis, but since they weren't actually being paid for cleaning the commercial space, there was not much money coming in.

Jason learned that Seth was more of a talker than a doer. He also learned that Seth's "professional contacts" were friends who did not have decision-making authority to hire a cleaning company. Every time Jason tried to schedule a meeting with Seth in order to develop a strategy, Seth would tell him not to worry.

"Bro, it's under control. No worries," he would assure him.

But Jason was frustrated—he wanted to know exactly to whom Seth was talking and what sorts of results he might expect. Seth, however, wasn't willing to share that information. "I'm networking," Seth would say. "The only way to grow this business is networking."

Over time, Jason was spending more and more time in their small office, while Seth was out drumming up business. "How the hell did I end up sitting in an office all day," Jason wondered. "I was the one who knew that I wasn't an office person, and yet, here I am!"

Things began to come to a head when Jason found out from a mutual friend that Seth was actually out partying with his buddies and not selling their new business idea. Jason immediately called Seth's cell, which went right to voice mail.

"Seth," Jason yelled. "Gimme a call immediately! We really need to talk about this business of yours."

Seth never called back, but the next day he came into the office and sought to reassure Jason.

"Look, Jason, I know things aren't going the way you would like, but I really need you," Seth explained. "Without your expertise, there is no way this can happen. I know you don't need me and my business, but I need you. Please, would you just stick it out for another month? One more month, and you can go back to travelling the world."

Jason had no reason to stick it out other than his friendship with Seth. But Seth seemed ready to work.

"One month," Jason replied. "But that is ONLY if we spend the next few hours mapping out a game plan, which includes who you will be speaking with and what you will be talking about. No more partying with friends. That is NOT how you are going to grow this business."

"Totally," Seth agreed. "Just . . . uh . . . don't tell anyone else that it's only going to be a month, okay? The workers seem to really respect you, and I don't want them to mutiny before we get everything straight."

During the remainder of the day, Seth was focused, and he agreed with all of Jason's suggestions. Jason left at the end of the day satisfied that the business could work, and that he would be out of it in just a few short weeks.

Within a week, however, things went back to the way they had been before. Jason had prepared the payroll, and he needed Seth to sign the checks. But Seth seemed to disappear for days at a time, leaving Jason to try to explain to the employees why they were not being paid.

The final straw was when the same mutual friend who had informed Jason that Seth was out drinking with buddies contacted him again and told Jason that Seth was bragging that he was "living the dream." According to the mutual friend, Seth gloated that "I've got one guy doing all the work, and he isn't even getting paid, and I've got a bunch of illegals doing the cleaning, so they can't complain if they don't get paid!"

Jason paid the employees out of his own pocket, went back to his hotel, and packed his belongings, and left Florida. The next day, Jason started getting voice mails and texts from Seth. Jason tapped Seth's number, then tapped "block caller" on his phone.

Questions for Consideration

1. What politeness strategies did Jason use with Seth? What politeness strategies did Seth use with Jason? Use politeness theory to explain why or why not these were appropriate.

2. Using social exchange theory, consider the friendship between Seth and Jason. Identify the rewards and costs for each person. Using the concepts of comparison level and comparison level of alternatives, why did Jason end the friendship?

3. Identify any internal and external dialectics that appear in the story. What strategies were used to manage these tensions? What strategies might have been better?

4. What private information and privacy rules exist in this story? How was boundary coordination used by the various characters? Did anyone violate boundary ownership? If so, who, and how did they do so?

5. Do any of the IPC theories provide a better explanation than the others? Why do you believe this to be the case? What additional factors might have been included to make a different theory or combination of theories better at explaining the situation?

5 CULTURE

LEARNING OBJECTIVES

After reading this chapter, you will be able to do the following:

1. Define culture, cross-cultural communication, and intercultural communication

2. Explain each of Hofstede's six primary cultural dimensions

3. Discuss the positive and negative consequences of accommodation

4. Identify the strategies used by members of non-dominant groups when communicating with members of dominant groups

5. Describe the two types of prejudice central to role of congruity theory

Culture matters when it comes to communication competence. In Chapter 1, we defined communication competence as a balance between effectiveness and appropriateness. Effectiveness, we explained, is the ability to achieve your goals, whereas appropriateness is following social rules. However, social rules vary across cultures. What is considered appropriate in one culture is not appropriate in another culture. Imagine that you are trying to cross a busy street and a driver stops to allow you to cross the street. What type of gesture might you make to acknowledge the driver who stopped? In the United States you likely would raise your hand in thanks. However, the outward hand gesture in Greece is highly offensive. Instead of thanking someone for their kindness, you are calling them worse than an idiot.

Social rules also vary across cultural groups within the United States. For example, White Americans often engage in "civil inattention" when in public places, especially if they think they might be invading other people's space (such as in an elevator). However, Latino/a cultural norms are to acknowledge others in public places—to ignore someone is to be rude (Lozano, 2015). Understanding the dynamics of cross-cultural and intercultural communication is critical in today's multicultural society and global economy. Although the challenges of cross-cultural and intercultural communication are probably not new to you, the implications of, difficulties with, and strategies for improving these exchanges is profound, particularly considering the high failure rate of such interaction. In fact, within the United States a failure to embrace diversity and inclusion has the potential of costing organizations $1.05 trillion in profits (Ward, 2020).

Clearly, there are many financial, personal, and social benefits—and costs—associated with the power of effectively communicating across cultural differences.

DEFINING CULTURE

Recognizing the diversity of today's personal and professional landscape is one thing, but what exactly is culture? We embrace Collier's (1989) notion of **culture** as one's identification with and acceptance into a group that shares symbols, meanings, experiences, and behavior. Cross-cultural communication and intercultural communication expand on this notion. **Cross-cultural communication** is the comparison of two or more cultural communities (Ting-Toomey, 1991); for example, comparing conflict styles of US managers with those of Korean managers. Somewhat differently, **intercultural communication** involves the actual interaction between members of different cultures; for instance, examining what happens when a German executive reprimands a Chinese subordinate. However, you should know that cultures are not only national cultures; there are also cultural variations within a dominant culture such as ethnic cultures, racial cultures, and gender cultures. Accordingly, when a Mexican-American and an Indian-American communicate, this can also be considered intercultural communication, as would communication between the sexes.

Using these definitions, we have selected four theories that examine broadly defined notions of culture and emphasize how culture shapes and is shaped by communication. First, Hofstede's cultural dimensions provide a typology useful for assessing cultural differences across social contexts. Next, we look at communication accommodation theory (CAT) as a way of predicting when individuals adapt to or diverge from the communication practices of a member of another cultural group. Third, co-cultural theory examines the strategies used by members of nondominant social groups when communicating with members of dominant groups. Finally, we consider social role theory, which argues that perceptions of men and women's behavior are always filtered through our stereotypes of how men and women should behave. We specifically apply this theory to research investigating women and leadership. Table 5.1 provides an overview of each of these theories.

TABLE 5.1 ■ Overview of Intercultural Communication Theories	
Theory	**Main Idea**
Cultural Dimensions	Cultures vary in terms of fundamental values and beliefs, which influences communication practices.
Communication Accommodation Theory	The extent to which an individual does, or does not, adapt their communication to their conversational partners affects how the individual is perceived.
Co-Cultural Theory	Members of nondominant groups select particular communication strategies to achieve their desired outcomes when interacting with members of dominant groups.
Social Role Theory	Because women are presumed to be different than men, they experience two types of prejudice in the workplace.

HOFSTEDE'S CULTURAL DIMENSIONS

Geert Hofstede was a Dutch management researcher who developed an inductive theory of culture. Specifically, he gathered statistical data from 100,000 employees of IBM around the world to determine the values on which cultures vary (Hofstede, 1980). In the process, he surveyed workers from 50 countries and three regions. Ultimately his analysis resulted in six dimensions with which to differentiate and rank cultures (Hofstede, 1980, 1991; Hofstede & Bond, 1984). Each dimension is described as a continuum, with distinct cultures classified somewhere along the continuum.

Individualism–Collectivism

Hofstede's (1980) first dimension is individualism–collectivism. This dimension addresses how people define themselves and their relationships with others. Cultures that fall on the **individualism** side of the continuum share four characteristics (Triandis, 1995). First, such cultures consider the individual to be the most important entity in any social setting. Think about some common phrases you have heard in the United States (a highly individualistic culture). When asked to do something beyond one's responsibilities, an American is likely to ask, "What's in it for me?" In explaining why an individual is ending a romantic relationship, the person might say, "I was putting more into it than I was getting out of it." In short, in individualistic cultures, the focus is on the self before all other relationships.

Second, individualistic cultures stress independence rather than dependence (Triandis, 1995). Recall the description of face needs in Chapter 4. Positive face is the desire to be appreciated and liked. Negative face is the desire to be free from impositions. Ting-Toomey (1988) argued that people from individualistic cultures tend to place relatively more emphasis on negative face needs compared with individuals from collectivistic cultures; there is a cultural preference to be free from imposition, which is in essence a desire to be independent.

Third, individualistic cultures reward individual achievement (Triandis, 1995). To illustrate, US organizations frequently use merit pay and employee recognition programs. These programs focus on recognizing particular individuals and their performance, raising them above other employees in the organization. Likewise, individual achievement tends to accompany the value of competition. In individualistic cultures, competition is viewed as a good thing. This is not always the case in collectivistic cultures.

Finally, individualistic cultures value each individual's uniqueness (Triandis, 1995). In such cultures, standing out from the crowd is highly valued, whereas in collectivistic cultures, standing out from others is a source of embarrassment. Consider the variations in two cultural proverbs (Mieder, 1986). The American proverb "the squeaky wheel gets the grease" implies you will receive rewards by distinguishing yourself from others; you ought to speak up and be noticed. The Japanese proverb "the tallest nail gets hammered down" implies punishment is associated with being different—you are better off being the same as others.

Thus far we have talked at length about individualism but have not addressed collectivism in detail. **Collectivism** refers to a social system based on in-groups and out-groups. In collectivistic cultures, groups (relatives, clans, organizations) are the central way of understanding relations between people; identity is understood solely through group membership.

There are also four characteristics associated with collectivism (Triandis, 1995). First, in collectivistic cultures the views, needs, and goals of the group are more important than any individual views, needs, or goals. For many Americans, the idea of kamikaze pilots or suicide bombers makes no sense. Yet, in collectivistic cultures, the needs of the group supersede the needs of the individual. In these sorts of systems, dying for the good of a group makes sense.

Second, obligation to the group is the norm in collectivistic cultures; behavior is guided by duty, not by individual pleasure or rewards (Triandis, 1995). This focus on duty over pleasure is apparent in mate selection. In individualistic cultures, people are "free" to marry the mate of their choice. In collectivistic cultures, acceptance of the potential mate by the family is of central importance (Dion & Dion, 1993).

Third, in collectivistic cultures, the self is defined in relation to others, not as distinct from others (Triandis, 1995). Jandt's (2004) example best illustrates this point. Imagine a person from Colombia (a more collectivistic culture) coming to the United States. In the United States, a common question for the visitor would be "What do you do for a living?" because Americans are understood by their individual accomplishments. In Colombia, however, the first question asked of this same person would likely be "Who are you related to?" Knowing a person's "connections" enables strangers to place that person into particular groups; knowing where a person comes from is the same as knowing who that person is.

Fourth and finally, those from collectivistic cultures focus on cooperation rather than competition (Triandis, 1995). This characteristic manifests in particular communication patterns in collectivistic cultures. Collectivistic cultures tend to use a **high-context communication** style (Hall, 1976). A high-context message privileges relational harmony over clarity or directness; messages tend to be indirect, circular, or unspoken so as not to offend. It is assumed the receiver will actively seek to understand what is really meant. By contrast, a **low-context communication** style, characteristic of individualistic cultures, values direct, explicit expression of ideas. In low-context communication, the meaning is in the message, and sometimes "the truth hurts."

We have presented a number of details unique to individualism and collectivism, but individualism and collectivism exist together in all cultures—they are, in essence, two sides of the same coin. Certain cultures, however, tend to operate at one end of the continuum or the other. We turn next to the second dimension of culture as described by Hofstede (1980), uncertainty avoidance.

High Uncertainty Avoidance—Low Uncertainty Avoidance

We talked about the concept of uncertainty in Chapter 3. As a cultural dimension, **uncertainty avoidance** refers to the extent to which "people within a culture are made nervous by situations which they perceive as unstructured, unclear, or unpredictable" (Hofstede, 1986, p. 308). Those cultures that seek to avoid ambiguity are known as high-uncertainty-avoidance cultures. Typically, cultures high in uncertainty avoidance maintain strict codes of behavior and support a belief in absolute truths. For instance, in high-uncertainty-avoidance cultures, the workplace is typified by rules, precision, and punctuality (Jandt, 2004). The preference for a business meeting would be a structured agenda, which would be rigidly followed (Lewis, 2000).

Cultures low in uncertainty avoidance tend to accept ambiguity and lack of structure more easily (Hofstede, 1986). Individuals in low-uncertainty-avoidance cultures are more inclined to take risks, innovate, and value "thinking outside of the box." Clearly, American culture is a low-uncertainty-avoidance culture. In the workplace, individuals from low-uncertainty-avoidance cultures tend to work hard only when needed (Jandt, 2004). Rules are often rejected or ignored, and punctuality has to be taught and reinforced.

High Power Distance—Low Power Distance

The third dimension uncovered by Hofstede (1980) is power distance, or the extent to which people with little power in society consider inequity normal and acceptable. Cultures with **high power distance** accept power as a scarce resource; power differences are natural and inevitable. In these sorts of cultures, there is greater centralization of power and a great importance placed on status and rank. In the workplace, high-power-distance cultures tend to have a large number of supervisors, a rigid system that classifies each job along a hierarchy, and decision-making only among those at the high end of the hierarchy (Adler, 1997). There also tends to be a wide salary gap between those high and low in the hierarchy (Jandt, 2004).

Cultures with **low power distance** value the minimization of power differences (Hofstede, 1980). Although hierarchy might exist, people higher in the hierarchy are not assumed to be superior to people lower in the hierarchy; people at all levels reach out to people at all other levels. Moreover, people lower in power believe that through motivation and hard work they can achieve power (Hofstede, 1980). In the workplace, low-power-distance cultures view shared decision-making with subordinates as empowering (Jandt, 2004).

The United States falls on the lower end of this power distance spectrum but is not extremely low. A pervasive management style in the United States is that of "status-achievement," meaning status can be earned "via hard work, personal ambition, and competitiveness . . . and displayed effectively and proudly (e.g., by driving expensive cars or having the spacious corner office)" (Ting-Toomey, 2005, p. 75). And when you consider the following statistics, it appears the United States is becoming increasingly higher in power distance. According to 2013 Bloomberg financial data, CEO salary for Fortune 500 CEOs had increased 1,000% since 1950 (Smith & Kuntz, 2013). In 1980, the average salary of a CEO was 42 times that of the average worker. After the "great recession" and stock market collapse of 2008–2009, CEO salaries took a dive but quickly bounced back. By 2015, top CEOs made 300 times as much as the average worker (Mishel & Davis, 2015). In 2019 that number increased to 320 times as much as the average worker (Mishel & Kandra, 2020). These figures mirror statistics indicating the difference between the "haves" and "have-nots" is growing in the United States; the rich are growing richer, but real income for the middle class and the working class has declined relative to the gains made by the wealthy (Horowitz et al., 2020). The extent to which American citizens believe this power differential is acceptable and normative demonstrates an acceptance of increasingly higher power distance.

Masculinity–Femininity

Hofstede's (1980) fourth dimension focuses on the relationship between biological sex and what is considered sex-appropriate behavior. **Masculine cultures** use the reality of biological sex in the creation of distinct roles for men and women. In masculine cultures, men are expected to be assertive, ambitious, and competitive; women are expected to be supportive, nurturing, and deferent. Translating these values to the workplace, countries with a masculine orientation believe managers are supposed to be decisive and assertive (Jandt, 2004). More important, women have a difficult time achieving workplace equality; they are given lower wages, less stable work, and few opportunities to advance (Kim, 2001).

The United States is a masculine country. Although women are making inroads in organizational life, there is still a significant wage gap (Brown & Patton, 2017), and the glass ceiling remains a reality (Ezzedeen et al., 2015). Moreover, women are often expected to conform to masculine norms if they hope to succeed at work, as we will see shortly when discussing social role theory (Brands, 2015).

By contrast, **feminine cultures** have fewer rigid roles for behavior based on biological sex (Hofstede, 1980). Men and women are equally permitted to be assertive or deferent, competitive or nurturing. Instead of rigid sex roles, the focus in feminine cultures tends to be on the facilitation of interpersonal relationships and concern for the weak (Jandt, 2004). In the workplace, feminine cultures manifest consensus seeking and a preference for quality of life over material success. To illustrate, consider Sweden, a highly feminine culture. In Sweden, the law allows both men and women to balance parenthood and employment. At the birth or adoption of a child, parents are jointly eligible for 480 days of paid, child-rearing leave ("Gender Equality in Sweden," 2013).

Long-Term—Short-Term Orientation

Hofstede's (1980) original research stopped after the first four dimensions. Responding to accusations of a Western bias to his work, Hofstede collected additional data with the assistance of Chinese scholars and ultimately added two additional cultural dimensions. Grounded in Confucian thinking, Hofstede (1991, 2001) called the fifth dimension the orientation toward long term versus short term. A **long-term orientation** is associated with a future orientation. Accordingly, individuals in these sorts of cultures tend to focus on thrift and perseverance in order to achieve prospective goals. In cultures with a long-term orientation, employees typically have a strong work ethic and keep their eyes toward the achievement of distant objectives (Hofstede, 2001). A **short-term orientation** is characterized by a present or past orientation (Hofstede, 2001). Employees focus on what is happening right now or look to the past for the way things should be. Individuals from short-term orientation cultures tend to have a mañana attitude; they will worry about tomorrow when tomorrow comes.

Indulgence—Restraint

The final cultural dimension identified by Hofstede focuses on the role of happiness in culture (Hofstede et al., 2010). Cultures that fall on the **indulgence** side of the continuum value the individuals' ability to satisfy their desires and meet their needs. Alternatively, cultures on the **restraint** side of the continuum frown on the pursuit of personal pleasure, focusing instead on conforming to social norms. As you might expect, individuals from indulgent cultures tend to seek immediate gratification. Individuals in these cultures tend to spend money to "keep up with the Joneses" and prefer quick results to long-term gain (Hofstede, 2001). On the other hand, individuals from restrain cultures tend to be more cynical and pessimistic (Hofstede et al., 2010).

Table 5.2 plots eight countries or regions on each of the six dimensions (Hofstede et al., 2010). Note that just because two countries are similar in one dimension does not mean they will be similar in another. Moreover, recognize that the rankings described are generalizations about each culture; it should come as no surprise that individual variations exist within each culture. Finally, in many countries, including the United States, different groups in the same culture might rank quite differently within a given dimension. For example, although the dominant US culture is individualistic, researchers believe that African Americans and Hispanics tend more toward collectivism (e.g., Hecht et al., 1993).

TABLE 5.2 ■ Rankings of Select Countries or Regions on Hofstede's Dimensions						
	Individualism–Collectivism	Uncertainty Avoidance	Power Distance	Masculinity–Femininity	Long-Term — Short-Term	Indulgence — Restraint
India	Both	Moderate	High	Masculine	Middle of the Road	Restraint
Italy	High individualism	Moderate	Moderate	Extreme masculinity	Middle of the Road	Restraint
Japan	Both	Extremely high	Moderate	Extreme masculinity	Long term	Restraint
Mexico	Moderate collectivism	High	High	Extreme masculinity	Short term	Very Indulgent
Nigeria	Collectivism	No preference	High	Masculine	Short term	Indulgent
Saudi Arabia	Collectivism	High	High	Masculine	Short term	Restraint
South Korea	High collectivism	High	Moderate	Moderate femininity	Long term	Restraint
Sweden	Moderate individualism	Extremely low	Very low	Extreme femininity	Middle of the Road	Indulgent
United States	Extreme individualism	Low	Moderate	High masculinity	Short term	Indulgent
Venezuela	Extreme collectivism	Moderate	High	Extreme masculinity	Short term	Very Indulgent

COMMUNICATION ACCOMMODATION THEORY

Have you ever caught yourself slipping into a southern drawl or using *y'all* while speaking to a native Texan? Maybe you have found yourself speaking in fast, clipped tones when talking with a New Yorker, or upon returning from a European vacation, friends point out that you suddenly sound more like Tom Holland than Tom Brady. Do you speed up while talking with some colleagues but slow your speech when speaking with others? Communication accommodation theory (CAT) can explain many of the changes in your speech and language use.

Originally conceived as speech accommodation theory (Giles et al., 1987) and later refined as communication accommodation theory (Giles & Coupland, 1991), CAT provides an informative platform from which to understand how and why we adapt our communication when we interact with others. Essentially, Giles and colleagues argue that when interacting with others, individuals will **accommodate** their speech and language patterns, either by matching their partners' speech or by differentiating their speech and language use. In this section, we explain Giles and colleagues' notion of accommodation through both convergence and divergence.

Assumptions of Communication Accommodation Theory

Giles and Coupland (1991) assumed individuals belong to a wide variety of social groups based on ethnicity, gender, race, and religion. Moreover, they maintained that these groups shape each person's collective identity. For example, "most ethnic minority groups in the United States have tended to form communities, however small, where they have other people of similar heritage to sustain their ethnic values, socialization practices, and culture" (Vivero & Jenkins, 1999, p. 9). Similarly, your marital status (e.g., married), your political alignment (e.g., Republican), your career (e.g., public relations director), and your ethnicity (e.g., Irish American) all represent social groups that influence the way you perceive yourself and others perceive you.

Like it or not, human beings categorize information to simplify and create understanding. One way in which we commonly categorize others and ourselves is through these social identity groups; these clusters are divided into in-groups and out-groups. **In-groups** are social affiliations to which an individual feels they belong (Giles & Coupland, 1991). **Out-groups** are those social affiliations to which a person feels they do not belong. In the workplace, for example, you may go to happy hour with members from your team or department but would feel out of place socializing with members of another department. Similarly, if you play on a company softball league, your teammates may become an in-group, even if you had not interacted previously.

In-groups and out-groups are important for understanding CAT. According to Giles and Coupland (1991), language, speech, and nonverbal messages all communicate one's in-group and out-group status. For example, if you have been around a group of teenagers recently, you may feel very much part of the out-group because you are wearing mom jeans or dad sneakers unironically? When your teenage son mumbles, "NONYA," in response to your simple question of "Where are you going tonight?" he has differentiated himself (a hip teen) from you (a stodgy middle-aged parent). Instead of simply saying, "It's none of your business," his use of Twitter slang leaves you wondering what the heck he is talking about, thereby creating a gap between his generation and yours.

The use of slang to create in-group and out-group status applies to the workplace as well. Each profession has its own set of jargon, or specialized language that not only gives precision to words and meanings but also helps create and maintain a distinct in-group. Thus, jargon includes those individuals who have similar training and experience and excludes everyone else. A member of your company's information technology (IT) department may use computer jargon that intimidates the nontechnology minded. For instance, when Karen calls her company's IT department with a question about a problem she is having with a website password, the help desk manager asks her, "What's your ISP?" Karen has no idea what an ISP is, much less which one she is using. In this instance, the help desk manager may use the jargon unintentionally when communicating with out-group members such as Karen and employees from other departments simply out of habit. Conversely, the manager may intentionally rely on jargon so as to intimidate the out-group members or to promote one's own credibility. Because she doesn't know what her ISP is, Karen may feel inferior, or she may perceive the help desk manager as possessing complex and invaluable information. Karen may even feel frustrated or annoyed because members of the help desk can't seem to explain things in plain English. Importantly, then, jargon is both inclusive and exclusive and should be used cautiously with out-group members.

Accommodation Through Convergence or Divergence

Individuals regulate their speech and conversational patterns either in an effort to assimilate with or to deviate from others (Giles & Coupland, 1991). And as Giles and Gasiorek (2014) argue, this ability to adjust "is a fundamental part of successful interaction" (p. 155). When a person wants to be viewed as part of an in-group, CAT predicts this person will accommodate by **convergence**. That is, you will alter your speech and behavior so that it matches that of your conversational partner. Speech includes word choice, pronunciation, pitch, rate, and even gestures such as smiling and gaze. For instance, elementary school teachers often converge their speech, using more expressive registers, slower speaking rates, and shorter words or phrases to accommodate their young pupils. When individuals match their speech, they convey acceptance and understanding. Interpersonal attraction also leads to convergence (Giles et al., 1987). That is, the more a person is likable, charismatic, and socially skilled, the more likely you are to try to match their communication patterns.

Conversely, there are times when individuals don't want to be associated with a certain group or do not find a person interpersonally attractive; sometimes you want to differentiate yourself from a particular crowd. In this instance, you will alter your speech through **divergence**. Rather than match your partner's communication patterns, you will seek to make your speech different. Deliberately diverging from the speech of your partner signals disagreement or rejection. A kindergarten teacher may use a sterner tone when disciplining the class for misbehavior. Similarly, you may overhear you're a group of teenagers conversing in strings of expletives with their friends simply as a way of countering adult authority. In addition to expressing disagreement or rejection of a speaker, divergence also illustrates one's cultural identity (e.g., maintaining a Scottish accent despite living in the United States) or differences in one's status (e.g., a physician's use of elaborate medical terminology when talking with a patient).

Extending the Theory: Maintenance and Nonaccommodation

Convergence and divergence are not the only options for approaching in-group/out-group interaction. Extending the theory, Giles and colleagues advanced two additional ways of managing, or failing to manage, such interactions (Giles et al., 2007). **Maintenance** simply is the absence of adjustment. Perhaps the out-group member is unaware of the perceived social distance between himself or herself and the in-group. Or maybe the out-group member doesn't care or isn't able to make the adjustment. Somewhat different, **nonaccommodation** includes over- and underaccommodation—that is, the person uses too much or too little adjustment in an effort to engage in a successful interaction. Much like Goldilocks who had to try three of everything to get it "just right," attempting to regulate one's interaction in real time, just enough to show social affiliation or be understood can be challenging. Importantly, Giles and Gasiorek (2014) remind us that nonaccommodation is a subjective evaluation. You may appreciate a physician's attempt to simplify vocabulary while your friend may view it as condescending. In the first case, the physician's attempt to simplify vocabulary is viewed as convergence, but in the second case, it is viewed as overaccommodation.

Influences and Effects of Accommodation

It is worthy to note differences in **accommodation** across groups because these differences say a great deal about the importance of perceived status, authority, and cultural and social identity within our multicultural society. In her review of research, Larkey (1996) reported that when looking at race, ethnicity, and sex in the workplace, White American male employees typically maintain; that is, they maintain their communicative style regardless of conversational partner because it is commonly defined as the "standard" in both the United States and much of Europe.

Conversely, minority employees (including women and members of racial and ethnic minorities) typically are expected to converge to this "standard" to achieve status within the organization. Persistent convergence may create cognitive dissonance for minority members by placing them in a dilemma; maintaining their cultural and social identity is sacrificed when using the mainstream speech patterns that are expected and rewarded.

Notably, accommodation is not always appropriate or effective (Giles & Coupland, 1991). When in doubt, individuals rely on social norms to inform their decision to accommodate or not. Norms are implicit expectations that guide social behavior; thus, we must rely on our perceptions of social appropriateness when determining whether to converge or diverge. Table 5.3 provides some consequences of accommodation. Note both positive and negative consequences for both types of accommodation.

All told, CAT explains and predicts the experience of convergence and divergence in interpersonal communication. The more we like a person or perceive ourselves as part of an in-group, the more likely we are to adapt and match our speech patterns. The more we want to communicate our difference, status, or unique cultural identity, the more likely we are to differentiate our speech from our partner's. Communicators must be aware, however, that accommodation is not always effective or well received and can have implications for workplace relationships.

TABLE 5.3 ■ Consequences of Accommodation		
	Positive Effects	**Negative Effects**
Convergence	Increased attraction; social approval; increased persuasion	Incorrect stereotypes of out-group; perceived condescension; loss of personal identity
Maintenance	Upholds personal identity	Apparent lack of interest or effort; perceived as overly rigid
Divergence	Asserts power differences; increased sympathy	Perceived disdain for out-group; increased psychological distance

CO-CULTURAL THEORY

Earlier in this chapter we indicated that not all cultures are international cultures; social groups such as ethnic groups, racial groups, and gender groups within a national culture might have varying values, beliefs, and ways of communicating. Co-cultural theory focuses on interactions between members of different **co-cultural groups**, which are nondominant social groups that are embedded in a larger culture (Orbe, 1998). It's important to note that co-cultural theory does not simply assume that there are variations among different subcultures; instead, the focus is on how power and privilege influences the interactions between those who are disadvantaged (**nondominant groups**) and those who have a more privileged position within the larger culture (**dominant groups**). The theory focuses on people who are marginalized based on race, ethnicity, gender, differences in ability, and sexual orientation, among others.

Co-cultural theory was greatly influenced by two earlier theories. The first, **muted group theory**, was developed by social anthropologists based on their observation that within every society the communication practices of those who have power are different from those who do not (Ardener, 1975a, 1975b). Specifically, the theory suggests that people who do not have power are muted groups; their membership in a nondominant group influences what they talk about, how much they talk, the channels they use, the words and concepts that are used, and the impact of their speech. The second theoretical influence was standpoint theory. **Standpoint theory** suggests that people's experiences stem from their position in society (Wood, 1992). Based on these experiences, people develop a way of seeing the world (called a standpoint) that is distinct from others who do not share the same experiences. Accordingly, a Latina has a different standpoint than a Black woman, an Asian-American woman, or a White woman.

Orbe's co-cultural theory focuses "on the various ways in which persons reinforce, manage, alter, and overcome a societal position that renders them outside the center of power" (Orbe, 1998, p. 65). That is, co-cultural theory identifies the strategies used by members of nondominant groups when they interact with dominant group members, as well as the factors that influence the selection of a strategy, and the goals that the strategy is designed to achieve.

Goals and Strategies

First, co-cultural theory identifies three possible interactional goals (Orbe, 1998). **Assimilation** is an effort to become more similar to the dominant group, which in essence lessens the perception of being a member of a co-culture. **Accommodation,** on the other hand, is when people seek to fit in with the dominant group without losing their co-cultural identity. It is a both/and goal that recognizes difference but seeks to maintain equal treatment. Lastly, **separation** is when the co-cultural member avoids interactions with the dominant group.

Given a specific desired outcome for co-cultural communication, the member of a non-dominant group has to determine which communication approach they will use (Orbe, 1998). A **nonassertive** approach is when individuals put others' goals above their own. An **assertive** approach seeks to achieve the individual's goal without impinging on the goals of the other person. Finally, an **aggressive** approach centers on achieving one's own goals without consideration of the other person's goals.

Based on these varying goals and communication approaches, co-cultural theory identifies a set of strategies, listed in Table 5.4. For example, a nonassertive approach to achieving assimilation can include censoring the self, which means that the nondominant group member refrains from saying something they would normally say. An aggressive accommodation approach might be to confront someone without concern for the other person's face needs.

TABLE 5.4 ■ Co-Cultural Communication Strategies			
	Assimilation	**Accommodation**	**Separation**
Nonassertive	• Emphasizing Commonality • Developing Positive Face • Censoring Self • Averting Controversy	• Increasing Visibility • Dispelling Stereotypes	• Avoiding • Maintaining Barriers
Assertive	• Extensive Preparation • Overcompensating • Manipulating Stereotypes • Bargaining	• Communicating Self • Intragroup Networking • Utilizing Liaisons • Educating Others	• Exemplifying Strength • Embracing Stereotypes
Aggressive	• Dissociating • Mirroring • Strategic Distancing • Ridiculing Self	• Confronting • Gaining Advantage	• Attacking • Sabotaging Others

Source: Camara & Orbe (2010)

Finally, an assertive separation approach includes exemplifying strength, which such as a focus on the achievements of the co-cultural group (Camara & Orbe, 2010).

Remember that the theory also articulates some of the factors that might influence a nondominant group member to select a particular goal and communication approach (Orbe & Roberts, 2012). First, remember that co-cultural theory was based on standpoint theory. Accordingly, the individual considers their own **field of experience** or standpoint. What has worked in the past for them? What has been less successful? Second, the individual considers their own **abilities**. Regardless of group membership, people vary in their interpersonal communication skill. Third, the **situational context** is considered. For example, if the individual has a formal position of power in the interaction, such as being someone's manager, more assertive and aggressive approaches might be perceived as appropriate. Fourth, the individual considers the **perceived rewards and costs** of engaging in a particular behavior. What is the best that can happen? What is the worst that could happen? Fifth, the individual considers the **preferred outcome**; does the person wish to assimilate, accommodate, or separate? Lastly, the co-cultural groups' **typical communication approach** influences the strategy that is chosen. For example, if you are a member of an individualistic culture it might be easier to engage in an aggressive behavior, but if you are a member of a collectivistic culture you might feel more comfortable with a passive approach.

SOCIAL ROLE THEORY OF GENDER

Co-cultural theory provides some insight into the communication between members of different sexes. For example, because women have historically been a muted group, the strategies and goals outlined by Orbe (1998) can be used to understand how women adjust their communication when interacting with men. However, a theory that more specifically focuses on how sex differences impact professional communication is social role theory.

Examining sex and gender differences in communication is perhaps one of the most controversial and widely debated areas of communication research in recent decades (see Canary & Hause, 1993; Wood & Dindia, 1998). Despite the number of popular self-help books proclaiming the idea that men inhabit one planet while women occupy another (see Gray, 1992, 1997/2005) or alleging men and women "just don't understand" each other (see Tannen, 1990), there is actually very little communication theory—or research—to support these stereotypical claims of widespread sex differences (Anderson, 1998; Canary et al., 1997; Canary & Hause, 1993; Crawford, 2004).

Yet there has to be a reason why these books are bestsellers. According to social role theory, perhaps one of the reasons we find it so tempting to believe men and women are fundamentally different is because sex is the single easiest characteristic we can use to classify people into categories; it is easier, even, than using race, age, or other easily observable groupings (Eagly & Karau, 2002). Not only that, but stereotypes based on sex can be activated at very low levels of consciousness. Much like expectancy violations theory (EVT) described in Chapter 3, social role theory focuses on our expectations for behavior and how we respond when our expectations are violated. Unlike EVT, however, social role theory suggests that violations of our expectations almost always lead to negative responses.

SEX AND GENDER: WHAT'S THE DIFFERENCE?

"Not biology, but gender prescriptions for women and men account for most differences in priorities, behaviors, attitudes, feelings, and self-concepts of the sexes" (Julia Wood in a dialogue with Kathryn Dindia, see Wood & Dindia, 1998, p. 30). How often have you filled out a survey or questionnaire that asks for your gender and then has boxes for "male" or "female"? What the survey is probably trying to determine is your sex. You may scratch your head and wonder, "What's the difference?" The difference could be drastic or insignificant, depending on the context. When discussing messages and communication patterns between women and men, it is helpful to understand there is a substantial difference between sex and gender.

Social role theory assumes that **sex** is genetically determined; it is your biological makeup as either a male (with XY chromosomes) or a female (with XX chromosomes). Whereas sex is a biological categorization determined at conception, gender is far more fluid. **Gender** is "the consensual beliefs about the attributes of women and men" (Eagly & Karau, 2002, p. 574). Importantly, all societies assign certain behaviors to each sex; in this way, gender is related to, but not equated with, sex. In Western culture, for instance, girls typically receive baby dolls and kitchen sets and are told to be "sugar and spice and everything nice," while their brothers typically receive trucks and toy guns and are told not to "cry like a girl." As adults, women are still expected to be primary caregivers, while men are expected to be primary breadwinners. When boys and girls and men and women behave outside of these prescriptions, eyebrows raise, a person's sexuality may be questioned (e.g., assuming male dancers are gay), and boundaries are pushed. It's important to note that although the theory focuses on sex as a biological reality, it does not dismiss the experiences of transgendered or nonbinary individuals; the focus on the theory instead is on social expectations for sex and gender, not how individuals perceive themselves and experience the world (Eagly & Wood, 2017).

One of the central ways people stereotype women and men is in terms of communal and agentic qualities (Eagly, 1987). **Communal qualities** include behaviors that demonstrate concern for other people through the expression of affection and exhibiting sympathy, helpfulness, sensitivity, nurturance, and gentility. **Agentic qualities**, on the other hand, include being assertive, controlling, confident, ambitious, and forceful. Whereas communal attributes are stereotypically associated with women, agentic behaviors are stereotypically associated with men. Social role theory suggests people assume this connection between gender roles and individual dispositions. In other words, we expect a woman to show sympathy and helpfulness while we expect a man to demonstrate confidence and assertiveness. Even when faced with evidence to the contrary (e.g., a very dominant woman or a very nurturing man) people cling to social role expectations.

ROLE CONGRUITY THEORY AND LEADERSHIP

Because leadership is most often described in masculine terms (i.e., leaders are supposed to be ambitious, assertive, and direct), social role theory has been extended to focus on sex differences in the realm of organizational leadership. Called role congruity theory, the theory suggests women in leadership positions are likely to experience two types of prejudice (Eagly & Karau, 2002). **Descriptive prejudice** refers to stereotypes that women have less leadership potential than men because they lack agentic qualities. **Prescriptive prejudice** (also called injunctive prejudice) refers to actual evaluations of women as less effective than men. Combined, these prejudices leave women in a **double bind**. "If they conform to their traditional gender role, women are not seen as having the potential for leadership; if they adopt the agentic characteristics associated with successful leaders, then they are evaluated negatively for behaving in an unfeminine manner" (Elsesser & Lever, 2011, p. 1557).

Eagly and Karau (2002) and Koenig et al. (2011) predict that because of this role incongruity women are actually less likely to emerge as leaders in professional settings than are men. Of course, some might question whether the stereotypes might be based on reality. Research suggests this is not the case, however; even when women possess agentic qualities they are less likely to emerge as leaders in a mixed-sex group than are men (Offor, 2012; Ritter & Yoder, 2004). Unfortunately, these negative stereotypes can be exacerbated by the context of the workplace. Garcia-Retamero and López-Zafra (2006) found that people showed stronger prejudice against female leaders who worked in a stereotypically male industry (e.g., the auto industry as compared to the clothing industry) and that older individuals reported more prejudice against female leaders than did younger individuals.

Research has found some support for the predictions made by role congruity theory. Surveying over 60,000 workers, a recent study found evidence for a strong descriptive prejudice against female leaders (Elsesser & Lever, 2011). The good news is that competence ratings for actual male and female bosses were similar, and respondents did not view leaders who behaved in a counter stereotypical style (e.g., a sensitive male manager or a direct female manager) as less competent than those who behaved in a stereotypical fashion. However, although it appears prescriptive prejudices may be fading, the results suggested that a cross-sex preference might exist such that women reported having better relationships with male managers and vice versa.

WHAT ABOUT ACTUAL DIFFERENCES IN COMMUNICATION?

Beyond the stereotypes we hold about men and women, and our evaluations of actual men and women because of these stereotypes, communication research shows little support for the notion that men and women differ with regard to their actual communication behavior simply because of their biological sex. In fact, research suggests we are more similar to the opposite sex than we are different. For example, Canary and Hause (1993) used a statistical procedure known as meta-analysis to compare more than 1,200 studies looking at sex differences in communication. When combined, they found that one's biological sex accounts for less than 1% of differences in communication behavior! This means that 99% of differences in communication behavior are likely created by something other than simply having XX or XY chromosomes.

On the other hand, there is support for the idea that gender roles influence communication styles. Regardless of biological sex, having a relationship partner who exhibits a feminine (i.e., communal) style of communication is positively related to romantic relationship satisfaction (Lamke et al., 1994), the use of positive and collaborative strategies for dealing with romantic relationship jealousy (Aylor & Dainton, 2001), and decreased loneliness among long-distance friends (Dainton et al., 2002). Masculinity (i.e., engaging in agentic behavior) has been associated with more effective political campaign ads (Wadsworth et al., 1987) and more strategic uses of communication (Aylor & Dainton, 2004).

Despite little evidence of actual sex differences in communication, social role theory provides a way to understand how social expectations for behavior result in stereotypes. Although these stereotypes affect both men and women, they have a particularly insidious effect on women leaders, placing them in a double bind of being judged negatively regardless of the leadership style they adopt.

CHAPTER SUMMARY AND RESEARCH APPLICATIONS

In this chapter we discussed four ways of examining culture and communication. First, Hofstede's six cultural dimensions provide systematic understanding of communication differences across cultures. This model has been used successfully to explain health outcomes during the COVID-19 pandemic. Specifically, Erman and Medeiros (2021) found that cultures that were higher in uncertainty avoidance, long-term orientation, individualism, and indulgence had higher fatalities, and suggested that messaging about the pandemic should vary based on cultural features.

Next, Giles and Coupland's (1991) CAT predicts an individual's desire to join the in-group will lead to attempts at convergence, while one's wish to remain an out-group member will result in divergence. Recent research on nonaccommodation found that instructors who did not accommodate to their students were viewed as less credible and less competent, even when controlling for the students' expected grade (Frey & Lane, 2021).

Third, we introduced co-cultural theory (Orbe, 1998), which highlights the ways that members of nondominant groups select communication strategies to meet their goals when communicating with members of a dominant group. Orbe (2021) recently investigated how attorneys of color (Black, Asian American, and Latinx) manage microaggressions that assume inferiority and criminality. He found that "doing nothing," a nonassertive assimilation tactic, was a strategic choice that many of his participants made.

Finally, we described the social role theory of gender, which highlights how assumptions about appropriate behavior for men and women influence our judgments about individual men and

TABLE 5.5 ■ Additional Theories of Intercultural Communication	
Theory	**Main Idea**
Cross-Cultural Adaptation Theory	Individual's intercultural competence transforms through a stress-adaptation-growth process (Kim, 2001).
Face Negotiation Theory	Differing face needs influence one's approach to conflict (Ting-Toomey, 2017).
Speech Codes Theory	Every culture has a distinctive speech code, which involves a culturally distinctive psychology, sociology, and rhetoric (Philipsen, 2008).

women in the workplace. To illustrate, Thomas and Petrow (2020) studied perceptions of men and women candidates for high-level political office. Consistent with social role theory, female candidates were perceived to have higher integrity than male candidates in general, but people judged female candidates with integrity failures more harshly than they did male candidates with integrity failures.

As always, the four theories we have featured in this chapter are not the only theories of intercultural communication that might provide insight into your personal and professional lives. Table 5.5 provides an overview of additional theories of intercultural communication.

DISCUSSION QUESTIONS

1. Hofstede's cultural dimensions focuses on differences in values and beliefs among cultures. For each of the dimensions, speculate about communication differences between each pole of the dimension. For example, how might people from masculine cultures communicate differently from people from feminine cultures? What about power distance (and so forth)?

2. Have you ever failed to accommodate appropriately? If so, what did you do/not do, and what happened? Did your experience support the predictions made by CAT?

3. Co-cultural theory identifies five factors that influence the strategy that a member of a co-cultural group might enact when interacting with a member of a dominant groups, including perceived rewards and costs. What might be some rewards and costs of the three outcomes? What about the rewards and costs of the three communication approaches?

4. Social role theory suggests that women are expected to behave like men, but when they do so they are judged negatively. Can you come up with an exception to this general trend? That is, can you name a woman who has behaved in a very masculine style and been judged favorably? If so, why do you think this is the case?

KEY TERMS

Abilities (p. 83)
Accommodate (p. 78)
Accommodation (p. 80)
Agentic qualities (p. 84)
Aggressive (p. 82)
Assertive (p. 82)
Assimilation (p. 82)
Co-cultural groups (p. 81)
Collectivism (p. 73)
Communal qualities (p. 84)
Convergence (p. 79)
Cross-cultural communication (p. 72)
Culture (p. 72)
Descriptive prejudice (p. 85)
Divergence (p. 79)
Dominant groups (p. 81)
Double bind (p. 85)
Feminine cultures (p. 76)
Field of experience (p. 83)
Gender (p. 84)
High-context communication (p. 74)
High power distance (p. 75)
Individualism (p. 73)
Indulgence (p. 76)

In-groups (p. 78)
Intercultural communication (p. 72)
Long-term orientation (p. 76)
Low-context communication (p. 74)
Low power distance (p. 75)
Maintenance (p. 80)
Masculine cultures (p. 75)
Muted group theory (p. 81)
Nonaccommodation (p. 80)
Nonassertive (p. 82)
Nondominant groups (p. 81)
Out-groups (p. 78)
Perceived rewards and costs (p. 83)
Preferred outcome (p. 83)
Prescriptive prejudice (p. 85)
Restraint (p. 76)
Separation (p. 82)
Sex (p. 84)
Short-term orientation (p. 76)
Situational context (p. 83)
Standpoint theory (p. 81)
Typical communication approach (p. 83)
Uncertainty avoidance (p. 74)

CASE STUDY 5
A Different Vue

A mid-sized financial software development firm, The Financial Enterprise Group (TFEG) specializes in creating technology solutions for financial institutions such as banks and brokerage firms. Like many of its competitors trying to survive in difficult economic times, TFEG had cut its full-time workforce in half. The organization had kept the younger (and cheaper) employees as well as the senior talent while laying off much of its mid-level staff. And with fewer fulltime employees, TFEG now relied heavily on lower-priced "contractors"—skilled technology professionals hired on a project-by-project basis—to fill the void. Contractors were often hired from outside the United States on temporary work visas, with the vast majority from India. As a result, half of TFEG's current workforce was American-born, while 40% were from India and the remaining 10% of workers came from other parts of Asia and Eastern Europe.

To improve their software development process while minimizing costs, TFEG had recently purchased a new program called Vue. Vue was vastly different from other types of software and required extensive implementation training. One of Vue's brightest consultants, Imani Williams, along with a team of several others, was assigned to train with TFEG's employees over a twelve-month period. Although only 27 years old, Imani was an expert in software implementation and held an MBA along with a master's degree in technology engineering. She could answer virtually any question, and better yet, she could explain technology in a very direct and easy-to-understand manner. She knew that as an African American woman in the tech field she faced a number of preconceived notions, so she knew that she had to work harder than everyone else, but she also made sure to communicate in an open and authentic fashion.

Each time Imani began a new training session, she would explain to the employees that Vue was radically different from the traditional software development process. Instead of a single developer "owning" the product through all development stages and operating with a great sense of autonomy, Imani described Vue's team-based approach. Each person on the team had a single, specific role in the technology development cycle, and each person had narrowly defined goals related only to that development component. Imani also emphasized that Vue required careful documentation of each stage in the development cycle. This documentation allowed the project manager to supervise the work closely during each phase.

As the training progressed, Imani and the other consultants noticed discernible differences between the Indian and American workers. Indian employees completed the required self-managed training modules, not only in advance of their American colleagues but also ahead of deadline. An online bulletin board that Imani had created to share ideas and best practices was heavily utilized by Indian employees but was virtually ignored by American employees. When a new utility for logging hours was introduced, it was widely disregarded by American employees but used faithfully by Indian employees. Similarly, the requirement to create documentation was closely adhered to by Indian employees, but once again ignored by American employees. The weekly briefings she and her colleagues held to keep employees informed of the progress of the Vue rollout were attended almost exclusively by Indian employees. Because she spent so much time communicating with the Indian employees (and so little with the American employees) Imani found herself communicating more and more like the Indians; she started being more polite and indirect.

Uncomfortable chastising the employees' behavior directly, Imani scheduled a meeting with the company's CEO, Phil Moore. "The other consultants and I are all noticing a problem with the employees' lack of compliance," she began. Phil interrupted "What exactly do you mean by 'lack of compliance'?" Imani responded "I mean, half of the trainees actually follow our protocols. The other half seem to do whatever they please." "And who are 'some'?" probed Phil. Imani hesitated, desiring to remain polite and indirect. "Imani, stop beating around the bush. I can't help if I don't know the problem," Phil insisted. Imani acquiesced, "Look, Phil, it seems to be mostly the Americans. Especially the TFEG veterans. They just don't do what we require. Maybe they're overworked or aren't used to having consultants tell them what to do," she hedged. "I'm sure they're good at their jobs, it's just that without their compliance, we'll never finish this training on schedule."

Phil was astounded, "Get me a list of their names!" he demanded. "We can't afford delays in implementation." Imani carefully explained that it wasn't her intent to embarrass anyone or get anyone in trouble. She just wanted management to encourage everyone to participate, at least for the weekly meetings. "If we could all routinely meet together," Imani reasoned, "I think we could get past some of these tensions. Vue depends on people working together, not against one another." Persuaded, Phil seemed agreed to assist, and Imani left the meeting hopeful.

Her hopes sank the next morning when she read the company-wide memo Phil sent, stating that weekly meetings were now mandatory. This wasn't what she had in mind when she said she wanted Phil to "encourage" participation. And if things weren't bad enough before the mandate, subsequent weekly meetings dissolved into "gripe sessions," with American employees candidly expressing their displeasure with the new process, while openly questioning whether Vue could produce the desired results. They also challenged Imani and her ability to lead the team, arguing that she lacked credibility and was too unassertive.

By the end of the year, the disparity in Vue adoption between Indian and American employees was common knowledge. When conducting year-end performance appraisals and calculating bonus awards, management made good on their threat to penalize employees who had failed to achieve the stated adoption goals. As a result, many American employees received unflattering performance reviews and a corresponding reduction in their level of compensation. Although contractors employed on a "temporary" basis were not eligible for the company's salary bonus program, many Indian employees were recognized by their immediate managers for their success with Vue adoption, and were compensated with paid vacation days, gift certificates, and public recognition of their achievement at the year-end Town Hall meeting. The difference in (perceived) compensation and public recognition frustrated the younger American employees and angered the senior American workers, who already bore strong feelings of resentment at the role lower-priced foreign workers were playing in displacing US-born technologists from their jobs. Meanwhile, a number of the younger American employees left TFEG for opportunities elsewhere. Imani left the company after her contract ended feeling like a failure; she was so confident before taking on this position, but the experience left her doubting her skills.

Questions for Consideration

1. How would Hofstede's dimensions of culture help to make sense of the difficulties experienced by Imani and the other Vue consultants? Make sure to look at both Indian and American cultures.

2. Do you see any evidence of accommodation or nonaccommodation? By whom? How?

3. What strategies has Imani used when engaging in co-cultural communication?

4. To what extent did gender play a role in the problems? Do you see evidence of any descriptive or prescriptive prejudice?

5. Do any of the theories emerge as "better" than the others? Why do you believe this to be the case? What situations might surface that would make a different theory or theories better at explaining the situation?

6 PERSUASION

LEARNING OBJECTIVES

After reading this chapter, you will be able to do the following:

1. Define persuasion, attitudes, and influence

2. Explain the function of Aristotle's three rhetorical proofs

3. Describe the process individuals use to determine narrative rationality

4. Explain the concepts of anchors, acceptance, noncommitment, and rejection to determine the likely effectiveness of a persuasive message

5. Identify central and peripheral messages

For nearly a century, the manner of how to persuade others has been both a popular and profitable subject in the United States, beginning with Dale Carnegie's (1936) best-selling book *How to Win Friends and Influence People.* The rise of mass media and pervasiveness of propaganda used in both World Wars led to the recognition and study of persuasive messages as critical to understanding political and social change. Given the global influence of social media, understanding the power of persuasive messages is greater than ever. In the early 2000s, around the time when digital marketing, social media, and smartphones converged, market researchers approximated that Americans encountered an average of 5,000 ads per day; fast-forward to 2021, and this estimate has nearly doubled to between 6,000 and 10,000 ads per day (Carr, 2021). As Marshall (2015) noted, "As media channels emerge, so do new advertising opportunities. Today, Americans (and most folks in modernized countries) are bombarded with advertisements. I'm talking about a tsunami of commercials. Print ads, brand labels, Facebook Ads, Google Ads, ads on your phone. Anything a business can produce to get your attention and compel you to buy" (¶1). We are inundated with messages of persuasion and influence in all aspects of our lives—relational, social, political, and economic. Consequently, we believe understanding how persuasive messages work (or don't work!) is central for surviving in today's advertising and media-saturated society.

DEFINING PERSUASION

Communication scholars define **persuasion** as "human communication that is designed to influence others by modifying their beliefs, values, or attitudes" (Simons, 1976, p. 21). O'Keefe (1990) argued there are requirements for the sender, the means, and the recipient to consider something persuasive. First, persuasion involves the intent to achieve a goal on the part of the message sender (see Chapter 3 for a discussion of goals). Second, communication is the means to achieve that goal. Third, the message recipient must have free will (i.e., threatening physical harm if the recipient doesn't comply is usually considered force, not persuasion). Accordingly, persuasion is not accidental—nor is it coercive. It is inherently a form of strategic communication (see Chapter 7).

Many persuasion theories focus on shifts in attitude, so it is important to clarify the term. An **attitude** is a "relatively enduring predisposition to respond favorably or unfavorably" toward something (Simons, 1976, p. 80). We have attitudes toward people, places, events, products, policies, ideas, and so forth (O'Keefe, 1990). Attitudes are *learned* evaluations; people don't enter the world holding specific attitudes. Rather, we develop attitudes over time based on direct and indirect experiences, making them relatively enduring—neither fleeting nor based on whims. At the same time, attitudes are also adjustable. That is, if we encounter new or different experiences, our attitudes *can* shift. Finally, and perhaps most important to the study of persuasion, attitudes are presumed to influence behavior; although, as we will see later, this influence is not always as strong as we might presume.

Related, the term **influence** is often used interchangeably with persuasion. Originating from Latin, the word *influere* meant influx or an inflow, and later, in Shakespearean times, the word referred more specifically to a cosmic force affecting one's destiny (Scott, 2019). While we may not ponder our cosmic destiny in the same way as did *Romeo and Juliet*, think of how we use the word "star" to mean someone with exceptional talent or a prominence in a way that affects others. Likewise, today's term "influencer" includes someone who has the ability, through digital connectivity, to promote products, behaviors, and even ideologies. In this way, influence is related to persuasion; while persuasion is a strategic action, we hold that influence is the capacity to affect others, albeit indirectly.

In this chapter, we present four very different theories of persuasive communication: Aristotle's *Rhetoric*, the narrative paradigm, social judgment theory, and the elaboration likelihood model. Although portrayed as theories of persuasion, each of these viewpoints can be applied to a wide variety of communication contexts. From well-crafted public relations campaigns designed to foster positive attitudes about a company to strategically forewarning a friend that they are about to hear something upsetting, these four theories highlight varied ways to consider and develop persuasive messages. Table 6.1 provides an overview of the theories.

TABLE 6.1 ■ Overview of Persuasion Theories	
Theory	**Main Idea**
Aristotle's *Rhetoric*	The ability to persuade an audience relies on a speaker's ability to determine and use rhetorical proofs: logos, ethos, and pathos.
Narrative Paradigm	Because storytelling unites the human experience, narratives—cohesive stories that align with the receiver's experiences—are meaningful, persuasive tools.
Social Judgment Theory	Understanding a person's latitude of acceptance (or rejection) and their ego-involvement with the attitude explains the likelihood of attitude change.
Elaboration Likelihood Model	A motivated and capable audience calls for a strong, centrally routed message for persuasion to occur, whereas peripheral messages are best suited for an audience that lacks either motivation or ability.

ARISTOTLE'S *RHETORIC*

Our first theory of persuasion, Aristotle's *Rhetoric* (367-322 BCE), lays the foundation for communication as a discipline unto itself. Written in Athens over a period of several decades, it is still considered one of the most significant texts in Western civilization. The three-book treatise carefully describes the means by which "common man" can use public address to persuade. Not surprisingly, a text that has survived more than 2,000 years has numerous interpretations. For the purposes of this chapter, we focus on the widely agreed upon tenets that make Aristotle's theory practically relevant today, rather than seek to provide an exhaustive review of scholarly debate.

Assumptions of the *Rhetoric*

Three assumptions guide our understanding of Aristotle's *Rhetoric*. First, humans are rational, therefore persuasion should be an intellectually rational event. Second, there exist three types of rational arguments, called **rhetorical proofs**, that can be used in various combinations—logos, ethos, and pathos. Finally, audience members play an integral role in any persuasive event, and audience members are not homogeneous entities. Therefore, a persuader must consider the unique composition of each audience.

While the first assumption of emphasizing intellectually rational arguments might appear self-evident in our data-saturated world, understanding the Classical era in which Aristotle lived and wrote contextualizes the significance of this premise. During this period, sophists emerged as professional educators who emphasized skill in public speaking, not only as a means to participatory democracy but also as a way for man (literally) to achieve virtue by searching for truth. A student first, and then teacher at Plato's *Academy*, Aristotle also believed in the necessity of one's ability to speak well in the public sphere. While Aristotle disagreed with his mentor in many areas, they both criticized the sophists' tradition, claiming that sophistry didn't truly prioritize the search for an absolute or a rational means of persuasion. They viewed the sophists as "intellectual charlatans," who often promoted persuasion through exaggerated claims and fallacious reasoning (Duke, n.d.). This disapproval of the sophists' approach is thought to have influenced the focus of Aristotle's three-book treatise, the *Rhetoric*.

Aristotle defined **rhetoric** as "the art of discovering the means of persuasion available for any subject" (Bizzell & Herzberg, 1990, p. 29) or the ability "to see what is possibly persuasive" in each situation (Rapp, 2010, para. 4.1). Others have interpreted Aristotle's definition more concisely to say that rhetoric is simply the "art of persuasion." Scholars generally believe that Aristotle saw rhetoric as a "morally neutral art"; that is, multiple sides of an argument can reasonably be argued with various means. This morally neutral stance also gives way to modern connotations of the word, which often imply empty promises, or "empty rhetoric." As we will see, however, just because a persuader can *see* all of the available means to persuade, doesn't meant that they should *use* any available means. Rational thought should prevail, leading to our second assumption, the use of *rhetorical proofs*.

Sometimes referred to as the rhetorical triangle, three elements called *proofs* make up persuasive rhetoric: **logos**, the argument; **ethos**, the speaker's character; and **pathos**, the emotional state of the audience. Aristotle wrote the most about argumentation (logos), contending that everyday citizens predictably rely on practical reason to guide real-world decisions, far more so than on scientific evidence (Neher & Sandin, 2017). Importantly, then, the persuader must think about the type of reasoning that typical people find convincing; it is here that Aristotle turns to the syllogism and enthymeme as two methods of reasoning. A **syllogism** is a type of *if—then* deductive reasoning that typically includes a major premise, a minor premise, and a conclusion (Kennedy, 1994). For example: if *humans are mortal* (major premise), and if *Aristotle is human* (minor premise), then *Aristotle is mortal*. Likewise, if *dogs bark*, and if *Fluffy is a dog*, then *Fluffy barks* (conclusion).

An **enthymeme** is a type of syllogism that emphasizes probabilities, signs, and examples, while omitting either a premise or the conclusion (Bitzer, 1959). In this way, the enthymeme provides a type of shortcut to logical deduction by assuming that the audience either already registers one of the premises or receivers can supply their own conclusion, therefore it doesn't need to be presented. As Lee noted (2011), the persuasive power of an enthymeme relies on "social truths," assumptions that the audience already accepts, therefore, the persuader doesn't need to spell them out. For example, *humans are mortal; therefore Aristotle is mortal*. You can deduce that Aristotle is (likely) human. Similarly, *dogs bark; therefore Fluffy barks*. Here, we don't tell you that Fluffy is a dog—we assume that you can logically deduce this (likely) fact. In the same way, we might claim, *dogs bark; Fluffy is a dog*. Again, we assume you are rational and can supply the conclusion yourself—Fluffy must bark. Importantly, however, social truths used in enthymemes are not scientific certainties. Thus, the enthymeme deals with probabilities not absolutes (Kennedy, 1994). For example, while dogs do bark, and the authors can hear Fluffy barking, it doesn't mean for certain that Fluffy is a dog. Foxes, coyotes, and seals also bark. Is it likely that a seal is barking outside our windows? Not likely at all, considering our location! Therefore, we go to the probability that Fluffy is a dog.

While these are very simplistic examples, what makes the enthymeme particularly persuasive is that the speaker and the audience members now share a connection by way of sharing a social truth. Because audience members have filled in the unsaid portion themselves, they are cognitively invested and more likely to be persuaded.

Enthymemes prevail in political communication and in advertising more broadly. Take the ubiquitous slogan, *America Runs on Dunkin.* The effectiveness of the catchphrase relies not so much on the stated premise (Americans "run"; we are busy), but more on an unstated assumption truth—getting coffee, and getting coffee quickly—is how to keep up the pace. The conclusion then is that Dunkin's quickly prepared coffee is the fundamental boost that helps us get it all done. While the American lifestyle may be busy, we don't empirically require swiftly served coffee to accomplish our daily grind. The implied social truth and conclusion are logical, but not a certainty. The cosmetic company L'Oréal Paris uses the tag line, *"Because you're worth it."* Here, a social truth is that being physically beautiful is important, and women in particular need products to achieve this beauty. Another is that appearance and beauty influence self-esteem. In both cases, the implied conclusion is that, because you deserve the opportunity to look beautiful, and because L'Oréal's products can fulfill that claim, you should buy L'Oréal. As well, L'Oréal has a reputation of being slightly more expensive than other drugstore brands, so the "you're worth it" tagline also implicitly justifies the price because you "deserve" to spend a little more! While it seems logical, think more deeply; it's like saying you deserve to work a little more.

This brings us to our second rhetorical proof, **ethos**. While logos is critical, it doesn't eclipse the relationship between the persuader and the audience. Aristotle understood that even the most sound arguments are ineffective if the audience doesn't trust in the persuader. Comprised of "good sense, good moral character, and goodwill," (Aristotle, qtd. in Bizzell & Herzberg, 1990, p. 161), ethos relies on the audience maintaining favorable impressions of the persuader. Current scholarship extends Aristotle's speaker-centered understanding of ethos beyond the individual to include cultural and social ethos (Condit, 2019). In other words, social and cultural expectations influence what we perceived to be credible and vice versa. Case in point, students often view alumni guest speakers as more credible purveyors of career advice than faculty, even when the advice is the same. When alumni professionals advise students to "get an internship!" students seem to hear it with more credibility than when professors share the same message. While students likely view professors as trustworthy, there is also a social belief that faculty are out of touch with the "real world."

The third pillar, **pathos**, recognizes the manner in which the audience members' feelings about the issue influences the success of various arguments. An emotionally charged audience will likely interpret a speaker's reasoning differently than a calm audience. Therefore, a persuader must consider the "the pathetic appeal [that] seeks to align the audience's emotions with the speaker's position" (Bizzell & Herzberg, 1990, p. 29). Aristotle argued that knowing the emotional state is not enough; the persuader must consider why the audience feels a certain way and under what conditions. Using the counterparts of anger and calm, as examples, we'd first need to the ability to identify a hostile audience as well as with whom and why they are angry. Then, we'd need to know how to effect calmness in this audience, to mitigate the anger in order to have our arguments be heard. Aristotle noted that the reverse also works.

While oratory was *the* mode of rhetorical persuasion in Ancient Greece, Aristotle's rhetorical proofs are commonly evident in today's emphasis on written, visual, and multimodal persuasion (e.g., Kjeldsen & Hess, 2021). Consider the ways in which companies visibly employ rhetorical proofs, particularly with advertising. Verizon uses a map of the United States to show their coast-to-coast coverage (logos), while Adidas' partnership with Beyoncé emphasizes the ethos of someone who had big dreams and worked hard to achieve them. Pathos is used extensively in advertising because multimedia can images quickly trigger our emotions, whether its feelings of nostalgia, distress, excitement, or a tug at the heartstrings. Amazon's commercial for their redesigned Echo smart-speaker relies on humor and sex appeal by featuring Michael B. Jordan as a daydream version of "Alexa's Body." Conversely, Dove's "Real Beauty" campaign inspires self-confidence by featuring everyday women with all different body shapes, sizes, and colors.

Canons of Rhetoric

Importantly, Aristotle's view of rhetoric demands the persuader understand one's own capabilities *and* the rhetorical situation *before* engaging in the rhetorical event (Table 6.2). Regarding the former demand, a persuader should assess their own abilities and resources. Aristotle affirmed a 5-step process as a way to self-assess: invention, arrangement, style, memory, and delivery (Bizzell & Herzberg, 1990).

Regarding the latter demand, the **rhetorical situation** presumes a specific type of persuasive event, for example political, legal, or epideictic (ceremonial). While sometimes underestimated, the audience's cultural beliefs and emotions are also situational elements.

TABLE 6.2 ■ Canons of Rhetoric	
Invention	**Brainstorm all possible arguments**
Arrangement	Evaluate the merits of each argument so as to organize the claims for maximum effect
Style	Select the words and phrases that will express the argument most clearly and appropriately (see Fortenbaugh, 1986)
Memory	Learn the speech so it can be recalled at will
Delivery	Use verbal and nonverbal strategies, including voice, silence, gestures, and appearance

Aristotle considered the first three steps to be the foundation of rhetoric, and they clearly align with logical, ethical, and pathetic arguments. Although not unimportant, Aristotle wrote far less about memory and delivery in the *Rhetoric*. As Cicero studied the Greek model of rhetoric some 200 years later, his interpretation expanded the focus on eloquence, reinvigorating discussion on the importance of memory and delivery for conveying. Together, these steps are commonly known as the *five canons of rhetoric*.

Consider the rhetorical situation of a public health crises coupled with government officials' (in)abilities to invent, arrange, and style rhetorical proofs within this context. Five years before the COVID-19 global pandemic, US government agencies responded to the Ebola health crisis (Condit, 2019). The situation included a global outbreak, set amidst much uncertainty and a "deeply polarized partisan context" (p. 192). While the disease itself was largely contained in the United States, the messaging strategy has been widely criticized by rhetoricians, health experts, and the public alike. Rhetorically, Condit has argued that CDC and NIH officials failed to arrange the rhetorical proofs effectively—overemphasizing logos and miscalculating the importance of *situational ethos*. While an experienced physician-scientist such as an immunologist has undeniable credibility in the scientific community, that same physician-scientist may appear as overreaching their claims or expertise when put in the context of public health advisor. Stated another way, when the same person's role shifted from physician-scientist to a politically appointed advisor, the ethos granted previously did not automatically transfer.

At the same time, messages from these officials stressed the absoluteness of known facts (logos) on a newly emerging infectious disease, where there was conflicting information. They also incorrectly assumed that the public would view the experts conveying the messages as having goodness and goodwill (ethos). These errors exacerbated tensions between citizens and public health officials. Rather than move toward a common health goal, the public increasingly viewed public health officials as partisan adversaries. As Condit (2019) argued, the nature of expertise must be recast; ethos is critical and extends well beyond credentials. Experts "must invent ways to form their characters as bridges between... their area of expertise and the public" (p. 207). Unfortunately, her advice was not heeded. Fast-forward to the COVID-19 pandemic; partisan distrust between nonexperts and experts again erupted as a key factor in the US government's inability to respond effectively (Altman, 2020).

Although the three proofs are often treated separately or hierarchically in practice, scholarly understanding of the *Rhetoric* maintains that Aristotle viewed "rhetoric as legitimately appealing to the whole person, not just to the 'rational being' alone" (Grimaldi, cited in Bizzell & Herzberg, 1990, p. 146). Thus for rhetoric to succeed, the persuader must fully appreciate the relationship between logos, ethos, and pathos.

NARRATIVE PARADIGM

Whereas Aristotle's *Rhetoric* emphasizes logical arguments that are situated among the persuader's ethos and emotional understanding of the audience, the narrative paradigm stresses the effectiveness of persuasion through storytelling (Fisher, 1984, 1987). Specifically, Fisher (1984, 1987) argues that human beings are fundamentally storytelling creatures; therefore, the most persuasive or influential message is not that of rational deduction but instead a narrative that convinces us of "good reasons" for engaging in a particular action or belief.

Turning back to advertising, the most notable ads don't flood you with facts about the product; they craft a memorable story. Progressive Insurance uses satire to make a not-so-fun product (insurance) funny with the help of Dr. Rick. In the "Afraid Of Becoming Your Parents?" series, the fictitious therapist guides young homeowners through a series of daily activities that stereotypically confuse older generations. Rather than bore the audience with actuarial tables or deductible comparisons, the ad playfully emphasizes that insurance doesn't prevent us from becoming our parents; but it can protect our home, auto, and possessions. The subtext: while insurance may seem stodgy, we need it.

Subaru America has also won awards for expertly employed storytelling "by connecting their product to a particular emotion—love—rather than focusing on the features or functions of their vehicles" (Jax, 2020, para. 1). Not known for flashy cars, Subaru is recognized for reliable, safe, and rough-road functionality across its vehicles. Yet, it's through storytelling that the brand can show how these "mundane" features play out in real life; through a variety of narratives, Subaru emphasizes love, across life styles and life stages. The "Baby Driver" storyline features a father and daughter, whom he still pictures as a young child. As he hands over the car keys while reminding her to stay off the freeway, we then see the driver is actually a teen driver. In a parallel story, "Moving Out" shows a child packing the family's Subaru, but then we see that the child is actually a young adult, presumably heading off to college or a first job. These nostalgic stories capture our attention far more than the usual visual of a car driving on a winding road in the middle of nowhere or simulating a crash to view safety features.

Narrative advertisements don't have to be long-term campaigns. Cheetos playfully incorporates the popularity of homemade song parodies in their "It Wasn't Me" campaign. Mila Kunis tries to convince her real-life spouse, Ashton Kutcher, that she's not guilty of eating the bag of Cheetos, all while singing to Shaggy's *It Wasn't Me*. iPhone's "Fumble" ad features no dialogue, only a feverish beat and the visual of a person's failed attempt to catch their "fumbled" phone while walking along a city street. When the phone finally succumbs to gravity, it remains unscratched.

In each case, stories facilitate emotional connections between people; "telling a good story is the most effective strategy in establishing productive relationships with people, regardless of one's communication goals" (Moraru, 2015, p. 195). Today's marketing experts understand that narration is a powerful way for organizations "to convey brand or product messages, position them in the minds of consumers, and, ultimately, achieve satisfactory levels of retention" (p. 195).

As we explain subsequently, Fisher's (1984, 1987) view of communication contrasts much of a Western emphasis on rational decision-making. Yet, by juxtaposing a narrative worldview with a rational worldview, we hope you will give some thought to this strikingly different way of considering communication and influence.

Narrative Assumptions

Fisher (1985, 1987) didn't develop the paradigm with the intent of theorizing persuasive communication specifically. Rather, he argued that narration is a "metaparadigm," synthesizing work from both humanistic and social scientific disciplines that emphasize narrativity. Further, he differentiated narration as related to but separate from rhetoric, stating that narration is "the foundation on which a complete rhetoric needs to be built" (Fisher, 1987, p. 184). While not intending his work to be a "theory of persuasion," the relevance to understanding persuasion is undeniable. Using this reasoning, we posit three assumptions that help relate the paradigm to persuasive communication.

First, Fisher (1985) reaffirmed others' assertions that humans' desire to hear and ability to tell stories not only makes humans unique but is also central to our experience of the world. Second, all narratives aren't equal; people need a way to judge which stories are believable and which are not. Third, the world as humans know it is based primarily on sets of both cooperative and competing stories. We will elaborate on these ideas below.

Related to the first assumption, narratives are not necessarily fantasy or fairytales; instead, a **narrative** broadly includes the symbolic words and actions people use to assign meaning (Fisher, 1987). Further, "narratives utilize elements of plot, tone, imagery, and language" (Stache, 2017, p. 577). Extending Aristotle's notion of rhetorical proofs, Fisher (1987) evoked the Greek term **mythos** to explain human communication as a collection of stories expressing "ideas that cannot be verified or proved in any absolute way. Such ideas arise in metaphor, values, gestures, and so on" (p. 19). Not even the wisest expert knows everything about everything in their area of specialization; there is an element of subjectivity in even the most "logical" of messages. Consequently, individuals relay messages and experiences through stories in an attempt to capture these subjective experiences. As Roberts (2004) asserted, "people are not essentially arguers, but rather storytellers" (p. 130); we construct reality through our creation and understanding of stories.

This brings us to our second assumption; while we rely on stories as a way to make sense of the world, we don't automatically accept every story. As rational beings, we have ways of evaluating the merits or veracity of narratives. While a child may believe in the magic of the Tooth Fairy, as we mature and our ability to reason develops, the idea that a tiny fantasy figure flies in to swap a baby tooth for money, all while you're asleep, seems ridiculous. Here, Fisher argued that individuals use **narrative rationality**—a logical method of reasoning by which a person can determine how believable another's narrative is. This narrative rationality relies on the twin tests of narrative fidelity and narrative coherence. First, we say there is **narrative fidelity** when a story maintains "truthful qualities." The narrative's facts should be relevant and credible; the story also must align with the receiver's values, experiences, and so forth. Importantly, the acceptance of facts and values are not guaranteed; rather they are embedded in culture, history, character, and experiences (Fisher, 1985, 1987). What seems plausible or truthful to one person may seem ridiculous to another person who has a different lived experience.

Take the simplistic narrative of what happens when a child loses a baby tooth. While the Tooth Fairy is known and accepted by American children, in Spain, Mexico, Guatemala, and Chile, a little mouse (El Ratoncito Pérez) replaces the tooth with a coin or treat. Culturally, the story featuring a cute mouse scurrying by to exchange the tooth seems far more "logical" than a winged fairy swooping in. A more realistic example for adults might be narratives about near-death experiences. Here, cultural and religious influences profoundly affect which narratives we will accept. In some faiths, sacred texts claim a person's soul transitions either to a paradise or hell; narratives in other faiths convey the belief that soul is reborn into another body or being. Stories of people claiming to recall a past life will be more or less accepted to the extent that the experience complements the recipient's belief about the "truth" of death. All told, we judge a story based not only on the factual or logical elements but also by comparing it to our own culture, character, history, values, and experience. This assessment process is what Fisher regarded as the "logic of good reasons."

Assuming the test of fidelity is met, we can then assess the second aspect of narrative rationality—**narrative coherence** (sometimes called narrative probability). Fisher (1987) outlined three categories of coherence: structural, material, and characterological. ***Structural coherence*** refers to a story's flow and arrangement. Is the story conveyed sequentially, logically, and without contradictions? Or does it bounce around or contain inconsistencies that make it hard to follow? ***Material coherence*** refers to the extent to which this story matches or is consistent with other stories already accepted by the receiver. Finally, and perhaps most importantly, ***characterological coherence*** involves the credibility or believability of the story's "characters." It should be noted that without fidelity, coherence is irrelevant; therefore, the receiver must accept the narrative's fidelity first.

Finally, the narrative paradigm presumes that our understanding of the world is based on sets of both cooperative and competing stories (Fisher, 1987). Cooperative stories build on, or mirror, other similar stories to form a common or shared understanding. Students who examined college recruiting materials found cooperative narratives—that is, stories matching their own expectations of university life—to be most influential (Burns, 2015). The idea that "hey, I've had that happened to me, too" adds to a story's fidelity. Social media and "review-based" websites like TripAdvisor or RateMyProfessor encourage both cooperative and competing stories. Cooperative stories could include individual users' anecdotes that complement each other, for example, multiple reviews that praise a hotel's staff and service add legitimacy to the review. Whereas competing stories could include contrasting reviews—one user's account of the hotel's service is completely different from another's experience. Here, we have to decide which narrative to believe.

Competing or counternarratives can also be used strategically "to mute and dismantle social movements" (Ray et al., 2017, p. 1798). For example, The Black Lives Matter movement emerged, in part, through shared cooperative narratives of racial injustice. This common narrative led to a collective movement protesting institutional police violence towards Black Americans. The unified sharing of outrage gave way to competing or counternarratives such as All Lives Matter and Blue Lives Matter. In the first counternarrative, All Lives Matter has shifted the focus away from discrimination and "the importance of race" in police violence (Langford & Speight, 2015, p. 83); in the second counternarrative, Blue Lives Matter has justified institutionalized force with the claim that "law enforcement lives are under attack" (Thornhill, 2017, p. 7). Here, the narratives are portrayed as a dichotomy; by virtue of accepting one, we seemingly must reject the other.

These examples bring us back to the logic of good reasons as the method for choosing among narratives. We will accept the narrative that most aligns with our own values, culture, and experience. Moreover, the narratives we choose to accept or reject can fundamentally affect our life.

Stated at the beginning of this section, Fisher didn't intend for his development of a narrative paradigm to be a prescriptive theory of persuasion. At the same time, if we consider the centrality of narrative thinking, it stands to reason that narratives can be used strategically to persuade. In other words, if narratives are central to humans' way of understanding the world, it stands to reason that narratives can be persuasive.

Narrative and Rational Paradigms

Mentioned earlier, the narrative paradigm diverges from a traditional Western that emphasizes rational arguments. Table 6.3 presents several points of contrast between the narrative paradigm and a rational paradigm. Fisher (1987) argued that **logos**, or logical argument, has been unfairly privileged as the ultimate measure of truthfulness. While an Aristotelian view of rhetoric assumes that "truth can be grasped through language" (Humphreys, 2020, para. d1), the narrative view assumes that most of what we "know" is shaded with the subjectivity of individual values and experiences. Rather than using argument to prove something as true, narratives seek to explain "What does this mean?" In this way, Fisher (1985) suggested that narrative rationality is really "an attempt to recapture Aristotle's concept of *phronesis*, 'practical wisdom'" (p. 355). Accordingly, Fisher posited that mythos (narratives) and pathos (emotional appeals) are more meaningful to humans and, consequently, more persuasive. Stated differently, the narrative paradigm does not exclude logic; rather it extends our understanding of what it means to be logical. No rhetorical proof (credibility, emotion, or reason) should be regarded as superior. Moreover, he advised that we move away from dualistic approaches (i.e., that we are either rational *or* narrative) and embrace more integrated perspectives (i.e., that we are both rational *and* narrative).

According to the narrative paradigm, then, human communication and our understanding of "reality" relies heavily on narration as the means to create meaning. What's more, Fisher (1987) believed that narration is a more effective means of influence than traditional forms

TABLE 6.3 ■ Comparing the Narrative and Rational-World Paradigms	
Narrative Paradigm	**Rational-World Paradigm**
1. Human beings are storytellers.	1. Human beings are rational.
2. Communication, persuasion, and decision-making are based on the logic of good reasons.	2. Communication, persuasion, and decision-making are based on sound arguments.
3. What one accepts as "good reasons" is determined individually by a person's culture, character, experiences, and values.	3. Strong arguments adhere to specific criteria for soundness and logic (e.g., using the premise-inference-conclusion model).
4. Rationality is based on one's awareness of how consistent and truthful a story appears when compared with one's own (and others') lived experiences.	4. Rationality is based on the accuracy of information presented and on the reliability of the reasoning processes used.
5. People experience the world as a series of stories from which to choose. As we make these choices, we create and re-create reality.	5. The world and reality can be viewed as a series of logical relationships revealed through reasoned argument.

of logic based on reasoning. However, only when a narrative exhibits good reasons and narrative coherence will it be convincing enough to permeate a receiver's consciousness and become translated into a change in action.

Organizational Storytelling

If the narrative paradigm seems too intangible for practical use, consider the influence of organizational storytelling. Barker and Gower (2010) cited numerous examples of the power of organizational narratives: conveying organizational culture, encouraging organizational learning, promoting employee expertise, and to conveying authenticity of leadership, a narrative approach has numerous applications for leaders of organizational development.

Organizations also use narratives to support employee recruitment, assimilation, and community by "effectively convey[ing] the company's values and mission" internally and externally (Boguszewicz-Kreft et al., 2019, p. 30). Perhaps one of the most famous organizations, the Walt Disney Company actively and intentionally uses organizational storytelling to maintain and commodify the organization's cultural heritage. Organizational storytelling is so engrained, Disney's origins, values, products, and conflicts have become "mythologized" into exaggerated ideas of family-like unity and fairytale drama.

Likewise, integrating good storytelling in diverse, multicultural work environments has tremendous benefit to the organization and its workforce "by representing personal, interpersonal, and corporate perspectives" (Barker & Gower, 2010, p. 304). Adding the current prominence of multimedia to the mix, public relations practitioners have predicted that *digital storytelling* will only increase as a driving force in effective organizational communication (Verghese, 2019). Bosch Global is realizing this trend. Not only does its public website feature an "Explore Our Stories" channel for external communications, Bosch also emphasizes internal storytelling to develop and sustain a unified, albeit global, workforce. The organization has incorporated podcasts and a multimedia presentation series, *The Spark;* similar to a TED-talk format, *The Spark* features engaging, employee-generated stories that link the organization, its products, and employee relationships (Staffbase, 2021).

SOCIAL JUDGMENT THEORY

Consider your personal and professional network. It is likely easy for you to come up with the name of at least one person with whom you cannot talk about a particular topic. Perhaps your mother is a die-hard Democrat who will not listen to any conservative viewpoints. Or perhaps you know that your boss is incapable of having a discussion that involves spending any money. Social judgment theory suggests that knowing a person's attitudes on subjects can provide you with clues about how to approach a persuasive effort. Developed by Sherif and associates, the theory focuses on peoples' assessment of persuasive messages (Sherif & Hovland, 1961; Sherif et al., 1965). Research using this theory has often focused on cognitive processes, but there are numerous implications for communicators seeking to persuade others.

The Importance of Attitudes

Social judgment theory explains how the strength of a person's attitude affects that individual's evaluation of an issue (Sherif & Hovland, 1961; Sherif et al., 1965). While not a theory of "how to persuade," understanding this relationship between attitude strength and judgments can help a persuader determine the types of messaging needed to be effective. As such, three assumptions ground our discussion. First, preexisting attitudes influence our evaluations or judgments of objects, issues, messages, and people. Second, individuals make these judgments based on **anchors**—that is, their stance or position on a particular topic, issue, or messages. Although attitudes are unobservable, cognitive structures, the theory's third assumption presumes that we can capture another's attitude by mapping "how an individual evaluates and categorizes relevant objects, persons or communications" as either acceptable or objectionable" (Rand, 1967, pp. 3-4). Consequently, if we want to persuade someone, we need to first determine that individual's preexisting attitude.

Stated above, an individual's anchor represents that person's viewpoint on an issue. According to Sherif and associates, each person's attitudes can be mapped or placed into one of three categories. First, there is the **latitude of acceptance**, which includes all those ideas that a person finds acceptable. Second, there is the **latitude of rejection**, which includes all those ideas that a person finds unacceptable. Finally, there is the **latitude of noncommitment**, which includes ideas for which you have no opinion—you neither accept nor reject these ideas.

Relating these assumptions to persuasion, one's reaction to a persuasive message depends on their position on the topic (Sherif & Hovland, 1961). Accordingly, the first step in the social judgment process is to map the receiver's attitudes toward a topic. Sherif and Hovland argued that the map of an individual's attitudes about any given topic is a function of the receiver's **ego involvement**, or how personally significant the issue is. When individuals are highly ego-involved with a topic, they perceive the issue as personally salient and typically hold an intense position (O'Keefe, 1990). When the topic has personal significance, it is considered to be central to that person's sense of self—hence, they are ego-nvolved.

Knowing a person's ego involvement allows the persuader to make certain predictions about the recipient of a persuasive message. The first prediction states that the greater the receiver's ego involvement, the larger their latitude of rejection. This prediction is based on logic; if you feel strongly about something, you are likely to reject anything that doesn't match your precise point of view. If you don't care as much about the topic, you are likely to be open to alternative possibilities. Likewise, the second prediction states that the greater one's ego involvement, the smaller one's latitude of noncommitment. Again, this hypothesis makes sense. If you believe a topic is important, you are likely to have thought about it, leaving little room for having no opinion or no knowledge. If you don't view the topic as important, you probably haven't spent much time developing an opinion about it.

Our introduction of social judgment theory stated that people make judgments about messages based on their preexisting attitudes. How does this translate to the real world? Imagine that you work in the human resources department of a major corporation, and you want to convince your manager to do something about the lack of diversity in your company. The first thing you need to do is to determine your boss's attitudes about the topic. How might you map their latitudes? What might their anchor be? How ego involved are they? Once you do this form of audience analysis, you can predict how she might respond to particular messages. Quite simply, the theory asserts that messages falling within the audience's latitude of acceptance will be viewed positively, while messages falling within the audience's latitude of rejection will be viewed negatively.

Effects of Messages Sent in Different Latitudes

Social judgment explains these positive and negative responses through two complementary processes, the contrast effect and the assimilation effect (O'Keefe, 1990). The **contrast effect** occurs when a message is perceived as further away from that person's anchor than it really is—the receiver subconsciously exaggerates the difference between the message's position and one's own position. This response happens when the message falls within an individual's latitude of rejection. In contrast, the **assimilation effect** occurs when a message falls within the receiver's latitude of acceptance; here, the individual subconsciously minimizes the difference between the message's position and their own position. True persuasion can only occur, according to this theory, if the message you send falls within an individual's latitude of noncommitment, or at the very edges of their latitude of acceptance (Miller, 2002).

To illustrate, returning to your concern about increasing diversity at your company, imagine that your manager is slightly in favor of considering race and ethnicity when making hiring decisions. Your manager is familiar with the concept of groupthink and recognizes that increased diversity leads to better decisions. However, your manager is uncomfortable with using race or ethnicity as the single most important criteria for hiring an employee. Given those beliefs, you might map your manager's latitudes as shown in Figure 6.1. The anchor, or specific stance, is that there should be some consideration of racial or ethnic background when making a hiring decision. However, either extreme is uncomfortable. Now imagine that you craft two proposals. Option A would simply be a request to add a sentence to all job ads stating "We welcome applicants from all backgrounds to apply." As you can see on the map of latitudes, this option is not very far away from your manager's specific anchor. In Option B, you add recruiting events at Historically Black Colleges and Universities (HBCUs). This option is slightly further away from your boss's anchor. Which would be a more persuasive option? In this case it would be Option B. Option A, although not far from your manager's anchor, falls in the latitude of rejection—it literally doesn't go far enough to address the problem of increasing diversity. Note that simply looking at how close a message is to an anchor is not sufficient; you must also consider the placement of the message relative to the latitudes. In this case, Option A is likely to be contrasted because it falls within your manager's latitude of rejection; it will seem further from the anchor than it actually is. Conversely, because Option B is in your manager's latitude of noncommitment, this message might be assimilated, and ultimately it might persuade your boss to do something differently. By the way, the map in figure 6.1 gives you some additional information. When looking at the relative sizes of your boss's latitudes, how ego-involved do you think your manager is about the topic of workplace diversity?

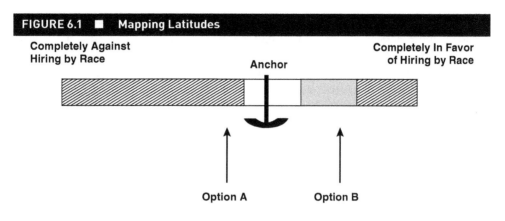

FIGURE 6.1 ■ Mapping Latitudes

Completely Against
Hiring by Race

Anchor

Completely In Favor
of Hiring by Race

Option A   Option B

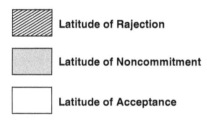

Latitude of Rejection

Latitude of Noncommitment

Latitude of Acceptance

In sum, social judgment theory proposes that persuaders must carefully consider the pre-existing attitudes an audience might hold about a topic before crafting a message. If you send a message that falls in a receiver's latitude of rejection, you will not be successful in your persuasive effort. Moreover, if you send a message that is clearly in a person's latitude of acceptance, you are not persuading that receiver, you are only reinforcing existing beliefs.

ELABORATION LIKELIHOOD MODEL

Turning to our final theory of persuasion, the elaboration likelihood model (ELM) views persuasion primarily as a cognitive event, meaning the targets of persuasive messages use mental processes of motivation and reasoning (or a lack thereof) to accept or reject persuasive messages. Developed by Petty and Cacioppo (1986), ELM posits two possible routes, or methods, of influence: centrally routed messages and peripherally routed messages. Each route targets a widely different audience. Accordingly, ELM emphasizes the importance of understanding audience members before creating a persuasive message.

The Central Route to Persuasion

Petty and Cacioppo's (1986) model depicts persuasion as a process in which the success of influence depends largely on the way the receivers make sense of the message. As mentioned earlier, ELM presents two divergent pathways one can use when trying to influence others. The more complex of the two paths is known as the **central route**, also referred to as the **elaborated route**. Centrally routed messages include a wealth of information, rational arguments, and evidence to support a particular conclusion. For example, during each election season, political hopefuls engage in speeches, debates, and roundtable discussions; each message is filled with elaborated and presumably rational information regarding the candidate's viewpoints, platform, and political history.

Centrally routed messages are much more likely to create long-term change for the recipient than are peripheral messages (discussed later); however, not all individuals are capable of receiving centrally routed messages. ELM argues that centrally routed messages succeed in long-term change only when two factors are met: the target must be highly motivated to process all the information given, and the target must be **able** to process the message cognitively. For example, if you are not willing to sit through a 2-hour televised debate between presidential candidates, then ELM suggests you do not have the motivation required to process an elaborated message in this instance. Alternatively, imagine you are motivated to watch the candidates' debate, but the politicians' messages are filled with complex issues of international policy that you simply do not understand. In this case, ELM suggests that despite being motivated, your ability to understand the highly specific and intricate messages is not present. The theory states that without *both* motivation and ability, a centrally routed, elaborated message is of little value.

Types of Elaborated Arguments

It should be apparent that understanding one's audience is critical when choosing the appropriate route; it is also imperative to understand the audience when constructing an **elaborated argument** (Petty & Cacioppo, 1986). In other words, it isn't enough to view your audience as motivated and able when considering the central route of persuasion. You must also consider how the audience members will likely react to the quality and arrangement of the arguments presented. Elaborated arguments can be measured as strong, neutral, or weak.

Strong arguments create a positive cognitive response in the minds of receivers while also positively aligning receivers' beliefs with those views of the persuader (Petty & Cacioppo, 1986). Strong arguments inoculate the audience against counterpersuasion and are most likely to create long-term attitude change that leads to predictable behavior. Repetition is thought to enhance the persuasive effect of strong arguments; conversely, interruptions will diminish their effectiveness. Neutral arguments generate a noncommittal cognitive response from the receiver. In other words, no attitude change occurs, and the ambivalent receiver may instead turn to peripheral cues, or shortcuts, to persuasion. Finally, weak arguments produce a negative cognitive response to the persuasive message. This negative response not only prevents attitude change but may also have a reverse or boomerang effect, thereby reinforcing the opposing point of view.

The Peripheral Route to Persuasion

Noted earlier, elaborated messages are ineffective when targeted participants are neither capable nor interested in the information (Petty & Cacioppo, 1986). Although the persuader might prefer an involved audience so as to produce enduring change, it is unreasonable to expect every persuasive target to be motivated or skilled enough to understand the barrage of influential messages put forth each day. As a result, when motivation or ability is missing from the target audience, the persuader can use the **peripheral route** to persuasion. Peripheral messages rely on a receiver's emotional involvement and persuade through more superficial means. Consider the ASPCA ads that feature images of neglected and abused animals. A montage of dirty and injured animals is shown with a background of sad music. These ads attempt to influence donations by pulling on viewers' heart strings, not by presenting reasoned arguments on animal cruelty. Thus, ELM predicts that when the audience is unmotivated or unable to process an elaborated message, persuaders should focus on quick and easy ways to produce change. One significant drawback is that the peripheral route leads only to short-term change, if any change at all.

Cialdini (1993, 1994) identified seven common cues of a peripheral message: authority, commitment, contrast, liking, reciprocity, scarcity, and social proof.

With the first peripheral cue, the persuader uses the perception of **authority** to convince the audience to accept the beliefs or behaviors presented. Parents often use this peripheral cue with their children: "Clean up your room because I said so!" This message may influence children to straighten the covers and hide the toys in the closet before Grandma's visit, but it probably won't create long-term neatness.

Peripheral messages that rely on **commitment** emphasize a person's dedication to a product, social cause, group affiliation, political party, and so on (Cialdini, 1993, 1994). For example, some people publicly announce their commitment to a certain group or cause. They attend rallies; run for office; or wear pins, hats, and other logos that symbolize the affiliation (Canary et al., 2008). Similarly, wearing a polo shirt that displays your company's corporate logo demonstrates some amount of dedication to the organization. Other people demonstrate their commitment more privately, for example, by sending anonymous donations to political campaigns or charitable organizations. However, "people usually feel greater commitment to a cause if they are publicly committed to it" (Canary et al., 2008, p. 369).

One very common tactic that emphasizes the commitment principle is the *foot-in-the-door tactic* (Cialdini, 1994). Here, a persuader convinces you to do something small first, like wear a campaign sticker or button. Then the persuader asks to put a campaign sign in your yard. Next, the persuader may ask you to make a donation or to host a reception. The strategy is to convince you to agree to a small, seemingly innocuous request first. Once you agree and commit yourself to the campaign, it becomes harder to refuse larger requests because there is a threat of appearing inconsistent with your commitment.

Persuading through the **contrast effect** requires the communicator to set up uneven points of comparison (Cialdini, 1993, 1994). For example, asking a coworker if she could do you a "giant favor" and then contrasting the statement with a simple request ("Would you text me if FedEx drops off a package while I am in a client meeting?") sets up a disparity. By inflating the coworker's expectations for the "giant favor" requested and then contrasting it with a simple favor, it is more likely to result in compliance. Retail salespeople also use this contrast principle by "reducing" prices or by showing customers the most expensive item first (because anything else will seem cheaper in comparison).

Liking messages stress affinity toward a person, place, or object (Cialdini, 1993, 1994). That is, if we like you, we will like your ideas. Many companies often rely on such messages of liking in their advertisements. By using basketball sensation Kevin Durant to sell Nike shoes or actress Sophia Vergara to endorse Pepsi products, these companies expect that if you like Durant or Vergara, you will also like their products (and will—they hope—buy them).

Messages of **reciprocity** try to influence by emphasizing a give-and-take relationship (Cialdini, 1993, 1994). For example, it is easier to persuade your sister-in-law to babysit your children if you have done something similar for her. Advertisers also use reciprocity: "Buy these steak knives in the next 10 minutes, and we'll throw in a free cutting board!" Here, the advertiser tries to influence the receiver by throwing in some extras. If you do this for us, we'll give you a freebie. Similarly, **scarcity** is a peripheral message that preys on people's worry of missing out on something. This "Quick! Get it before they're all gone!" approach creates a sense of urgency for receivers. Home shopping channels, department stores, car dealers, and furniture stores all rely on this strategy by imposing time limits on the sale of items; presumably, you won't be able to purchase the deluxe salad spinner after the sales event expires. Realtors also use this approach; alerting prospective buyers that an offer has been placed on a property creates a sense of urgency and may start a bidding war. A house that was "of interest" now seems that much more appealing when it may disappear from the market.

Finally, the peripheral cue of **social proof** relies on the age-old notion of peer pressure (Cialdini, 1993, 1994). Although you might mistakenly believe only teenagers succumb to the "everyone's doing it" mentality, adults are also swayed by messages of social proof. Within the workplace, for instance, many corporations participate in charity drives such as with the Red Cross or the United Way. Here, employees who participate in blood drives or fundraising are given pins to wear or balloons to display, thereby gaining influence by putting subtle pressure on other employees to "get on board."

If unaware of these techniques in the past, you should now be able to identify these seven peripheral cues—they are everywhere! Again, however, it is important to stress that these peripheral messages emphasize fleeting emotional responses and are not likely to create long-lasting change.

Types of Peripheral Messages

As with centrally routed arguments, peripheral messages can be evaluated as positive, neutral, or negative (Petty & Cacioppo, 1986). Positive peripheral messages are those perceived favorably by the audience and create a positive affective state. Positive peripheral messages have a chance at yielding weak, positive changes in attitude. For example, if you're a fan of *Full Frontal with Samantha Bee* and Bee endorses Candidate X over Candidate Y, you may feel more positively about Candidate X. However, a change in attitude does not necessarily predict a change in behavior. For instance, you may believe voting is an essential civic duty for American citizens, yet you may not vote in your local primary election because you don't think you are knowledgeable of the candidates. Here, we see incongruence between an attitude (voting is important) and behavior (failing to vote).

Neutral peripheral messages leave receivers feeling emotionally ambivalent; they really don't know or care about the cue used to capture their interest (Petty & Cacioppo, 1986). If you don't know who Samantha Bee is or don't really care about her political views, then her endorsement of Candidate X will not create any attitude change—nor is it likely to influence your voting behavior. Finally, negative peripheral messages produce negative or disapproving emotional responses within the receiver. If you can't stand *Full Frontal*, then Samantha Bee's comments endorsing Candidate X will likely irritate you. Thus, you are now left with a negative impression of Candidate X because of this person's "association" with an actor, personality, or TV show you find objectionable.

ELM makes very clear predictions, summarized in Figure 6.2. The theory predicts that if receivers are motivated and able to consider an elaborated message, persuaders should rely on strong, factually based arguments. Arguments can backfire if they are weak or poorly presented, however. Conversely, persuaders should focus on emotionally based peripheral messages if receivers cannot or will not consider an elaborated message. Persuaders must recognize that using a peripheral route guarantees no long-term change. Instead, effects, if any, will be minimal and fleeting.

FIGURE 6.2 ■ Elaboration Likelihood Model

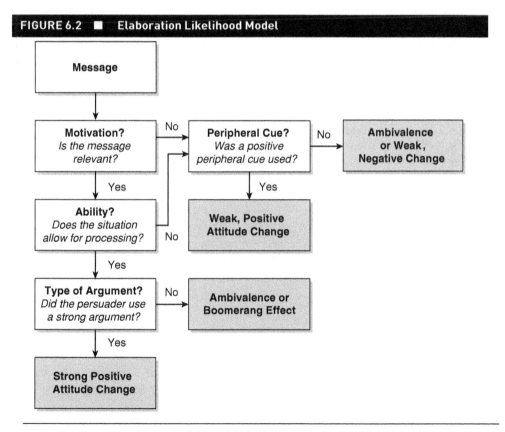

Source: Communication and Persuasion (p. 4) by R. E. Petty and J. T. Cacioppo, 1986, Springer-Verlag.

CHAPTER SUMMARY AND RESEARCH APPLICATIONS

This chapter examined four theories of persuasion. We began with the one of the oldest, most influential theories, Aristotle's *The Rhetoric*. Aristotle separated rhetoric into three appeals: logos, ethos, and pathos. Persuasion, then, is the function of appropriately and effectively combining these rhetorical proofs. Discourse analysis of political rhetoric remains a common research application, and also has extended our understanding of ethos, pathos, and logos to climate change discourse (Spoel et al., 2008), in the courtroom (McCormack, 2014), and for understanding the role of personality in political messaging (Reyes, 2020). Moving into analysis of digital media, Fahmy and Ibrahim (2021) explored the use of logos, pathos, and ethos in framing #MeToo memes on Twitter. They found that promovement memes incorporated logos appeals almost twice as often as did antimovement memes, while antimovement memes relied on significantly more emotional (pathos) appeals.

Discussed second, the narrative paradigm looks at persuasive messages through a descriptive lens. Persuasion isn't so much a rational process as it is an emotional one based on storytelling. At the same time, all stories are not equal; fidelity and coherence are needed for a narrative to have influence. In addition to the ways in which narratives can benefit organizations discussed previously, persuasive storytelling shapes our understanding of politics (Seargeant, 2020) and public health, such as the role of storytelling in vaccine hesitancy and resistance (Hoppin, 2016). Blending narrative persuasion with the effect of social media influencers on corporate reputation campaigns, researchers found that influencers' narrative endorsements of the organization led to more favorable corporate attitudes, so long as a "paid sponsorship" disclosure didn't accompany the narrative (Kim et al., 2021). The influencers' stories of their positive experiences with the organization seemingly "reduc[ed] perceptions of manipulative intent" p. 133).

Next, social judgment theory considers the importance of examining receivers' preexisting attitudes; sending a message that falls in their latitude of rejection will not result in successful persuasion. "True persuasion" occurs only when the message falls within audience members' latitude of noncommitment or at the edges of their latitude of acceptance. The US Department of Agriculture has used social judgment theory to explore consumers' attitudes toward genetically modified food (Ruth & Rumble, 2019). Understanding consumers' latitudes of acceptance, rejection, and noncommitment can help agricultural campaigns address the "moveable middle"—those who have a large latitude of noncommitment, particularly around the safety of genetically modified foods.

Our fourth and final theory, ELM, also argued that persuaders must carefully consider the audience before crafting a message. Receivers must be motivated and able to process objective, elaborated messages. When audience members are unmotivated or unable to process such messages (or both), peripheral cues should be used. Recent research has used ELM to explore online shopping strategies (Levy & Gvili, 2020) and message strategies of entrepreneurs when they engage in crowdfunding (Xian et al., 2019). In a study that combined principles of ELM

TABLE 6.4 ■ Additional Theories of Persuasive Communication	
Theory	**Main Idea**
Cognitive dissonance theory	Cognitive dissonance theory explains persuasion as a postreactive response to inconsistencies in beliefs and actions (Festinger, 1957). Persuaders can take advantage of receivers' dissonance by proposing a solution, product, or action that attempts to close the disparity between incongruent beliefs and behaviors.
Goals-Plans-Action Theory (GPA)	GPA focuses on how and why people send persuasive messages (Dillard, 2015). The theory suggests that individuals have both primary and secondary goals that must be achieved, and that there are cultural, interpersonal, and individual scripts that are followed during influence events.
Heuristic-Systematic Model (HSM)	Similar to ELM, HSM assumes two routes to persuasion, one relying on superficial processing, the other relying on cognitive processing. Unlike ELM, however, HSM proposes that heuristic (superficial) and systematic (cognitive) processing can cooccur. As well, the model suggests that individuals rely on heuristic processing to defend existing beliefs (Chaiken, 1980).
Visual persuasion theory	Emerging from advertising, visual persuasion theory examines the influence of images through the dual roles of semantic and syntactic properties (Messaris, 1997). The theory holds that visual messages can convey shared meanings, generalizations, and ambiguous meanings in ways that words cannot, making visual imagery a unique persuasive tool.

and social judgment theory, researchers assessed the effectiveness of reputation-repair messages for the New England Patriots organization and for the National Rifle Association (NRA) after each faced public reputation threats (McDermott & Lachlan, 2020).

There are numerous other theories that focus on persuasive communication.

Table 6.4 highlights three such theories.

DISCUSSION QUESTIONS

1. Think about the last time someone tried to persuade you. What examples of logos, ethos, and pathos were used? Which proof or combination of proofs did you find most convincing? Why? Now think about the last time you tried to persuade someone else. What examples of logos, ethos, and pathos did you use? Which proof or combination of proofs do you think was most convincing for your target? Why?

2. Watch part of a daytime TV court show (e.g., *Judge Greg Mathis; The People's Court*). Pay attention to the narratives used by the plaintiff and the defendant. Whose side of the story

do you find more believable? Why? Relate the concepts of narrative fidelity and narrative coherence to explain your choice.

3. Brainstorm a few debatable topics (e.g., veganism, self-driving vehicles). Then, select one and consider how you could map audience members' preexisting attitudes (that is, their latitudes of acceptance, noncommitment, and rejection). Come up with some sample statements for each latitude and then ask a few classmates to rank your statements as acceptable, unacceptable, or undecided. Based on these findings, how wide is your audience's latitude of noncommitment? What messages could you use to persuade them toward one side or the other?

4. Compare the elaborated or central route of persuasion with Aristotle's rhetorical proofs. Where do you see similarities and differences? How might the peripheral route align with Aristotle's notion of sophistry or irrational persuasion? Are these fair comparisons? Why or why not?

KEY TERMS

Able (p. 108)

Anchors (p. 105)

Assimilation effect (p. 106)

Attitude (p. 94)

Authority (p. 109)

Central route (p. 108)

Characterological coherence (p. 102)

Commitment (p. 109)

Contrast effect (p. 106)

Ego involvement (p. 105)

Elaborated argument (p. 108)

Enthymeme (p. 96)

Ethos (p. 96)

Foot-in-the-door tactic (p. 109)

Influence (p. 94)

Latitude of acceptance (p. 105)

Latitude of noncommitment (p. 105)

Latitude of rejection (p. 105)

Liking (p. 110)

Logos (p. 96)

Material coherence (p. 102)

Mythos (p. 101)

Narrative (p. 101)

Narrative coherence (p. 102)

Narrative fidelity (p. 101)

Narrative rationality (p. 101)

Pathos (p. 96)

Peripheral route (p. 109)

Persuasion (p. 94)

Reciprocity (p. 110)

Rhetoric (p. 96)

Rhetorical proofs (p. 95)

Rhetorical situation (p. 98)

Scarcity (p. 110)

Social proof (p. 110)

Structural coherence (p. 102)

Syllogism (p. 96)

CASE STUDY 6
Problems CONNECTing

An up-and-coming tech business, CONNECT offers interactive, virtual event platforms. The company employs roughly 80 people and currently offers three web-based products: interactive team meetings, virtual conferencing, and large-scale digital networking. Three separate Product Managers (PMs) oversee each of the three services. These PMs are accountable for their product and their staff.

The company's small size coupled with upper management's open-door attitude has created a unique environment where individual opinions, even contrary ones, are encouraged. Employees generally value each other and the work they do because their own success relies on the company's success.

A collaborative work environment also has downsides. For example, one drawback is the sheer abundance of new ideas (some good, some bad). Every idea and every suggestion get attention and need to be researched—a time-consuming and sometimes frustrating process because many ideas lack the resources, practicality, and efficiency to be used.

Part of CONNECT's Marketing Department, Bryn Hopkins is the Social Media Manager and currently supervises two marketing assistants. Bryn's chief responsibility is to generate a variety themed content, manage schedules of posts for the company's three services, and monitor the effectiveness of the posts. To the untrained eye, managing social media may seem simple; however, for content to be effective, it must be visually engaging, communicate a clear story, and be frequently updated. And because CONNECT's products all emphasize aspects of web-based video conferencing, the company uses a lot of videos in their social media marketing.

CONNECT's procedure for developing and approving content is detailed because of the different products and parties involved. Each quarter, the entire Marketing Department brainstorms a series of marketing themes that can span each of the company's three products; once a theme is selected, one of Bryn's marketing assistants jumps in to develop the theme into social media content for each product line. Regardless of the theme, content emphasizes realistic but inspirational narratives that focus on a "typical" CONNECT client, typically smaller business owners and employees who are trying to work smarter with a variety of remote-work options. Bryn's marketing assistant drafts scripts for video posts and related blurbs, then takes these scripts to the Media Production Department. There, a **graphic designer and video editor** create the visual images and video needed for each piece of content. This whole package (of videos and blurbs) then goes back to Marketing for proofing and Bryn's final approval. Only after this final approval is the content scheduled and eventually posted to the particular social media platforms. Although it seems tedious, Bryn developed this procedure to maintain the company's brand vision and the quarter's theme. Ultimately,

Bryn knows she will be held responsible for any social media blunders, so she wants to have the final say before any post goes live.

One of CONNECT's PMs, Gerald Martin oversees their Interactive Team Meeting (ITM) product. While Gerald thinks of himself as very enthusiastic, Bryn views him as a perfectionist who tends to overanalyze things. Recently, Gerald mentioned to Bryn that CONNECT should change its social media procedures. He wanted to schedule a meeting with Bryn to discuss the proposed changes. Gerald also causally mentioned that *he* would also like to be a part of the social media development process; for example, the marketing assistant should include Gerald in drafting the scripts so that he could have input into the storyline. Also, the graphic designer and video editor could show Gerald each package that related to ITMs before getting Marketing's final approval. As Social Media Manager, it was up to Bryn to determine the procedure, not Gerald. Besides, Bryn didn't want someone peering over her shoulder and questioning her department's decisions. She had been managing social media for a number of years prior to joining CONNECT and had the experience to understand what would engage current and prospective clients.

"No way am I going to show this guy every post that comes along!" Bryn thought to herself, "Gerald will want to haggle over each comma or question mark and it'll take weeks to get content posted!"

Not wanting to appear difficult, however, Bryn didn't say anything. She planned to wait until the next Marketing Department meeting when she and the other marketing staff could discuss Gerald's ideas in more depth.

Later that same afternoon, Bryn passed by the Media Production Department's studio and spotted Gerald talking with Anaya, one of Bryn's marketing assistants. Gerald caught Bryn's eye and waved Bryn in to the room. "Hey, Bryn! Come here—just for a minute. I've worked everything out." Puzzled, Bryn poked her head into the studio. "Hey, Gerald. I'm on my way to a meeting. What's up?"

"I'm glad we ran into you! The problem's all solved. From now on, the marketing assistants will show me all of the scripts and plans related to my division before going to Media Production. Then, I will work with the graphic designers before they create the visual content. Then you can give final, final approval," Gerald declared, as if he had just solved a major world problem.

"Gerald, I thought we were going to discuss this at our next staff meeting. I'm not even sure that there *is* a problem," Bryn replied.

"Well, Bryn, you're always saying that you're on a deadline here. I want to get things in place before next quarter's posts are planned. You know what they say! 'Time is of the essence'!"

Bryn didn't know what to say. Keeping in mind Gerald's overzealous approach and recognizing that her own stress level was high, Bryn answered with a quick "Uh… Okay, sounds good, I'll get back to you," and headed back out the door. Although she firmly believed that Gerald's idea wasn't a good idea, Bryn also knew that discussing it while on her way to a meeting wasn't the proper time.

Later that afternoon, Bryn sent Gerald a meeting request to discuss his new social media procedure. It looked like Bryn would have to convince Gerald that the Marketing Department's current social media strategy was a good one and that it worked! At the very least, Bryn figured they could come up with a modified procedure that wouldn't inconvenience anyone involved.

A day later, the two colleagues met in an unoccupied conference room. Bryn started the meeting, "Hi Gerald, thanks for meeting today to discuss your new social media posting strategy. Although I think your intentions are good, as the person responsible for our social media engagement, I have concerns with your plan." Bryn went on to say that Gerald's idea simply was impractical for their deadline driven industry. "We need a constant cycle of themed posts, ranging from full-blown videos, short videos, and blurbs. We need to keep a lean process and stay on our marketing themes. Content creation is already a difficult process; plus, I can't run around, chasing Project Managers for approval of every post." Bryn expressed that Gerald's new procedure created unnecessary steps making it inefficient.

"I have an alternative solution," Bryn suggested, "one that combines your idea of having extra eyes look over the posts along with my belief that we shouldn't put up additional barriers in the approval process." Gerald nodded, "Okay, I'm game – what's your idea?"

Bryn went on to explain her idea—Marketing could share their theme and concept ideas to the Project Managers before taking the ideas to Media Production. Bryn explained, "This way, the Marketing Department's flow wouldn't be disrupted, and it would allow for Marketing's content creators and the Project Managers to collaborate so that everything is just right. Then, when Marketing does receive the complete package, we could just do our normal checking routine before scheduling the posts."

Gerald indicated that he originally had suggested this to Anaya, but that she had expressed the same concerns that Bryn just did. "Essentially," Gerald said, "Anaya told me it's simply too inefficient; Marketing doesn't have time to chase down Project Managers for approvals either."

Bryn probed a little farther and asked some more questions aimed at finding out exactly what the "problem" was. It turned out, Gerald felt that their social media themes were too "abstract" and the videos seemed like unrealistic "fairy tales." The content focused more on users' lifestyles rather than on the features of the product. He thought that content should focus on differentiating CONNECT from other interactive meeting platforms. Gerald believed that if he had participated in the initial content development, he would have requested that more information about the product be included in the posts. Bryn pressed Gerald for more details; it turned out that Gerald was worried about larger, better known competitors. He felt that by focusing primarily on user stories, rather than on information as to what makes CONNECT different from other platforms, they were missing their mark. This was a sore spot for Gerald; he explained that at his previous job, the competitor eventually ended up acquiring his company and in doing so, Gerald lost his job.

Based on his story, Bryn recognized that Gerald's problem was not with Marketing's social media procedure, but rather, a misunderstanding about the role of social media marketing as compared to other types of traditional advertising. Bryn felt confident in her strategy and knew that changing the procedure was not going to fix Gerald's perception.

By listening to Gerald's experience, Bryn also realized that Gerald (and perhaps the other PMs) needed to "see" how their quarterly social media content actually did increase awareness and interest in their company, thereby adding to CONNECT's growing credibility. Together, Bryn and Anaya explained that social media marketing wasn't replacing other types of traditional advertising; rather, it was engaging a different base of clients, primarily Gen Y and Gen Z users who responded to the storytelling approach. By showing Gerald analytics from the last six months, they convinced him that their method was working!

As well, Bryn, Gerald, and Anaya came up with a joint proposal. Marketing would set up a shared drop box with folders for each Project Manager's office. Once Marketing determined the quarter's theme and general approach to the content, they would reach out to the Project Manager's input on "featured" content. This featured input would include a select piece of tangible information, such as a new product feature, that the Project Manager felt should be emphasized in that quarter's posts.

This solution allowed Marketing to maintain their storytelling approach while also encouraging collaboration with PMs. Selectively incorporating a key piece of information into the quarter's schedule facilitated the sharing of product information while staying on theme and without overwhelming posts with lots of details. Amazingly, all staff members involved agreed to this joint solution. A month later, all were satisfied with the new procedure.

Questions for Consideration

1. Apply Aristotle's rhetorical proofs of logos, ethos, and pathos to Bryn and Gerald's misunderstanding for what should be included in CONNECT's social media content. Which rhetorical proof(s) does Bryn's marketing approach seem to emphasize? Which rhetorical proof(s) does Gerald's plan seem to emphasize? How does their solution seem to rebalance the use of logos, ethos, and pathos?

2. Explain how *mythos* functions in the case. First, consider how Gerald's narrative and Bryn's response helped the co-workers better understand each party's frustrations. Second, consider the role of *mythos* in CONNECT's social media content. While the content itself was not fully described in the case study, use your own experiences

to imagine how the narratives that Bryn's team used could employ the *logic of good reasons* and work as a marketing tool. You might also consider creating your own social media narrative that Bryn could use for her Gen Y or Gen Z clients.

3. What peripheral strategies did Gerald try to use to convince Bryn that there was a problem with the current ad approval method? Why didn't these strategies work? Create examples of other peripheral strategies that Gerald could have used; do you think these tactics would have worked any better? Why/why not? Would an elaborated message produce a different result? Explain.

4. Consider the tenets of Social Judgment Theory. Where would you place Gerald's anchor on the relevance of social media marketing? How do both party's ego-involvement influence their latitudes of rejection and acceptance? What about the latitude of acceptance? How could Gerald and Bryn both have used SJT principles early on to avoid the confusion and conflict that ensued following Gerald's initial proposal?

5. Which persuasion theory seems to explain the situation "better" than the others? Why do you believe this to be the case? What situations might surface that would make a different theory or theories better at explaining the situation? What theories could you combine to make for an even "better" explanation of the encounter?

7 STRATEGIC COMMUNICATION

After reading this chapter, you will be able to do the following:

1. Define goals, strategy, mission and vision statements

2. Explain the theory of planned behavior and how the interplay of attitudes, normative beliefs, and perceived behavioral control is critical in persuading people to change their behavior

3. Describe the Extended Parallel Processing Model, and detail the ways that message strategies should be adapted based on the combination of perceived threat and perceived efficacy

4. Illustrate the Inoculation Theory, and explain refutational preemption and identify examples of counterpersuasion efforts

5. Explain the Situational Crisis Communication Theory and articulate how the nature of a crisis influences reputational threat, and the crisis response strategies that can mitigate that threat

Upon receiving your degree, many of you will work in the field of strategic communication. **Strategic communication** is a catch-all label for fields such as advertising, public relations, marketing, and management communication. In general, it references the purposeful communication used by organizations to achieve organizational goals. Those goals might be to sell the organization's products or services, to develop and maintain a positive reputation in the minds of the public, to launch a public health campaign, or to engage employees during organizational change. Regardless of the specific focus of the communication, there are two characteristics associated with strategic communication: strategy and influence.

DEFINING STRATEGIC COMMUNICATION

Every organization exists to achieve some sort of collective goal. A **goal** is a long-term outcome desired by the organization (Labelle & Waldeck, 2020). Often these are framed in terms of an organizational **mission** statement, which is a formal statement of the organization's purpose, or a **vision** statement, which articulates what the organization would like to achieve. For example, Southwest Airline's vision statement is "to be the world's most loved, most efficient, and most profitable airline." TikTok's mission statement is "to inspire creativity and bring joy." And the American Cancer Society's mission is "to save lives, celebrate lives, and lead the fight for a world without cancer." In general, you can find an organization's mission and vision by visiting its website.

So, how does Southwest Airlines become loved, efficient, and profitable? They do so by using **strategy**, which is a process of determining what should be done to achieve a goal. In essence a strategy "is a clear roadmap, consisting of a set of guiding principles or rules, that defines the actions people in the business should take (and not take) and the actions they should prioritize (or not prioritize) to achieve desired goals" (Watkins, 2007, p. 2).

Communication efforts are considered strategic when they assist the organization in achieving its goals (Wilson & Ogden, 2004). Accordingly, communication professionals at Southwest Airlines should craft messages that foster a sense of affection for the company, that assist the company in becoming more efficient, and that engender profitability. Each of these activities is symbolic efforts to **influence** others' thoughts, emotions, or behaviors. To be loved, you need to craft public relations messages to positively affect stakeholders' views of the company. To be efficient, you need to craft messages to employees regarding resources and costs. To be profitable, you need to craft advertising messages that will convince customers to fly with the airline.

In this chapter, we present four theories that are useful for strategic communication. The first two theories could have been described in Chapter 6, as they are theories of persuasion. However, they have significant implications for strategic communications. They are the theory of planned behavior and the extended parallel processing model. We then explain inoculation theory, which is in essence a counterpersuasion theory; it focuses on how to prevent people from being persuaded. The final theory, situational crisis communication theory, centers specifically on strategies public relations professionals should use when confronted by unexpected and uncertainty-inducing events. Table 7.1 provides an overview of the theories.

TABLE 7.1 ■ Overview of Strategic Communication Theories	
Theory	**Main Idea**
Theory of Planned Behavior	Three concepts can predict an individual's behavior: attitude, normative beliefs, and controllability.
Extended Parallel Processing Model	The effectiveness of fear appeals are dependent on the severity and susceptibility of the threat, as well as beliefs about response efficacy and self-efficacy.
Inoculation Theory	In order to prevent persuasion from happening, a communicator can offer a weak form of the persuasive effort and then negate it.
Situational Crisis Communication Theory	Strategic communicators should match their crisis response to the level of organizational responsibility for the crisis and the reputational threat of the crisis.

THEORY OF PLANNED BEHAVIOR

The theories in Chapter 6 provide advice if you are trying to persuade someone to think or feel a particular way about an organization, a person, an idea, or a product. But what if your goal is to move beyond attitude change to actually changing someone's behavior? What if you want someone to buy your product, act on your proposal, or comply with instructions? Our first theory, the theory of planned behavior, may provide a template for how to persuade people to change their behavior.

The roots of the theory of planned behavior can be traced to an earlier theory, the theory of reasoned action, developed by Martin Fishbein and Icek Ajzen in the 1960s (Fishbein & Ajzen, 1975). Fishbein was frustrated by the body of persuasion research at the time; although the notion of an attitude had been well developed, studies could not provide evidence linking attitudes and behavior. Simply being *in favor* of a particular political candidate doesn't guarantee votes for him or her, and supporting the notion of environmental conservation does not necessarily lead to consistent recycling behavior. Fishbein, who later worked with Ajzen, recognized that something likely mediates the relationship between an attitude and behavior.

First, Fishbein and Ajzen (1975) assumed all behavior is intentional: We don't accidentally behave in a particular manner; we have reasons for doing so. The idiot who cut you off on your drive to work this morning likely did so because he was in a hurry. The coworker who leaves work early may be doing so to care for a sick child. The assumption that there are reasons for all of our actions led Fishbein and Ajzen to develop the notion of **behavioral intention**, which simply means you plan to act a particular way.

The next step for these authors was to determine what creates behavioral intention. Fishbein and Ajzen (1975) believed there are two predictors of behavioral intention: attitudes and normative beliefs. We discussed attitudes in Chapter 6; **attitude** is defined as the sum of beliefs about something. The theory of reasoned action states that our attitudes are made up of two components: our evaluation of the object and our belief strength. Take, for example, your attitude toward climate change. Do you think it is one of the most important issues facing the world, or do you think that the threats associated with climate change are overstated or unwarranted? Clearly, your attitude about climate change will play a significant role in any efforts to change behaviors that might affect the impact of climate change. Of course, these variations reference your evaluation of the object, but your belief strength must also be taken into account. Do you feel very strongly that climate change is a significant threat, or are your concerns fairly weak? Your attitudes provide one indication of your behavioral intent.

According to the theory of reasoned action, the second predictor of behavioral intention is **normative beliefs**, which are your perceptions about what others in your social network expect you to do. Notably, behavioral intention is not formed by beliefs about all others in our social network but only our valued others. A disliked associate is unlikely to persuade us to behave in a particular way, but a respected colleague is likely to have that power. In addition to the value you place on others in your network, the theory suggests you must also consider the motivation to comply with these others. Some people are conformists and likely to succumb to peer pressure because of their people-pleasing ways. Others rebel, intentionally doing the opposite of what even valued others expect of them. Returning to our example of climate change, if your close friends are climate change warriors, you are more likely to follow their lead in adopting a vegetarian diet or relying on public transportation. However, if you have a nagging relative who you don't really like harping on climate change very much, you are unlikely to change your ways.

The determination of behavioral intention is achieved by looking at the relative weights of the two predictors. In some cases, attitudes might be weighted more strongly, and in others normative beliefs will be weighted more strongly. In order to persuade someone to act a particular way, then, the persuader has to send a message to affect the proper predictor. Consider trying to convince someone to adopt a vegetarian diet. If attitudes are very strong and normative beliefs are not, then a message should be sent to address attitudes ("You will look and feel better if you become a vegetarian, and think about the positive effects on the environment!"). If the opposite is true, you should focus your message on complying with valued others ("The people you love the most are committed to an environmentally friendly diet."). Finally, the persuader can try to change the relative weights of the attitudinal and normative components. If, for example, normative beliefs are weighted more than an attitude, you can try to reduce the strength of the normative beliefs ("It's your life; you need to decide what's important for you.").

Although research has provided some strong support for the tenets of the theory of reasoned action, Ajzen (1988, 1991) extended the theory by adding a third major predictor, changing the name to the theory of planned behavior. Ajzen recognized that sometimes we might intend to behave a certain way, but our plans are not carried through because we don't have control over the situation. Like attitudes and normative beliefs, **perceived behavioral control** is also comprised of two elements: self-efficacy and controllability. **Self-efficacy** refers to an individual's belief that they can actually perform the behavior. As regards becoming a vegetarian, do you believe that you can refrain from eating beef at a barbecue? Do you think that you can dine in a restaurant with nonvegetarians and feel satisfied? People often "talk themselves out" of doing something because they fear they won't be successful. In short, you need to believe you can truly do something in order to develop the intention to do so. The second component, **controllability**, recognizes that sometimes things are simply out of our control—or are at least perceived that way. Do you have a gluten intolerance or soy or nut allergies that will make getting enough protein in a vegetarian diet challenging for you? Do you suffer from an eating disorder that might be triggered by food restrictions? Figure 7.1 pulls all of these components together.

The theory of planned behavior provides an explanation for why public relations and marketing campaigns that focus only on providing information are unlikely to have any behavioral effect. Simply changing someone's attitude is not enough. If your goal as a persuader is to convince someone to act in a particular way (e.g., buy your product, donate blood, or engage in fewer arguments), you need to provide attitudinal, social norm, and controllability incentives.

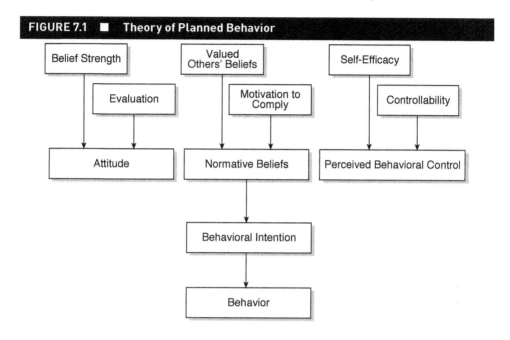

FIGURE 7.1 ■ Theory of Planned Behavior

EXTENDED PARALLEL PROCESSING MODEL

You can easily imagine a public health campaign focused on the situation we just discussed: encouraging people to adopt a plant-based diet. One temptation might to be to use a fear appeal to do so. If you have seen the documentaries *Food, Inc.* or *Cowspiracy,* you have been exposed to some fear appeals about the effects of eating meat. A **fear appeal** is a persuasive message that emphasizes the danger or harm that will occur if the receiver does not adopt the recommendations of the persuader. The classic example of fear appeals is cigarette labelling in the US Food and Drug Administration (FDA) has mandated that every package and carton of cigarettes must include a permanent warning accompanied by a graphic image depicting one of 11 identified negative effects of smoking. The warnings range from an image of a sick child with an oxygen mask accompanied by the statement "Warning: Tobacco smoke can harm your children" to a close-up image of disease-riddled feet with missing toes and the statement "Warning: Smoking reduces blood flow to the limbs, which can require amputation."

The question is, do fear appeals actually work? Shadel et al. (2019) conducted an experiment to test whether graphic health warnings influenced smokers' purchases of cigarettes. They found that the warnings did not have a direct overall effect on purchases. Instead, the graphic warnings influenced only those smokers with a low dependence on nicotine. So, why don't these fear appeals work more broadly? The next theory we introduce is the Extended Parallel Processing Model (EPPM), which can shed light on these findings.

The EPPM was developed by Witte (1992), who merged two previous theories focused on fear appeals—the Parallel Process Theory (PPM, Leventhal, 1970) and the Protection Motivation Theory (PTM, Rogers, 1975, 1983). The theory focuses on how rational decisions and emotional decisions work in conjunction to determine behavior. The theory identifies four important variables: two threat variables, and two efficacy variables.

The two threat variables are perceived severity and perceived susceptibility (Witte, 1992). **Perceived severity** refers to how serious the individual thinks the consequences of the behavior might be. Think about the common side effects listed in advertisements for prescription drugs. Often these ads list a host of conditions such as headaches and nausea (not so bad), to anal leakage (ew), to death (pretty damn serious). **Perceived susceptibility** references the individual's belief in the likelihood of experiencing these negative consequences. Although most of us have an optimism bias, discounting the likelihood that bad things will happen to us (Weinstein, 1984), teenagers in particular are subject to this pattern of thinking.

The two efficacy variables are response efficacy and self-efficacy (Witte, 1992). **Response efficacy** is defined as the effectiveness of the proposed solution. For example, when talking about the efficacy of birth control methods, according to the FDA sterilization and Intrauterine Devices (IUDs) are the most effective methods (less than 1% likelihood of pregnancy), and condoms and spermicide are the least effective methods (18% and 28% chance of pregnancy; US FDA, 2021). Of course, even the least effective methods do prevent pregnancy compared to using no contraceptive at all. Yet, if an individual believes that using a condom is not very effective, and it includes a number of costs, they are less likely to believe that using a condom is "worth it."

We have already introduced the notion of self-efficacy when we described TPB. **Self-efficacy** references an individual's confidence that they can perform the proposed action (Witte, 1992). Using the example of switching to a plant-based diet, do you believe that you can actually go meat-free? In terms of birth control, do you trust yourself to use a condom when you are in the moment?

EPPM combines these variables in to a two-by-two matrix of different audience types, and proposes different message strategies depending on the audience type (Witte, 1992). Table 7.2 provides an overview of the matrix. The theory considers the two types of threat variables and the two types of efficacy variables as **multiplicative** rather than additive (Witte, 1994). To illustrate, imagine you are determining the threat of contracting a deadly disease like malaria. Your perceived severity of the disease is likely high; malaria is one of the most common causes of death around the world. On a scale of 1-10, malaria might be rated about an eight. However, if you live in the United States and do not travel to countries with high incidences of the disease,

TABLE 7.2 ■ The Extended Parallel Processing Model		
	High Efficacy	**Low Efficacy**
High Threat	Danger Control	Fear Control
Low Threat	Lesser Danger Control	No Response

your likelihood of actually getting malaria is close to zero. To determine an overall perception of threat, you multiply the two scores (getting a 0) rather than adding the two scores (getting an 8). What this means is that although malaria might be perceived as a serious illness, the individual in question is unlikely to perceive it as a threat because they are unlikely to be susceptible to it.

Returning to the matrix, audiences who perceive a high threat and also perceive high efficacy can be reached using a **danger control** strategy; these individuals are likely to take protective action or avoid or reduce the threat if they are given a call to action. In this case, individuals are using a rational decision-making process ("Here's how you can prevent x"). However, in cases of high perceived threat but low efficacy beliefs, individuals are likely to respond emotionally and engage in maladaptive behaviors such as denial or rejection of possible solutions. Fear appeals are likely to backfire in this situation, as they will only exacerbate negative emotions. In this case, strategic communicators should engage in **fear control** by educating the audience about their abilities to enact solutions.

In situations perceived as low threat, but the individuals perceive high efficacy, the appropriate strategy is a weaker form of danger control, in which messages focus on information about the risk (Witte, 1992). In general, audience members in this quadrant aren't particularly motivated to do anything because they don't think that they personally are at risk. In this situation, messages should seek to educate audience members about the actual risks of the threat. For example, the Well Project is a nonprofit organization that seeks to dispel the myths about HIV/AIDS. They target girls and women, seeking to educate them about the actual risks of contracting HIV/AIDS, even among virgins, straight women, and women in monogamous relationships.

Finally, among low threat and low efficacy audience members, people don't feel at risk and don't know what to do about it anyway (Witte, 1992). They will be unlikely to process any messages centering on the issue. At best, a strategic communicator can seek to increase perceived threat and increase perceived efficacy by informing the audience members about the nature of the risk and the ways that the risk can be mitigated.

In summary, EPPM provides a means for strategic communicators to target audiences with the types of messages that are most likely to be persuasive given their perceived threat and efficacy levels. The theory cautions that fear appeals without corresponding efficacy information might result in maladaptive behaviors, pushing individuals to behave in an opposite fashion than what is desired. Accordingly, fear appeals should also include information that empowers audience members with tools to combat the risk.

INOCULATION THEORY

Thus far, we have discussed theories that give advice about how to persuade someone. But what if your goal is to persuade someone *not* to be persuaded? Given the plethora of persuasive attempts that surround us on a daily basis, knowing how to resist persuasion is also a useful tool. McGuire's inoculation theory (1961) presents a way to understand how resistance to persuasion might be achieved. Using a medical metaphor, McGuire argued that like a vaccine that prevents you from getting a disease, particular messages might "inoculate" you from attacks on your beliefs. Specifically, an **inoculation** message presents a weaker form (i.e., a "small dose") of a contrary argument, much like a vaccine includes a weakened form of a virus. Once exposed to this weaker argument, people are less likely to change their attitudes when presented with a stronger form of the argument; they have, in essence, developed a formidable defense system. Research has supported this assertion, indicating people are more resistant to persuasion when an inoculation process takes place than when original beliefs were simply bolstered by stronger evidence (Banas & Rains, 2008; McGuire & Papageorgis, 1961).

McGuire's original theory focused solely on what he called "cultural truisms" (1962), such as "you should brush your teeth after every meal" and "mental illness is not contagious." Critics challenged this focus, suggesting these noncontroversial issues did not provide an adequate test of how well people will resist persuasive efforts about controversial subjects (Ullman & Bodaken, 1975, as cited in Banas & Rains, 2008). In recent years, a communication scholar named Michael Pfau and his colleagues have examined how inoculation theory might work in broader persuasive contexts, particularly in terms of health communication (Godbold & Pfau, 2000), political communication (An & Pfau, 2004), employees' organizational commitment (Haigh & Pfau, 2006), and corporate advocacy (Burgoon et al., 1995). The result is that inoculation theory has "almost limitless application" (Banas & Rains, 2008, p. 1).

Pfau (1997) suggests there are two major components to an inoculation message: threat and refutational preemption. First, **threat** is a necessary component of any inoculation effort. Note that threat is not the same as fear appeal. Instead, threat simply involves a forewarning of a potential persuasive attack on beliefs, making sure the target of the persuasive effort is aware of their susceptibility to the attack. According to Pfau, making you aware of a threat should motivate you to defend your attitudes or beliefs. For example, Wong (2016) investigated the effectiveness of inoculation theory in generating resistance to persuasive messages attacking the safety and effectiveness of the human papilloma virus (HPV) vaccine. To stimulate perceived threat, he had participants read a message that stated the following:

> Despite your positive attitude and feelings towards the HPV vaccine, there exists out there many reports and stories by the media and various interest groups aimed at attacking your attitude and feelings on the issue, and there is a real possibility that you will come into contact with these arguments in the near future, some of which will be so persuasive that they may cause you to question your attitude and feelings toward getting the HPV vaccine. (Wong, 2016, p. 130)

The threat need not be a strong warning; Banas and Rains (2008) found that even low levels of threat provided inoculation.

The second component of an inoculation effort is **refutational preemption**. Not only should targets receive information about potential threats, but the inoculation message should also anticipate the counterpersuasive effort by raising specific challenges and then contesting them. In the study by Wong (2016) described previously, two news reports and two messages from the Centers for Disease Control and Prevention (CDC) served as refutational preemption.

The news reports interviewed doctors about the questions and concerns they have heard raised by parents and the media, with the doctors reassuring the viewing audience of the safety and the effectiveness of the vaccine. The messages by the CDC reinforced these arguments by describing the safety of vaccines in general, and the HPV vaccine specifically.

Research consistently shows that "matching" the content of refutations exactly to what actually occurs in the counterargument is unnecessary; any preemptive refutation seems to bolster the inoculation effect (Banas & Rains, 2008). In the study just described, Wong (2016) found that the messages focused on the safety of vaccines in general were just as effective as the messages focused on the HPV vaccine in particular. The bigger question appears to be how strong the preemptive arguments need to be. Using the vaccine analogy, how much "disease" in the vaccine protects the recipient, and how much is too much? McGuire (1964) argued that inoculation efforts should be "threatening enough to be defense-stimulating, but not so strong as to overwhelm" (p. 202). In testing this issue, Compton and Pfau (2004) concluded that even weak refutations provide protection.

Inoculation theory provides clear advice for professional communicators challenged (or who think they may be challenged) by "bad press." Consider the efforts of the soda industry. In 2013, there were no "sin" taxes focused on reducing the consumption of pop or other sugary drinks. As of 2021, 10 cities in the United States have sugary-drink taxes, and New York state, Connecticut, and Hawaii are considering adopting this type of tax (Boeson, 2021). The goals of such efforts are twofold: to address the rising obesity epidemic in the United States and to provide a means to reduce budget shortfalls in an uncertain economy. The industry leaders (Coca-Cola and PespsiCo) have partnered with the American Beverage Association (ABA) to make sure the public is not persuaded to vote in favor of these tax increases, however. It's estimated the ABA has spent over $100 million in efforts to prevent the public from being persuaded to tax soft drinks, including nearly $10 million in California alone. Table 7.3 depicts the argument presented in one advertisement called "Your Cart Your Choice," which clearly demonstrates an inoculation effort.

TABLE 7.3 ■ Inoculation Campaign Against Proposed Sweetened Beverage Taxes	
	Example
Threat	"Some politicians still don't think we can choose what's best for our families without new laws, regulations, or taxes telling us what to buy."
Refutational pre-emption	"Getting serious about obesity starts with education, not laws and regulations." "Look around your grocery store lately? There are more choices and more information than ever before. New kinds of beverages. Different portion sizes. Calories right up front."
Conclusion	"The fact is, it's not the government's job to grocery shop for my family. It's mine."

SITUATIONAL CRISIS COMMUNICATION THEORY

The first two theories we have discussed in this chapter were proactive; they focused on developing messages to meet organizational goals. The third theory, inoculation, is preventative, as it seeks to make sure that others' persuasive efforts do not negatively impact the organization. The final theory we discuss in this chapter, Situational Crisis Communication Theory (SCCT), is entirely reactive. The theory centers on best practices for responding to an organizational **crisis**, which is defined as a "sudden and unexpected event that threatens to disrupt an organization's operations and poses both a financial and a reputational threat" (Coombs, 2007, p. 163).

W. Timothy Coombs developed SCCT in 2007, using the tenets of Attribution Theory as the foundation for his theory (Attribution Theory was described in the case study sections of Chapters 1 and 2). In short, SCCT suggests that strategic communication professionals should use different crisis responses based on how the organization's publics will likely attribute responsibility for the crisis. To determine which crisis response to use, the theory identifies three important considerations: the nature of the crisis, the responsibility for the crisis, and the reputational threat the crisis poses for the organization.

First, SCCT suggests that the strategic communicator should determine the nature of the crisis itself (Coombs, 2007). He identified three clusters, or types, of crises. The first is called the **victim cluster**. In these types of crises, the organization is one of the victims of the crisis itself. Examples of these sorts of crises include natural disasters, workplace violence, false rumors, and product tampering. Coombs (2007) labeled the second cluster the **accidental cluster**; these types of crises occur when the organizational actions associated with the crisis were unintentional. Examples include stakeholder challenges (i.e., a claim that the organization is operating inappropriately), technical-error industrial accidents, and technical-error product harm (i.e., recalls). The final cluster was labeled the **intentional cluster**. In these sorts of crises the organization knowingly engaged in actions that sparked the crisis. This cluster includes human errors that result in either an industrial accident or product recalls, organizational deception, management misconduct, or risky management decisions that put people at risk.

Classification of the type of crisis allows strategic communicators to determine the level of reputational threat the organization faces. A **reputational threat** is a challenge to the image that an organization has developed that has the potential to affect the organization's position in the field (Fombrun, 1996). The three crisis types vary in terms of reputational threat, with the victim cluster associated with only weak attributions of crisis responsibility (and therefore only a mild reputational threat), the accidental cluster associated with minimal attributions of responsibility (and therefore a moderate reputational threat), and the intentional cluster associated with strong attribution of crisis responsibility (and a corresponding severe reputational threat; Coombs, 2014).

However, the type of crisis is not the sole consideration when determining reputational threat. The organization's history also affects reputational threat. If the organization has a history of experiencing crises, or if it has done a poor job of managing a crisis in the past, then the reputational threat is increased. Consider two companies, Starbucks and Facebook. In 2018, a manager of a Starbucks store in Philadelphia called the police to arrest two Black men for trespassing because they had not purchased anything and were using the store as a meeting location. The incident quickly went viral, leading to claims of racism and boycotts of the company. The company's response to the incident is considered to be a textbook case of how to handle a crisis. Starbucks' CEO immediately apologized, saying "I'm embarrassed, ashamed. I think what occurred was reprehensible at every single level. I take it very personally, as everyone in our company does, and we're committed to making it right." He then shut down 8,000 stores for a day of racial bias training. Closing the stores resulted in approximately $12 million in lost revenue. However, the rapid response and acknowledgement of culpability has given the company a boost to its reputation, which can potentially translate to more good will if and when Starbucks faces another crisis.

Conversely, Facebook has faced several crises in the past few years, from selling users' data without their consent in 2018, to advertising boycotts over allowing hate speech to be promulgated on the platform, to an FTC lawsuit claiming that the company illegally eliminated competitors. Given the plethora of crises the company has faced, even a crisis that would be considered in the victim cluster might be a large reputational threat because of the company's history.

Crisis Response Strategies

Given the type of crisis and the company's history of crisis management into consideration, SCCT articulates four general crisis response strategies, three of which are considered primary strategies, and one of which is considered a secondary strategy (Coombs, 2014). Details about each of the strategies can be found in Table 7.4. The **deny** strategies attempt to distance the organization from the crisis and should be used when the crisis is in the victim cluster and there is no history of similar crises. Deny strategies are particularly useful for rumors and challenge crises. If the organization uses these strategies effectively, no reputational harm will be done (Coombs, 2007).

The **diminish** strategies should be used when there is little crisis responsibility (Coombs, 2007). These strategies seek to reassure stakeholders that the crisis is either not as bad as it seems or that the organization had nothing to do with the crisis. They should be used for victim crises if there is a history of previous similar crises, or during accident crises when there is no history of similar crises and the organization has a positive reputation.

The **rebuild** strategies are used to change the perception of the organization (Coombs, 2007). They should always be used when there is a strong attribution of responsibility, although they are also appropriate for accident crises when the organization has a history of similar crises. The use of these strategies should be accompanied by credible information; if conflicting information appears in the media, the organization's publics will choose the interpretation that seems most credible to them.

Coombs (2007) also identified a secondary strategy called **bolstering**, which involves presenting either new, positive information about the organization, or reminding stakeholders about previous good works. Bolstering strategies seek to cultivate feelings of sympathy and good will, but they do not replace the primary strategies.

TABLE 7.4 ■ Crisis Response Strategies		
Primary Strategies	**Strategy**	**Description**
• Deny		
	Attack the accuser	*Confront the person making a crisis claim.*
	Denial	*Assert that there is no crisis.*
	Scapegoat	*Blame a person or group outside of the organization.*
• Diminish		
	Excuse	*Minimize the organization's responsibility for the crisis.*
	Justification	*Minimize the damage associated with the crisis.*
• Rebuild		
	Compensation	*Offer money or gifts to victims.*
	Apology	*Takes responsibility and asks for forgiveness.*
Secondary Strategies		
• Bolster		
	Reminder	*Revisit the organization's past good works.*
	Ingratiation	*Praise stakeholders.*
	Victimage	*Remind people that the organization is a victim, too.*

Finally, SCCT posits that organizations should pick one crisis response strategy and stick with it. Using multiple different strategies diminishes the credibility of the organization and will ultimately damage the organization's reputation (Coombs, 2007).

CHAPTER SUMMARY AND RESEARCH APPLICATIONS

This chapter examined four theories central to strategic communication. The theory of planned behavior says that three concepts can predict an individual's behavior: attitude, normative beliefs, and controllability. A wide range of actions have been studied using this theory, including the likelihood that someone will post selfies on social networking sites (Kim et al., 2016), willingness to intervene when a friend is the victim of relational violence (Lemay et al., 2017), and college students' intentions to cheat on exams (Chudzicka-Czupała et al., 2016).

Second, the extended parallel processing model provides insight into how and why fear appeals might motivate people to behave in a particular way. For example, Roberto et al. (2021) found that the theory was accurate in predicting college students' social distancing behavior during the COVID-19 pandemic. Similarly, Myrick (2019) found that using celebrities in health campaigns can be effective, especially if the celebrity focuses on optimism versus fear in their message about health preventions.

Next, inoculation theory provides a means to argue proactively in support of a position by sending preemptive messages that include forewarning of the threat and refutations to anticipated arguments. The theory's application has wide reach, including public relations' research demonstrating that inoculation messages are a viable proactive strategy in crisis communication (Kim, 2013) and also work to prevent people from falling prey to conspiracy propaganda (Banas & Miller, 2013). Inoculation theory has also been used to craft resistance messages applicable to public health communication professionals. From trying to uphold one's exercise motivation (Dimmock et al., 2016), to studying the efficacy of alcohol media literacy interventions among school students (Gordon et al., 2016) to protecting positive attitudes toward the HPV vaccine (Wong, 2016), inoculation theory is frequently employed either as a means of discouraging behaviors that negatively affect public health or of protecting positive health behaviors in the face of temptation to do otherwise.

Finally, the situational crisis communication model provides advice for public relations practitioners seeking to prevent negative outcomes of an organizational crisis. For example, Kochigina (2020) used a case study of Tesla's financial crisis in her analysis of the role of faith-holders (organizational supporters) during a crisis. She found that faith-holders provide a powerful voice when managing a crisis. Also looking at the way that organizations can leverage outsiders when dealing with a crisis, Fan and Jiang (2021) studied the use of Twitter during Hurricane Harvey in 2017. They found that local influencers served as an information hub during the disaster, and they recommend that organizations make use of local influencers to better spread organizational messages during a crisis.

In addition to the four theories that we have spotlighted, additional theories that provide insight into strategic communications are described in Table 7.5.

TABLE 7.5 ■ Additional Theories of Strategic Communication	
Theory	**Main Idea**
Framing Theory	How information is presented influences how people interpret the information (Goffman, 1974).
Image Repair Theory	Identifies approaches and strategies for responding to accusations or suspicions (Benoit, 2015).
Risk Information Processing Model	People will seek and process information when they have insufficient information, when they perceive that they have the ability to gather information, and when they believe communication sources are trustworthy and useful (Griffin et al., 1999).
Situational Theory of Problem Solving	The more committed an individual is to problem-solving, the more likely they will acquire information, select information, and transmit information related to the problem (Kim & Grunig, 2011).

DISCUSSION QUESTIONS

1. Think of something about which you have a negative attitude. It might be a type of food, a genre of music, or a media franchise (i.e, the *Twilight* saga, *The Fast and the Furious* films, or the *Marvel Universe*). For the item you have selected, which is stronger—your negative attitude or your normative beliefs? Using the Theory of Planned Behavior, how might someone convince you to try the food, listen to the music, or view the film?

2. EPPM says that even if the perceived threat of something is high, if an individual has low efficacy beliefs they are likely to engage in maladaptive behavior. Have you ever found yourself doubting your ability to do something, even if you perceived it to be very important or very serious? Was EPPM correct in its predictions—did you engage in maladaptive behavior such as avoidance, denial, or rejection?

3. The examples we used for Inoculation theory focused on the HPV vaccine. Consider the campaign to persuade Americans to get the COVID-19 vaccine. How might the government have used inoculation theory to increase the number of Americans who got vaccinated?

4. Because organizational crises happen on a regular basis, select a crisis that has appeared in the news recently. What strategy did the organization use? What strategy should the organization have used based on the principles of SCCT?

KEY TERMS

Accidental cluster (p. 130)

Attitude (p. 123)

Behavioral intention (p. 123)

Bolstering (p. 131)

Controllability (p. 124)

Crisis (p. 130)

Danger control (p. 127)

Deny (p. 131)

Diminish (p. 131)

Fear appeal (p. 125)

Fear control (p. 127)

Goal (p. 121)

Influence (p. 122)

Inoculation (p. 128)

Intentional cluster (p. 130)

Mission (p. 121)

Multiplicative (p. 126)

Normative beliefs (p. 123)

Perceived behavioral control (p. 124)

Perceived severity (p. 126)

Perceived susceptibility (p. 126)

Rebuild (p. 131)

Refutational preemption (p. 128)

Reputational threat (p. 130)

Response efficacy (p. 126)

Self-efficacy (p. 124)

Strategic communication (p. 121)

Strategy (p. 122)

Threat (p. 128)

Victim cluster (p. 130)

Vision (p. 122)

CASE STUDY 7
Million-Dollar Manipulation

Trina had always loved her job at the Columbus AIDS Confederation (CAC). She was part of a small nonprofit that served poor people who had been diagnosed with HIV/AIDS. As a case worker, Trina provided one-on-one support for her clients, helping them cope with their diagnosis and assisting them with developing a plan of care. A big part of her job was to facilitate her clients' access to community resources that might help them, whether it was housing, nutrition, or medical care. It was important work, and she loved her coworkers, her clients, and the CAC.

As a small nonprofit in a relatively large urban area, the CAC was almost always struggling to meet a sizable pool of potential clients given a modest (at best) budget. The organization had just five social workers, an executive director, and an administrator on staff. The executive director, Mohammad Bacho, not only had to oversee the work that was being done by the organization, he also had to do fund-raising, marketing, and community outreach. As a licensed social worker, he also occasionally met with clients when needed, especially to cover the vacations and sick days of the social workers on staff. And, of course, there was the ongoing tension of working with the board of trustees. This tension particularly became an issue when Albert Brothman rose to chairman of the board for the CAC. Brothman was a successful CEO who managed a multi-million-dollar company based in Columbus. His demeanor was a bit brash for the "people-first" mindset typical in the nonprofit sector; Brothman was confident to the point of arrogance and aggressive to the point of bullying.

The first board meeting with Brothman at the helm did not go well. Brothman challenged Mohammad's leadership skill, questioned his fund-raising numbers, and criticized Mohammad's care for clients. As an executive director of a nonprofit, Mohammed was skilled at the delicate balance of reassuring board members while simultaneously fighting for the integrity of the nonprofit. He remained calm and simply asked the board to help him to live the mission of the organization. Little did he know that his modest request would have such troubling consequences.

At the next month's board meeting, Brothman announced that he had finalized a deal with BRcd Enterprises, a pharmaceutical company that was seeking to develop a new protease inhibitor for HIV/AIDS. BRcd had promised to donate $1 million to the CAC, which was a large and potentially transformational gift. Mohammad was excited but also concerned. What was the catch? He didn't have to wait long to find out.

BRcd had already filled out its Investigational New Drug Application with the FDA and had completed Phase 1 clinical trials for the new protease inhibitor. The Phase I Trials, which were conducted on healthy volunteers, indicated that the drug was safe. The company was about to launch Phase II, which focuses on the effectiveness of the drug. For this phase, they needed to study people who had been diagnosed with HIV/AIDS. And they wanted the CAC to do the recruiting for them.

Mohammad knew that such a request had the potential of being unethical; the ethical code of the National Association of Social Workers was clear about conflict of interest. However, he also knew that his social workers had a great deal of integrity, and he could trust them to practice ethically. He called a staff meeting the day after the board meeting.

"I've got some really great news, and I have a small request," Mohammad began. "The really great news is that we have received a $1 million gift."

Trina and her colleagues couldn't help themselves. They cheered and high-fived each other. "That is incredible, Mohammad!" Trina exclaimed. "How did you manage that?" she asked.

"It wasn't me. It was Mr. Brothman. Apparently, he's got some connections to a pharmaceutical company, and he convinced them to make the gift."

"Wait, what? A pharmaceutical company?" Gavin asked. "What would a pharmaceutical company want with us?"

"Just like us, they are committed to serving people with HIV/AIDS," Mohammad explained. "They just wanted to put their money where their mouth is."

"Huh. Well, that's pretty awesome. I'm down with that," Darryl exclaimed. The other social workers mumbled their acceptance as well.

"So that was the great news, what's the small request? Would you like us to start purchasing all of our supplies at Brothman's company?" Tiffany asked. The group chuckled at her facetious comment, knowing that none of them could afford the high-end products Brothman's companies sold.

"No," Mohammad said solemnly, immediately dampening the enthusiasm of the group. "No, but this is serious. Listen, as part of the deal with the pharmaceutical company, Brothman did make a promise, and I want you to hear it from me first, and I want to make sure you understand that I have the same strong ethical commitments that you do. The pharmaceutical company, BRcd, is seeking approval from the FDA for a new HIV/AIDS drug. They are about to launch the Phase II study, and they are looking for participants for the drug trial."

"Please tell me . . ." Gavin began.

Mohammad held up his hand to hold off the question. "I informed the board that we would not violate our ethical standards as social workers. I explained conflict of interest to them, and I reminded them that many of our clients are vulnerable, and it would be inappropriate to try to persuade them to take part in the study. The board agreed. They have merely asked that we post information about the drug trial in our offices, and if we think it is appropriate, that we disseminate information about the study to any suitable clients. We will not directly solicit participants."

The social workers were mollified but still concerned. Their jobs were to advocate for their clients, not pander to the needs of a donor.

"Look, we don't exactly have many million-dollar donors beating down our door. Beggars can't be choosers, right? I'm convinced we can accept this money without compromising our integrity," Mohammad reassured.

Within a month, the money had come in, a poster about the clinical trial was displayed in the CAC lobby, and each social worker was given a handful of pamphlets about the study to distribute to any appropriate clients.

Four weeks later, Mohammad answered his office phone to a very irate chairman of the board. "Bacho, I thought I was clear with you about this BRcd deal. They gave us money. We give them subjects for their drug trial. I can see that we got the money. Why the hell don't they have any subjects for their damn study?" Brothman shouted.

"Mr. Brothman," Mohammad began. "You know that we are bound by the ethical guidelines of our profession. We simply cannot coerce our clients to take part in a study."

"I'm not talking about coercion, Bacho, I'm talking about persuasion. BRcd needs 100 people for their study, and they need them as soon as possible. Every delay means that your clients don't have another potential drug that can help them. Work harder at getting subjects."

Mohammad hung up the phone and considered how to best create a win/win solution. He decided to craft an e-mail to his staff, which read as follows:

Dear Colleagues:

We do important work at the CAC. Most of you may not think about it, but just a few years ago I was one of you; I was out in the field, doing my best to help people that society wants to ignore. I remember one of my clients, Rosa. Rosa was 26 when she was diagnosed with HIV. Unfortunately, she wasn't diagnosed until after she had 3 children, and two of her children subsequently were diagnosed with HIV. Like many of our clients, Rosa was a substance abuser, and her willingness to be treated for HIV varied depending on her sobriety. It would be easy to judge Rosa, but that's not our job. Our job is to do our very best for the Rosas out there and to work tirelessly to make sure that her kids have a chance for a healthy life, too.

I know that you are doing everything you can for your clients. It's great that we at the CAC provide the support that we do, but isn't the real end goal to try to prevent people from needing our support? Don't we want a future where we aren't attending the funerals of our clients, or worse yet, kids who didn't deserve to deal with the issues they have to deal with?

Yes, we have come a long way in the drug treatments we have available to people with HIV/AIDS, but don't we want to stop treating the disease and start curing it?

We have the opportunity to contribute to finding a cure for HIV/AIDS. You have the information pamphlets provided by BRcd. Please consider talking about the opportunity to be a part of the study with your clients.

Yours in Service, Mohammad

Within 5 minutes of the e-mail being sent, Trina was on the phone with Tiffany. "Did you see Mohammad's e-mail?" she fumed. "Can you believe this? I thought he said that we didn't have to solicit participants!" she fumed.

"Hmmm. I didn't read it that way at all. I trust Mohammad. If he wants me to talk to my clients, I will. I mean, I won't be pressuring them, just informing them about an opportunity," Tiffany replied.

"Are you kidding me?" Trina was aghast. "I am not going to be controlled by some money-grubbing pharma company! My integrity is worth more than a million dollars."

Tiffany sighed. "Trina, Mohammad has reassured us again and again that he won't compromise our integrity. Finding volunteers for the study is a good thing. Things aren't so black and white."

"Uh, yes they are. There is right, and there is wrong! This is wrong, Tiffany. BRcd should just find participants the same way every other pharma company does. And I'm going to let Mohammad know that it is wrong." Trina hung up, exasperated.

Trina was so angry she didn't know what to do with herself. After pacing her living room for a half an hour, she sat down at her computer and began typing. First, she wrote a letter of resignation. Then, she wrote a letter to the National Association of Social Workers (NASW), detailing what she perceived to be a violation of ethical behavior and requesting a professional review of Mohammad Bacho, and another letter to the state licensing board, asking for the same. Finally, she wrote an e-mail to her former colleagues at the CAC.

Dear Tiffany, Gavin, Darryl, and Shanae:

I want to let you know that I have resigned from my position at the CAC, and I have filed a professional complaint with the NASW and the state licensing board. I have worked with each of you for at least 5 years (and Tiff, we have worked together for 12!), and I have always been proud to be a part of a group of caring and committed social workers. I cannot in good conscience continue my employment there given the questionable ethical conditions at the CAC.

I know you—all of you. I know that you are outstanding professionals who are dedicated to doing the very best for our clients. I know you are honorable and honest and hardworking. Please do not fall prey to the questionable "deal" negotiated by the chairman of the board, Albert Brothman, and please don't be persuaded by Mohammad's reassurances that he wants us to behave ethically. First, he swore to us that we did not have to directly solicit participants for the drug trial. Then, he asked us to "talk" to our clients about the opportunity. What's next? Have us drive our clients to the study? Make sure they're taking the study meds? Think about it. This is not just a little thing he is asking, he is asking us to violate our own code of ethics. As social workers, we are dedicated to service and the right to self-determination. We cannot use our position of power to manipulate people into doing something that might not be in their own best interests.

All my Best.

Trina

Questions for Consideration

1. How do Trina's attitudes and normative beliefs affect her behavioral intention to solicit participants for the study? How does perceived behavioral control come into play for her? Now contrast these elements with Tiffany's attitudes, normative beliefs, and behavioral intentions.

2. Consider the variations in Trina and Tiffany's interpretations of the email that Mohammed sent. Using EPPM, do you think that Trina and Tiffany perceived a different level of threat in the situation? What impact did it have? What about efficacy; did they seem to vary in their efficacy perceptions? What were the results of these variations in perceptions?

3. How did Trina use inoculation theory to try to persuade her fellow social workers?

4. The CAC is now facing a crisis; explain which type of crisis it is, and then use the situational crisis communication theory to suggest the appropriate crisis communication strategy.

5. Which strategic communication theory seems to explain the situation better than the others? Why do you believe this to be the case? What situations might surface to make a different theory or theories better at explaining the situation? What theories could you combine to make for an even better explanation of the encounter?

GROUP COMMUNICATION

After reading this chapter, you will be able to do the following:

1. Define basic terms associated with group and team communication

2. Describe the axioms of communication identified by the systems/interactional perspective

3. Articulate the four functions identified in the functional approach to decision-making

4. Recommend strategies to prevent groupthink

5. Explain the development of a rhetorical vision using symbolic convergence theory

Whether you work for a publishing company, a retail organization, or a Fortune 500 corporation, US businesses have adopted a "team" structure. To succeed as a communication professional, understanding *how* groups work, as well as the principles and pitfalls of group decision-making, is crucial to your career. In this chapter, we explain a broad range of group theories—from those that focus specifically on group decision-making to those that emphasize the ways group communication creates the norms for group behavior.

DEFINING GROUP COMMUNICATION

Popular understanding implies a group is simply a collection of people. Scholars studying group communication are more precise when using the term *group*, however. According to scholars, a **group** refers to a system of three or more individuals who are focused on achieving a common purpose and who influence and are influenced by each other (Rothwell, 1998). A group is different from an **aggregate**, which is simply a set number of individuals—say, the people standing at a bus stop or the people on an elevator. Moreover, a group is distinct from an organization. Organizations typically involve formal hierarchies (e.g., CEO, director, manager) and structured channels of communication (e.g., annual performance reviews, employee newsletters). In contrast, a group's structure and patterns of communication typically emerge through interaction (Rothwell, 1998).

Because of the increased use of team-based structures in organizations, it is also of interest to articulate the nature of a **team**. In an organizational setting, a team is an ongoing, coordinated group of people working together (Dyer, 1987). Teams are typically self-directed and self-regulating, meaning typical chains of organizational command are suspended; teams are empowered to complete a task from start to finish. Not all groups are teams (if control is primarily external, for example), but all teams meet the qualification of being a group.

Group communication is distinct from other types of communication because all groups must balance **task communication** (communication focused on achieving the instrumental goal the group is trying to achieve) with **socioemotional communication** (communication focused on developing, maintaining, and repairing the relationships between group members). Put simply, the more time the group members spend on the task, the less their focus on relationship needs, and vice versa. Because group members likely have different orientations toward the importance of these two activities, balancing task communication and socioemotional communication is often quite challenging and usually leads to group members enacting group roles. A **group role** refers to a pattern of communicative behaviors performed by one individual in light of expectations held by other group members. Typically, group roles are classified as task-oriented roles, maintenance-oriented roles, and disruptive roles, which are roles that meet individual versus group needs. For example, the isolate is someone who withdraws from participating in the group, the zealot is someone who tries to convert all group members to their belief system, and the stage hog monopolizes the conversational floor and prevents others from expressing their thoughts and opinions (Rothwell, 1998).

This chapter emphasizes understanding the communication that takes place within groups and teams. The four theories we present vary in focus. First, the systems/interactional perspective focuses on patterns of communication that develop through interaction with others. Next, functional group decision-making centers on the tasks communication achieves in the decision-making process. Continuing with a focus on decision-making, the third theory, groupthink, provides a mechanism for explaining poor or ineffective group decision-making. Finally, symbolic convergence theory (SCT) explains the development of a group consciousness, including shared emotions, motives, and meanings. Table 8.1 provides an overview of each theory.

TABLE 8.1 ■ Overview of Group Communication Theories	
Theory	**Main Idea**
Systems/Interactional Perspective	In order to understand group functioning, you need to understand the communication within the group.
Functional Group Decision-Making	Effective decision-making requires meeting requisite functions.
Groupthink	Poor decisions occur based on cohesion, structural faults, and situational characteristics.
Symbolic Convergence Theory	Group members create and sustain a group identity, which in turn influences norms for behavior.

SYSTEMS/INTERACTIONAL PERSPECTIVE

Rather than one specific theory, systems approaches are a constellation of theories that share common assumptions and concepts. Although we have classified this approach as a group communication theory, in reality systems theories are used to explain nearly all communication contexts, from interpersonal to organizational settings. The core of all systems approaches is a focus on the interdependence that develops whenever people interact with each other. In this chapter, we focus on some common assumptions of systems perspectives and then the axioms of one specific approach, the work of the Palo Alto Group.

Assumptions of the Systems Perspective

A central assumption of systems approaches is that communication is the means by which systems are created and sustained (Monge, 1973). Systems approaches provide both macro and micro approaches to studying the communication that takes place in relationships. As a macro approach, systems approaches allow for a recognition of how larger social institutions (such as a company or, larger still, a national culture) might influence smaller groups of people such as work groups or families. As a micro approach, systems theories provide a way to understand how individuals and interpersonal relationships between individuals might influence the group as a whole. In short, systems approaches center on the mutual influence between system members, as well as between subsystems, systems, and suprasystems.

First, of course, we have to define what is meant by the term system. A **system** is a group of individuals who interrelate to form a whole (Hall & Fagen, 1968). Examples of systems are a family, a work group, and a sports team. Any time that a group of people has repeated interaction with each other, they represent a system. Systems are embedded in a **hierarchy**, with systems existing within other systems (Pattee, 1973). Accordingly, a **subsystem** is a smaller part of the group as a whole: the defensive line of a football team or the accounting department of an organization. A **suprasystem** is the larger system within which the system operates: the National Football League is a suprasystem for an individual football team, and the industry of an organization is a suprasystem for that organization.

More than simply focusing on these sorts of interrelationships, however, there are several assumptions inherent in systems approaches. Systems theories hinge on **nonsummativity**, which means that the whole is greater than the sum of its parts (Fisher, 1978). Think of your favorite sports teams. Some sports teams have few superstars, but when they work together, they win a lot of games. On the other hand, some teams have "big-name" athletes, but as systems, these teams are not successful. From a systems perspective, individuals in and of themselves don't make or break the system. Instead, the system as a whole might work together to create more than what might be accomplished by those individuals alone. This ability to achieve more through group effort than individual effort is positive **synergy** (Salazar, 1995). Of course, occasionally negative synergy occurs, meaning the group achieves less than the individual parts would suggest (Salazar, 1995). Nevertheless, the point of nonsummativity is that the whole is qualitatively and quantitatively different from the individual components.

A major reason nonsummativity takes place is because of interdependence (Rapoport, 1968). **Interdependence** means that all system members are dependent on all other system members; if one group member drops the ball, literally or figuratively, the group as a whole is unlikely to achieve its goals. Many of you probably have had this experience at work because there are few professional positions in which an individual operates completely independently. In the example of a magazine, the failure of an advertising sales rep to meet their deadline means the editor can't determine how many pages an issue will have, which means a writer doesn't know whether their story will run in that issue, and also that the production people can't do preproduction. Every member of a system is dependent on every other member.

Another principle central to systems approaches is **homeostasis** (Ashby, 1962). Homeostasis refers to the natural balance or equilibrium within groups. From a systems perspective, homeostasis is not meant to imply that change doesn't happen. Instead, it is the tendency for a given system to maintain stability in the face of change. This effort at stability can be either functional or dysfunctional for the system. On one hand, a successful system that achieves homeostasis is likely to continue to be successful. However, imagine a system that has a great deal of conflict, which impedes the system's ability to achieve its goals. Homeostasis would suggest that efforts to reduce the conflict might only engender more conflict because conflict is the "natural" balance of that group. Thus, systems theory recognizes that when a system experiences a novel situation, whether positive or negative, its members will somehow adjust to maintain stability, whether that stability is positive or negative.

A final systems concept of interest in the study of interpersonal communication is equifinality. **Equifinality** suggests that there are multiple ways to achieve the same goal (von Bertalanffy, 1968). Let's say a production group is challenged with the goal of increasing revenues by 10 percent. They can do so by selling more product, increasing the prices of the old product, reducing manufacturing costs of the old product, developing new products, or reducing the workforce needed to make the product, among other things. In short, there are multiple paths the group might take to achieve its goals. In addition, at any given time, there are multiple goals that the group can address. If a group is not only trying to increase revenues but also trying to increase employee morale, it might choose to develop new products, which would simultaneously increase revenues and morale. The group might decide that morale is more important than revenues, however, and focus on that rather than the revenue issue.

In summary, systems approaches focus on the communication that takes place among groups of interacting individuals. It focuses on patterns of communication that exist to sustain homeostasis and achieve systemic goals. The approach also recognizes the influences of larger suprasystems as well as subsystems. As a theoretical approach, it is typically perceived as a description of communication, rather than as providing specific testable principles (Fitzpatrick & Ritchie, 1992). One specific systems approach, the Interactional Perspective, has, however, had a profound impact on the study of communication. We turn to this specific systems theory next.

The Interactional Perspective

In 1967, a group of psychiatrists at the Mental Research Institute in Palo Alto, California, published a book called *Pragmatics of Human Communication*. In the book, the three authors, Watzlawick et al. (1967) presented a model for human communication that was grounded in systems thinking. Called the interactional perspective, Watzlawick et al.'s view profoundly influenced our assumptions about communication and has been applied to everything from understanding foreign policy problems (Calhoun, 2008) to understanding brand relationships in advertising (Heath et al., 2006).

According to the Palo Alto Group, there are five axioms of communication (Watzlawick et al., 1967). Summarized in Table 8.2, the first axiom is *on the impossibility of not communicating*. Widely misinterpreted and debated, the axiom suggests that all behavior has the potential to be communicative, regardless of whether the sender intended the behavior to be interpreted as a message. For example, according to this axiom the "silent treatment" is indeed communicative because the recipient of the silent treatment is clearly receiving the message: "I'm angry with you." Within a work setting, the person who is chronically tardy might be perceived as communicating their disinterest in the work activities. The group member who answers a cell phone in the middle of a meeting might be perceived as sending the message to their teammates that "I'm more important than you are." Intentionality is a complex issue in the field of communication,

TABLE 8.2 ■ Systems Axioms and Implications for Group Communication	
Axiom	**Implication for Group Communication**
The impossibility of not communicating	Interactional partners' interpretations of your behavior will affect your relationship, regardless of whether you intended that interpretation.
Content and relationship Levels	How you say what you say will affect your partners' interpretations and will also give others clues about the relationships between the interactants.
The problem of punctuation	What you view as the cause and effect is not necessarily how an interactional partner will view it. To resolve the problem, forget about assigning blame.
Digital and analogic Communication	Digital communication can express detailed meaning if the interactants share the same set of symbols; analogic communication can express powerful feelings directly.
Complementary and symmetrical communication	Within systems, patterns of interaction develop such that people behave differently or behave similarly. These patterns particularly illustrate power in the relationship.

with scholars on both sides of the debate passionate about the role of intent. The Palo Alto group is firmly committed to the belief that communication need not be intentional.

The second axiom is that *all communication has both content and relationship levels* (Watzlawick et al., 1967). When people interact with each other, they are sending particular messages, which are considered the **content level**. These messages may be verbal or nonverbal. At the same time that they are sending content, they are also sending additional information. The **relationship level** is characterized as how the content should be understood, particularly in terms of the relationship between the communicators. To illustrate, consider the following statements: "Peter, can you work on getting that brochure copy done?" and "Peter, get the brochure copy done." The content is virtually the same; however, the relationship level gives us quite different information in the two scenarios. The first statement can be understood as a request, whereas the second can be understood as a command. More than that, in the first situation you understand that the two people are on an equal footing and that their relationship is respectful. In the second situation, the speaker either has a legitimate superior status over the listener or the speaker is trying to exert dominance over a status equal. The implications of this information are likely to affect the patterns of communication throughout the entire system.

The third axiom focuses on the *tendency of communicators to punctuate sequences of behavior* (Watzlawick et al., 1967). The grammatical definition of the term **punctuation** refers to the use of marks to separate sentences, clauses, and so forth. For example, the previous sentence has a capital *T* to indicate the beginning of the sentence, two commas to indicate pauses between a series, and a period to indicate the end of the sentence. Watzlawick et al.'s notion of punctuation is similar. They believe that interaction is understood by the people involved in it as a series of beginnings and ends, of causes and effects. For example, in the example used for content and relationship levels, Peter might respond to the command by sarcastically responding, "Why yes, ma'am, right away ma'am, whatever you say, ma'am." Peter would likely view the perceived inappropriate command as the cause of his sarcasm, whereas the person who gave the command might view his flippant attitude as the reason why she had to give a command rather than a request in the first place. The point of this axiom is that although communicators tend to assign causes and effects to interactions, it is likely that interactants will view the same interaction as having different causes and effects; punctuation is always a matter of individual perception, with no perception being wholly correct or incorrect. Moreover, Watzlawick et al. argued that differences in punctuation frequently lead to conflict among system members.

The fourth axiom is that communication entails both digital and analogic codes. According to Watzlawick et al. (1967), apart from a few exceptions, **analogic communication** "is virtually all nonverbal communication" (p. 43). Importantly, Watzlawick et al. emphasize the nonverbal communication is more than movement and gestures; it includes "posture, gesture, facial expression, voice inflection, the sequence, rhythm, and cadence of the words themselves" (p. 43). For example, holding two fingers up to indicate the number 2 is an analogue. Crying is an analogue to represent sadness; the tears are a physical representation of the emotion. Onomatopoeia, in which the word sounds like what it means (such as buzz or click), can also be considered examples of analogic communication because the tone or inflection of the word helps to define the word. The point is that analogic communication is rarely misunderstood because of the direct connection between the symbol and its meaning; even people from vastly different cultures can typically understand each other's analogic communication.

Digital communication refers to linguistic symbols that are arbitrarily linked to meaning—usually words (Watzlawick et al., 1967). Digital messages are more complex, more flexible, and more abstract than analogues. Digital messages rely on syntax and logic to convey meaning; they can refer to the past, present, or future, and the meanings of these symbols are culturally determined. Whereas a kiss from your significant other demonstrates analogic communication, having them say "I love you" exemplifies digital communication.

As with analogic communication, there are some exceptions to the rule. Some gestures, particularly emblems (which have dictionary-type definitions), can be considered digital. The OK symbol, wherein you make a circle with your thumb and forefinger, is an example of digital communication (which is why it has different meanings in different cultures). The challenge with digital communication is that two people operating from different digital codes (e.g., different language systems or different rules for nonverbal expression) likely don't understand that misunderstandings might be due to the nuances inherent in the use of digital codes.

The fifth and final axiom proposes that *communication can be symmetrical or complementary.* When communicators behave in the same manner, they are using a **symmetrical pattern**. For example, Mike is sarcastic to you, and you are sarcastic to Mike. Mike defers to you, and you defer to Mike. When the communicators behave in different ways, they are using a **complementary pattern**. For example, Mike commands, and you defer. Mike is sarcastic, and you whine. Notice that behaving in a complementary fashion does not mean interactants are behaving in an opposite fashion, just that the patterns of behavior are different. This axiom has most frequently been used to study control behaviors (Millar & Rogers, 1976).

In sum, systems theories recognize the complexities of interaction. They focus on the patterns of relationships that develop when groups of people interact. The Palo Alto Group's interactional perspective places emphasis on how communication happens in communication systems.

FUNCTIONAL GROUP DECISION-MAKING

Although groups have a number of purposes, one of the central purposes is decision-making. Gouran and Hirokawa (1983, 1986, 1996) are the key researchers associated with developing the functional approach to group communication. A function refers to what communication do. Although groups have a number of purposes, one of the central purposes is decision-making. Gouran and Hirokawa (1983, 1986, 1996) are the key researchers associated with developing the functional approach to group communication. A **function** refers to what communication does. For example, an apology serves the function of relationship repair, and a joke can serve the function of tension release. As such, the functional approach to decision-making focuses less on what is actually said and more on what the communication in groups *does*; how does it function?

Gouran and Hirokawa began theory development by asking the basic question, "Why do some groups make good decisions while others make bad ones?" (Hirokawa, see Miller, 2002,

p. 219). Their model argues that the answer to this question has to do with whether or not the group has successfully accomplished five functions, which they call *requisite functions* (Gouran & Hirokawa, 1983, 1996). These functions are highlighted in Table 8.3.

The first function is **problem analysis** (Gouran & Hirokawa, 1983). This means the group must take a realistic look at the nature, extent, and likely causes of the problem. This function also necessitates all members are clear about what they are trying to accomplish. A thorough analysis often involves information gathering. As an example, let's consider a group convened to address the larger organization's continued budget shortfall. The functional group decision-making theory suggests the group should spend a significant amount of time analyzing the actual gap between essential and realized revenues, the implications of the budget shortfall, and the possible causes for the shortfall. Were there too many expenditures? Slow growth in sales? Or is it just a normal downturn in the economy, which might bounce back? The answers to these questions are important because recognizing the root cause and implications of the problem determines the form the solution should take.

The second function is to **determine minimal standards** or characteristics of an acceptable solution (Gouran & Hirokawa, 1996). Returning to our example, the group members studying the budget shortfall need to be clear about their goals (e.g., are they an advisory group that can only make recommendations or are they an actual decision-making group?). Typically, this function requires group members to develop criteria; these criteria, or standards, will be used to evaluate workable solutions. Thus, our example group should also determine the requirements for a solution. Some sample criteria might include the following: budget cuts shouldn't exceed more than 5%, the implementation of the solution must be achievable within 6 months, and the solution must support the organization's mission.

The third function is to **identify alternatives**. Here, group members brainstorm to generate many possible solutions, maximizing the likelihood that a good solution is ultimately chosen (Gouran & Hirokawa, 1983). **Brainstorming** requires group members to come up with as many

TABLE 8.3 ■ Five Functions of Decision-making	
Function	**Means of Achievement**
Problem analysis	Focus on the nature, extent, and likely causes of the problem. Be careful to differentiate between problems and symptoms of problems.
Determine standards	Identify what an ideal solution would "look like." What are necessary elements, and what would be ideal but not necessary?
Identify alternatives	Generate a large number of possible solutions: Quantity matters more than quality at this point.
Evaluate	Evaluate each alternative using the established goals.
Select	Based on the evaluation of alternatives, group members select the "best" alternative, the alternative that best fulfills the characteristics and criteria established.

solutions as possible while following these rules: don't evaluate ideas; don't clarify ideas; encourage zany ideas; expand on others' ideas; record all ideas with no reference as to who contributed; and encourage participation from everyone (Putnam & Paulus, 2009).

Fourth, the group must **evaluate** the viable solutions (Gouran & Hirokawa, 1983, 1996). To accomplish this, group members must assess the viable solutions generated in the previous function; specifically, the members must compare the possible solutions with the criteria they developed in the second function. Both positive and negative characteristics of the proposed solutions should be considered before selecting the solution that best meets the group's goals (Gouran & Hirokawa, 1983). Returning to our example decision-making group, the chosen solution will likely be altered if the group determined the problem was slow sales growth rather than overexpenditure. The fifth and final function is to **select** the best alternative based on the analysis of available options completed in function four.

Functional group decision-making theory states that all five functions need to be accomplished to maximize the likelihood of an effective decision and that no one function is more important than another. Hirokawa (1994) acknowledged, however, that a specific problem might make a particular function challenging to accomplish. For example, because some problems are particularly obvious, problem analysis is relatively easy. Other problems might naturally have many workable solutions; here, generating alternatives might be a time-consuming endeavor. Perhaps more important than task complexity, however, are group members' awareness of and ability to reflect on their process, recognizing that process is just as, if not more, important than the product itself (Gouran & Hirokawa, 1996).

Despite appearance of a logical order to the requisite functions, research suggests it doesn't matter whether they are completed in a particular order; it only matters that the functions are completed (Hirokawa, 1994). Nevertheless, Hirokawa (1994) found that groups tackling complex problems tend to follow a similar path. Specifically, the pattern suggests that an analysis of the problem tends to happen first but that the group then cycles back and forth between problem analysis and identifying alternatives. Once criteria are established and the group is satisfied with the proposed alternatives, they move on to evaluation and selection.

Finally, functional group decision-making theory makes particular claims about communication in groups. The theory argues that "communication is a social tool used to accomplish effective decision-making" (Hirokawa & Salazar, 1999, p. 169). As such, it proposes that human beings actively construct group experience based on their communication. Gouran and Hirokawa (1986) specifically delineated three types of communication in small groups. **Promotive communication** is geared toward one of the requisite functions. **Disruptive communication** diverts, retards, or frustrates the ability of the group to achieve the requisite functions. Disruptive communication might include social communication. Finally, **counteractive communication**, or messages that return a disrupted group back to the requisite functions, is likely to be most important for group decision-making.

Relatively narrow in scope, the functional perspective focuses solely on task communication associated with group decision-making. Gouran (2010, 2011) has more recently emphasized the role of rationality and leadership within group decision-making while attempting to identify what factors most often compromise a group's ability to complete the requisite functions.

Individual and collective ignorance of the task requirements, procedures, and roles, along with ego, hierarchy, and poor leadership contribute to the difficulties workgroups face (Gouran, 2010). It is the promise of improved group success that makes this theory a significant practical application for communication, business, and other professions.

GROUPTHINK

Whether or not you know the details of the theory, it's likely you've heard the term *groupthink*. Developed by Janis (1972), the notion of groupthink has bridged the gap from the realm of academics into popular culture. We performed a Google search of the term and found more than five million hits, with the term referenced in major newspapers, magazines, trade journals, and even blogs. Clearly the concept is being used—but is it being used the way Janis intended?

Groupthink is a dysfunctional "way of deliberating that group members use when their desire for unanimity overrides their motivation to assess all available plans of action" (Janis, see Miller, 2002, p. 193). As such, groupthink was designed to explain and predict how poor decisions are made by groups. At its core, the notion of groupthink represents a failure of the group to demonstrate critical thinking. When groups "go along to get along," the end result of the decision-making process is likely to be less effective than if group members question the information at hand, being careful to look at the problem from a variety of perspectives.

Antecedent Conditions

Janis (1982) articulated three **antecedent conditions** to groupthink. According to Janis, these preexisting conditions make groupthink more likely. Note that the existence of the antecedent conditions does not guarantee groupthink. Instead, Janis calls these "necessary but not sufficient" conditions. The antecedent conditions are high cohesion, structural flaws, and situational characteristics.

First, **cohesion** refers to the degree of connection, or sense of solidarity, between group members (Janis, 1982). Because groupthink emphasizes the preservation of group harmony, a high degree of cohesion is necessary for groupthink to occur. Yet Janis's notion that cohesion might engender unwise decision making is novel. Think about your own work experiences; in how many "team-building" activities have you taken part? If you are a full-time student, how many of your classes have started with "icebreakers" so the class members might feel more connected to each other? Typically, workplace cohesion is viewed positively, but Janis warns cohesion might make people reluctant to "rock the boat"; yet rocking the boat might be necessary to make the best possible decision.

The second antecedent condition, **structural flaws**, refers to problems with the way the group is organized (Janis, 1982). Janis identified four specific structural flaws, any one of which might lead to groupthink. First, *group insulation* means the group is somehow isolated from the larger world. Perhaps they meet so frequently with each other and so infrequently with others outside the group that they are disconnected from the larger system. Perhaps the group hasn't had direct experience with the problem at hand. This insulation might lead to an inability to process adequately all of the information necessary to make an effective decision. The second structural flaw is *biased leadership*. If the leader already has their mind made up or has a personal stake in the decision, group members might defer to the leader simply because of the power differential, regardless of whether the leader's solution is good. Third, *a lack of procedural norms* can lead to groupthink. Not having a process in place for how to make a decision can happen either because the group has not taken the time to create the process or because the group fails to follow the process. In either case, following a standard process can prevent the group from inadvertently missing a key component of the decision-making process. Last, too much *homogeneity* is problematic. Homogeneity refers to similarity; group members who are remarkably similar—in background, values, or beliefs—are less likely to challenge each other's ideas.

The third and final antecedent condition is **situational characteristics** (Janis, 1982). In short, groupthink is more likely to occur in times of high stress. This high stress might come from pressures outside the group. Groups that work in the pharmaceutical industry experience stress from Federal Drug Administration requirements. Television network executives experience pressure from advertisers. Sometimes external forces place undue pressure on the group through operating constraints, threats, or legal requirements. High stress might also come in the form of time pressures; the more rapidly a decision has to be made, the less likely all possible solutions have been adequately studied.

Stressors don't always come from outside the group, however (Janis, 1982). Groups that have experienced recent failures may lose confidence in their decision-making ability, and the loss of confidence might create a self-fulfilling prophecy. The final category of situational characteristics is moral dilemmas; if group members feel the viable alternatives represent ethical challenges, they are more likely to fall prey to groupthink. Consider a situation where a group can come up with only three solutions to a problem, but two of the three are deemed ethically inappropriate—the group is likely to pursue the third option, regardless of how good it might be.

Again, these three antecedent conditions are necessary, but not sufficient, for groupthink. In other words, all three conditions must be present to some degree for groupthink to occur; however, these circumstances alone don't guarantee groupthink. Instead, Janis (1982) argued you have to examine how the group operates to observe symptoms of the groupthink process.

Symptoms of Groupthink

Janis (1982) identified eight symptoms of groupthink, which he grouped into three categories: overestimation, closed-mindedness, and pressure toward uniformity. The first classification of symptoms, **overestimation of the group**, occurs when group members have an inflated view of the group's abilities. Two specific symptoms to look for are an illusion of invulnerability (a belief that the group won't or can't fail) and a belief in the inherent morality of the group (because the group is good, the decisions the group makes have to be good). Note that both of these symptoms are representative of unwavering confidence in the group and its abilities. As such, group members might not feel it necessary to analyze critically the decisions being made.

The second category of groupthink symptoms includes **closed-mindedness** (Janis, 1982). These symptoms demonstrate polarized thinking, which means viewing the world in extremes.

Things are perceived either as good or bad, right or wrong. If they are good, they are wholly good; if they are bad, they are wholly bad. If a decision is right, it must be completely right. Two specific instances of this category are stereotyping out-groups and collective rationalization. First, *stereotyping* out-groups refers to the process of demonizing other groups and their leaders. In the United States in 2022, both major political parties have engaged in stereotyping out-groups. On the left, conservatives have been deemed racist, misogynistic, and deplorable. On the right, the mainstream liberal media cannot be believed, Democrats have been labeled "libtards," and Democratic politicians are called smug, arrogant, and anti-American. When other groups are portrayed as uncompromisingly bad, it is easier to ignore information that might challenge that belief. *Collective rationalization* means that the group members tend to justify their decisions by talking themselves into it. As an example, consider a group that spends only 5 minutes coming up with a solution and 25 minutes discussing why they are right in making the decision. Rather than critically analyzing the decision, group members come up with a litany of reasons to defend why it's a good decision.

The third and final symptom of groupthink is organized around the notion of **pressure toward uniformity** (Janis, 1982). When groupthink occurs, it is not only because the group members have an inflated view of themselves or because they demonstrate polarized thinking; it is also because individual group members actively suppress critical thinking. Self-censorship means group members tend to keep their mouths shut when experiencing doubts. Often they feel as though everyone else is "on board" with the decision, so they are afraid to go out on a limb with their concerns. This tendency also highlights the illusion of unanimity, which means group members perceive a consensus, even if one hasn't been reached. As such, silence tends to be interpreted as consent. In fact, self-appointed mind guards are careful not to present any contrary information, even if they know it exists; in other words, a self-appointed mind guard engages in self-censorship. If someone actually does question the decision, a group experiencing groupthink will often place pressure on dissenters; challenges to the group are squashed.

To prevent groupthink, Janis (1982) recommends group members take the following steps: encourage critical evaluation; avoid having the leader state a preference; set up several independent subgroups to study the problem and propose solutions; discuss what is happening in the group with people outside of the group; invite outsiders into the group; assign someone to be a devil's advocate; monitor the group for the symptoms; and take time between the initial decision and the confirmation of the decision to analyze the decision critically.

Table 8.4 presents an overview of the antecedents and symptoms of groupthink. As you can see, Janis (1982) identified a large number of factors present before the group begins deliberating, as well as factors recognizable while the group is deliberating. Groupthink itself—the tendency to avoid critical thinking so cohesion can be maintained—occurs somewhere in between antecedent conditions and the symptoms.

TABLE 8.4 ■ Antecedents and Symptoms of Groupthink		
Antecedents	**Groupthink**	**Symptoms**
Cohesion		*Overestimation of group*
		• Illusion of invulnerability
		• Belief in morality
Structural flaws		*Closed-mindedness*
• Insulation		• Stereotypes
• Biased leadership		• Collective rationalizations
• No procedural norms		
• Homogeneity		
Situational characteristics		*Uniformity pressures*
• High stress		• Self-censorship
• Time pressure		• Illusion of unanimity
• Recent failures		• Self-appointed mindguards
• Moral dilemmas		• Direct pressure on dissenters

SYMBOLIC CONVERGENCE THEORY

The final group theory we discuss is symbolic convergence theory (SCT). Although considered a general theory of communication, SCT was developed within the traditions of group communication and has been applied most frequently to this context (Bormann, 1982). SCT is based on the notion that group members cooperatively create and sustain a shared consciousness, including shared meaning, through interaction. Specifically, SCT focuses on two aspects of group communication: the creation of a group identity and the ways group identity influences norms for behavior.

Central Concepts of SCT

As with many theories, a number of concepts are critical for understanding the explanation of group communication provided by SCT. The most important concept is a fantasy theme. The term *fantasy* can be misleading. According to SCT, **fantasy** does not refer to something desired or something fictional; rather, it refers to a creative understanding of events that fulfills a psychological or rhetorical need (Bormann, 1982).

A fantasy theme starts with a **dramatizing message**—such as a joke, anecdote, innuendo, pun, figure of speech, double entendre, or metaphor, among other things (Bormann, 1996). Importantly, these messages do not refer to present happenings; instead they reference events that have happened in the past or that are anticipated for the future. Moreover, dramatizing messages always include some level of emotional revelation, typically including both a surface level and a deeper level (Bales, 1970). Imagine Trevor, the youngest member of his work team, has recently solved a seemingly impossible problem. When walking into his next team meeting, Kyle playfully waves an imaginary magic wand and calls him Harry Potter ("What magic spell did you dig out to solve this one?"). This message serves the surface function of tension release but also serves the deeper function of recognizing the value of Trevor's work. Sometimes these messages are sent and then immediately dropped, but if the rest of the group responds to the dramatizing message, a **fantasy theme** has emerged.

Continued embellishment of the fantasy theme can result in a **fantasy chain** when the fantasy theme is developed through group interaction and enters group consciousness (Bormann, 1982). If, for example, the "Harry Potter" theme develops and is built on by other group members, a fantasy chain has emerged. At a later meeting, group members might refer to an incompetent supervisor as a "muggle" or might joke about the magic spells needed to accomplish a project on time.

According to SCT, building fantasy chains results in group cohesion, a process termed **symbolic convergence** (Bormann, 1982). In other words, the emergence of a fantasy chain transforms the group from a collection of individuals to an identifiable group with a group consciousness. Consider the Harry Potter fantasy chain. Imagine a subsequent meeting that includes the original work team as well as other organizational members not part of that team. Again, Kyle mentions their secret weapon, "Harry," and all of the original team members laugh—they understand the reference. The individuals who were not a part of the original team may feel left out, however, because they don't understand the joke. Bormann et al. (1994) argued that when people have a shared fantasy theme, they have come to share a consciousness that can be set off by a commonly agreed upon symbolic cue. Much like an inside joke, only those who were a part of creating the fantasy theme to which the inside joke refers will respond appropriately.

Any given group might have numerous fantasy chains. That is, the same group that chains the Harry Potter fantasy theme might also use sports metaphors when referring to business situations ("You really hit that one out of the park, Jane" or "It's third and long, and we have to go for it if we're gonna win"). In addition, the group might have a stock story about a team member who failed to follow procedure and lost his job. New members might be told the story as a cautionary tale, and current members might be sanctioned by being told, "Don't be a Don!" The ways fantasy chains combine within a group leads to a **rhetorical vision**. A rhetorical vision is a unified way of viewing the world. Consider the three fantasy chains just described: Harry Potter, sports, and sanctions against violating rules. All three fantasy chains share a common way of viewing the world. All three suggest the world is clearly divided: right and wrong, good and evil, winners and losers. If you are on the side of good, you play hard and win; if you are on the side of evil, you will lose. This rhetorical vision provides a set of implicit norms for group behavior.

In addition, the process of symbolic convergence affects decision-making (Bormann, 1996). For instance, building a sense of common identity and shared meaning fosters group members' creativity in decision-making. Moreover, group consciousness and shared motivation also influence assumptions and preferred processes by which decisions are made. In fact, Bormann contended that group members might create fantasy themes about the decision-making process itself.

Figure 8.1 provides a visual representation of the process of symbolic convergence. Starting at the upper left-hand side of the diagram, a group member sends a dramatizing message. If others in the group interact as a result of that message, a fantasy theme has emerged. If and when group members embellish that fantasy theme, a fantasy chain results. When studying a group, observers can examine the fantasy chains to uncover the underlying rhetorical vision that provides the group with a sense of cohesion and implicit norms for behavior.

The discussion of SCT thus far implies the theory is concerned only with events internal to a group. One of the strengths of the theory, however, is that it links groups to other social systems, such as a larger organization or social movement (Poole, 1999). For example, a rhetorical vision might start in a group and spread to other parts of an organization. Conversely, the rhetorical vision of a larger organization might restrict the types of fantasy themes generated within a group.

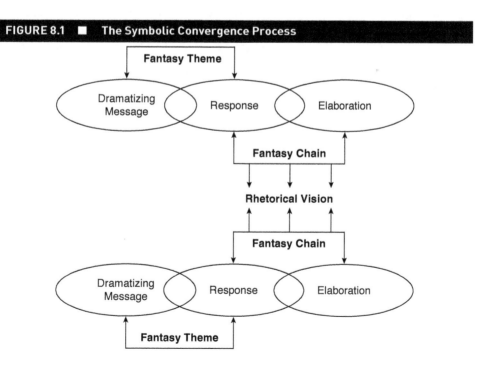

FIGURE 8.1 ■ The Symbolic Convergence Process

CHAPTER SUMMARY AND RESEARCH APPLICATIONS

In this chapter, we discussed four distinct theories of group communication. Our first theory, the systems/interactional perspective, proposed five axioms of communication. The axioms highlight how and why miscommunication might occur, and ways in which contemporary organizations might need to adapt their communication. For example, Altabbaa et al. (2019) used the axioms of the interactional perspective to develop a tool to improve communication among healthcare teams.

The second theory, functional group decision-making, delineates specific tasks or functions group members need to complete to make an effective decision. Although it sounds simple enough, poor group decision-making still plagues the workplace. Many scholars believe that decision-making is influenced by the use of mediated communication channels. To assess this, Dobosh et al. (2019) conducted an experiment with three groups: a face-to-face group, a 2D group (i.e., a group that used Skype), and a 3D group (i.e., a group that used immerse, virtual reality technology). They found that there were few differences in the accuracy or speed of decisions made in the face-to-face group, but that the 3D group performed worse and took longer to complete the task. Of course, this may be because of a lack of familiarity with the mechanisms of virtual reality.

Next, groupthink provides a means for understanding why group members make poor decisions through a particular focus on cohesion, structural faults, and situational constraints (Janis, 1982). The theory has been used to explain extremism and polarization in American politics (Willis, 2017) as well in the "courage" required of subcabinet officials to make difficult political decisions (Kelman et al., 2016).

Finally, SCT suggests that particular types of messages called fantasy themes contribute to a rhetorical vision and sense of group identity. An examination of these fantasy themes and how they might combine provides a rhetorical vision that provides the principles by which the group operates. Social media provides another powerful mechanism by which groups can create, share, and elaborate on fantasy themes. In recent research that included Facebook interactions between team members, two complementary and competing rhetorical visions emerged (Zanin et al., 2016). In some cases, the themes increased a sense of belonging and identification, where in other instances, they created divided loyalties between those who felt included in the themes and those who felt left out. Zanin et al. (2016) offered suggestions by which SCT might benefit from more research on group divergence on fantasy themes.

The four theories we have highlighted are not the only theories of group communication that can increase out understand of what happens in groups. Table 8.5 identifies some other prominent theories of group communication.

TABLE 8.5 ■ Additional Theories of Group Communication	
Theory	**Main Idea**
Adaptive Structuration Theory	Structures, or enduring patterns of relationships, develop based on group interaction, and how these structures in turn constrain group interaction (Poole et al., 1985, 1986).
Image Theory	Decision-makers use three types of knowledge (or images) in making decisions: value images (ethics, morals, and core values/beliefs), trajectory images (goals), and strategic images (plans, or strategies and tactics, for how to achieve goals, Beach, 1990).
Leader-Member Exchange Theory	Because of limited resources, organizational supervisors have in-group relationships with some team members (called a Leader Member Exchange relationship, or LMX), and an out-group relationship with others (called a Supervisory Exchange relationship, or SX (Dansereau et al., 1975).

DISCUSSION QUESTIONS

1. Think about a time that you and someone you are close with had a misunderstanding. Do any of the axioms of the interactional perspective explain why you had the misunderstanding?

2. Functional group decision-making labels any communication that does not meet one of the requisite functions "disruptive." Do you think engaging in social communication is actually disruptive? What functions might social communication serve?

3. Have you ever been in a group and thought that the group was making a poor decision? What did you do? How does the situation relate to groupthink?

4. We used an example of a Harry Potter fantasy chain. Try to imagine a situation using a different example of a fantasy chain. What terms, phrases, or labels might evoke the fantasy chain?

KEY TERMS

Aggregate (p. 141)

Analogic communication (p. 146)

Antecedent conditions (p. 150)

Brainstorming (p. 148)

Closed-mindedness (p. 151)

Cohesion (p. 150)

Complementary pattern (p. 147)

Content level (p. 146)

Counteractive communication (p. 149)

Determine minimal standards (p. 148)

Digital communication (p. 147)

Disruptive communication (p. 149)

Dramatizing message (p. 154)

Equifinality (p. 144)

Evaluate (p. 149)

Fantasy (p. 153)

Fantasy chain (p. 154)

Fantasy theme (p. 154)

Function (p. 147)

Group (p. 141)

Group role (p. 142)

Groupthink (p. 150)

Hierarchy (p. 143)

Homeostasis (p. 144)

Identify alternatives (p. 148)

Interdependence (p. 144)

Nonsummativity (p. 143)

Overestimation of the group (p. 151)

Pressure toward uniformity (p. 152)

Problem analysis (p. 148)

Promotive communication (p. 149)

Punctuation (p. 146)

Relationship level (p. 146)

Rhetorical vision (p. 154)

Select (p. 149)

Situational characteristics (p. 151)

Socioemotional communication (p. 142)

Structural flaws (p. 150)

Subsystem (p. 143)

Suprasystem (p. 143)

Symbolic convergence (p. 154)

Symmetrical pattern (p. 147)

Synergy (p. 143)

System (p. 143)

Task communication (p. 142)

Team (p. 142)

CASE STUDY 8
The Gifted Group

A new leader brought renewed enthusiasm to the Brunswick County Conference & Visitors Bureau (BCCVB), the official tourism promotion agency for Brunswick County, Pennsylvania. Under her leadership, the bureau underwent both programmatic and physical expansion. Shortly after the BCCVB relocated its offices and visitor center to a newly constructed building, the executive director decided to create a gift center committee. The purpose of the committee was to devise a plan for a visitor gift center shop—something the BCCVB had never had—in which a variety of merchandise bearing the Brunswick County logo could be sold to visitors.

The committee consisted of the following five BCCVB staff members: John Maher, communication assistant; Laura Doherty, office manager; Nannette Kearny, membership director; Lisa Berman, assistant director; and Donald Johnson, corporate sales manager. The newly formed group was highly cohesive; they had worked together for more than 5 years, and they were all committed to the vision of the visitor's bureau developed by the executive director. The committee was given 3 weeks, meeting as often as they deemed necessary to devise a plan detailing how the BCCVB would establish a visitor center gift shop. The time frame was difficult to achieve given that the group members still had to perform the duties of their regular jobs, but all of the members were committed to doing so.

The first meeting turned out to be a "meeting of the minds" to establish a consensus as to how the group would move forward. Because of their cohesion, committee members were sociable, gregarious, and comfortable working with one another. As a result, members spent a good 15 minutes at the onset of the meeting catching up with one another. Donald, the group clown, decided that an important first step was to come up with a name for the committee, and he decided the group members should be known as the "gifted group." This name led to much laughter and joking that it would be the first time Donald had ever been called "gifted" in his life.

Lisa Berman also participated in this social interaction but took naturally to a leader-type role when it came time to discuss business matters. She made an effort to focus the committee's attention to the matter at hand—the gift shop—and enabled the group to transition from social-related to more task-related communication. At that point, the committee began discussing the overall idea of a gift shop and how to devise a plan to initiate such a venture. The group quickly came to a rather dramatic realization following this discussion: Nobody on the committee had any retail or gift shop experience. Committee members, undoubtedly discouraged by this realization, became reluctant to move forward. The meeting closed, however, with John recommending that each member research visitor center gift shops before the next gathering. Donald and Nanette initially disagreed with the proposal, saying they didn't have time to do so. Nannette asked Laura if she would be willing to do the research, and Laura quickly complied. However, Lisa pointed out that if each person did a little research, no one person would be overburdened. She persuaded the group members to take on the task as a whole.

At the second meeting, each committee member arrived with an impressive arsenal of visitor center gift shop research. Again, the first 10 or 15 minutes were devoted to socializing. And again, Lisa had to work to get people back on task. At first, Donald fought with Lisa for control of the meeting. He continued joking around, calling one of the organizational members not on the committee "special Ned." When Lisa tried to get the group back on task again, Nanette responded, "Hey, not everyone can be considered gifted," and the group continued laughing. Lisa tried to remain lighthearted because she wasn't the official leader, but she was frustrated that others were wasting time. She remarked, "We won't continue to be considered gifted if we don't get this done." Donald teased, "Uh oh, teacher is mad. Are you gonna keep us after school if we don't hit the books?" At this, everyone laughed, including Lisa.

Finally turning to the job at hand, the meeting entailed a thorough investigation of each member's materials and a lengthy discussion about how the group would use the research to proceed. The committee decided to compile the research that related most directly to the BCCVB and to set a calendar indicating how, armed with such information, they would move forward with subsequent meetings. Collectively, the committee established a heavy meeting schedule, with a meeting scheduled every day for the remainder of the 2-week time frame.

Each meeting flowed in a manner very similar to that of the first and second meetings. The first 10 or 15 minutes of every meeting, even as the deadline drew near, were set aside for social interaction. Donald would joke around, and the others would follow his lead. Then, the committee would either progress naturally toward the task at hand, or Lisa Berman would comment about moving forward or getting down to business, and eventually the group would do so.

Toward the end of the second week, group energy was sagging. Everyone had been devoting a significant amount of time not only to the meetings but to "homework" each tackled in between the meetings. At this point, John's role shifted from group member to group cheerleader. He encouraged others when they became frustrated or tired. He reminded everyone that although the short time frame meant they weren't running a marathon, the work they were doing wasn't a sprint either. Donald responded, "What, we're doing the 800 meter?" Nanette retorted, "Well, hell, that's my problem, I'm out of shape!" John joined in, saying, "Actually, the hurdles were always my specialty! But yes, it is an 800-meter race; we need to keep a rapid pace, but we can't all-out sprint the whole time."

After the 3 weeks were over, the group presented their final proposal to the executive director. Following the meeting, Laura presented all of the members a track jersey with the words "The Gifted Group" written across the chest.

Questions for Consideration

1. What was the homeostasis of the gifted group? Do you see any evidence of any of the axioms of the interactional perspective? Which? Where?

2. Using the functional model, was the decision on how to establish the gift shop likely to be effective? Why, or why not? Describe how and when each function emerged.

3. What antecedents of groupthink are present? What symptoms of groupthink are present? What could the group do to prevent groupthink from occurring?

4. Discuss the elements of symbolic convergence as related to the group. How do you think symbolic convergence might have affected the decision-making process? How might symbolic convergence theory and groupthink influence each other?

5. Do any of the theories emerge as better than the others? Why do you believe this to be the case? What situations might surface that would make a different theory or theories better at explaining the situation?

9 ORGANIZATIONAL COMMUNICATION

One of the most intriguing paradoxes of corporate life is how often organizational members stress the importance of communication yet how few of these members exhibit effective organizational communication. In Chapter 1, we argue that popular culture tends to oversimplify the communication process. Nowhere is this more evident than in the organizational setting.

DEFINING ORGANIZATIONAL COMMUNICATION

While there is no single definition of organizations or organizational communication, there are common features for both that we will emphasize. The term "organization" can have communicative, social, and legal definitions (Kramer & Bisel, 2017). In all three cases, **organizations** systematically and consciously coordinate people and/or activities to accomplish a broader goal (Tompkins, 1989). Unsurprisingly, it is through communication that we actually "organize" other. While this interdependent relationship appears concise on paper, it is quite complex to enact. Contemporary approaches to **organizational communication** center on the extent to which meaning is created between individuals in an organizational setting, between individuals and organizations, and between organizations and societies (Feldner & D'Urso,

TABLE 9.1 ■ Overview of Organizational Communication Theories	
Organizational Culture	Schein's (1990, 1992) cultural approach provides a language for understanding how and why organizations develop certain behavioral norms and ways of communicating, and why culture is so difficult to change.
Organizational Assimilation Theory (OAT)	OAT focuses on how individuals become socialized into an organization, with a recognition of the role that organizational culture plays in this socialization
Organizational Identification and Control (OIC)	Extending the notions of culture and assimilation, OIC focuses on how organizations establish and maintain power, particularly in team-based environments.
Organizing Theory	Weick's (1969) approach argues that communication *is* the foundation of organizing, making it the basis for organizational success and failure

2010). Rejecting the oversimplified idea that an organization is simply a "container" in which communication occurs, organizational communication scholars focus on communication as a process rather than an event. Indeed, as Simon (1976) argued, "without communication there can be no organization, for there is no possibility then of the group influencing the behavior of the individual" (p. 154).

Specific communication processes of interest to organizational communication scholars include: the development and maintenance of workplace relationships, the socialization of new organizational members, the development of organizational cultures, the ways organizations and organizational members exert and resist power, the ways communication processes create organizational structures, and the ways organizational structures alter communication processes.

This chapter focuses on four theories of organizational communication: Schein's model of organizational culture, organizational assimilation, organizational identification and control (OIC), and Weick's organizing theory. Table 9.1 provides an overview of the perspectives.

ORGANIZATIONAL CULTURE

Few of the concepts covered in this book are more popular than the notion of **organizational culture**. Bookshelves are overflowing with tomes like *The Culture Blueprint: A Guide to Building the High-Performance Workplace* and *The Culture Question: How to Create a Workplace Where People Like to Work*. While there are numerous theories of organizational culture (e.g., Deal & Kennedy, 1982; Likert, 1967), we focus on Edgar Schein's (1985, 1990, 1992) model that focuses on culture as a dynamic process. In their updated discussion that emphasizes the interplay of organizational culture and leadership, Schein and Schein (2016) defined organizational culture as "the accumulated shared learning of [a] group as it solves its problems of external adaptation and internal integration" (p. 6). Importantly, this shared learning is "taught to new members as the correct way to perceive, think, feel, and behave" (p. 6), and over time, becomes taken for granted as normative.

Schein's (1990, 1992) model includes three levels of culture: artifacts, beliefs and values, and assumptions. Although all three make up a culture, he believed the third level, assumptions, is at the crux of organizational culture and that the first two levels, artifacts and beliefs and values, may simply reflect the more abstract and subconscious assumptions shared by organizational members.

Level 1: Artifacts

Schein's (1990, 1992, 2010; Schein & Schein, 2016) notion of **artifacts** refers to observable and "feelable" evidence of culture. Artifacts may take the form of physical entities, such as architecture, office lay-outs, dress, organizational charts, and mission statements, but they also consist of patterns of behavior. These patterns of behavior can take the form of routines and rituals, acronyms, forms of address, approaches to decision-making, and management style. Table 9.1 lists some examples of artifacts.

While artifacts are visible by definition, their meanings may be difficult to decipher (Schein & Schein, 2016). For example, what does it *mean* when an organization develops an informal, playful, and relaxed pattern of interaction? We might observe a jeans and t-shirt dress code, ping pong tables in conference rooms, and flexible working hours, but making sense of these artifacts is difficult. According to Schein and Schein, you might view the informal organization as "inefficient" or immature. On the other hand, you might assume the playfulness and flexibility leads to innovation and cohesiveness. Thus, while artifacts are readily apparent, they do not provide enough substance to understand the organizational culture. Attention must be turned to higher levels for such perception. Table 9.2 presents some examples of artifacts.

TABLE 9.2 ■ Cultural Artifacts and Behaviors	
Artifact/Behavior	**Examples**
Architecture	Open floor plan, cubicles; offices with windows; size of offices; rented suites versus owned campus
Technology	Up-to-date versus archaic computer systems; availability/type of Internet connection, email, tablets, smartphones
Dress	Business attire versus casual attire; uniforms, casual Fridays; dress codes
Forms of address	Titles used versus first names; differences in address by hierarchical level
Decision-making style	Autocratic versus participatory; rapid versus slow; conservative versus risk-taking
Communication patterns	Formal versus informal; friendly versus distant; use of acronyms, unique terms, myths, stories; rituals

Source: Miller, *Organizational Communication, 3rd ed.* © 2003 Wadsworth.

Level 2: Beliefs and Values

The second level of culture is organizational members' espoused beliefs and values, defined as preferences about what "ought to happen" (Schein, 1992, 2010). These preferences represent shared beliefs about how things should work. By nature, values are intangible, but organizational members are typically able to articulate them. Organizational leaders are frequently the source of values; for instance, research shows the values held by the founder of a company strongly influence the values described by other employees (Giberson et al., 2005; McCown, 2008; Morley & Shockley-Zalabak, 1991). Certainly, literature suggests leadership is, by definition, the ability to shape members' perceptions of the task and the mission of the organization (Barge, 1994). Accordingly, it's not surprising organizational members are persuaded to adopt the values of organizational leaders.

Still, simply because a leader articulates a value system does not make it so. Championed values are not always authentic values, as evident when the ideals expressed do not match behavior (Schein, 1992, 2010). Consider, for instance, two organizations that claim to value innovation. When scrutinizing the artifacts of the first organization, observers notice the company encourages risk and gives employees time to experiment. Failures are not punished; in fact, the company encourages employees to talk about failures because one person's failure might be the solution to another person's problem. A significant portion of the annual budget is earmarked for research and development. In this case, the artifacts seem to support the value of innovation. At the second company, however, failure is not an option; people who fail are reprimanded. The organization is resistant to change and has very rigid systems to implement even the smallest change. Little of the budget is slated for research and development, and employees are kept so busy maintaining the current product or service that they have virtually no time to develop any new ideas. In fact, employees have facetiously created the following company slogan: "We don't innovate; we duplicate." Clearly, these artifacts do not seem to suggest innovation is actually practiced. The point is that espoused values are not always identical to the actual values of the organization; just because it appears in the mission statement does not mean it reaches the level of everyday practice.

Whole Foods and IKEA are two examples of companies routinely praised for actually practicing their proclaimed organizational values (Brooks, 2018). Conversely, Uber suffered a well-publicized "toxic culture" crisis when its initial set of core values didn't reflect employees' day-to-day experience. As the exemplar, one of Whole Foods Market's core values states, "We care about our community and the environment" (Whole Foods Market, n.d.). One model of practicing this value is through supporting local producers as well as funding nutritious food access and food education programs, particularly in food insecure communities, domestically and globally. Another example of walking the walk is through their design of energy efficient stores. As of the end of 2021, the organization had achieved green buildings certifications (LEED) in more than 20 of its North American stores. On the other hand, Uber's founding core values included being "super-pumped" and having a "champion's mindset" (The HR Capitalist, 2019). While these values imply enthusiasm, they were practiced in a way that fostered sexual harassment and bullying.

Level 3: Assumptions

The final level of culture is the most difficult to identify because it is taken for granted—"assumed"—by organizational members, and over time, goes unquestioned as the "correct" way to behave. **Assumptions** refers to the organizational consensus that "results from repeated success in implementing certain beliefs and values" (Schein & Schein, 2016, p. 21). In other words, when the beliefs and behaviors of Level 2 become so ingrained, and organizational members can no longer imagine an alternative, assumptions have developed.

These assumptions are subconscious because they have been reinforced over and over again as the organization faces challenges. Assumptions lie at the heart of organizational culture because actions based on these beliefs are made uniformly throughout the organization (Schein, 1992, 2010).

Assumptions develop about the organization's relationship to the larger environment (e.g., adversarial or collaborative), the nature of reality (e.g., the meaning of time, space), the nature of human nature (e.g., the value of human relationships) among other things (Schein, 1992, 2010). These concepts are profound philosophical commitments, such as the "right" way for people to interact with each other, whether human beings are by nature good or evil, and whether truth is singular (i.e., there is one absolute "truth") or conditional (e.g., some things are true at some times in some places for some people).

Although this notion sounds complex, such assumptions have a substantial effect on organizational life. Consider two different employment programs for former prisoners. A fundamental assumption of one program might be that people are capable of changing. Such an assumption will affect the everyday decisions made because organizational members will spend energy seeking to develop and reward individuals rather than punish them for past infractions. Yet a different organization might assume the best predictor of future behavior is past behavior. In this case, organizational members are likely to view individuals who have made mistakes as risky prospects likely to repeat those mistakes.

According to Schein's (1992, 2010) model of organizational culture, an analysis of assumptions could assist organizational members in generating a coherent blueprint for how the organization should operate, yet this postulation is not always the case. Some organizations might simultaneously hold seemingly conflicting assumptions. For example, employees of a Catholic institution of higher learning may be challenged by incompatible assumptions; assumptions the Catholic Church makes about "truth" may contrast the assumptions some of the university's academic disciplines hold about "truth." Such contradictory assumptions might cause problems for members seeking to behave in concert with organizational assumptions. How the organization reconciles these inconsistent assumptions determines the overarching organizational culture.

The COVID-19 pandemic brought to light a number of organizational assumptions that otherwise may not have been exposed. For example, the assumptions held by organizations about the value of remote work were challenged when many organizations *had* to engage in remote work during various state shutdowns. "The great work-from-home experiment occasioned by the pandemic has divided opinion in the corporate suite and sparked endless debates about whether employees work as effectively from the kitchen table as they do from the office" (Curran, 2021, para 1). Case in point, Goldman Sachs' CEO stated that having employees work from home is "'an aberration' that the investment bank will 'correct as quickly as possible'" (Solomon, qtd. in Curran, 2021, para. 4). The assumption here is that onsite work is the *only* way to work on Wall Street. Conversely, Facebook's CEO had a different take, noting that the shift to remote work "opened up new pools of talent" (para. 5) and in locations far from its head-quarters. Rather than revert back to an in-person format, Facebook plans to continue remote work, and offer salaries that match employees' remote locations. Where one organization saw remote work as a threat to its assumptions about the value of in-person work, another came to view the situation as an opportunity to redefine how and *where* work will happen so as to attract better talent.

In sum, Schein (1985, 1992, 2010) proposed three levels of culture: artifacts, beliefs and values, and assumptions. Although there may be surface inconsistencies within and across these levels, a careful analysis of the patterns that emerge will give observers an understanding of the organizational culture. Cultures are created and recreated by organizational members, with particular emphasis placed on the influence of those at the highest levels in the organization. Accordingly, organizational cultures both aid and constrain organizational communication.

ORGANIZATIONAL ASSIMILATION

Many of us have learned very quickly that we don't "fit" with a particular organization. You might find, for example, you are a blue jeans kind of person in a three-piece-suit kind of world. Or you might find an organization's values (e.g., slow and steady wins the race) don't mesh with your personality (e.g., Type A). We've just finished discussing what organizational cultures are and how we might identify a particular organization's culture. Taking this a step further, Jablin (1987, 2001) created **organizational assimilation** theory as a way to explain how individuals become integrated into the culture of an organization.

Jablin (2001) argued the process of being socialized into an organization is complex and takes place over years. The process of assimilation can be planned, for example, through a potential employee's active researching of a company or formal training procedures. On the other hand, assimilation is often unplanned. Coworkers' interaction styles might not be intended to send messages about the organizational culture, but the new organizational member might perceive these messages regardless. The theory identifies four stages that organizational newcomers go through before becoming full members of an organization, as well as a fifth stage for disengaging from the organization. These stages are summarized in Table 9.3.

Vocational Anticipatory

Socialization Before we ever get our first job, we learn about the nature of work and what means to work a "real jobs" (Jablin, 1985). Beginning in childhood, we might have watched a parent or parents leave in the morning and return in the evening, oftentimes frazzled and grumpy. Or we witnessed parents who worked weekends, were "on call," or had less predictable schedules.

TABLE 9.3 ■ Stages of Assimilation	
Stage	**Description**
Vocational anticipatory socialization	Developing a set of expectations and beliefs about the nature of work and work settings
	Examples: I should be paid for my work; The people I work with will be my close friends.
Anticipatory socialization	Learning about a particular vocation, position, and organization
	Examples: Renee's sister routinely works 10-hour days in advertising; Jared did an informational interview with a PR manager at DanCo.
Encounter/Entry	Joining the organization and making sense of its culture
	Example: Unlike my last job, people at DanCo are expected to speak up at meetings.
Metamorphosis	Transitioning from outsider to insider, understanding roles, and negotiating roles
	Example: We work hard and don't complain—it's just what we do here at DanCo.
Exit	Departure from the organization; can be voluntary or involuntary
	Example: I am leaving DanCo for another opportunity

We had guest speakers at school "career days" and listened to our teachers tell us that we've done a "good job" or that we need to "work harder." We've heard tales of dream jobs as well as office horror stories. We have laughed at the incompetence of Michael Scott on *The Office* or cringed at the cruelty of the bosses in the movie *Horrible Bosses*. We've had part-time jobs and even full-time jobs, and we have listened as our professors tell us what it's really like to be a journalist, a PR account manager, or a communications director.

While we spend years collecting information about diverse types of jobs as well as the nature of work, much of what we learn is distorted, biased, or just plain wrong. Jablin (2001) described a host of studies indicating ways in which the media overrepresent managerial and professional work and underrepresent skilled-labor jobs. For example, medical, military, legal, and law enforcement careers have been significantly overrepresented on TV (Signorielli, 2009; Sink & Mastro, 2017). As well, characters on TV and in film hold jobs that are often stereotyped by age, race, gender, and sexual orientation. Moreover, the nature of communication in these scripted workplaces is distorted, with much of the characters' conversation focused on socializing, giving orders, or giving advice. Together, these notions of work and jobs make up **vocational anticipatory socialization**—our expectations and beliefs about work and careers, all before we even begin to assimilate into a specific organization.

Anticipatory Socialization

The second stage of OAT is **anticipatory socialization** (Jablin, 1985, 2001). Here, individuals gather information about a specific organization and includes what Kramer and Bisel (2017) term "recruitment and reconnaissance." From both a newcomer and an organizational prospective, the anticipatory socialization stage includes the process of selection, information gathering, and potentially preparing for entry into the organization. Caldwell and O'Reilly (1990) argued that organizations should emphasize **person–job fit (PJ fit)**, that is, matching the right person's abilities to fulfill the demands of a specific role, by looking at skill set and personality. Considered equally if not more important is **person–organization fit (PO fit)**, or how well an individual's values and beliefs align with the organization's values and beliefs, and vice versa (Chatman, 1991). While a person might have all of the skills needed to perform well in a specific job, that same person may not mesh well within a given organization. As Jablin (2001) and others have argued, an individual is not just accepting a job, the individual is preparing to join an entire culture.

Like preparing for a first date, the anticipatory socialization stage often includes unrealistic and inflated notions, in part because institutions (and recruits) typically communicate only their positive aspects during this phase (Jablin, 2001). As we will see in the encounter phase, unrealistic expectations are often problematic, as newcomers and existing organizational members may grow dissatisfied when expectancies aren't met.

Many organizations now spend considerable time and resources recruiting and interviewing for PO fit, recognizing that numerous job skills can be honed on the job but "fit" cannot (Rivera, 2012). For example, online retailer Zappos is famously known for paying new recruits to quit during training—a 4-week process that occurs prior to entering the organization. The reason? Zappos wanted to maintain its unique and quirky organizational culture. By weeding out less committed recruits early on, the organization can "make sure that employees aren't here just for paychecks and truly believe this is the right place for them" (Hsieh, qtd. in Feloni, 2016, para. 28).

On the other hand, recruiting and selecting for a match in core values can diminish efforts to recruit a diverse and inclusive workforce (Powell, 1998). In her interviews with 120 executive and midlevel hiring managers, Rivera (2012) found that while the vast majority explicitly sought candidates who "fit in" with the organization, few recruitment evaluators had clear descriptions of what organization fit actually looked like for their firm. Rivera's analysis concluded that the evaluators typically used "similarity to self" as a proxy for true organizational fit. Specifically, candidates who signaled extracurricular and extraprofessional similarities were viewed as a "good fit," particularly when they shared "activities associated with the white-middle class" (p. 1017). Consequently, without training in *how* to hire for PO fit, organizations may unintentionally perpetuate biased selection in hiring (Spiegelman, 2021).

All told, anticipatory socialization generates expectations. And while much of the activity happens prior to entering an organization, the process is not necessarily linear, as we will see with the remaining phases (Fox, 2019).

Encounter

The third phase is one of high uncertainty, surprise, and anxiety. In the **encounter** (or entry) phase, the newcomer enters the organization and begins to learn the normal patterns and expectations (Jablin, 2001). As described in Chapter 3, there are many ways people reduce uncertainty, including observation and asking questions. Typically, newcomers rely on organizational insiders—coworkers and supervisors—for uncertainty reduction. Individuals in this stage frequently undergo "culture shock" as they compare their expectations with the new reality. Jablin noted that social support from insiders can significantly reduce the newcomer's anxiety when they experience gaps between expectations and reality.

The encounter is not a one-way phase; organizational insiders also engage in uncertainty reduction. Insiders share (or not) information *with* the newcomer and *about* the newcomer between themselves (Jablin, 2001). As Mornata and Cassar (2018) found, the interpersonal skills of insiders, as either supportive or undermining, influenced new members' learning and assimilation during the encounter phase. Thus, veterans of the organization play an important role in the newcomer's uncertainty reduction during the encounter.

Socializing newcomers also affects existing insiders, both individually and the organization as a whole. In a review of the literature, Feldman (1994) noted that helping to socialize a newcomer may increase the veteran's motivation, attitude, and professional knowledge. Conversely, supporting a newcomer may create work overload, increase stress, and aggravate perceived inequities. Positive outcomes of onboarding relative to the organization included elevating morale, discovering opportunities to analyze strengths and weaknesses, and gaining external feedback from the newcomer's viewpoint. Equally, bringing in newcomers may slow productivity, exacerbate intraorganizational tensions, and tarnish morale, if new hires prove ineffective.

All in all, encountering the organization is not a one-time event. Rather, it is a key part of the socialization process that moves newcomers toward becoming insiders and provides existing insiders with opportunities to incorporate newcomers.

Metamorphosis

The fourth stage of assimilation, **metamorphosis**, reflects the movement of the individual from an outsider to an insider (Jablin, 2001). During this phase, the newcomer and the organization exert mutual influence in the process of developing a "fit" between the organization and the employee. Here, the newcomer moves towards being an insider by internalizing values and behaviors in order to fulfill organizational expectations (known as **socialization**). At the same time, the new insider seeks to make an impact on their role and work environment (known as **individualization**). Imagine you have begun working at an organization that rigidly follows the rules of the employee handbook. You have reached metamorphosis if you still allow the handbook to guide your behavior, but you also use inconsistencies and missing areas of the handbook to achieve your goals. In this case, you have been socialized to rely on the handbook, as is the organizational culture, but you have adapted the culture to your own needs by taking advantage of the handbook's limitations to get what you think you need to accomplish your job.

Notably, metamorphosis is also not a steady state. For example, when a newcomer arrives, existing members need to readjust and renegotiate their roles within the organization.

Exit

Exit, or departing from the organization, makes up the final stage of assimilation (Jablin, 1985, 2001). While organizational members may cycle somewhat between encounter and metamorphosis as the organization grows or changes, exit is more concrete. Researchers typically distinguish between voluntary and involuntary exits (Kramer, 2010). **Voluntary exit** often includes three phases: (1) preannouncement, (2) announcement, and (3) exit (Jablin, 2001). During the *preannouncement* phase, the member gathers information and makes the decision to leave the organization. Reasons for voluntary exit might include dissatisfaction with the organization, finding another job or opportunity, taking extended caregiving leave, or even retiring altogether. If the exit is planned, such as with retirement, there is likely to be a lot of open communication and discussion. For other types of leave, the process may be highly secretive. During the *announcement phase*, the member actively declares the intention to leave. Communication during this phase largely centers around maintaining self-presentation goals. For example, Alex ambiguously tells coworkers that they're leaving for "a different opportunity," when, Alex sought out a different opportunity because they can't stand their manager's constant criticism and controlling oversight. Additionally, the member may show concern for disrupting the organizational system. For example, Alex may help to create a job announcement for their role or spend time transitioning projects over to a coworker. Finally, *exit* begins when the insider is no longer an employee or member. While it may be possible to maintain relationships with organizational members, it will likely become more challenging to do so (no more chats over the department's Keurig or pickup basketball in the parking lot on Fridays). Likewise, access to organizational resources ends.

Note that while the departing member typically has a clear separation from the organization, the remaining members now must make sense of and adjust to the departure. If a newcomer is brought in, the encounter process reemerges; if the workload gets divided among remaining members, metamorphosis and "how we do things" may be reexamined. As well, there is emerging research to suggest that voluntary departures may have a *contagion effect* (Felps, et al., 2009). When one well-regarded member leaves, remaining members begin to question their own value and fit with the role and organization. For example, a record number of US employees resigned in the first half of 2021, right as the disruption from the COVID-19 pandemic was stabilizing (U.S. Bureau of Labor Statistics [BLS], 2021). Coined the "Great Resignation," workforce experts have explained the mass exodus, in part, as a response to job dissatisfaction coupled with the realization that life is fragile (Kelly, 2021). Seeing friends, family, and coworkers leave their jobs in search of something else has emboldened others to leap as well. Felps et al. (2009) research concluded that organizations would do well to (re)emphasize organizational and individual embeddedness through collective socialization.

Distinct from voluntary separations, **involuntary exits** are forced removals such as layoffs or being fired (Kramer, 2010). Such exits are typically abrupt and unpleasant and may create uncertainty with remaining members. There also recent consideration of a hybrid type of separation—a **bridge exit**. In one example of this situation, the member is given opportunities to improve performance, assuming this is a key factor in being separated (Kramer, 2010). In another example such as involuntary retirement, the organization may help the member transition from a role within the organization to a role outside the organization (Dingemans & Henkens, 2014). Similar to voluntary exits, however, self-presentation needs of the departing member and readjustment of the remaining members need attention.

The next theory, organizational identification and control, takes this notion of organizational assimilation a step further by articulating the hidden aspects of becoming a member of an organizational culture.

ORGANIZATIONAL IDENTIFICATION AND CONTROL

As indicated in Chapter 8, organizations routinely use team-based structures to improve quality, engender creativity, and increase employee involvement (Deetz et al., 2000). Although these are the *stated* goals of work teams, research suggests team-based structures also serve another purpose: control over employees (Barker, 1999). Consequently, organizational identification and control (OIC) theory centers on the way an individual's connection to the organization influences behavior and decision-making in team-based structures. Three main concepts tie the theory together: identification, control, and discipline.

Identification

OIC's first major concept, **identification**, refers to the sense of oneness with or belongingness to an organization; when individuals experience identification, they define themselves in terms of the organization (Mael & Ashforth, 1992). Identification happens most frequently in the metamorphosis stage of organizational assimilation, as described earlier in the chapter. Evidence of identification happens when you listen to organizational members speak. Often, they will say things such as, "We don't operate that way here" or "We launched a new product today." In these cases, the organizational member's is adopting the persona of the organization—while the individual may have had little to do with the new product, there is a sense of pride in and ownership of the product because of identification. This process of identification plays a central, yet subtle, role in how organizations control their employees. As Sias and Duncan (2020) summarized, organizational identification is linked with positive outcomes such as commitment and performance. Importantly, organizational identification doesn't just occur. Communication scholars maintain that identification is a complex, socially constructed process in which communication plays a central role (Walker, 2021). For example, research suggests that leaders who use motivating language can strategically enhance members' organizational identification (Mayfield et al, 2021). Moreover, this identification is championed; to become high performing, today's organizations are advised to make a pointed effort at creating strong identification (Ryckman, n.d.).

Control

Organizations need power "to control the contributions of others toward a goal," and one way to establish power is through control (McPhee & Tompkins, 1985, p. 180). OIC suggests there are several forms of control an organization might use. Based on Edwards's (1981) delineation, an organization may exert control through three traditional methods. **Simple control** involves direct, authoritarian control. If a manager makes threats (e.g., "do this, or you'll get fired") or places conditions on an employee (e.g., "you can leave early if you finish the Kegway project"), they are using a classic way of controlling employees by simply directing the employee as to what can or should be done.

The second method of control is slightly more subtle. **Technological control** involves the use of technology to manage what can and can't be done in the workplace (Edwards, 1981). A factory assembly line is a perfect example; employees must go exactly as fast as the assembly line is moving—no faster and no slower (as the classic episode of *I Love Lucy* in the candy factory illustrated). Employees on an assembly line can only take prescribed breaks, as well, because the whole line must be shut down if one person takes a break. A more contemporary example of this type of control is the limitation of computer technology. How often have you been told by someone, "The computer program won't let us do that"? The technology you can access and the way technology works (or doesn't!) serve as a means of organizational control.

The third kind of control is **bureaucratic control** (Edwards, 1981). Undoubtedly, you are familiar with the term *bureaucracy*, and it is usually associated with negative perceptions. Edwards, however, was referring to the vision of bureaucracy first articulated by Max Weber, a German sociologist. Writing at the turn of the 20th century, Weber argued that modern organizations are served best by a hierarchical system of rules, with rewards and punishments drawn from those rules. That hierarchy is evident in contemporary organizations through company policies and formal procedures. Employee handbooks and other such formalized rule systems are the clearest example of bureaucratic control.

These first three forms of control are typical ways in which power has been exerted in organizations. In developing OIC, however, Tompkins and Cheney (1985) suggested that changes in organizations during the latter part of the 20th century have shifted the way control is wielded. With the growing use of team-based organizations and organizations grounded in participation and empowerment, Tompkins and Cheney identified two additional types of control: unobtrusive and concertive. **Unobtrusive control** is based on shared values within the organization. Put simply, in the modern organization, management's job is to create a vision and mission for the organization. When organizational members make decisions based on the vision or credo of the organization, they are not making those decisions because they are forced to but because they believe in the mission of the organization—they *identify* with the organization. Thus, the commitment to organizational values controls employees. This commitment can also have potentially unethical consequences. According to Ploeger and Bisel (2013), organizational members who demonstrated strong identification with their organization were more likely to defend the organization, even when the organization's wrongdoing was certain.

Based on interpersonal relationships and teamwork, **concertive control** happens when peers develop mechanisms to reward and control behavior that influences the team (Tompkins & Cheney, 1985). For example, group members can discipline nonconforming coworkers through criticizing, monitoring, giving the silent treatment, or exerting social pressure, among other tactics (Barker, 1999). Importantly, concertive control is not a managerial or role-based function; concertive control happens among hierarchical equals. Because of this peer-to-peer relationship, it is often described as a hidden form of control. Table 9.4 provides an overview of the types of control.

TABLE 9.4 ■ Organizational Identification and Control		
Type of Control	**Examples**	**Types of Organizations**
Simple	<ul><li>Commands</li><li>Threats</li></ul>	<ul><li>Law enforcement agencies, military, and emergency services providers all rely on aspects of simple control</li></ul>
Technological	<ul><li>Swipe cards to enter building</li><li>Firewalls on workplace computers</li></ul>	<ul><li>Amazon uses AI surveillance to track drivers and warehouse employees (Hunter, 2021)</li><li>In a survey of more than 1,000 employees, nearly two-thirds of workers reported that their employers restricted access to certain websites, streaming services, social media apps, and shopping websites (Lindzon, 2020)</li></ul>
Bureaucratic	<ul><li>Employee handbooks</li><li>Employment contracts</li></ul>	<ul><li>Ford's (2007) code of conduct handbook communicates the company's culture and policies. (Your college or university likely has a Handbook or Code of Conduct for students, staff, and faculty, too!)</li></ul>
Unobtrusive	<ul><li>Identification with organizational values</li><li>Decision-making based on organizational mission</li></ul>	<ul><li>Women's activewear retailer, Athleta demonstrates its organizational value of sustainability by choosing recyclable and environmentally friendly fabrics for its products (Chen, 2019)</li><li>When CVS rebranded as a health services company in 2014, it also stopped selling tobacco products. Despite a $2 billion loss in sales, the company relied on their updated values (Glazer, 2021)</li></ul>
Concertive	<ul><li>Monitoring of other team members' performance</li><li>Coworker pressure on nonconforming members</li></ul>	<ul><li>Universities rely on concertive control in on-campus housing contexts. For example, Resident Assistants are peers who monitor other students.</li><li>Since 2014, Zappos (n.d.) has employed a self-managed work system called Holacracy in which decision-making power is distributed among teams rather than top-down.</li></ul>

Discipline

Pulling together the concepts of identification and control, Barker (1999) and colleagues (see also Tompkins & Cheney, 1985) suggested **discipline** is achieved through a sense of responsibility to the work group because members identify with their organization and because they share common values and a vision for the organization. When individuals are faced with a decision, they will rely on organizational values to make that decision—there is no need for top-down management directives. If an individual is not behaving in concert with organizational values, work group members tend to censure that individual.

Notably, according to OIC theory, superiors need not do the disciplining themselves; the norms for behavior generated by the organizational mission and values coupled with the identification of organizational members work together to maintain organizational control. Thus, the creation of organizational missions and visions might have the explicit function of driving the organization's business, and work teams might provide a mechanism for employee empowerment, but these initiatives also serve the implicit function of controlling employees.

ORGANIZING THEORY

The previous theories in this chapter have linked communication processes to organizational processes. The fourth and final perspective, Weick's (1969) organizing theory, takes this link one step further by stating that communication *is* the organization. Instead of viewing organizations as containers in which communication occurs, Weick argued communication *is* what constitutes an organization. Instead of examining an organization (a noun), Weick examined the process of **organizing** (a verb).

With roots in Darwin's theory of evolution, information theory, and systems theory, organizing theory assumes organizations exist in an **information environment** (Weick, 1969). Rather than focusing on the physical environment, Weick's theory is concerned with the massive amounts of information organizations have available to them, from internal and external sources. Organizations depend on information to accomplish their goals, and the Herculean challenge of processing it all.

In addition to issues of quantity, managing the information environment is difficult because much of the information organizations deal with is unpredictable. The term **equivocality** references the ambiguity of information available to organizations (Weick, 1969). Messages are equivocal to the extent there may be multiple understandings of the information. Equivocality is different from the concept of uncertainty. When individuals are uncertain about a message, they can gather more information to reduce uncertainty. However, when individuals find a message to be equivocal, they do not need additional information; instead, they must decide which one of multiple interpretations is the best fit. Consider the example of Kristine, who has to decide how to invest her money. The state of the economy is equivocal; some financial planners argue that real estate will pick up, and so she should invest in property, whereas others suggest that because real estate is recovering so slowly, Kristine should invest in the stock market. Gathering more information is likely only to add to the equivocality. In the end, Kristine has to interpret the state of the economy for herself, but this interpretation is only one of many.

According to Weick (1969), one way to reduce equivocality is to rely on **rules** (also called recipes). The term *rule* most often refers to guidelines for behavior, and Weick's use of the term is consistent with this conceptualization. Typically, organizations have rules, or guidelines, for analyzing both the equivocality of a message and how to respond to it. These rules are developed to make a process more efficient and are generally based on past successes. There are many obvious examples of rules, such as rules for whom to contact to accomplish certain tasks, rules about specific forms to be used, and rules about processes to be followed. Rules can also be less formalized, too. For example, an organization might have had past success with increasing profits by reducing packaging costs for its products. Accordingly, the next time corporate earnings are in question, the standard response is to seek to reduce packaging costs: Cost reduction has become a rule.

Rules don't always work, and there isn't always a rule for every situation. Organizing theory suggests a second way to reduce equivocality is for organizational members to engage in communication cycles known as double interacts (Weick, 1969). Double interacts are suited for instances of high equivocality because they require organizational members to develop interdependent relationships in the process of communicating. According to the systems perspective of **nonsummativity** (Fisher, 1978), the whole is greater than the sum of its parts. Grounded in systems principles, Weick argued that greater involvement among organizational members can produce greater results in reducing equivocality.

A **double interact** consists of an act, a response, and an adjustment (Weick, 1969). An act is a communication behavior initiated by one person or group of people. The receivers of the message communicate in return, which is considered a response. This two-way exchange of messages is most typically used to understand the communication process. Weick proposed genuine communication requires a third step, an adjustment to the information originally received. This adjustment can take several forms. It might be a confirmation that the information has been understood. If the information is still equivocal, the adjustment might be additional information gathering.

To illustrate, the marketing department of a major manufacturing company has created a new product to be sold exclusively at Walmart. They approach production with the new idea, but members of the production team respond by telling marketing the configuration they have sold cannot be produced on the current assembly lines. Marketing amends the proposal so the customer receives the specialty product, and the production department can use existing equipment and materials: act, response, adjustment.

Sociocultural Evolution

At the beginning of this section, we stated Weick (1969) was more concerned with the process of organizing than with the entity of an organization. Double interacts are the process of organizing; according to Weick, they are the links that hold an organization together. Weick also believed, however, that organizing is an evolutionary process. Much like Darwin's theory of evolution, which suggests organisms become extinct if they can't adapt to their environment, organizing theory maintains organizations that don't adapt to their environment will collapse. Accordingly, Weick (1969) proposed a three-stage process of **sociocultural evolution** for organizations.

The first stage of sociocultural evolution is **enactment**. Enactment occurs when members of an organization take note of equivocal information in their information environment. Recall that equivocal information can be interpreted in multiple ways. Recognizing multiple interpretations and putting into practice a mechanism for making sense of the information are at the heart of enactment.

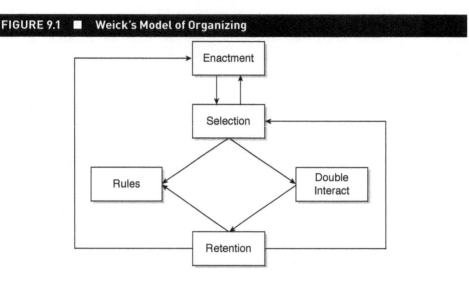

FIGURE 9.1 ■ Weick's Model of Organizing

The second stage is **selection**. In seeking to reduce equivocality, organizational members must choose how to respond. As described earlier, organizational members can choose between rules, or standard guidelines for how to respond, and a double interact, which is a communication process that allows members to adapt solutions to the problem.

The third stage is **retention**. Retention is a form of organizational memory. What was done and how it was done is stored, formally or informally, so organizational members can refer to it again. Notice what is happening here; even if organizational members go through a double interact to reduce equivocality, in this stage, the double interact is retained as a new rule or guideline for behavior in the future. Accordingly, retention should be used sparingly. Figure 9.1 provides a visual illustration of sociocultural evolution.

To complete the analogy with Darwin's theory of evolution, Weick's (1969) theory of organizing posits that organizations exist in a complex information environment. This environment is complex because organizations have to deal with equivocal information. Organizations that don't adapt to equivocality, whose members don't use double interacts to resolve new forms of ambiguity, will not survive and flourish. In short, change is the key to organizational success, and change occurs through the process of communicating.

SUMMARY AND RESEARCH APPLICATIONS

This chapter introduced four theories of organizational communication. We first looked at organizational culture. Schein's (1985, 1990, 1992) model proposes that, while difficult to identify, assumptions lie at the heart of organizational culture. Organizational values and artifacts develop from and are reinforced by these assumptions. The now familiar business development paradigm of corporate sustainability was developed using Schein's model (see Baumgartner, 2009). Specifically, an organization can only become socially, environmentally, and economically viable with a strong organizational culture that supports these sustainable values. Not only relevant for business organizations, Harkins (2021) used Schein's model of culture to analyze membership and leadership challenges faced by the Boy Scouts of America (BSA), a national, nonprofit organization. Harkins pointed to the discrepancy between current societal attitudes about race, sexual orientation, and gender-inclusiveness versus the BSA's long-held values and assumptions that are repeatedly reenacted through rituals, uniforms, and language. In an empirical test of Schein's model of culture in law firms, Hogan and Coote (2014) found that firms' artifacts, norms, and innovative behaviors influenced values and, subsequently, members' performance.

Second, organizational assimilation theory details five stages of socialization as members blend into a new organization. While much research has focused on socializing new members, understanding the impact of exits on remaining organizational members is of increased interest. Benedict (2020) studied the message characteristics of organizational members' following a coworker's involuntary dismissal. Employees were more likely to learn about the peer's dismissal from grapevine sources than from a manager. Additionally, the source and channel of the message influenced remaining employees' levels of uncertainty. When informed of the dismissal quickly, by a superior, and in a face-to-face context, the remaining employees had less uncertainty and perceived lower social costs for information seeking. Benedict advised organizations to ward off the grapevine by using more formal, downward communications to share key information about dismissals, as well as "task-oriented information" as to how current workers' should proceed.

Next, organizational identification and control proposes that when organizational members identify with the values of an organization, they can be controlled through self-discipline and peer pressure. For example, researchers found that peers' use of concertive control helped to explain why employees, in public and private sectors, often did not take full advantage of the organization's work–life balance policies (ter Hoeven et al., 2017). Use of jokes and reprimands between colleagues served as powerful signals about when and how often one should use flexible arrangements so as not to leave coworkers overburdened.

Finally, Weick's theory of organizing argues organizations and their members must process equivocal information in order to succeed. Recent research has applied Weick's notion of organizing and equivocality to "high reliability organizations" (HROs)—those that operate in complex, hazardous environments yet have minimal catastrophic accidents themselves, such as emergency response organizations. Jahn (2019) explored how wildland firefighters used voice enactments, that is, assertive and upward communications, as part of their after-action-reviews (AARs). Firefighters' language during these scripted reflections stressed complementary rather than hierarchical relationships; instead of emphasizing role-based authority, the AAR routine encouraged collaborative sensemaking. This critical examination of a previous incident also decreased equivocality by comparing how others perceived the same situation. Jahn argued that it is through such mindful organizing, that HROs such as firefighters, can regularly avoid catastrophic failure.

TABLE 9.5 ■ Additional Theories of Organizational Communication

Theory	Main Idea
Attraction-Selection-Attrition (ASA) Theory	ASA proposes that members' collective characteristics come to define the organization (Schneider, 1987). Organizational members tend to attract and select newcomers based on perceived similarities. If the similarities don't hold up, people will leave the organization.
Leader–Member Exchange (LMX)	LMX proposes that differential supervisor-subordinate relationships influence organizational socialization, employee performance, and retention (Dansereau et al., 1975).
Systems Perspective	A systems perspectives suggest that we need to study the interrelated patterns of communication of people in a relationship in order to understand the relationship (Monge, 1977). As related to organizational communication, a systems approach summarizes the complexity of organizations by explaining the relationship between the interdependent components that make up the whole as a unit and how that unit interacts with the environment (Poole, 2014)
Transformational Leadership	Bass's (1997) theory suggests that exchange-based (transactional) leadership is less effective than transformational leadership. Transformational leadership is associated with emotional intelligence and consists of charisma, motivation, intellectual stimulation, and individual consideration.

The four theories we have highlighted are not the only theories of organizational communication used by scholars. Table 9.5 identifies some other prominent theories of organizational communication.

DISCUSSION QUESTIONS

1.   Take a closer look around your classroom, office, buildings, and campus. What artifacts represent your university's (or workplace's) culture? What meaning do those artifacts have in relation to your organization's espoused values? What assumptions underlie these values and artifacts?

2.   Think about an organization you have joined (you might consider your university, an extracurricular group such as a sports team or performing group, a job or internship). In what ways did the members help to socialize you into the organization? Now that you are part of the organization, in what ways do you help socialize newcomers? If anyone has left the organization during your time, discuss how remaining members readjusted to the exit.

3. Table 9.4 presents several examples for the different types of organizational control. Brainstorm some organizations with which you are familiar. How might the organizations on your list use different types of control? You could also do a quick web search to see if you can find examples of organizational handbooks, technological control, and so forth. Then, consider how organizational culture might influence how strongly one identifies with an organization or with the types of control an organization uses.

4. Weick's organizing theory recommends retrospective sensemaking—that is, there is an act, a response, and an adjustment. By looking back, we can make sense of what occurred, adjust, and move forward. How have you experienced this double interact? Or how might you apply this method yourself?

KEY TERMS

Anticipatory socialization (p. 167)

Artifacts (p. 163)

Assumptions (p. 165)

Bridge exit (p. 170)

Bureaucratic control (p. 172)

Concertive control (p. 172)

Discipline (p. 173)

Double interact (p. 175)

Enactment (p. 175)

Encounter (p. 168)

Equivocality (p. 174)

Identification (p. 171)

Individualization (p. 169)

Information environment (p. 174)

Involuntary exits (p. 170)

Metamorphosis (p. 169)

Nonsummativity (p. 175)

Organizations (p. 161)

Organizational communication (p. 161)

Organizational assimilation (p. 166)

Organizational culture (p. 162)

Organizing (p. 174)

Person–job fit (p. 168)

Person–organization fit (p. 168)

Retention (p. 176)

Rules (p. 174)

Selection (p. 176)

Simple control (p. 171)

Socialization (p. 169)

Sociocultural evolution (p. 175)

Technological control (p. 172)

Unobtrusive control (p. 172)

Vocational anticipatory socialization (p. 167)

Voluntary exit (p. 170)

CASE STUDY 9
Losing Hope

For more than 80 years, Hope Medical Center had serviced its local residents as a privately run, not-for-profit community hospital. However, with the rapidly escalating cost of medical care, last year, Hope's board of directors agreed that, for the hospital to survive, it was in their best interest to partner with the Greater Valley Hospital Alliance (GVHA)—a for-profit hospital management group. Under GVHA's management, resources could be used more efficiently, the hospital would have more financial security, and patients and doctors alike would have access to other facilities in GVHA's network of hospitals. GVHA had promised that Hope's daily operations would remain untouched after the merger. When announced in the local newspaper, nearby residents and the hospital staff enthusiastically supported the partnership.

Stella Brindle had worked for Hope for the last 8 years in its community relations department. She helped publicize the hospital's services, success stories, and awards. She also helped the hospital raise money, and she was particularly proud of her work directing the most recent fund-raising campaign that helped finance the hospital's pediatric unit renovations. Stella was excited by the merger; by sharing resources, she believed the partnership would free her from some of the more tedious job duties and allow her team to focus more on fund-raising and developing the hospital's services.

Additionally, Stella's team had spearheaded an initiative called the Beacon of Hope, a mission statement and motto for all employees. Called the Beacon for short, its purpose was to "inspire all members of the Hope community to realize what it means to be truly exceptional caregivers." The Beacon had emerged after the American Medical Association named Hope as "the nation's most compassionate hospital." The director of community relations, Devin Au'berge, wanted to formalize this standard of care and assigned Stella to lead the Beacon initiative.

With support from the entire hospital community, the Beacon was to serve as a code of conduct for all physicians, nurses, staff members, and volunteers. Stella ran a number of focus groups and sought input from various stakeholders. As a result, Hope employees were quite proud of the Beacon and what it stood for. The mission statement appeared prominently on all of the hospital's promotional materials, and a framed copy hung in each patient's room. The hospital gift shop even sold a variety of items with the Beacon's logo. Hope's physicians were invited to use the Beacon in their patient office areas, and the Beacon logo was stitched on all hospital lab coats and scrubs.

Despite the Beacon initiative's success and the initial community support for merging with GVHA, however, tough times were on the horizon for Hope. Six months into the merger, Stella and many other employees had serious regrets about joining the GVHA network. When initially proposed by the board, Hope employees were led to believe that a partnership with GVHA would have minimal impact on their day-to-day tasks. The CEO of GVHA even told hospital staff that "a partnership would not disrupt the wonderful community culture of Hope Medical Center." However, only days after the deal was signed, this promise seemed moot. First, a bright red and purple GVHA banner was hung, overshadowing the Beacon. Next, GVHA administrators sent an email informing Hope employees that as part of the GVHA network, Hope employees must wear the GVHA-approved uniforms or lab coats. Although seemingly a trivial issue, Stella and the rest of the community relations team were upset. Not only were they being forced to wear a uniform, but the demand also meant the Beacon logo could no longer be worn because it wasn't "consistent" with the other GVHA hospitals.

Transformations appeared in the gift shop, too. The Beacon merchandise was still there but on a back shelf where it was hard to see. And several weeks after that, Stella noticed changes to the hospital's website. The Beacon logo was no longer featured prominently; instead it was a tiny link, buried halfway down the page. Stella was confused; normally, her department managed the website and all changes were made as a team. Yet, no one in community relations knew anything about the changes. When Stella called GVHA to find out about the new website, she was told, "Oh, you don't need to worry about maintaining your site anymore. We'll do all of that for you so you have more time to work on fund-raising." Stella felt conflicted. On one hand, no one in community relations liked the tedious task of constantly updating the website; however, she wished the team would have been asked, or at least informed, about this shift.

The changes weren't just about logos and merchandise. Hope had always prided itself on its family-like atmosphere where all of the doctors, nurses, and staff members knew each other by first name. The cafeteria and elevators were typically jovial places because people would chat with each other. Since the merger, however, physicians and nurses could be required to work at several of GVHA's hospitals, depending on which hospital had the most need. This meant there was an ongoing influx and exodus of medical personnel and more unfamiliar faces. Although always busy, the pace at Hope now felt more intense as doctors dashed from room to room trying to see all of their patients before driving to another location.

Community relations started receiving complaints—first from the nurses, then from the doctors, and even from patients. A letter to the editor was published in the local newspaper, and comments were surfacing on local social media pages, all criticizing Hope for "going commercial." Reported medical mistakes had risen since the partnership, and patient satisfaction had declined. Stella's boss, Devin, asked the community relations team to start categorizing these complaints. After a month, Devin prepared a report and called a meeting with the board of directors. She showed them all of the data along with her conclusion: Hope was losing what had made it such an exceptional hospital. The medical staff felt more overworked than ever, while patients felt like numbers, rather than people. The whole philosophy behind the Beacon had become overshadowed by GVHA's corporate atmosphere. The board was at a loss. If the hospital's record of medical mistakes was too high, or if too many patients filed complaints, GVHA would void their contract and withdraw hospital funding. Clearly, something had to be done, but what?

Questions for Consideration

1. Compare and contrast the culture of Hope Medical Center (before the merger) with that of GVHA. Make sure to describe the artifacts, values, and assumptions

apparent in both organizations. Using Schein's theory of organizational culture, analyze the assumptions, values, and artifacts of both organizations. Can the cultures of Hope and GVHA coexist? Why, or why not?

2. Using organizational assimilation theory, describe the stages of Stella's adjustment (or failure to adjust) to the "new" hospital after the GVHA merger. Do you believe metamorphosis will occur? Why, or why not?

3. What types of organizational control did Hope Medical Center use before the partnership? Compare this with the types of control GVHA uses to manage its hospital network.

4. Using organizing theory, what evidence is there of the use of double interacts? What might sociocultural evolution predict will happen to Hope?

5. Do any of the theories emerge as better than the others? Why do you believe this to be the case? How could the story be altered so as to make a different theory or combination of theories better at explaining the situation?

10 MASS COMMUNICATION

LEARNING OBJECTIVES

After reading this chapter, you will be able to do the following:

1. Discuss the five characteristics of mass communication/mass media

2. Apply the elements of first- and second-level agenda setting to news stories

3. Explain the process of cultivation theory via mainstreaming, resonance, and symbolic double jeopardy

4. Relate the process of observational learning and modeling to media violence as pertaining to social cognitive theory

5. Differentiate between three ways of encoding/decoding messages, using preferred, negotiated, or oppositional codes

"The past decades have witnessed thousands of empirical studies into the cognitive, emotional, attitudinal, and behavioral effects of media on children and adults" (Valkenburg & Peter, 2013, p. 221). Results suggest that exposure to TV, movies, music, and other media forms is associated with childhood obesity, sexual activity, use of tobacco products, drug and alcohol use, low academic achievement, and attention-deficit/hyperactivity disorder (American College of Pediatrics, 2016; Robidoux et al., 2019). With such negative consequences, why do we continue to allow the media into our lives? Perhaps it is because such a dismal view oversimplifies our complex relationship with the media. For many of us, the media provide both personal and professional opportunities for development. After all, *Sesame Street* really can instruct our children, and the opportunity to surf the web can simplify our quest for information. Moreover, despite the commonly held view of negative media effects, scholarly research often conflicts with popular beliefs and even contradicts other scholars' work. Intellectual and political debate remain over *who* are most affected, *to what extent* these individuals are influenced, and *why* some people are more affected than others. In this chapter, we present four influential and often controversial theories that attempt to explain and predict media use and media effects: agenda-setting theory, cultivation theory, social cognitive theory of mass media, and encoding/decoding theory. First, however, we discuss exactly what we mean by mass media.

DEFINING MASS COMMUNICATION

Mass communication and mass media are decidedly different from mediated communication and social media. Discussed in Chapter 11, mediated communication includes all messages in which there is a device, third party, or electronic mechanism that facilitates communication between the sender and receiver. Mediated communication isn't bound by audience size and can occur in both mass and interpersonal contexts, such as calling a family member, texting a friend, or emailing your boss. By contrast, **mass communication** "is a process in which professional communicators use technology to share messages over great distances to influence large audiences" (Pearson et al., 2008, p. 3). Note the source could be an announcer, reporter, writer, and so on, while the technology used to mediate the mass message could include fiber optics, satellites, cable, radio waves, and printing presses to name a few. In turn, the **mass media** include organizations, or parts of large media conglomerates, responsible for using technology to send mass messages to the public. Mass communication and the mass media are intertwined; without organizations and agencies to create, produce, and transmit the message content, reaching a mass audience would be difficult. If all these distinctions seem confusing, remember this: *all mass communication is mediated but not all mediated messages are mass communication.*

Another distinction within mass media involves traditional media as compared with new media. **Traditional (or legacy) media** include "media originally distributed using a pre-Internet medium (print, radio, television), and media companies whose original business was in pre-Internet media, regardless of how much of their content is now available online" (Miel & Faris, 2008, p. 3). For example, newspapers, magazines, television, and film all predate the information age. Meanwhile, new media include both digital-native and participatory media. **Digital-native (or web-native) media** are outlets that originated online and distribute content primarily (or solely) via the Internet. **Participatory media** include formats and entities where audience engagement or contribution is significant to the platform. With participatory media, the media is transactional such that the "audience" is also part-creator. Borrowing from Jay Rosen (2011), "people formerly known as the audience" are essential.

These particularities are important and not just because of technological advancements. While many think of traditional media as old-fashioned, they still set the content for many digital platforms, particularly with news. As Diel (2017) contended, both legacy and new media depend heavily on the same initial content; however, most original reporting is generated by traditional media, while new media use those reports to redevelop the material and create feature-type stories. Furthermore, new media's dependence on traditional media "is especially significant because of the continuing decline in employment in legacy media, as it suggests that new media are not filling the news vacuum left by the decline in the number of professional journalists but are instead giving consumers aggregated content re-purposed as features" (p. 106).

Importantly, five key characteristics of traditional mass media have stood the test of time, despite advances in technology and the decrease in some mediums (McQuail, 2010). First, the mass media can reach an enormous amount of people instantly or almost instantly with information, entertainment, or opinions. However, while the mass communication sender can promptly reach a large audience, feedback from these receivers back to the source is typically much slower. For example, if you want to comment on an article written in your local print newspaper or favorite magazine, you need to send an email or write a letter to the editor. The letter may or may not be read, published, or otherwise acknowledged. Likewise, if you want to complain about inappropriate content on a "family-friendly" TV show, you must email, write, or attempt a phone call. Again, the show's producer may or may not receive, read, or otherwise acknowledge your message. With emerging and interactive media technologies, this slow feedback process is not always the case (think about texting your vote to *America's Got Talent* or tweeting your feelings about the latest *WandaVision* episode). Nonetheless, the quality of feedback the audience can provide is often much less rich than in interpersonal communication.

A second characteristic offered by McQuail (2010) argues that the media continue to inspire universal fascination. Again, the popular technologies may change (from sitting around the radio listening to Abbott and Costello to watching streaming video via Netflix), but people's preoccupation with shared stories continues. Likewise, a third feature of mass media is that it can rouse, in equal measure, hope and fear in audiences. Think about the COVID-19 pandemic. People world-wide watched, read, and posted about the never-ending news coverage of lockdowns, case numbers, death rates, vaccine developments, and conspiracy theories.

The fourth property of mass media noted by McQuail (2010) concerns the relationship between the media and other sources of societal power. Unlike other types of communication noted in this book, the mass media influence and are influenced by the four sources of social power identified by Mann (2012): economic, ideological, military, and political. Most mass media, at least in the United States, are funded by advertising. By emphasizing consumerism, either directly through advertisements or indirectly through product placement, sponsoring a national sporting event, or drawing attention to characters' dress, hairstyles, and homes, the media can encourage our shopping and spending habits. To illustrate, research indicates that the younger adults watch or read about celebrity culture and lifestyles, the more materialistic they are themselves (Lewallen et al., 2016).

In terms of ideological power, most Americans can agree that a key term associated with the 2020 American presidential election was "fake news." What is fascinating is what people consider to be fake news; it seems that one's political ideology influences what people view as "fake." Even before the contentious 2016 and 2020 US elections, researchers found that using biased news sites promotes inaccurate beliefs, leading to partisan belief gaps (Garrett et al., 2016). More simply put, the media outlet that one chooses to watch can lead to vastly different beliefs about the political world.

Indeed, consider the role of the media during political campaigns. According to the Center for Responsive Politics, candidates in the 2020 US elections (both presidential and congressional) spent a record $14.4 billion in their efforts to win (Evers-Hillstrom, 2020). This amount is roughly equivalent to the entire gross domestic product (GDP) of Jamaica, and more than what was spent in 2016 and 2012 elections combined. We may not like those slickly edited and often negative campaign ads squeezed in between our primetime TV viewing or the news (real or fake) that appears on our social media feeds, but clearly it is influential.

Economic power also influences and is influenced by the media. In the United States, nearly all mass media organizations operate as privately owned businesses, with profits as their primary goal (Marger, 2019). The old saying, "if it bleeds, it leads," exemplifies the relationship between content and economics. More people will tune in to, turn on, or click links to stories covering tragedy and disasters, and all those viewers, readers, and "clickers" generate advertising revenue. Thus, the economics of mass media as a business influences content selection. As well, research shows that "journalists are asymmetrically responsive to economic conditions" such that there is much heavier reporting on negative than on positive economic developments (Damstra & Boukes, 2021, p. 27). While journalists serve an important "watch dog" role to keep the government in check, the unevenness in coverage also influences perceptions of the economy. When the public perceives a negative economic outlook, it affects their spending as well as their political leanings. As another example of the relationship between media and economics, consider how US business journalists initially reported on "subprime mortgages" as opposed to "predatory lending practices" in the early 2000s. This rhetorical distinction is believed to have influenced the public's opinions about the safety of home loans and subsequent panic when the housing bubble burst, contributing to the 2008 market collapse (Longobardi, 2009).

Finally, McQuail's (2010) fifth characteristic of the media is the assumption that it is a source of enormous power and influence. For instance, the media influence social reality—that which we perceive to be true. The evening news provides viewers with information, but that information is edited, and other stories are omitted. The news stories presented may or may not be complete, accurate, or reliable. During the height of the COVID-19 pandemic, for example, numerous news outlets reported on Sweden's strategy of "herd immunity" for managing the pandemic; some reports praised it, others criticized it. Regardless, the mass media typically treated the Swedish response as a monolithic, single-step solution to avoid the lockdowns that became common (but controversial) practice elsewhere in the world. However, Irwin (2020) argued that this reporting was not only misleading, but it was also irresponsible. According to Irwin, the media ignored cultural, regional, and county differences that influence strategy use. As well, "Sweden, and the Swedish approach, is much more multilayered than portrayed in the media, and this hinders serious policy evaluation" (p. 370). Thus, while the reporting was not wholly inaccurate, the way in which the story was framed omitted critical features that would influence the use of such policy elsewhere.

Regarding inaccuracy, initial news reports of George Floyd's murder in 2020 was that "Man Dies After Medical Incident During Police Interaction" (McCarthy, 2021). News outlets relied on a police statement, which is frequent practice when reporting on crime and violence (Craven, 2021). The statement emphasized the suspect appeared to be "under the influence" and that no "weapons of any type" were used. While accurate, the statement was incomplete. Police reports rely on text-based communications logs written in a "passive-voice" that doesn't capture the full narrative (McCarthy, 2021). It was only after video taken by teenage bystander Darnella Frazier and shared on social media that the reporting narrative changed from one of seeming accidental death to that of murder. As Jackson (2020) argued, the way in which news media cover crime matters profoundly to a democracy because the media can influence public support or rejection

TABLE 10.1 ■ Overview of Mass Communication Theories	
Agenda-Setting Theory	The news media influence the public's view of what issues are most important by choosing the topics on which to report and by stressing certain characteristics of these issues.
Cultivation Theory	Because of its pervasive storytelling influence, television cultivates attitudes such that heavy viewers have a distorted perception of reality that mirrors TV reality more than actual life.
Social Cognitive Theory of Mass Media	When actions shown in the media (e.g., violence) are attention-grabbing, memorable, reproducible, and incentivized through perceived rewards, viewers are more likely to model these behaviors.
Encoding/Decoding	Audiences can decode or understand mass media messages in one of three ways—as upholding the dominant position, through a negotiated understanding, or through an oppositional understanding that rejects the dominant framework.

of policies that might solve social ills such as racism and police brutality (para. 2). The point here isn't to demonize news organizations; rather, it is to highlight the power the media have.

The theories featured in this chapter focus on the media's power and influence—the ways and the extent to which various media influence receivers. Again, the four theories are agenda-setting theory, cultivation theory, social cognitive theory of mass communication, and encoding/decoding theory. According to these theories of mass communication influence, although mass media can't make us watch, read, or listen, when we do participate as audience members, we are transformed in some way. Table 10.1 provides an overview of each theory.

AGENDA-SETTING THEORY

McCombs and Shaw (1972) and McCombs et al. (2014) were among the first communication scholars to test and support their ideas of media influence within the realm of political news. Before their study of the 1968 presidential campaign, it was widely held that the news media simply reflected the public's interests, covering issues about which audience members already knew or wanted to understand in more detail. In this way, many assumed the news media simply act as mirrors of public interest. According to this viewpoint, extensive coverage of Britney Spears' attempt to end her conservatorship was because the American viewing public demanded to learn about it.

McCombs and Shaw (1972), however, had a hunch that something wasn't quite right with the "news media as a reflection of society" theory. Instead, they argued that public opinion is shaped, in part, *by* media coverage—particularly about political news and campaigns. Rather than the news media simply providing a reflection of the public's interests, McCombs and Shaw posited the reverse equation—that is, the public mirrors what is presented by the news media. In other words, McCombs and Shaw conceived the news media present audiences with an **agenda** for what events the public should consider as important—this view is known as **first-level**

agenda setting. Going back to Britney Spears, then, we wanted to know more *because* the story was put out by the press, not the reverse.

McCombs and Shaw (1972) tested this first-level agenda-setting function of the news media, relying on two key assumptions. First, they argued that the news media have an agenda. That is, the news media tell audiences what "news" to consider as important. However, the media's agenda is somewhat limited. That is, the primary agenda-setting function proposes that news media provide "not *what* to think . . . but what to think *about*" (emphasis added; Cohen, 1963, p. 13).

Second, McCombs and colleagues (McCombs & Shaw, 1972; McCombs & Weaver, 1973; McCombs et al., 2014) posited that people's **need for orientation** (NFO) influences the extent to which the agenda-setting function shapes public thought. Defined as a blend of relevance and uncertainty, NFO depends on an individual's assessment of an issue—how significant is the topic to that person and how uncertain does that person feel (McCombs & Weaver, 1973).

McCombs and Shaw (1972) argued that most people need—and want— assistance when trying to understand and evaluate the complex world of politics. Consequently, audience members who need help determining political realities rely on news media to point out topics of importance. For example, in 2017, the city of Philadelphia levied a beverage tax on all sweetened drinks—from juice to sports drinks, to soda (locally known as the "soda tax")—as a means of increasing revenue to fund the city's early childhood education initiatives, public library renovations, and city park maintenance (Aubrey, 2017). As this legislation was introduced, debated, and passed, the city's residents, merchants, and beverage workers likely had a high NFO. How much will this tax increase my family's grocery bill? Or a college student's meal plan? How will this tax affect consumer spending, vender revenue, and manufacturing? How will profits of the tax be spent? Is such a tax even legal? Whereas people living just outside the city limits and who don't work or regularly visit the city likely wouldn't have an NFO. They don't care much about the issue because it really didn't affect them.

Returning to McCombs and Shaw (1972), they drew on these assumptions and used media coverage of the 1968 presidential election as an opportunity to study agenda-setting theory. They predicted a causal relationship between the news media's coverage of the candidates (Richard Nixon and Hubert Humphrey) and subsequent voters' perceptions. In other words, McCombs and Shaw hypothesized that voter perceptions of Nixon and Humphrey and their campaign election issues would form *after* and *based on* the content of campaign coverage presented within various media outlets.

To test their prediction, McCombs and Shaw (1972) used two central criteria for measuring the media's agenda: **length** and **position** of a news story. When considering traditional media such as newsprint and broadcast TV or radio, there is limited physical space or time for reporting a given story. Time and space are costly; advertisers and subscribers support publications and broadcasts to the extent that not every news story can possibly be reported in any one publication. Thus, the length of a story (measured by airtime or print space) signifies its importance.

The position of a news story is also significant. Stories that "lead" the newscast or that appear on the front page or homepage are perceived as more important. Even with cable news and digital media where you can have infinite time or "space," there is little value to being aired at 3 a.m. or positioned at the bottom of a website or on later pages. Think about your last Google search; how many pages of results did you consult? If you're like most people, you likely stuck to the first five results on the first page. In fact, two-thirds of searches rely on the first five results that appear on the first page, and it is estimated that between 75% and 91% of Google users never click past the first page of results at all (Shelton, 2017). All to say, the position of a story signals importance.

Importantly, McCombs and Shaw's research found not only that news media tell audiences what topics to consider "but also how much importance to attach to that issue from the amount of information in a news story and its position" (p. 176). Although their initial study could only find a correlation, not causality (see Chapter 2 for a discussion of causation), subsequent researchers were able to support the causal relationship through experimental research studies (e.g., Iyengar et al., 1982). Moreover, decades of research on the subject continues to support McCombs and Shaw's groundbreaking work; there is a clear and consistent link between what the news media present to audiences and what the audiences then perceive to be critical issues (see Luo et al., 2019; McCombs et al. 2014). The causal notion of agenda setting is further developed through second-level agenda setting and framing.

Second-Level Agenda Setting

The news media's success in telling viewers and readers "what issues to think about" stems from how the media frame issues (McCombs & Shaw, 1972). Much like an art gallery director's choice of which frame to place around a given painting, the media have been shown to frame news events. Whereas the gallery vents. Whereas the gallery director chooses a frame that highlights or deemphasizes certain features of the painting, perhaps nuances in color or angular shaping of objects, news media **gatekeepers**—the handful of news editors who set the agenda— also select, emphasize, elaborate, and even exclude news stories or parts of news stories to create a certain effect for the audience. As Griffin (2003) reported, "75% of stories that come across a news desk are never printed or broadcast" (p. 394). This is probably a good thing because it is estimated the average person can only follow three to five ongoing news stories at a time. However, when considering the considerable number of news stories, or parts of news stories, left on the editing room floor, it may give you pause to wonder what *has* been left out. If you are interested, Project Censored, associated with the media literacy organization Media Freedom Foundation, identifies "the News that Didn't Make the News" every year. Although it is difficult to know which stories or aspects of stories have been excluded, a savvy reader or viewer can take a critical examination of the news event presented. Table 10.2 provides an overview of **framing** through the processes of **selection**, **emphasis**, **elaboration**, and **exclusion**.

We should note that although agenda setting focuses on the gatekeeping ability of the media, other people besides journalists, editors, and broadcasters can influence the media agenda. Public relations professionals, lobbyists, advertisers, and even the President of the United States can influence what the media cover as news (Eshbaugh-Soha, 2013; Huckins, 1999; Peake, 2001). Accordingly, media professionals might, either consciously or unconsciously, frame news coverage, but it can also be deliberately manipulated by other parties.

TABLE 10.2 ■ Framing the News	
Process	**Example in Action**
Selection: What stories are chosen?	● "Since the 2001 terrorist attacks on the United States, covering the type of violence inspired by al-Qaeda and the Islamic State (IS) has become a staple of the news media's repertoire. Collectively, this reporting increases the public's sense of vulnerability: An evil is out there, unpredictable, and ferocious, sure to strike again." (Seib, 2017, ¶2)
Emphasis: What focus, or tone is taken?	● "Cell phone videos of screaming victims; details of first responders' hectic efforts; "Was it terrorism?" guesswork; speculation about the perpetrator" (Seib, 2017, ¶1)
Elaboration: What details are included to round out the story?	● "Western reporting about IS-inspired terrorist attacks almost always, explicitly or implicitly, notes a connection to Islam." (Seib, 2017, ¶6) ● "The news media do not cover all terrorist attacks the same way. Rather, they give drastically more coverage to attacks by Muslims, particularly foreign-born Muslims—even though those are far less common than other kinds of terrorist attacks." (Kearns et al., 2017, ¶4)
Exclusion: What aspects of the situation are not reported?	● "The complexities of terrorism and Islam. Who are these people who murder so wantonly? Why do they do it? And most importantly, how might such attacks be stopped?" (Seib, 2017, ¶4) ● "Islam usually disappears from the news until the next tragedy, even though approximately 80 percent of Muslims live outside the Arab world in countries of rising importance such as Indonesia, Pakistan and Nigeria." (Seib, 2017, ¶8) ● "Coverage should also address state-sponsored extremism, most notably Saudi Arabia's well-funded promotion of Wahabbist Muslim ideology. This fundamentalist doctrine is intrinsically separatist and lends itself to militancy. It provides a purported theological rationale for treating moderate Muslims—as well as non-Muslims—as enemies." (Seib, 2017, ¶9)

Framing also brings us to the theory's growth by extension and addition of **second-level agenda setting**, or **attribute agenda setting** (Ghanem, 1997; McCombs & Evatt, 1995; McCombs et al., 2014). Whereas first-level agenda setting focuses on the media telling audiences what issues to think about through length and position of a selected story, expansion of the theory led to the investigation of attributes, or how a story is told. Second-level agenda setting proposes that the way stories are framed influences audiences' attitudes and *how* to think about the issues covered (Ghanem, 1997). That is, the way a frame is prepared—how and what features of a story are selected, emphasized, elaborated, and excluded—affects public opinion about that issue. There has been extensive research on the influence of second-level agenda setting, ranging from coverage and framing of mass shootings (Holody & Daniel, 2017), to coverage and framing of environmental crises such as the BP oil spill (Kleinnijenhuis et al., 2015), to the coverage and framing of the COVID-19 pandemic (Buturoiu & Gavrilescu, 2021).

Third-Level Agenda Setting

Current research developing the theory goes another step farther and emphasizes a third level of agenda setting. Known as **network agenda setting**, Guo and colleagues proposed that news media not only tell us what issues to think about (issue salience), and how to evaluate the issues based on characteristics and tone (attribute salience), but also how issues and attributes are, or may be, connected (Guo, 2014; Guo & McCombs, 2011; McCombs et al., 2014).That is, when news media repeatedly report on several issues concurrently, the public then makes mind-maps or mental associations between these issues and the tone (attributes) used. For example, if news media routinely report on the "immigration" and "unemployment" together, these two issues not only transfer to public's agenda, but the issues also become "bundled" or intertwined in the public's mind and memory. Rather than assume the public internalizes news issues as separate topics, network agenda setting argues that the way in which news media bundles issues subsequently influences individuals' perceptions of reality; audiences adopt the media-formed combinations of issues as opposed to viewing them as discrete. As Buturoiu and Gavrilescu (2021) found, for instance, participants descriptions of the COVID-19 pandemic mirrored the media's language that highlighted negative effects such as isolation, loneliness, lockdown, and quarantine. Additionally, participants also associated the pandemic with the issues of misinformation and fake news suggesting that topics became combined in the public's mind.

Importantly, however, news media do not influence every issue or every audience member, and those who are affected will not necessarily be affected in the same way. As McCombs and Bell (1974) argued, even with the media's ability to influence, our thoughts, opinions, and actions are not predetermined by the news media's agenda. Certain issues are more likely to influence audience thought, and certain individuals are more likely to be influenced by these issues. Noted earlier and aligned with McCombs and Shaw's (1972) NFO, the media are particularly effective in creating public interest in political issues, such as stories about the candidates and their campaign strategies. Similarly, social issues such as human rights violations, chronic disease, and teen violence also seem to create a high NFO.

In sum, agenda-setting theory states that gatekeepers selectively determine an agenda for what's news. By selecting, excluding, emphasizing, and elaborating certain aspects of the news, public opinions are inevitably shaped and influenced. Thus, the news media influence their audiences to think about selected issues in a certain light.

CULTIVATION THEORY

Like agenda setting, cultivation theory emphasizes media effects. Unlike agenda-setting theory, which focuses on the framing of news within a variety of media, the origins of cultivation theory focused almost exclusively on one medium: television. Broadly speaking, cultivation theory (also termed cultivation analysis) predicts that the amount of time spent watching TV influences viewers' perceptions of reality due to repetitive exposure to common themes (Gerbner et al., 1980; Signorielli & Morgan, 1990). Consequently, individuals who watch more TV are more likely to view the world in "ways that reflect the most commonly repeated messages in television content" as compared with their peers who watch less TV (Bailey, 2006, p. 3).

One of those common and repeated themes found on TV is violence. Consequently, Gerbner and colleagues spent nearly 5 decades examining the portrayal of violence on TV (Gerbner, 1998, 2000; Gerbner et al., 1980; Signorelli et al., 1995). These researchers argued the inescapable violent content of TV programming influences audiences' view of social reality such that they begin to perceive the world as a "mean and scary" place. Before explaining cultivation theory's causal thesis and extension to topics beyond violence, we consider three assumptions.

Assumptions of Cultivation Theory

First, cultivation theory assumes TV is central to American life and culture (Gerbner, 1998). Nearly 99% of Americans have at least one television in their home, and adults watch an average of 5.5 hours of TV programming each day—including live, recorded, and streaming content (Hubbard, 2021). Because of its ubiquity, Gerbner (2000) argued that TV is now the principal source of stories and storytelling in the United States, noting "television is a centralized system of story-telling. Its drama, commercials, news and other programs bring a relatively coherent system of images and messages into every home" (p. 4). Whereas neighbors and family members used to gather around the dinner table, sit on the front porch, or stand at the street corner sharing stories about the day's events or recounting local gossip, now we watch hours of medical and legal dramas, crime series, and "reality" contests. Even the commercials use stories to sell their products. And while traditional, broadcast TV viewing has decreased, 78% of Americans now subscribe to streaming video on demand (SVOD) services such as Netflix and Hulu (Stoll, 2021). Whether your plugged in to watch *NCIS* or streaming *Ozark*, TV content has usurped personal conversation, books, religion, and any other medium as the primary source for storytelling. Moreover, and as Gerbner (1998) pointedly criticized, the stories being told are not "from anyone with anything relevant to tell. They come from a small group of distant conglomerates with something to sell" (p. 176).

Second, cultivation theory assumes TV influences audience perceptions of social reality, thereby shaping American culture in terms of how individuals' reason and relate with others (Gerbner, 1998). In other words, through TV's selective and mass-produced depiction of current events, stories, dramas, comedies, and the like, only certain aspects of social life are presented. Importantly, Gerbner does not suggest that TV programming intends to persuade audiences to think or act in a particular way; instead, he argues that the repetitive representation of commercialized social life is what audiences come to expect and believe as more or less normative.

A final assumption is that TV's effects are limited (Gerbner, 1998), meaning TV is not the only factor—or even the greatest factor—that affects an individual's view of social reality. Although this statement of "limited effects" sounds like backpedaling, Gerbner et al. (1980) argued that the consistency of TV's effect is more revealing than its magnitude. In other words, the effects of TV may not be huge, but they are consistently present and do make a significant difference in the way people think, feel, and interact.

TV's Content—Violence

Although current cultivation research now includes issues other than violence, Gerbner and colleagues were originally interested in the extent to which TV fostered a "mean and scary world" thanks to the frequency of violent programming. First, Gerbner and colleagues' definition of **violence** emphasizes physical force, hurting someone, or killing (Gerbner et al., 1980; Signorelli et al., 1995). More specifically, their research defines violence as the "overt expression of physical force (with or without weapon, against self or others) compelling action against one's will on pain of being hurt and/or killed or threatened to be so victimized as part of the plot" (p. 280). This definition includes cartoon violence, comedic or humorous violence, and so-called accidental violence. Notably, the definition excludes more ambiguous messages such as verbal assaults, threats, and inconsequential gestures, such as sticking out one's tongue or giving someone the finger.

Using this definition of violence, Gerbner and his associates (Gerbner et al., 1980; Signorelli et al., 1995) then developed the **violence index**, an objective research instrument that uses content analysis to measure the prevalence, frequency, and role of characters involved in TV violence (for an overview, see Chapter 2). Researchers have assessed violence annually and have studied more than 50 years of TV programming. Year after year, they have repeatedly found that the prevalence, frequency, and role of TV violence during daytime (8:00 a.m. to 2:00 p.m.) and primetime programming (8:00 p.m. to 11:00 p.m.) differ little. In fact, more than half of primetime programs contain violent content, with about five violent acts per episode and children's programs contain even more violence than adult show. In both cases, heroes and villains alike engage in equal amounts of violence. While TV violence is glamorized for both young and older audiences, it tends to be "sanitized" or "trivialized" within youth programming (Martins & Riddle, 2021).

In addition to demonstrating the pervasiveness of violence, cultivation research also illustrates an imbalance regarding who is victimized on TV (Gerbner, 1998). Specifically, the victims of TV violence are disproportionately of minority backgrounds; Black, Latino, underprivileged, elderly, disabled, or female TV characters are more likely to be victims of violence than are white, middle-class male characters. Recent research analyzing popular streaming series (Netflix original) found that white characters engaged in more "justified" violence, whereas non-white characters were more likely to be engaged in sexual violence, with non-white male characters as perpetrators and non-white female characters as victims (Krongard & Mina Tsay-Vogel, 2020).

Moreover, decades of research show these same minority groups are vastly underrepresented. For example, a content analysis of the most frequently viewed television shows over a 20-year period revealed a severe underrepresentation of Latino, Asian American, and Native American characters (Tukachinsky et al., 2015). In the last few years, representation has increased, and 78% of top programs have some presence of diversity (Nielsen, 2021). However, while quantity of diverse representation has increased, that does not mean the quality of character representation has increased. Case in point, even when a minority identity group is represented (e.g., women, LGBTQ, Hispanic), characters have a lower "share of screen," meaning that the identity group is not represented among the top 10 recurring or lead characters on a show or series. For example, while Black male and female characters were slightly overrepresented across broadcast, cable, and SVOD platforms in 2020, these identity groups were significantly underrepresented as portraying major characters. Only 9% of shows had a lead Black male character and only 8% of shows had a Black female lead. Moreover, TV portrayals of these groups continue to follow genre stereotypes. With regard to violent content, minority persons are significantly less visible on TV than in real life, and at the same time these minority characters are much more likely to be associated with violence. Fair (1993) labeled this paradox **symbolic double jeopardy**. Not surprisingly, then, minority audience members worry the most about being victimized because of TV viewing.

How Are Attitudes Cultivated?

The media do not affect everyone equally; cultivation theory predicts individuals' social attitudes change as their TV viewing increases. In other words, the more TV you watch, the more likely you are to view the world in a way consistent with TV reality. To better understand the relationship between TV viewing and attitudes, we will differentiate types of viewers and explore the two paths through which cultivation is thought to occur.

First, Gerbner et al. (1980) separated heavy viewers from light viewers. **Heavy viewers** average 4 or more hours of TV viewing each day, whereas **light viewers** watch less than 2 hours of televised content each day. As predicted, heavy television types erroneously believed their chances of being involved with violence were 1,000 times greater than crime statistics suggest; these viewers overestimated criminal and police activity and were more likely to agree with statements such as "most people will take advantage of you if they could" (Gerbner et al., 1980). Gerbner aptly named this phenomenon the **mean-world syndrome**, whereby heavy viewers significantly overestimated real-life danger, presumably due to their steady exposure to televised violence. Figure 10.1 depicts the differences between heavy and light TV viewers. TV "reality" doesn't match actual reality, and heavy viewers are more likely to be influenced by TV reality,

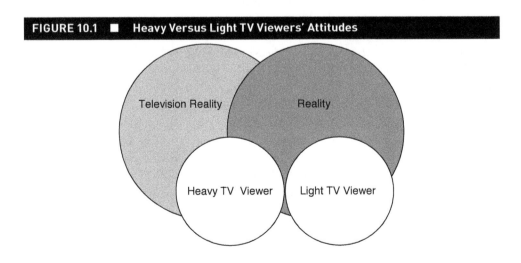

FIGURE 10.1 ■ Heavy Versus Light TV Viewers' Attitudes

whereas light viewers are not. Research also indicates that light viewers watch "selectively," choosing a program to watch and then turning it off, whereas heavy viewers tend to graze, watching whatever shows catch their attention (Gerbner, 1998).

Second, cultivation theory research suggests viewers' attitudes are cultivated in one of two ways: mainstreaming and resonance (Gerbner, 1998). **Mainstreaming** implies viewers—heavy viewers in particular—develop a common view of social reality based on their frequent exposure to the repetitive and dominating images, stories, and messages depicted on TV. Thus, these heavy television types are likely to perceive the world in ways that parallel TV's theatrical portrayal of life—as more corrupt, more crime ridden, more attractive, more sexualized, and so on.

Notably, cultivation theory can also be considered a form of critical theory. Discussed in Chapter 2 as well as later in this chapter, critical theory examines ways in which power is created and maintained, particularly through hidden structures (Craig, 1999). Shanahan and Morgan (1999) argued that cultivation acts as a form of social control such that there is "a slow, steady and cumulative internalization" of the issues and ideology portrayed (p. 18). Mainstreaming is exactly the process by which social control develops; through repeated representations of the same themes and images, audiences come to view these as normative.

Resonance is the second way cultivation is thought to occur (Gerbner, 1998). Resonance involves the viewer's own lived experience, specifically, congruency between one's own encounters and those they see on TV. When individuals who have faced an act of violence in their own lives, then watch violent TV programming, they are forced to replay their own life situations repeatedly. Thus, the TV violence reinforces, or resonates, with their individual experiences and only serves to amplify their suspicion of a mean and scary world. Similarly, if a person feels as though they have been victimized in other ways (being discriminated against because of sex, physical appearance, affectional preference, and so forth), viewing such actions on TV reinforces feelings that such behavior is the norm.

Growth Beyond TV Violence

While cultivation theory initially focused on violent TV content, television has come a long way. Noted earlier, we now have broadcast, cable, and SVOD options, not to mention other types of storytelling media, such as social media, video games, music, and film, each of which is easily accessible with today's smartphone capabilities. Many cable channels have very narrow genres; for example, programming on the Food Network is, you guessed it, all about cooking. While hosts may chop, scramble, whip, or beat their ingredients, that hardly constitutes violence. Thus, recent research on cultivation theory has gone beyond just looking at the amount of television. Today's research considers the ways in which TV genre and other media formats (e.g., video games, social media) influence perceptions of numerous social issues.

For instance, a number of studies have focused on the media's portrayal of obesity and body image, and how these repeated portrayals affect both men and women's attitudes about female bodies (e.g., Levine & Harrison, 2009; Van Vonderen & Kinnally, 2012), including a willingness to undergo plastic surgery (Nabi, 2009). Other research has looked at the cultivation effects of health beliefs and attitudes toward physicians after watching TV medical dramas (Chung, 2014; Serrone et al., 2018) and the relationship between materialism and the reality television genre (Lee et al., 2016). Still other researchers have explored video gamers' acceptance of racial stereotypes (Behm-Morawitz & Ta, 2014) and of sexist attitudes (Cunningham, 2018). While additional lines of research have examined ways in which television viewing affects attitudes toward racial and sexual diversity (Żerebecki et al., 2021), acceptance or rejection of same-sex attraction (Hefner et al., 2015), and teens' attitudes about sex (Malacane & Martins, 2017)

In a meta-analysis of cultivation research spanning five decades, Hermann et al. (2021) found that "cultivation effects remain stable over the decades, implying an enduring relationship between television's message system and viewers' conceptions of social reality, despite immense changes in the institutional structure and technology of television" (p. 515). In other words, while the topics of cultivation research have broadened beyond violence, and the scope of television has changed from primarily broadcast to a blend of technologies and genre-specific channels, the premise still holds—televised content influences perceptions of reality.

SOCIAL COGNITIVE THEORY OF MASS COMMUNICATION

Bandura's (1977, 1986, 1994, 2001) social cognitive theory of mass communication, developed as an extension of social learning theory, has been widely used to study the media's influence on behavior, particularly to understand the relationship between media use and violent behavior. In contrast to cultivation theory's prediction that heavy television viewing distorts people's attitudes and perceptions of social reality; social cognitive theory posits that mass media can play a significant role in influencing behavior through observational learning. We discuss three assumptions of social cognitive theory next.

Assumptions of Social Cognitive Theory

First, whereas social learning theory can apply quite broadly—from learning how to break up with a romantic partner to learning how to perform CPR—Bandura's development of social cognitive theory demonstrates specific concern with mass media's influence on cultural ideology. Like Gerbner, Bandura (2001) was particularly concerned with the mass media's ubiquity and social construction of reality, arguing that "heavy exposure to [television's] symbolic world may eventually make the televised images appear to be the authentic state of human affairs" (p. 282). In other words, the mass media, and TV, are tremendously influential in shaping our view of what is "normal."

A second assumption of social cognitive theory is one's ability to self-reflect (Bandura, 2001). Stated differently, humans are not only actors but also self-examiners of their behavior. This metacognitive activity can be both rightful as well as faulty. You can have accurate self-reflections about the appropriateness of your behavior at the office holiday party, just as you can have wildly distorted ones. The quality of the self-reflection depends in part on the deductive reasoning process, information used in the assessment, and one's own biases.

Beyond the cultivating power of the mass media and humans' self-reflective abilities, Bandura's (1977) most central claim is that "most human behavior is learned observationally through modeling: from observing others one forms an idea of how new behaviors are performed, and on later occasions this coded information serves as a guide for action" (p. 22). In other words, you can learn plenty about relationships, social norms, and acceptable behavior simply by taking note of what others do (and of the consequences) situations. This brings us to our third assumption; learning through vicarious, observational **modeling** saves individuals time and embarrassment from using a behavioral trial-and-error approach. As Bandura noted, "learning would be exceedingly laborious, not to mention hazardous, if people had to rely solely on the effects of their own actions to inform them what to do" (p. 22).

The notion of learning through vicarious observation contrasts classical learning theory. According to classical learning, humans learn primarily through the trial and error of doing, by improving on their own actions, not through observational modeling. Intuitively, however, Bandura's (1977, 1986) idea of learning through observation makes sense. For example, even if you are not a parent right now, you probably have learned quite a bit about raising children from observation—from reflecting on your own parents' child-rearing methods, as well as by watching friends, siblings, and TV parents interact with their children. Thus, social cognitive theorists believe you can learn quite a bit by watching what others do (and don't do) and by noting others' reactions to your behaviors. You can then decide which behaviors to emulate and which to overlook.

Observational Learning

Certainly, not every child who watches *SpongeBob* or the classic *Looney Tunes'* coyote chase the roadrunner lashes out and hits other kids over the head, just as not every adult who watches *Narcos* or *Ozarks* is trafficking drugs. Other factors come into play. Guided by four processes or "subfunctions," social cognitive theory maintains observational learning is more than monkey see, monkey do (Bandura, 2001). Rather, modeling is based on attention, retention, reproduction, and motivational processes. Figure 10.2 provides an overview.

Attention Processes Using social cognitive theory, you can't learn much if you don't observe and pay attention to a particular behavior. Thus, selective attention to a given situation is critical. Bandura (1977, 2001) noted an **attention process** is determined by both the observer's characteristics and the arrangement of intended behaviors. In other words, the observer needs to be attentive, and the actions in question need to be worthy of notice. Obviously, TV stations and other mass media outlets want to make money. To do so, they need audiences. Programmers, scriptwriters, advertisers, and even actors need viewers' attention. Bright colors, rapid edits, the use of popular songs, dazzling special effects, violence, and sex are just a few of the ways the media seek to gain our attention.

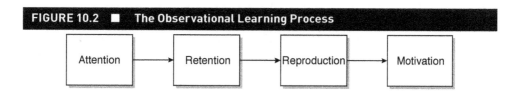

FIGURE 10.2 ■   The Observational Learning Process

Attention → Retention → Reproduction → Motivation

Retention Processes Learning through observational modeling is not inherently a negative process. In fact, learning by observing has many positive aspects. For example, you can learn how to cook by watching *The Kitchen* on the Food Network. Social cognitive theory posits humans can learn without engaging in a particular behavior if they can visually and verbally store the images to which they have attended (Bandura, 1977, 2001). In other words, the **retention process** allows you to learn from the observed behaviors.

That said, the modeling process is more complicated than simply watching and mirroring another's behavior. Instead, observational learning is a cognitive process wherein individuals observe, organize, remember, and mentally rehearse behavior (Bandura, 1977). "Observers who code modeled activities into either words, concise labels, or vivid imagery learn and retain behavior better than those who simply observe or are mentally preoccupied with other matters while watching" (p. 26).

Behavioral Reproduction Processes It only makes sense that to engage in a modeled behavior, one must have the self-efficacy and motor skills necessary to reproduce the activity in question. You might attend to and remember how to tie a chicken before roasting, but if you do not have the strength, coordination, or motor skills necessary, you will not be able to replicate the behavior with much success. As Bandura (1977) noted, in the **reproduction process**, individuals can typically execute a fairly accurate demonstration of a new behavior through modeling; they then refine the action through self-corrective adjustments based on feedback and focused demonstrations of behavioral segments only learned in part. Additionally, social cognitive theory maintains that "modeling is not merely a process of behavioral mimicry, as commonly misconstrued. . . . Subskills must be improvised to suit varying circumstances" (Bandura, 2001, p. 275). Think about learning how to parallel park. You might have practiced successfully in an empty parking lot, using orange cones, rather than automobiles, as markers. Now think about parallel parking between real cars in a congested downtown area during rush hour or on a decline with a crying baby in the backseat. The essential principles of parking and mechanics of the behavior are virtually the same; however, the conditions in which the behavior occurs can influence your ability to complete the task. Thus, you must assess and adjust the behavior based on the circumstance.

Motivational Processes The last piece of observational learning related to social cognitive theory is motivation (Bandura, 1977, 2001). To go from observation to action requires the ability to replicate the behavior as well as the desire, or motivation, to use the learned action. The **motivation process** is inspired by three types of incentives: direct, vicarious, and self-produced (Bandura, 2001). **Direct motivation** occurs when you anticipate receiving a valued reward as a result of displaying an observed behavior. Alternatively, if you anticipate being punished as a result, your motivation to use the behavior diminishes. **Vicarious motivation** occurs when individuals "are motivated by the successes of others who are similar to themselves" (p. 274). Like direct motivation, there are specific outcomes that a person wishes to obtain or avoid; however, instead of personally directed outcomes, the individual observes others benefiting. Perhaps you see your peers receive accolades or a bonus for tackling a difficult project; those valued incentives motivate you to mirror their work habits. Conversely, people are typically deterred when they see negative consequences for their peers. If Shelby gets fired for checking her cell phone while on the sales floor, that will likely deter others from using their phone as well. Finally, with **self-produced motivation**, individuals rely on their own personal standards, engaging in observed activities they find personally worthwhile and refusing to participate in those activities of which they disapprove. Instead of extrinsic rewards (or punishments) as incentives, self-produced motivation occurs from inherent self-satisfaction.

Dual Paths of Influence

Thus far, we've focused on what Bandura (2001) terms a **direct path of influence**. That is, the media influence viewers directly, from creating mass-produced, attention-getting messages, to enabling behavior, to providing vicarious incentives to replicate actions so the viewer changes their behavior. Bandura noted that industries such as food and fashion rely on this direct path of influence coupled with vicarious motivation. Ads show actors living their best lives while drinking a certain beverage or enjoying others' adoration because of their jewelry, hair style, or clothing selections; the very purpose of the ads is to encourage modeling through consumerism.

A second route, the **socially mediated path of influence**, also links mass media to behavior but does so indirectly through interpersonal networks. In this socially (or interpersonally) mediated path, mass media connect individuals to larger, more influential social networks or communities. These mediated influences occur in a variety of ways. For example, when individuals go on to discuss a show, song, or news story within their social networks, that media example becomes a "transactional experience." Consider shows, memes, videogames, or YouTube videos that get shared or talked about among friends, family, or colleagues; they live on and can become influential.

In another example of socially mediated influence, individuals receive guidance, incentives, and social support, making behavioral change more likely. For example, religiously watching *Dr. Phil* may not provide enough motivation for you to change your dead-end job or stand up to an exploitative relative. However, *Dr. Phil* also has resources, newsletters, and strategies on the show's website. Here, people can connect with a community of people with similar problems, get advice from experts, and receive referrals to therapists, ultimately providing the motivation necessary to change their lives. Here, the media's influence is facilitated by participation in a related social network.

A third way that the social mediated path can work is simply through an individual's connection to other adopters. Specifically, Bandura (2001) argued that the media's influence could be entirely socially mediated, with no personal exposure. In other words, " people who have had no exposure to the media are influenced by adopters who have the exposure and then, themselves, become the transmitters of the new ways" (p. 286). Thus, influence is spread through intermediaries. Think of how dance moves like the "Floss" spread. While many kids learned it directly from modeling the moves shown on the video game Fortnite (or maybe even from the original source, YouTuber sensation, "The Backpack Kid"), others learned the moves indirectly from watching their social network—those peers who had played the game and subsequently did the dance moves. Thus, you don't need to have ever played Fortnite or have even heard of The Backpack Kid videos to learn the floss. All told, while media can directly teach us behaviors, much of what we learn from the media is facilitated through interpersonal and social networks.

Modeling and Media Violence

As a theoretical construct, observational learning represents an impartial process; it is not inherently negative or positive. As Bandura (1977) argued, observational learning is simply a primary means by which humans learn. When applied within the realm of mass communication, however, research shows such modeled learning can be hazardous, particularly for viewers of media violence (Bandura, 1986). Television is but one mass medium in which violent action is both common and frequently rewarded. After all, Superman doesn't save Metropolis from Lex Luther by holding a sit-in.

Remember that for observational learning to occur, the first step is to gain attention. Violent content can be easily found in all types of entertainment programming and on TV newscasts. Violent acts grab viewers' attention (Bandura, 1986). Aggressive behaviors such as kicking, punching, stabbing, shooting, and biting are also easy to remember and reproduce, the second and third steps in the modeling process. Finally, positive motivation is easily introduced when fictitious characters as well as real-life heroes are rewarded (or not punished) for their aggression. As Bandura (2001) contended, aggression, particularly in entertainment media, is viewed as "a preferred solution to interpersonal conflicts; it is acceptable and relatively successful; and it is socially sanctioned by superheroes triumphing over evil by violent means. Such portrayals legitimize, glamorize, and trivialize human violence" (p. 277).

Importantly, the relationship between observing violence and having the motivation to engage in violence is critical. According to social cognitive theory, if viewers know how to do something, they are more likely to do it, particularly when they have positive incentives, such as getting 15 minutes of fame or getting peers' attention and respect. Thus, it is not as simple as "monkey see, monkey do." Simply watching aggressive content doesn't automatically lead one to engage in violent behavior; it is the positive reward associated with the action that entices one to model observed behaviors (Bandura, 1977, 1986; Bandura et al., 1963; Huesmann et al., 2003). If violent behavior is condemned, viewers are less likely to copy the aggression. Note it is not enough that "bad guys" are punished on television; many of the "good guys" are rewarded for using violence to triumph over the bad guy. Indeed, as Bandura (1986) argued, "Given that aggressive lifestyles are portrayed as prevalent, socially acceptable, and highly functional, it is not surprising that viewing violence is conducive to aggressive conduct" (p. 292).

Growth Beyond TV Violence: Where Else Does Modeling Occur?

Just like with cultivation theory, social cognitive theory of mass communication has grown through intension. That is, the theory has been used to understand media effects in contexts other than violence (e.g., health behaviors) and among other mediums (e.g., social media, videogames). Beyond violence, social cognitive theory has been used to understand other frequently televised behaviors such as materialism, altruism, celebrity behavior, and even teen pregnancy. In one experimental study, Aubrey et al. (2014) discovered that the teen viewers of *16 and*

Pregnant were actually "more likely to believe that the benefits of teen pregnancy outweigh risks" (p. 1156). Rather than serve as a deterrent from teen pregnancy, the authors posited that the celebrity associated with being on the show may serve as unintended, positive motivation rather than as negative reinforcement. While teen pregnancy has declined nationwide, there are real-life examples of teens purposefully engaging in "pregnancy pacts," such as intentionally attempting to become teenaged mothers (Kingsbury, 2008), possibly for the glamour they see on TV. Similarly, Stefanone and Lackaff (2009) found that heavy viewers of reality TV programming were more likely to model the characters' patterns of disclosure and to engage in "celebrity-like" behaviors such as broadcasting about themselves on social media platforms. Meanwhile, an analysis of the popular Netflix series, *13 Reasons Why*, investigated both positive and negative behavioral modeling opportunities related to bullying, sexual assault, substance abuse, and suicide (Wang & Parris, 2021).

Beyond television, social media has given way to new opportunities for media modeling. Indeed, social media platforms such as TikTok explicitly encourage modeling through "challenges," some of which are innocent dance competitions, while others encourage destructive or even violent behavior (Bellware, 2021). In a positive vein, Kashian and Liu (2020) applied the theory to examine the relationship between exercise efficacy and social media. They found that viewing others' posts about successful exercise experiences was positively correlated with the viewers' own self-efficacy—or belief that they could reproduce the maneuvers. That is, viewers of the posts subsequently felt more confident in their own abilities to be successful. While the study did not investigate whether the viewers actually modeled the behaviors, the research adds to the theory by applying it to a new medium.

All told, social cognitive theory predicts the mass media have noteworthy influence because humans learn observationally through a four-step process: attention, retention, motor reproduction, and motivation. For communication scholars, media producers, parents, and viewers, social cognitive theory adds a new level of complexity to TV and media. That is, if individuals are exposed to media content that is easily replicable and socially rewarding, viewers, particularly younger audience members, are more likely to try and emulate that content.

ENCODING/DECODING THEORY

At the same time American scholars were focusing on the extent to which the mass media affect their audience, scholars in other parts of the world were investigating the same issue but with a different focus. You may remember that in Chapter 2 we described the social scientific and humanistic approaches to understanding communication. We also mentioned a third perspective called a critical approach. Theories that take a critical perspective seek to uncover the extent to which communication processes create and reflect differences in power (Craig, 1999). Also mentioned in conjunction with cultivation theory (this chapter), the goal of such theories is to raise awareness of inequities. One critical approach that addresses media effects was created by British sociologist Stuart Hall. Most called encoding/decoding theory, it is also called cultural studies, preferred reading theory, or reception theory.

Assumptions of Encoding/Decoding Theory

Four assumptions set the foundation for understanding encoding/decoding theory (Hall, 1973). First, Hall calls the focus of his work **cultural studies** rather than media studies because he believes the media are simply one mechanism for the development and dissemination of cultural ideologies. An **ideology** is a mental framework used to understand the world; it includes language, concepts, categories, and images we use to make sense out of our experiences (Hall, 1986). Typically, ideologies work at a low level of consciousness. Because we live in a particular culture, we tend not to notice cultural ideologies; it is akin to asking a fish to describe water. For fish, water just is. The same is true of ideologies; they are taken-for-granted truisms. Hall believes the media tend to produce messages that support the **dominant ideology**, meaning a view of the world that supports the status quo. For example, an essential US. ideology is the power of the individual. Americans believe a single person can make a difference in the world. Now consider successful US novels and films such as the *Hunger Games* and *Divergent*. On the surface, both series are female empowerment action yarns. However, underneath the surface,

> [B]oth "Divergent" and "The Hunger Games" are fundamentally works of propaganda disguised as fantasy or science fiction. They're not propaganda on behalf of the left or the right, exactly, or at least not the way we generally use those words in America. They are propaganda for the ethos of individualism, the central ideology of consumer capitalism, which also undergirds both major political parties and almost all-American public discourse. It's an ideology that transcends notions of left and right and permeates the entire atmosphere with the seeming naturalness of oxygen in the air. (O'Hehir, 2014, para. 2)

O'Hehir (2014) concluded that both films are "designed to remind us how grateful we should be to live in a society where we can be 'ourselves,' where we can enjoy unspecified and entirely vague freedoms" (para. 5). Hall argues mass media messages are a cultural production because they provide a means to create, challenge, reproduce, or change cultural ideologies. According to Hall (1986), the process whereby our cultural ideologies are reinforced is called **articulation**.

The second assumption of encoding/decoding theory is that the meaning of a message is not fixed or determined entirely by the sender (Hall, 1973). In the process of **encoding** or creating a message, the sender typically develops a message using the signs and symbols of a cultural ideology. However, Hall suggests the interpretation, or **decoding**, of the message is not guaranteed. Consider the 2017 Pepsi ad featuring Kendall Jenner joining a protest movement and handing a police officer a Pepsi. Many viewers believed the advertisement trivialized the Black Lives Matter movement. The ad was quickly removed, and the company posted a statement saying "Pepsi was trying to project a global message of unity, peace, and understanding. Clearly, we missed the mark and apologize" (Victor, 2017, para. 2). Here is a clear case of variations in decoding.

Third, encoding/decoding theory assumes all messages are encoded using an ideology (Hall, 1973). That is, there is no such thing as "value-free" communication. Although we might not immediately perceive the meaning system embedded into a television show, song, or movie, Hall assures us that "every language—every symbol—coincides with an ideology" (Becker, 1984, p. 72). Because we are not likely to see the presence of ideologies we endorse, however, we do not often recognize the power built into the messages.

Finally, encoding/decoding theory is grounded in the belief in an active audience. Hall believes audience members can challenge the ideologies embedded in the messages they receive (Hall, 1973). Despite the level of optimism inherent in this belief, Hall does not believe recognizing and wrangling over ideology is easy. After all, it is much easier to become an unthinking recipient of media content than it is to critically confront who benefits and who loses from beliefs. Because he comes from a critical tradition, however, he encourages people to do so.

"Reading" a Message

To encourage a critical analysis of what we encounter in the media, the central idea of encoding/decoding theory is that even though the media present us with messages that support the dominant ideology, media consumers do not have to interpret the messages in this way (Hall, 1973). Hall describes three ways to interpret—or *read*—a message. To illustrate these ways of interpreting a message, consider a recent *Los Angeles Times* headline that read "Texas School Shooter Killed Girl Who Turned Down His Advances" (Hennessy-Fiske et al., 2018). The headline is descriptive: it indicates what happened to whom and why. But the headline itself has an embedded ideology when you look a bit deeper. Let's discuss the three ways the theory says you can interpret this headline.

First, encoding/decoding theory says the first way an audience can interpret a message is by engaging in a **preferred reading** (Hall, 1973). In this case, the receiver of the message uses the **dominant code** (i.e., the dominant ideology) to interpret the content of the message. That is, the receiver understands and accepts the values and beliefs embedded in the message; this type of reading is considered easy and natural. Because the dominant code is used, the reader does not recognize that there is an ideology inherent in the headline. In fact, many of you might be reading this and wondering what ideology is embedded in the headline. If so, it is because you have used the dominant code.

In contrast, some receivers use the **negotiated code**. When using the negotiated code, the receiver accepts the dominant ideology in general but engages in some selective interpretation to better fit their view of the world (Hall, 1973). "Essentially, the receiver only accepts the preferred meanings that he/she wants to accept, while 'misunderstanding' the meanings incompatible with his/her lifestyle" (Platt, 2004, p. 4). In the case of the Texas school shooting headline, perhaps the reader is overwhelmed by the number of school shootings in the United States, so the headline is interpreted yet another preventable tragedy. Or the reader might be a strong advocate of Second Amendment rights, so the headline is viewed as the precursor to another round of alarmist gun control rhetoric.

Finally, receivers might use the **oppositional code**, in which the receiver identifies the ideological bias in the message (Hall, 1973). Individuals who use the oppositional code see the preferred reading, but they deconstruct the message and then reconstruct it from a different point of view. To illustrate this, consider an alternative headline to the school shooting story: "Texas School Shooter Kills Girl He Had Stalked." Now do you see the ideology in the original headline. The original headline implicitly suggested that there was a reason for the shooting, and that the victim played a role in her own murder. When you change the phrasing, you realize that the shooter had wronged the victim twice, once through stalking her and then by killing her, and the media was also victimizing her by implying that she was in any way at fault for what happened. The dominant ideology in this case is one that implies that female victims "do something wrong" that causes a crime to occur. We see this when people question why female victims were at a particular location at a particular time, or by questioning a victim's choice of apparel as if what she wears explains why she was victimized.

Decoding is the Central Process

Although Hall's theory is called encoding/decoding theory, the main thrust of the theory focuses on the decoding process. According to Hall, it is only when mediated messages are decoded that they have any meaning, and we can consider possible media effects (Hall, 1973). Hall argues most theories of mass communication ignore the decoding process because decoding tends to happen at an extremely low level of consciousness. He also points out that a full understanding of decoding is difficult because most people tend to confuse denotative and connotative meaning. **Denotative** meaning refers to a literal meaning; you might think about it as a dictionary definition. **Connotative** meaning refers to all associated meanings. As an example, think about the meaning of the word *terrorist*. As Procter (2004) points out, most people might believe they are interpreting the term in a purely objective way, but it is virtually impossible to separate the meaning of a concept from feelings about the concept, previous experiences associated with it, and value judgments about it. As such, it is the connotative meanings that make up an ideology. According to Hall, media effects are insidious, not necessarily because the media encode messages supportive of the status quo but because audience members who use the dominant code to read the messages repeatedly eventually come to believe the dominant ideology is "not simply plausible and universal, but commonsense" (Procter, 2004, p. 67). To assist you with being able to read a media message from multiple points of view, select any text (e.g., a newscast, a magazine advertisement, a sitcom) and try to accomplish the tasks associated with each of the three codes in Figure 10.3.

Oppositional Does Not Mean Against

Before concluding our section on encoding/decoding theory, it is important to be clear that the term *oppositional* does not necessarily imply someone is against dominant values or beliefs; it simply means the individual doing an oppositional reading of a message understands the dominant ideology but chooses to interpret the message differently. When messages are reinterpreted in ways not intended by the source, new ideologies are formed and can take root (Pillai, 1992).

FIGURE 10.3   ■   Questions to Answer Using Each of the Codes

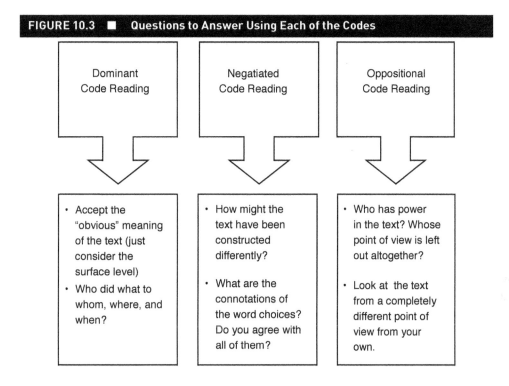

Similarly, Hall is not concerned with a personal or isolated oppositional reading; he is concerned with the use of an oppositional code among social groups, with a particular focus on minority groups, as a means for increasing power (Procter, 2004). The use of an oppositional code is likely to be viewed as deviant by those who endorse a dominant ideology, but Hall endorses as a critical approach any cultural resistance that might result in political empowerment.

SUMMARY AND RESEARCH APPLICATIONS

In this chapter, we discussed four theories of mass media—specifically, theories about how to understand the power and influence of the mass media. First, agenda-setting theory states that the news media do not tell us what to think, but they do tell us what to think about. Agenda-setting theory has been applied not only to political issues but also to social issues. Xu et al. (2022) examined the relationship between second-level agenda setting of influenza-related news coverage and actual flu vaccine uptake in the population. News frames that emphasized death and serious illness predicted greater vaccination uptake rates in both adults and children. News frames that also emphasized prevention strategies, knowledge about influenza viruses, and public accountability also predicted increased vaccine uptake among adults. In a different vein,

Trifiro and Zhang (2021) examined Twitter's role in political agenda setting, specifically coverage of the candidates in the US 2020 Democratic primary. Their analysis revealed that despite the diverse candidates (four women, four people of color), white male candidates received disproportionately more Twitter coverage. Furthermore, it was mainstream media's Twitter content that influenced public perception of the white male candidates, whereas minority candidates, who didn't receive such coverage, were able to impact public perception via their own tweets.

Our second mass media approach, cultivation theory, suggests that individuals who watch large quantities of TV develop skewed perceptions of reality that align more with the dramatized representations found on televised storytelling rather than real life. For example, cultivation research has found that heavy viewers hold more negative attitudes about immigrants (Atwell Seate & Mastro, 2016), while Elmore et al. (2020) found that participants who perceived media portrayals to be more realistic and congruent with their peers also were more likely to believe in rape myths, such as the victim "asked for it" or that the perpetrator "didn't mean to" do it. In a different vein, Foss and Blake (2019) found that entertainment education can positively influence attitudes about breastfeeding. After viewing television clips that showed characters breastfeeding in public, participants' own attitudes toward public breastfeeding improved.

Discussed third, social cognitive theory of the mass media is based on social learning theory, specifically the idea that when individuals are cognitively aware, physically able and motivated they will model their behavior after esteemed others, including people or characters shown in the media. Current research shows behavioral modeling is particularly visible with gender roles. For instance, Golden and Jacoby (2017) found that girls who consumed a lot of media associated with Disney Princesses tended to engage in more stereotypical, gender-based play. Comparably, straight adult males who remembered idolizing superheroes during childhood reported holding stricter ideals for appearance and valued traditional masculine norms (Roberts et al., 2021).

Lastly, Hall's encoding/decoding theory is also concerned with the power and influence of the media, contending the media develop, propagate, and reinforce cultural ideologies. In doing so, audience members who use the dominant code to interpret messages assume this dominant ideology is the "right" or "normal" way of viewing the world, when in fact, other interpretations exist. Molina-Guzmán's (2016) study investigated the preferred, negotiated, and oppositional readings of the 2014–2015 media coverage of #OscarsSoWhite. Meanwhile, Hall's encoding-decoding theory is extended to examine power differences that underscore interactive media affordances (Shaw, 2017). Shaw argued that "interactive communication technologies require that we treat audience activity as expected," but what happens when users find other affordances? Shaw used the topics of cheating and mudding in videogames, arguing these subversive activities could be considered oppositional uses of digital gaming (Table 10.3).

TABLE 10.3 ■ Additional Theories of Mass Media

Theory	Main Idea
Excitation-transfer theory	The theory posits that the emotional arousal experienced while viewing media can be transferred to other intense emotions, at least temporarily (Zillmann, 1991). Related to media effects such as aggression, the arousal induced by exposure to media violence may become misplaced. If the viewer is unaware of this transfer, the hostile emotion may be "re-energized" by real-life stressors and lead to aggressive behavior.
Framing theory	Framing theory extends second-level agenda setting by taking a macrolevel viewpoint and considering the impact of culture on frames. Framing theory emphasizes ways in which communicators "frame" media messages not only through topic selection and attribute salience but also through diagnosing, evaluating, and prescribing (Entman, 1993).
Priming	Priming theory, also considered an extension of agenda-setting theory, predicts that media coverage not only influences what topics the public considers important, but coverage also affects public opinion by making certain topics more accessible (Iyengar & Kinder, 1987; Weaver, 2007).
Differential Susceptibility to Media Effects Model (DSMM)	The DSMM seeks to explain media effects associated with disaster media coverage, particularly the behavioral and mental health effects of viewing televised trauma (Houston et al., 2018; Valkenburg & Peter, 2013). One media effect observed in the model is a transactional effect, whereby the anxiety created by exposure to disaster media only serves to promote more media consumption.

DISCUSSION QUESTIONS

1. Look at the front page (print or digital) of two different news sources. What is the agenda and how is it framed? Specifically, what stories are selected and given coverage? What stories are excluded (for example, a news story appears on one source but not the other)? Select one story that appears in both sources and look for examples of emphasis and elaboration.

2. Although cultivation research initially focused solely on television as the central source of storytelling, and violence as a central theme, consider ways in which other mediums might cultivate other attitudes (besides violence and fear). For example, how might the prevalence of filters on social media apps cultivate perceptions of reality?

3. Originally developed to understand the modeling of media violence, social cognitive theory can explain other behavioral modeling. What other activities are shown widely in the media that might also be ripe for modeling (consider the four-step process of observational learning)? Consider both positive and negative behaviors as well as different audiences (children, teens, adults).

4. Identify another example of ideology (children, teens, adults).

5. Identify another example of ideological messaging found in mass media that can be "read" differently. Analyze the message for the dominant code, negotiated code, and oppositional code. What power structures are in play that contribute to these different interpretations?

KEY TERMS

Agenda (p. 187)

Articulation (p. 202)

Attention process (p. 197)

Attribute agenda setting (p. 190)

Connotative (p. 204)

Cultural studies (p. 202)

Decoding (p. 202)

Denotative (p. 204)

Direct motivation (p. 198)

Legacy media (p. 184)

Digital-native media (p. 184)

Web-native media (p. 184)

Participatory media (p. 184)

Direct path of influence (p. 199)

Dominant code (p. 203)

Dominant ideology (p. 202)

Elaboration (p. 189)

Emphasis (p. 189)

Encoding (p. 202)

Exclusion (p. 189)

First-level agenda setting (p. 187)

Framing (p. 189)

Gatekeepers (p. 189)

Ideology (p. 202)

Length (p. 188)

Mainstreaming (p. 195)

Mass communication (p. 184)

Mass media (p. 184)

Mean-world syndrome (p. 194)

Modeling (p. 197)

Motivation process (p. 198)

Need for orientation (p. 188)

Negotiated code (p. 203)

Network agenda setting (p. 191)

Oppositional code (p. 203)

Position (p. 188)

Preferred reading (p. 203)

Reproduction process (p. 198)

Resonance (p. 195)

Retention process (p. 198)

Second-level agenda setting (p. 190)

Selection (p. 189)

Self-produced motivation (p. 199)

Socially mediated path of influence (p. 199)

Symbolic double jeopardy (p. 194)

Third-level agenda setting (p. 184)

Traditional media (p. 184)

Vicarious motivation (p. 198)

Violence index (p. 193)

CASE STUDY 10
TikToking for Attention

Chestnutville High School students Ginger Lane and Larissa Rogers were your average teenaged students. Not exactly in the "popular crowd," they weren't unpopular either. They had friends but didn't really feel important or remarkable, not in the way that others were celebrated for their athletic, academic, or musical talent. Particularly after suffering through remote learning and all the restrictions imposed during the COVID-19 pandemic, they longed to be extraordinary.

One Saturday, as the two friends scrolled through social media, they noticed a few of their peers had commented on some popular TikTok dance challenges. The pair decided this was it—their way to being insta-famous. They didn't want to be recognized for doing something awful; no, they just wanted to be noticed and to have people know their names. Plus, they were both good dancers, having taken gymnastics and jazz as kids. The friends spent the rest of the evening capturing their moves and uploading the videos for at least a dozen challenges.

Their plan worked! Several of their videos got immediate traction and received numerous likes, shares, and even comments from some of their classmates. These likes and shares encouraged the pair to start their own viral dance challenges. They searched YouTube for creative inspiration, and then over the next few weeks Ginger and Larissa choreographed their dances, recorded them in funny locations, and then posted the videos, inviting others to take up their challenges. Their latest challenge asked viewers to record themselves dancing the "cancan" on top of school cafeteria tables.

Meanwhile, another social media dare was circulating. In this challenge, students were encouraged to record themselves vandalizing school property (Doubek, 2021). News media outlets were quick to pick up on the story after school officials reported similarly strange acts of destruction, such as toilets clogged with food, stolen soap dispensers, and missing ceiling tiles. A student at a neighboring school got caught while filming himself trying to remove paper towel dispensers. Headlines and stories issued warnings, alerting school authorities, parents, and community members of what was happening. Not only was the challenge promoting illegal behavior, but students across the country were also actually trying it. News outlets reported on the "drastic" and "draconian" disciplinary measures some districts were taking at an effort to prevent such damage, such as closing school bathrooms altogether. Districts were also pressing criminal charges against violators and in some cases, holding parents responsible for the cost of long-term repairs, such as leaky pipes.

Parents of Chestnutville students were alarmed at what was happening elsewhere and demanded to know what their district was doing to stop the behavior. On high alert, the Chestnutville administration quickly passed a "zero-tolerance" policy for cell phone and media use. Students would be prohibited from having cell phones on their possession at any time during the school day. Phones had to be stored in their lockers. Additionally, anyone caught photographing, videoing, or recording anything not explicitly part of class instruction would be suspended and lose extracurricular privileges for the rest of the year. Ginger and Larissa's "Cafeteria Can-Can" challenge seemed doomed.

News stories continued to circulate the topic, discussing why these dangerous trends surface in the first place. One psychologist opined that the problem stems from a "dangerous combination" of narcissistic, attention-seeking teens coupled with a lack of parental control, citing the fact that many parents don't monitor their kids' social media use. Another story took a deep dive into TikTok, criticizing the company for not doing more to prevent viral spread of videos promoting dangerous activity.

While the new rules paused the girls' "Cafeteria Can-Can" dance challenge, they weren't deterred from exploiting their newfound popularity. Instead of curbing their activity, Ginger and Larissa found ways to sneak their phones into classes. Rather than share dance moves in silly locations, however, they started capturing photos of other students also illicitly using their phones during class. They used the pseudonym CHSPaparazzi and started an Instagram account where they posted the secretly taken photos along with the hashtag #freethephones. Within 72 hours, the #freethephones movement at Chestnutville High School had taken hold. Every day, latest photos were posted with students brazenly breaking the school's zero-tolerance policy, with catchphrases such as "zero tolerance for lonely phones."

Questions for Consideration

1. How did the news media "frame" the initial reports of school vandalism? How did that frame change?

2. Based on what you know about Ginger and Larissa and teenagers in general, how have the girls' attitudes been cultivated by repeated media exposure? How might mainstreaming and resonance play a part in Ginger and Larissa's cultivation?

3. Apply social cognitive theory's assumptions and observational learning process to the case study. Even after the school developed dire consequences for having phones and taking videos, how does the theory explain the fact that Ginger and Larissa still have sufficient motivation to carry on with their plan?

4. What is the dominant code presented in Chestnutville's "zero-tolerance" policy? Do Ginger and Larissa rely on the preferred reading, negotiated code, or oppositional code when interpreting the rule? Explain your reasoning.

5. Do any of the mass media theories provide "better" explanations than the others? Why do you believe this to be the case? What situations might surface that would make a different theory or combination of theories better at explaining the situation?

11 MEDIATED COMMUNICATION

Is your LinkedIn profile up to date? How often do you tweet? Do you know what time it is if you don't have your smartphone? Are you more likely to watch TV shows and movies on a television or on a tablet? There are a bewildering array of communication technologies available to us, with new platforms being launched nearly every month and old platforms slowly becoming obsolete (AOL anyone?). With so many communication channels available to us, being a competent communicator requires selecting the appropriate method to share a particular message. This chapter focuses on **mediated communication** channels—how mediated channels become popular as well as how and why we use them.

DEFINING MEDIATED COMMUNICATION

When we casually use the term *media*, we often mean the "mass media"—those large organizations responsible for producing the content we see on television and in the movies; the recordings we listen to on the radio and on our smart devices; and the books and periodicals we read in print, on an e-reader, or on the web (discussed in Chapter 10). This type of mass communication is decidedly different from mediated communication.**Mediated communication** includes any message in which there is a device, third party, or electronic mechanism that facilitates communication between the sender and receiver. Mediated communication can be further divided into interpersonal and masspersonal media. **Interpersonal media** include channels that provide individuals with direct and one-to-one interaction, such as texting or phone and video calls (Choi & Toma, 2014; Choi & Toma, 2017). In contrast, **masspersonal media** blend aspects of interpersonal media with mass communication to provide individuals with direct and large audience interaction (Choi & Toma, 2017; O'Sullivan, 2005). One obvious form of masspersonal media is **social media**— "digital technologies that allow people to connect, interact, produce and share content" (Lewis, 2010, p. 2). These user-generated media vary in nature and purpose and include blogs, microblogging sites like Twitter, wikis, social networking sites like Facebook and LinkedIn, podcasting, video and photo sharing sites such as YouTube and Instagram, and discussion forums. Social media are considered distinct from traditional media because they are based on user-generated content (versus "institutional" or "organizational" content). Additionally, the costs of creating and disseminating the content on social platforms are either free or relatively inexpensive.

Although the original focus of social media was on its ability to assist individuals with achieving their personal goals (Vorvoreanu, 2009), increasingly, people use social media to achieve professional goals. This is particularly evident in the realm of public relations; PR scholars such as Avery et al. (2010) claim "virtually no organization can afford to neglect its social media presence" (pp. 198–199). In part, this is because social media allow for one group or individual to easily persuade other groups or individuals (Blossom, 2009). Yet there is little evidence social media are different from any other channel available to communicators.

A critical understanding of the role of social media in our lives requires us to understand the nature of mediated forms of communication. Table 11.1 provides an overview of the four theories we discuss in this chapter. The first theory we discuss, channel expansion theory, extends media richness theory (MRT), which focuses on choosing the right channel for a given message, particularly within organizational settings. Second, social information processing model argues that, despite the "leanness" of online environments that lack many nonverbal cues, individuals adapt and use the tools available to create *pseudo*-rich interpersonal communication. Third, we discuss uses and gratifications theory, which centers on the choices audience members make in order to fulfill their needs. Finally, we offer spiral of silence as a way to understand how media and social media influence the perception of dominant ideas and the expression of public opinion.

TABLE 11.1 ■ Overview of Mediated Communication Theories	
Channel Expansion Theory	Individuals select communication channels based on channel characteristics, individual experiences, and social influence.
Social Information Processing Theory	Identifies three phases of computer mediated communication, which range from impersonal, to interpersonal, to hyperpersonal, with associated issues of impression management.
Uses and Gratifications 2.0	Users select particular media to both meet their own needs and because of the affordances the media provide (modality, agency, interactivity, and navigability).
Spiral of Silence	Individuals who believe they hold a minority point of view will refrain from expressing that point of view publicly.

CHANNEL EXPANSION THEORY

Controversial "Mandalorian" star Gina Carano apparently learned of her dismissal from Lucasfilm via Twitter (Cronin, 2021). And, according to an article in Harper's Bazaar, Chrishell Stause of Netflix "Selling Sunset" fame claimed her husband/co-star Justin Hartley texted her that he had filed for divorce (Mackelden, 2020). Meanwhile, Forbes reported that the electric scooter-sharing startup, Bird, laid off 400 workers in a 2-minute Zoom call (Kelly, 2020). Needless to say, none of the recipients of these messages were happy with the way in which the news was conveyed. While technology may be more efficient, is it really okay to conduct layoffs via Zoom call? Or announce an employee's termination via Twitter? Our first theory in this chapter, channel expansion theory provides guidance as to selecting a medium to fit the message.

Media Richness and Channel Selection

Channel expansion theory (Carlson & Zmud, 1999) provides an example of how theories change and grow by **extension** (see Chapter 2). Specifically, channel expansion theory was developed in response to inconsistencies in its predecessor, media richness theory (MRT). Developed by Daft and Lengel (1986), MRT recognizes that as new communication technologies or channels develop, the decision about the best way to send a message becomes more complex. Communicators should consider a message's complexity first, then select an appropriate channel based on that medium's richness. Channel expansion theory (Carlson & Zmud, 1999) builds on this premise by adding the concepts of individual experience and social influence.

Far from the days when there were only a handful of ways for managers to communicate with employees, technology has exploded, offering a wide variety of electronic communication channels or media. From email to SMS text, Teams, Slack, Yammer, and Remind, how do we know which one to use? In its original formulation, MRT was meant serve as a prescriptive theory for improved organizational communication. Specifically, a media richness framework advises management professionals to select the communication channel that best corresponds with the ambiguity of the message content (Daft & Lengel, 1986; Lengel & Daft, 1988). Moreover, managers who successfully match the channel with the message are considered more effective.

According to Daft and Lengel (1986), communication channels vary in their information carrying capacity, or **media richness**. They asserted that we can objectively determine the richness of a medium by assessing four **channel characteristics:** (1) speed of feedback, meaning synchronous or asynchronous capacities, (2) the ability to personalize the message, (3) the availability of multiple nonverbal cues, and (4) language variety. Consequently, face-to-face interactions are considered most "rich," with various electronic media falling in the middle, and mass-produced or mass-printed materials appearing as lean media (see Table 10.1). We can probably all understand the difference between an in-person, face-to-face lecture versus an asynchronous, online video lecture. In person, the professor can immediately recognize individuals and can craft or adjust messages to the needs of those individuals. As well, both the professor and the students can use tone, facial expressions, gestures, pauses, eye contact, and other nonverbal cues during the exchange. Finally, the instructor can repeat or change the vocabulary or jargon depending on the audience's needs. Contrast this example with an asynchronous, online class session. Here, you watch a prerecorded lecture on your own. If you don't understand something in the recording, the video can't be fine-tuned in the moment to adapt to your confusion; all that you can do is rewatch the same segment again. Moreover, a video lecture is likely produced for multiple sections of a course and not tailored to particular individuals or current events and experiences. As such, the asynchronous lecture is considered a "leaner" medium. Shown in Table 11.2, MRT richness theory organizes media from rich to lean based on each channel's characteristics.

A second consideration of MRT concerns the nature of the message to be sent. Influenced by Karl Weick (see Chapter 9), MRT focuses on message ambiguity (Daft & Lengel, 1984,

TABLE 11.2 ■ Continuum of Media Richness	
Rich Media	**Face-to-face**
↑	Video conferencing, interactive websites, social networking sites
	Telephone
	Email
	Texting, instant messaging, microblogs
	Video or audio recordings
↓	Memos, letters
Lean Media	Bulk mail, brochures, pamphlets, flyers

1986). **Ambiguity** refers to task complexity or the possibility of multiple interpretations. If the goal of communication is shared understanding (as Daft and Lengel assumed), then ambiguous messages run a greater risk of being misunderstood. Imagine working for an organization facing a financial crisis. The senior management team has decided that, rather than lay off employees, they will reduce employee benefits. You might have many questions about this decision. Will this affect all employees? Is it a permanent decision, or will benefits be returned once the crisis is over? Will the elimination of these benefits really solve the financial problems, or might there still be layoffs sometime in the future? Can individuals choose which benefits are reduced? Health care might be a major concern to some employees, and retirement benefits might be of greater concern to others. In short, this type of situation is highly ambiguous.

According to the original theory, the more ambiguous the message, the richer the medium should be used to communicate this message (Daft & Lengel, 1984, 1986). In the employment situation described above, MRT would recommend a synchronous townhall meeting or even small group meetings as the best channel to explain the decision and to answer questions; an email blast would not be an appropriate channel choice. On the other hand, using email might be perfectly appropriate for announcing the meeting itself, as the time and date of a meeting is not particularly ambiguous.

Channel Experience

As indicated earlier, channel expansion theory extends MRT. Both assume that communication effectiveness is more likely when the channel selected corresponds with the ambiguity of the message. An equivocal message that is communicated via lean media is likely to exacerbate uncertainty and create misunderstanding. Conversely, using a very rich medium to communicate straightforward information is overkill, potentially wasting time and money and possibly contributing to a sense of information overload. Imagine having a meeting about every bit of information and decision—it would be exhausting!

Where the theories diverge is with the categorization of "rich media." MRT has received empirical support when comparing traditional mediated communication options used in organizations—namely in-person, phone, letters, and memos (e.g., Russ et al., 1990). However, the theory receives inconsistent support when studies take into account the myriad of digital and new media now commonplace in organizations (Carlson & Zmud, 1999; Dennis et al., 1999). Noticing this deficit, Carlson and Zmud (1999; Carlson, 1995) argued that MRT be reconsidered in light of new media. They proposed that "richness" is not a purely objective characteristic; individuals' and organizational experiences with various channels also influence perceptions of richness. Indeed, we all know people who make a phone call for even the simplest of questions, whereas others prefer IM or email exchanges. Similarly, organizations have differing cultures related to the preferred ways of communication.

In their formulation of channel expansion theory, Carlson and Zmud (1999) proposed that richness includes: channel characteristics (as described in MRT), individual experiences, and social influence. Regarding the first addition, they developed the **index of channel experience** and argued four categories of experience shape our perceptions of richness: experience with (1) media channel, (2) message topic, (3) organizational context, and (4) one's communication partner(s). In other words, our view of a medium's richness develops as our familiarity with each of these factors increases, above and beyond the objective characteristics of rich media as laid out by MRT.

Regarding the second addition, **social influence** includes one's perception of how influential others—such as important peers and supervisors—refer to and/or use a medium (Schmitz & Fulk, 1991). If Keith's manager uses email to provide team members with updates and reminders, Keith will likely view texting as a richer medium than voicemail, even though voicemail's characteristics include more nonverbal cues.

A number of studies have found support for the addition of experiences and social influence as relevant in assessing channel richness, particularly that of email (e.g., Anders et al., 2020; Armengol et al., 2017; D'Urso & Rains, 2008). Regarding the index of experiences, user experience with the medium receives the most consistent support. Other experiential elements such as organizational context may not always have an effect (e.g., Armengol, et al., 2017).

With regard to choosing a medium to convey equivocal or ambiguous information, channel expansion theory suggests that, in addition to channel characteristics, senders consider the recipients' experience with, as well as the supervisor's support of, the medium. Consequently, organizations may want to increase user experience and familiarity by incorporating training for the communication technologies it depends upon. As well, organizations need to remember that employees' direct supervisors impact the degree to which a given channel is perceived as acceptably rich. All told, skilled communicators need to consider media richness in the communication process.

SOCIAL INFORMATION PROCESSING MODEL

While media richness and channel expansion theories emphasize mediated communication within organizations, Walther's (1992, 1996) social information processing (SIP) model examines the ways digital or computer mediated communication (CMC) in interpersonal contexts. As email and other CMC technologies blossomed in the 1990s, Walther noticed discrepancies in the emerging research. Experimental research showed CMC participants perceived less rich interaction; however, field studies revealed that real users perceived some mediated interaction as equivalent to face-to-face encounters. Given the fact that CMC is thought to limit or even eliminate nonverbal cues central to creating shared meaning in interpersonal interactions, Walther sought to understand how relational tone could be conveyed with digital media.

Blending properties of interpersonal communication with mediated communication, five assumptions ground the SIPmodel. First, and noted in other interpersonal theories (e.g., communication accommodation theory; expectancy violations theory, politeness theory, uncertainty reduction theory), humans are social creatures that seek connection. Second, we use a series of verbal and nonverbal exchanges to form interpersonal impressions of others. Third, the possibility of moving from an impersonal contact to a relational one depends on the impressions formed. Certainly, if you formed a negative impression of Angela based on a series of crisp exchanges, you're probably inclined to keep things impersonal rather than seek closeness. Conversely, if your exchanges with Angela led to a positive impression, you will be more motivated to increase relational messages. Presuming a positive impression and the motivation to increase relational communication, the fourth assumption characterizes relational messages as verbal or nonverbal, linguistic or text-based. In other words, relational messages are not limited only to verbally spoken or physically observed nonverbal exchanges. Pointedly, we can effectively use text forms to substitute for face-to-face, sensory-based conversations. The fifth and final assumption is temporal. That is, the processes of developing mutual understanding and relational communication take longer when using text forms and CMC. Together, these assumptions form six propositions that explain how "individuals use computer-mediated communication to develop interpersonal impressions and to advance relational communication over time online" (Walther, 2015, p. 1).

Three Phases of Mediated Communication

When relying on computer-mediated rather than face-to-face channels, Walther (1996) proposed that CMC interactions move from impersonal, to interpersonal, to hyperpersonal over time. Described in Table 11.3, the **impersonal phase** is task-oriented, wherein individuals simply use CMC to "get the job done." Early study of CMC focused on email and other text-based media. Noted in our previous discussion of MRT and channel expansion theories, text-based media averts much of the nonverbal richness inherent in face-to-face and even auditory-based communication (e.g., telephone, voicemail). Cues such as tone, pauses, posture, and facial expression are reduced. Still, we can use CMC effectively to organize, plan, and make decisions, particularly in group settings. Using text-based CMC to complete tasks can certainly be more efficient; for example, a series of email exchanges may eliminate the need to host an in-person meeting. Because impersonal communication lacks socioemotional aspects of interaction, performances often expected in face-to-face situations—such as navigating status differences, managing conflict, and conformity pressure—are also minimized. The impersonal phase typically occurs only when participants don't anticipate future interaction (i.e., uncertainty reduction theory) or when the communication goal is purely instrumental and socioemotional features would hinder the process.

Despite the medium's leaner features, most CMC quickly moves beyond the impersonal into the **interpersonal phase** (Walther, 1996). Walther argued that qualities of traditional interpersonal communication emerge in CMC environments "when users even so much *expect* to have a long-term association" (p. 33). While it takes longer in mediated environments, the same amount of information, impressions, and values are exchanged. Indeed, CMC users adapt to the environment and develop linguistic strategies to assist with impression formation, for example, responding more or less frequently, using emoticons, and inserting abbreviations to

TABLE 11.3 ■ The Three Phases of Mediated Communication	
Impersonal	Task-oriented communication with little personal information provided.
Interpersonal	Users adapt to the CMC environment in an effort to create more personal interactions.
Hyperpersonal	Individuals present a carefully monitored impression of themselves.

signal tone ("JK" just kidding). Consequently, relationships developed over CMC can be just as close as those relationships established in face-to-face contexts.

While relationships developed over CMC can be equivalent as those relationships established in face-to-face contexts, Walther (1996) posited that there is a marked difference in the **hyperpersonal phase**. Because CMC is largely asynchronous, senders have more time opportunity to control and manage their self-presentation. Discussed in Chapter 4, we routinely engage in **facework** to display our desired self-image. In face-to-face encounters, we must monitor eye contact, posture, expressions, tone, and the depth of our exchanges, all in real time. With CMC, however, monitoring one's physical self is irrelevant; we convey ourselves in text format only, allowing us to present an "idealized self." We can compose and edit our sentences to be wittier; we can select which features of ourselves we want to share. Our age, ethnicity, gender, and race are unknown, unless we choose to reveal them through language. Consequently, the hyperpersonal nature of CMC encourages users to present a more manicured or filtered version of self, producing "interaction that is more desirable than we can often manage in [face-to-face]" encounters (Walther, 1996, p. 28).

The Hyperpersonal Model and Warranting

As additional forms of CMC emerged, attention to the hyperpersonal phase has also evolved into a model of its own. Like its predecessor, SIP, the hyperpersonal model assumes that communicators adapt to the medium, expressing socioemotional messages with whatever digital characteristics exist (Walther & Whitty, 2021). For example, with more primitive messaging, users combined the grammatical symbols of a colon, dash, and closed parenthesis to signal smiling:-). Or using a less-than symbol and the number "3" to convey "love" <3. We "know" that typing in ALL CAPS means you're shouting, and so on. With today's graphic emojis, memes, and GIFs, we have even more options for expressing a vast range of emotions, humor, wit, and sarcasm.

The hyperpersonal model extends SIP by focusing on ways in which advances in communication technology influence previously unacquainted senders and receivers, as well as experiences of channels and feedback (Walther & Whitty, 2021). With present-day new media, the hyperpersonal model suggests that *senders* not only engage in selective self-presentation, senders also strategically exaggerate this digital self-image. For example, we may use filters, avatars, and color-enhanced selfies to control and present an embellished self.

Receivers also engage in exaggeration. Walther and Whitty argued that when hyperpersonal receivers assume an unknown sender is more similar to themselves, they put more trust in the sender. For example, we look at "likes," product ratings, and user reviews assuming that those making the evaluations are like us, without any real knowledge of the sender, or their tastes, values, or experiences. Thus, receivers distort assumed similarity with senders.

With regard to *channel*, the hyperpersonal model emphasizes the technological and temporal qualities of a medium as relevant to crafting and cultivating an edited self-image. Interpersonal media forms, such as texting, emailing, and direct messaging, afford control to the message creator. Consider even the notion of "scheduled" texts, posts, or emails, where the sender can set up a future time for the message to be sent and time-stamped. Creating a text now but setting it to be sent at a future point in time exaggerates the message's temporal quality. The receiver doesn't know that you crafted the response almost immediately upon receipt, but delayed sending it. This channel technology can make it seem as though an employee is working late at night or early in the morning, based on a message's time stamp. Similarly, a text exchange that includes intentionally delayed messages may convey a number of different meanings—ranging from indifference (the illusion of being "too busy" to respond right away) to thoughtful (the illusion that your response is based on "careful consideration" rather than a knee-jerk response).

Finally, *feedback* in today's hyperpersonal model is primarily one of scale (Walther & Whitty, 2021). Early CMC technology and research focused on dyads and small groups. However, the explosion of masspersonal has created large audiences for interpersonal messages. Users can "congratulate or condemn" virtual strangers via social media platforms. We can "like," "care," "follow," and "share" content, thereby acknowledging the message and reacting. Feedback can be overly positive or overly negative.

Beyond changes in sender, receiver, channel, and feedback, the hyperpersonal model addresses the fact that relationships formed over digital media may very well move from virtual to physical environments, or become "mixed-mode relationships" (Walther & Parks, 2002; Walther & Whitty, 2021). For example, online dating sites are meant to provide a pathway to real-world romance. Social media for professional networking may lead to in-person networking or interviews. Online enthusiast or hobby forums often have meet-up conferences. Yet how well does our "actual self" align with the idealized image we have created online? As Walther and Parks (2002) offered, "the connection between who we are and who we claim to be on the Internet is by no means obvious" (p. 551). Indeed, we can fake an entire online profile. Consequently, **warranting** behaviors seek to determine congruence between one's online presentation and that person's real-life attributes. In other words, CMC users who are savvy to the fact that others can and do exaggerate their online persona will look for other cues to determine the veracity of their partner's claims. As well, if online partners expect to meet face-to-face eventually, they will often provide each other with additional warranting information to "backup" self-presentation claims. Third-party photos, information on a company or organization's website, and friends' comments on a user's posts all help to affirm another's online identity (Walther et al., 2009).

All told, SIP and the proposes that computer-mediated relationships can be at least as rich as those established in face-to-face environments. The hyperpersonal model adds to theory by suggesting that qualities of CMC can influence the development of exaggerated forms of interpersonal relationships.

USES AND GRATIFICATIONS 2.0 (MEDIA AFFORDANCES)

Our third framework, uses and gratifications, represents a somewhat different means by which to analyze and explain the use of mediated communication. The **uses and gratifications approach** broadly emphasizes active audiences and focuses on receivers' motivations for using various media forms. That is, because humans have options and free will, individuals make specific decisions about which media to use and when to use them (Katz et al., 1973). The choices and decisions you make are based on personal needs and values you wish to fulfill. Thus, you can select among various media for **gratification**, or satisfaction, of your individual needs.

Assumptions of Uses and Gratifications

Three assumptions underlie the uses and gratifications (UG) approach. First, Katz et al. (1973) argued that media usage isn't passive, involuntary, or coerced; audience members actively choose and use media to fulfill certain needs. Likewise, media technologies represent numerous options available for a person to fulfill social or psychological needs, goals, and values. Indeed, the increase in communication technologies available to people in the 21st century only boosts the viability of choice (Ruggiero, 2000; Sundar & Limperos, 2013). In this way, media use is active and goal-driven based on individuals' needs.

Initially developed in contrast to other mass media effects theories (Ruggiero, 2000), a second assumption of UG is that **mass communication** (see Chapter 11) doesn't just happen to you; nor do the mass media *do* anything to you. There is no magic spell cast by media owners to coax you into viewing their programming. Instead, UG maintains a person must identify a need and make a media choice (Katz et al., 1973). Individuals *choose* to watch, read, or listen to mass media sources. While Katz et al. didn't have the plethora of interactive **social media** that we do today, the assumptions still holds. Individuals *choose* to blog, tweet, post, share, or create a Pinterest board. In this regard, the term "media effects" is misleading. UG does not support a simple "straight-line effect" whereby a given medium causes people to think or behave differently. Rather, the focus is on how users consume media. Termed "users" (rather than audience members), individuals select a medium and then allow themselves to be swayed, changed, and influenced—or not. You choose to view a YouTube video and watch; YouTube doesn't turn itself on and force you to watch.

Third, media outlets compete with other available means of satisfying personal needs (Katz et al., 1973). Stated differently, we have many ways to fulfill our needs. Feeling frazzled after a hectic day at work? You may fulfill your need (to relax and unwind) by choosing to watch a sitcom (mass media) or to scroll through Instagram (social media) or to videochat with a friend (interpersonal media). Alternatively, you may meet your needs by taking a run in the park, practicing yoga, or soaking in a warm bath with a glass of wine. Thus, the mediated options represent only a handful of alternatives available to you. Next, we present reasons individuals use the media and how media exposure can gratify various social and psychological needs.

Motivations for Media Selection

McQuail (1987) identified four broad classes of motivations that include several subcategories. For example, we can use interpersonal, masspersonal, or mass media for entertainment purposes. *Entertainment* includes some specific subtypes, for example, to: relax, escape, feel excitement or emotional catharsis, pass time, or enjoy an artistic pleasure. You may relax by listening to a podcast while commuting to or from work. You may have watched *The Ring* to experience an eerie thrill or *Casablanca* to experience a romantic heartbreak. Your children may watch a

Paw Patrol DVD while riding in the backseat of your car to prevent boredom. Similarly, you may turn on a TV sitcom as a diversion from the daily grind. Table 11.4 provides an overview of gratifications.

Second, media outlets and content provide information (McQuail, 1987). This media function presents individuals with opportunities to learn about current and historical events, to obtain advice, and to feel secure or satisfy curiosity by acquiring general knowledge. Thus, you may turn on news radio while driving for the weather, traffic updates, and local sports scores. You have probably watched or read about local, national, and world news to find out what is going on in your neighborhood and the world. You may read an advice column for investment strategies or etiquette protocols. You may use sites like Zillow and Houzz to scour real estate listings or source the perfect lamp for your bedroom.

Third, people use media to reflect, reinforce, or contrast their personal identity (McQuail, 1987). In other words, individuals can choose among various media and media content to gain insight into or assist in the development of their own attitudes or beliefs. For example, you might watch Dr. Phil to hear how others struggle with relationship issues. Likewise, a person often acquires a deeper sense of self by comparing, and perhaps contrasting, oneself with characters portrayed in various media. For instance, you are probably familiar with the hit show *The Office.* Although you may find the characters of Michael, Dwight, Kevin, and Angela to be hilarious with their lack of social skills, you also are apt to compare your own experiences and attitudes with theirs. Are you that self-centered? That neurotic? That immature? That insecure? We hope not! But that is exactly the point of the show—to present extreme personalities audience members can at once relate to and simultaneously ridicule for their triviality.

A fourth and final reason is that people turn to various media for personal relationships and social interaction (McQuail, 1987). Media exposure can help individuals learn about or connect

TABLE 11.4 ■ Media Gratifications	
Gratification	**Examples**
Entertainment	• Listening to the Coffee House channel on Spotify to help you concentrate • Watching *Psycho* to experience a thrill • Scrolling through TikTok videos because you're bored
Information	• Seeking advice about practical matters, such as how to cook hard-boiled eggs or roast a turkey • Scanning a weather app so you know what to wear
Personal identity	• Reading *Vogue* or *Esquire* to see the latest in high fashion • Putting together a Pinterest board to share your passions
Personal relationships and social interaction	• Listening to the Sports Radio Network on your drive to work so you can talk about it with your coworkers • Using Discord to play games with your friends

with others through comparisons of interpersonal relationships and social situations. Certain media can even serve as a substitute for real-life relationships by offering companionship or a sense of community. Watching *Trains, Planes, and Automobiles* every year with your family allows you to bond at Thanksgiving time. Gossiping with coworkers about the latest twist on *Succession* creates a sense of community. Reading an *Insider* article titled "12 Dating Horror Stories from Real People" may provide readers with an opportunity to (re)consider their own dating disasters.

Media Affordances

One criticism of UG is that the original framework doesn't predict specific media use; it only describes individuals' motivations for engaging with fairly traditional media (e.g., radio, TV, film, books, and periodicals). With the rise in new media, however, Ruggiero (2000) argued that "as new technologies present people with more and more media choices, motivation and satisfaction become even more crucial components of audience analysis" (p. 14). Indeed, with the plethora of competing mass, interpersonal, and masspersonal media options, the ability to predict channel or platform usage would be beneficial.

To that end, some media scholars have begun to explore the concept of media affordances as an extension of uses and gratifications (e.g., Rathnayake & Winter, 2018; Sundar, 2008; Sundar & Limperos, 2013). Adapted from Gibson's (1977) work, **media affordances** include users' perceptions of a given technology's "action possibilities" (Sundar, 2008). For example, what qualities of a medium do you view as helpful in achieving a particular goal or gratification? At the end of the 20th century, most people would have laughed at the idea of a *phone* being used to record and share video, shop online, or provide real-time, turn-by-turn directions. Fast-forward to today: we expect a phone to accomplish these goals and more! Thus, a phone's affordances or action possibilities have expanded from a fairly simple, home-based device used to connect with someone by voice transmission, to a user-generated source of entertainment (e.g., TikTok), to a pocket-sized, virtual shopping mall (e.g., Amazon), to a personal navigation system (e.g., Waze).

Media affordances help to extend UG to digital media use. Sundar (2008) identified four categories of affordances in digital media: modality, agency, interactivity, and navigability. Known as the **MAIN model**, *modality* includes ways in which a medium can appeal to different senses (e.g., visual, auditory). *Agency* implies that users are their own "gatekeepers of content"— they can create, contribute, share, and critique content. *Interactivity* presumes that users are simultaneously sources and receivers of content and can adapt or make changes to the content in real time (Sundar & Limperos, 2013). Last, *navigability* speaks to the ease with which users can "move through" or navigate a medium. Sundar also argued that a medium's features influence the nature of content. That is, each medium differs in qualities that either enable or inhibit messages, which in turn, affects the content. For example, an interactive website with linked content creates a nonlinear way to process information; you can click on a hyperlink that takes you out of, and then back to, the original page—or not. This back-and-forth quality makes reading an article on a website inherently different than in a print version. Likewise, think about a synchronous class or meeting held on a virtual conferencing site, such as Teams or Zoom. Even with video, audio, whiteboard, and chat features, there are still limits to the video conference medium which restrict what or how the instructor can present information.

The MAIN model is just one heuristic that broadly identifies digital media affordances. Looking specifically at interpersonal channels and social media, Choi and colleagues (Choi & Toma, 2014, 2017) found the affordances of ease of use, message visibility, nonverbal cues, and intrusiveness predicted social sharing via specific media. Regardless of which affordances, research indeed suggests that accounting for users' needs along with media affordances broadly writ provides a more useful construct for understanding and even predicting digital media selection (Rathnayake & Winter, 2018).

UG maintains people have many options from which they intentionally select to meet personal needs. The question, then, isn't about what effects the media have on us, but, rather, what and why people make the selections they do. With the addition of media affordances, particularly applied to social media, UG continues to evolve as a theory.

SPIRAL OF SILENCE

Everyone has opinions—from simple food preferences like vanilla or chocolate, to the camera quality of Samsung versus iPhone, to the efficacy of self-driving cars; it is human nature to judge the world around us. These views may be based on truth, myth, or falsehood, personal experience or conjecture. Our opinions are important because, and as discussed in Chapter 6, opinions influence attitudes and behavior. Our last theory in this chapter, Spiral of Silence, focuses on the complex interaction between individuals' opinions, interpersonal networks, media consumption, and the expression of public opinion (Noelle-Neumann, 1974, 1977, 1993). Specifically concerned with political communication, Noelle-Neumann hypothesized that when one's personal views don't align with what is perceived to be the majority view, particularly with moral, controversial, or highly emotional issues, that individual will remain silent out of fear of social isolation. Over time, these "minority" views become increasingly repressed to the point where a differing viewpoint is no longer considered relevant.

Understanding Noelle-Neumann's view of public opinion is central to understanding spiral of silence. While this may seem like a common-sense term on the surface, Glynn's (2018) analysis of public opinion research observed a multitude of ways to designate this term. Definitions of public opinion can range from: a collection of individual opinions; to the reflection of majority beliefs; to the processes by which individual opinions are cultivated and reach the masses; to a creation fabricated by media influencers. With regard to understanding the interplay of politics, public opinion, and the media, the Spiral of Silence emphasizes the second explanation. Specifically, Noelle-Neumann's theory (1974, 1993) defines **public opinion** as the sum of beliefs about controversial issues that one feels comfortable expressing publicly, without fear of social ostracism or isolation. In other words, it's a measure of comfort as to whether you will share your views on contentious or arguable issues; quite literally, are you comfortable publicizing your opinion? Public opinion, then, are those views that people are willing to express. Notably, the "true" majority opinion may not be what the public perceives to be the majority opinion.

At times, the opinion of a very vocal minority may seem as if it is the prevailing view. Known as **pluralistic ignorance**, distortions can exist in our perception of the dominant view such that we perceive public opinion to be farther from or closer to our own opinion than it actually is. As Manfredi et al. (2020) explained, pluralistic ignorance may inadvertently shift public opinion if "those who are in the majority stop expressing their views because they believe themselves to be in the minority" (p. 2). Consequently, minority opinions can "dominate public discourse" making these views seem more popular than in reality.

Assumptions of Spiral of Silence

A complex theory, Spiral of Silence rests on three assumptions. First, humans are social creatures who seek inclusion and fear social isolation. Arguing that society isolates people who don't conform, Noelle-Neumann's (1974, 1993) work complemented others' views of social conformity and comparison (e.g., Asch, 1956; Festinger, 1954). Known as **isolation pressure**, people will exclude or ridicule individuals who don't seem aligned with social norms or public opinion. Because we fear this exclusion, we avoid presenting ourselves in ways that are contrary to the majority

Second, Noelle-Neumann (1974) proposed that individuals routinely monitor the opinion climate on controversial topics, social issues, and political views. She later termed this personal assessment of the public's prevailing views a **quasi-statistical sense** (Noelle-Neumann, 1977). That is, while we don't use scientific methods to empirically determine the majority opinion, individuals have a sense or strong awareness of how our own views align with what is perceived to be socially acceptable. This quasi-statistical sense is particularly active in times of high uncertainty or instability. Noelle-Neumann argued that we use our interpersonal networks and mass media to gauge public views. Extending her work into the new media of the 21st century, social media also includes means by which we can ascertain the larger opinion climate (Stoycheff, 2016).

A third assumption is that our fear of isolation, coupled with our ability to sense public opinion, influences whether or not we will express our views publicly. Specifically, Noelle-Neumann (1974, 1993) argued that we will silence our opinions if we think they diverge from the larger opinion climate. In other words, if we believe that our views contradict popular sentiment, we will stifle these beliefs. Indeed, decades of public opinion research has "consistently showed that perception of hostile opinion climates—or when individuals belief their views differ from the majority—significantly chills one's willingness to publicly disclose political views" (Stoycheff, 2016, p. 296).

By way of example, Tatiana believes that removing statues or monuments is a misguided attempt to rewrite history by censoring speech; she finds it strange that suddenly people are upset over a Confederate flag or Civil War statue that they had paid no attention to previously. To her, it seems like a slippery slope. However, Tatiana sees the protests on various news outlets, photos of defaced monuments on Instagram, and #tearthemdown hashtags on Twitter. She recognizes that in her community, people equate these monuments with being racist. While she isn't a Confederate supporter or even all that political, she just thinks the larger issues of racism are being overlooked; knocking down a statue doesn't change the larger issues. However,

FIGURE 11.1 ■ Spiral of Silence

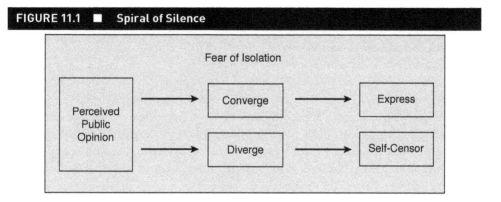

Tatiana doesn't want to be labeled "racist" so she keeps her views to herself. Importantly, notice that Tatiana doesn't change her opinion just because she perceives the majority holds a different view. Rather, she censors her public expression of the opinion. Figure 11.1 provides a depiction of this process.

Notably, not everyone is equally fearful of isolation, and not everyone squelches their opinions. As a caveat, Noelle-Neumann (1974, 1993) noted that there are some "hard core" or "avant-garde" individuals who continue to speak their views, regardless of social rejection.

Sources of Public Opinion

So far, we have looked at the assumptions that tie (1) public opinion, (2) our "quasi-statistical sense," and (3) a fear of social isolation to the likelihood of expressing our views in the public eye. As Hopkins (2015) summarized, "one's [expressed] opinion depends on the opinion of others" (para. 5). Connecting these assumptions, Noelle-Neumann (1974) sought to understand why some opinions gain public support, and others slip away. This begs the question: how do we derive our opinions on political, moral, or social issues? Noelle-Neumann argued that we derive many of our opinions from two sources: interpersonal interactions and media consumption. Certainly, personal conversations with our primary ties lead to an exchange of ideas and beliefs that help us to form opinions. Media organizations also act as opinion leaders. Discussed in Chapter 11, the mass media play an important role in setting the public's agenda for what topics considered newsworthy.

According to Noelle-Neumann (1974, 1993), three characteristics render media organizations uniquely poised to influence public opinion—ubiquity, cumulation, and consonance. First, **ubiquity** refers to the pervasiveness of mass media; it is everywhere. With smart devices, media can quite literally be carried in your pocket or worn on your wrist. Second, **cumulation** refers to the fact that news media repeat views and stories across and between outlets as well as over time. What you see, read, and hear regarding political and social issues is likely to mirror what some in another city, state, or region sees, reads, and hears. Sinclair Broadcast Group, a media conglomerate that owns more than 180 local TV stations across the United States, had dozens of anchors on it stations read nearly identical news scripts, cautioning viewers to beware of "fake news" and biased content running on other stations, outlets, and social media (Folkenflik, 2018). Third, **consonance** signifies congruence or similarity between journalists themselves; these shared values and mutual sources lead to reciprocal influence.

If you consider the pervasive, repetitive, and insular nature of news media, along with the fact that a function of the news media is report on "public opinion"—the opinions that people publicly express—it makes sense that the same dominant opinions get recycled in the media sphere. All the while the media is reinforcing the majority expressed view, those with minority opinions become less and less likely to express their viewpoints, making it less and less likely for minority voices to rise up. As Baran and Davis (2020) explained, individuals stop talking about viewpoints that are "ignored, marginalized, or trivialized by media reports" (p. 304). This silencing effect "spirals," as the media continue to pick up the opinions that are freely expressed, making them appear even stronger, while the views that aren't expressed become silenced in public decision-making.

Advancing the Spiral: Social Media

With the rise of media fragmentation, some scholars claimed the spiral of silence would become obsolete (Katz & Fialkoff, 2017). Certainly, when Noelle-Neumann's work was initially conceived and tested, the media landscape had more general and geographically defined audiences. As the number of distinct media outlets grew with the rise of cable news and the Internet, audiences now have many more niches from which to choose (Heath, 2013). With more choice, media consonance and the silencing of minority viewpoints seems less likely (e.g., Moy & Hussain, 2014).

Interestingly, however, the escalation of social media has reenergized researcher's examination of spiral silence (e.g., Matthes et al., 2018; Neubaum & Krämer, 2017). The initial conception of Noelle-Neumann's theory viewed opinion expression as a function of the interplay between interpersonal networks and (mass) media consumption. While these domains *were* largely separate, today's social media fuses interpersonal and mass media exchanges into a distinct and interactive opinion source and an opinion-monitoring source. Not only do social outlets often repeat mass media news, they also allow for user-generated commenting, liking, and sharing functions. Consequently, social media allows for real-time opinion monitoring, wherein participants can quickly gauge public opinion and immediately choose to voice or silence their views. Indeed, using meta-analysis, Matthes et al. (2018) analyzed 66 studies with more than 27,000 participants, and found continued support for the spiral of silence. That is, across multiple types of online environments, fear of rejection influenced individuals' willingness to voice contrary views. One difference Matthes et al. found, however, was that online opinion suppression was strongest with personal relationships (friends, family, neighbors) than with strangers or distant ties. Moreover, while selective social media exposure can exacerbate pluralistic ignorance (Chia & Sun, 2020), it is possible that the sheer number of online options encourages at least incidental exposure to alternative views. For example, researchers found that while online users primarily affiliated with "like-minded media," there was also more intentional and incidental exposure to alternative views than those individuals who relied on offline news media (Masip et al., 2020). While online users interacted and commented primarily in their like-minded groups, they also engaged in less selective exposure and therefore were more likely to encounter different ideologies. Their offline peers engaged in greater selective exposure, making them less likely to encounter different ideologies. While not examining the spiral of silence directly, the results suggest that individuals use social media to inform their quasi-statistical sense and self-censor on sites that present counter ideologies.

While previous researchers had studied the concepts individually, Noelle-Neumann's work uniquely advanced understanding of media effects by demonstrating that isolation pressure, a quasi-statistical sense, and self-censorship interact to create a chilling effect that "spirals" over time due to the media's pervasive influence. Extended to new media and social media, these silencing effects may persist but in different ways.

CHAPTER SUMMARY AND RESEARCH APPLICATIONS

In this chapter, we presented an overview of four theories that are useful for understanding the nuances of mediated communication. First, we described channel expansion theory as an extension of media richness theory. Both theories argue that when conveying ambiguous or equivocal messages, senders should consider a medium's richness. Channel expansion theory adds that, in addition to channel characteristics as laid out by MRT, user experience and social influence also contribute to the perception of richness. For example, in a comparative study of email versus phone/voicemail among business-to-business buyers, researchers found that both social influence and experience with email predicted the perception of email as a rich medium (Anders et al., 2020). Regarding phone/voicemail, only a supervisor's social influence increased the perception of phone messages as being rich.

Next, we looked at social information processing and the hyperpersonal model within mediated interpersonal contexts. Despite the leaner features of CMC as compared to face-to-face, users can and do adapt to the medium. Not only can users convey equivalent socioemotional content via CMC, they may engage in exaggerated or hyperpersonal relationships. A study of attraction and online dating compared text-based messaging with videoconferencing prior to meeting face-to-face and confirmed this hyperpersonal effect (Antheunis et al., 2020). Participants who communicated via text-based CMC reported greater social attraction than those who video-conferenced prior to meeting. Likewise, the same text-based CMC participants also rated their partners higher in social attraction even after meeting them in person. In both conditions, romantic attraction declined after meeting in person, suggesting that users perceived an exaggerated image of their online partner that didn't align with their in-person image.

Covered third, UG focuses on choices media users make, arguing that people actively seek and employ media forms that satisfy individual needs. By incorporating the notion of media affordances—that is, users' assumptions about a medium's ability to meet their needs—UG can be applied to newer forms of mediated communication. In a study of media uses and gratifications during the COVID-19 pandemic, Choi and Choung (2021) found that participants' need for information and entertainment predicted masspersonal media use. Conversely, users sought interpersonal media when seeking personal interaction and social connection. Interpersonal media afford intimate and synchronous features that signal presence, whereas masspersonal media afford "endless feed updates" that provide equally endless entertainment. These findings support the argument that "people use media whose affordances match their needs" (p. 2410).

Finally, research examining the spiral of silence in online environments reveals that "social media have fundamentally altered the way how individual opinions find their way into the public sphere" (Zerback & Fawzi, 2017, p. 1034). For example, Stoycheff's (2016) experimental study showed a significant chilling effect occurred when participants were primed to think about government surveillance on internet sites such as Facebook. For most of the participants, being made aware of the fact that the government uses internet surveillance for national security significantly decreased the expression of minority views in hostile opinion climates. Stoycheff's findings add the notion of "authority" to isolation pressure. Whereas Noelle-Neumann focused on the fear of "social" isolation, Stoycheff's research found that fear of authority contributed to silencing. Similarly, Zerback and Fawzi's (2017) research found that when confronted with a contradictory opinion climate, those who supported immigrant deportation silenced their opinion on Facebook and in offline discussions. This result suggests that individuals use social media exemplars, such as Facebook posts and comments, to gauge public opinion. As well, individuals whose views contradicted the exemplars stayed silent (Table 11.5).

TABLE 11.5 ■ Additional Theories of Mediated Communication	
Theory	**Main Idea**
Diffusion of Innovations Theory	Identifies the six stages through which a person, group, or organization progresses when adopting innovations such as new media (Rogers, 2003).
Media synchronicity theory	Proposes that communication effectiveness occurs when the communication task (either convergence or conveyance) aligns with a medium's synchronicity (Dennis et al., 2008). Asynchronous media are better suited for tasks requiring conveyance, or the creation of shared meaning. Synchronous media are more effective for tasks that emphasize convergence or collaboration based on preexisting understanding.
Social identity-deindividuation theory (SIDE)	When our CMC partner is unfamiliar and in the absence of nonverbal signals, receivers overestimate the cues they do receive. Relying on stereotypes, we inflate the importance of, or "overattribute," message characteristics, such as typos, all caps, and punctuation (Lea & Spears, 1992)
Social presence theory	Suggests that media vary based on engagement, or how closely media resemble the "presence" or involvement of face-to-face encounters (Short et al., 1976). Also termed "cues-filtered-out" theory.

DISCUSSION QUESTIONS

1. In what ways has your experience (or inexperience) with a channel influenced your perception of its richness? When has social influence contributed to your adoption of a channel?

2. Think about your own online interactions. When have you engaged in hyperpersonal relationships? When have you used warranting to determine if another's online persona was authentic?

3. Compare the MAIN model of general media affordances with Choi and colleagues' more specific affordances of social sharing media. Consider the different gratifications for media use (entertainment, information, social interaction, and personal identification). Can you come up with other affordances or qualities that might predict channel selection for one of these gratifications? For example, what affordances predict platform use for someone who is motivated by entertainment?

4. Think about your own self-censorship, both in person and online. How do you determine the opinion climate and decide whether to weigh in or remain silent? Do you think social media increases or decreases the spiral of silence?

KEY TERMS

Ambiguity (p. 215)

Channel characteristics (p. 214)

Consonance (p. 226)

Cumulation (p. 225)

Extension (p. 213)

Facework (p. 218)

Gratification (p. 220)

Hyperpersonal phase (p. 218)

Index of channel experience (p. 215)

Interpersonal media (p. 212)

Impersonal phase (p. 217)

Isolation pressure (p. 224)

MAIN model (p. 222)

Mass communication (p. 220)

Masspersonal media (p. 212)

Media (p. 212)

Media affordances (p. 222)

Media richness (p. 214)

Mediated communication (p. 211)

Pluralistic ignorance (p. 224)

Public opinion (p. 223)

Quasi-statistical sense (p. 224)

Social influence (p. 216)

Social media (p. 212)

Ubiquity (p. 225)

Uses and gratifications approach (p. 219)

Warranting (p. 219)

CASE STUDY 11
Silencing Refuge

The opioid epidemic has ravaged communities across the United States, and communities are clamoring for help. Philadelphia is no exception, with residents, politicians, and health professionals all exploring ways to relieve the devastation. However, when an organization came before Philadelphia's City Council announcing its desire to establish the nation's first "safe-injection site," controversy quickly ensued. The nonprofit group, Refuge, sought to open a medically supervised facility for opioid addicts and was looking for a suitable location within the city. Already operating in Canada, Australia, and several European countries, "safe consumption" organizations aim to curb drug use and associated crime by allowing addicts to use or inject under the supervision of medical professionals. By moving addicts off of the streets and into hygienic conditions, these safe site organizations reduce overdoses and increase access to medical care. While such facilities aim to "reduce harm," the effectiveness for reducing overall drug use remains unclear, however. Refuge contended that legally operating a safe site facility would dramatically improve the quality of life in portions of the city that had large numbers of addicts, as well as the associated homelessness, crime, and drug-related diseases. But a number of council members and residents of the neighborhood where Refuge's safe site was being proposed were outraged. Newspaper headlines, broadcasts, yard signs, tweets, and posts all had something to say about the proposed facility.

At first, brief news stories emphasized the site would bring relief to parts of the city most affected—with fewer users on the streets, fewer overdoses, and increased health services with medical staff better positioned to recommend addiction treatment. Residents like 45-year-old Gianna Johnson were thrilled; Gianna's cousin had died from an overdose, leaving behind two young children. She knew firsthand how addiction destroys families. In Gianna's mind, anything that could help save lives would be worth it. She often spoke to home-and-school parent groups, community organizations, and even church congregations to raise awareness about opioid addiction and to dispel myths that addiction is a personal weakness. These in-person events allowed audience members to ask questions and even share their own stories. Gianna also shared her support of Refuge's safe injection site plan, and explained how such a facility would have saved her cousin.

When Refuge announced its location for the safe site, however, a number of business owners and residents were furious. Kendra Winters, 37, was one such resident. Worried about her own children being exposed to illicit drugs, along with the potential for increased crime, and declining home values, Kendra organized a political action group called Philly Parents Against Injections in Neighborhoods (PhillyPAIN). Kendra made use of all of her network connections to get people involved with the group; she not only posted on her own social media pages, but she also posted information about the proposed injection site on pages of local businesses, local schools, and other local nonprofit groups. She created a website and posted information such as newspaper articles about the safe site proposal along with contact information for the politicians who were supporting the initiative. The website also featured an interactive "Comments" section where registered users could post information and organize meetings. She started following the Twitter accounts of local council members, tweeting responses to them with the hashtag # PhillyPAIN. As the action group's membership grew, PhillyPAIN began tweeting about potential protests and rallies around the city, including the historical tourist attractions like Independence Hall and the National Constitution Center. The aim was to attract as much media attention as possible, thereby creating widespread negative publicity for Refuge's safe site proposal.

PhillyPAIN's social media outreach was strong, but the group's efforts exploded after Wes Turnbull direct messaged Kendra with an idea. A doctoral student at nearby Franklin University, Wes studied political strategy and new media technologies. While personally ambivalent about Refuge's safe site plan, Wes's research focused on technology use among grassroot groups. He had seen the vast array of PhillyPAIN's media coverage and thought Kendra's tech-savvy group would benefit from a new application called Loke. Before responding, Kendra did a quick search on Franklin University's website and found several citations for Wes's work. Convinced he was authentic, the two exchanged a series of emails, Wes explained Loke provided real-time navigation information to users through their smartphones. He also emailed her examples of other grassroots groups that were trying the app. For #PhillyPAIN, he could help adjust the app to allow network members to see current #PhillyPAIN activities near the user's current location, as well as other members' current locations.

Kendra quickly took up Wes's help and convinced a core group of the activists to start using it to coordinate their efforts. Soon more than half of the #PhillyPAIN constituents had downloaded the app. They also learned to use the app to edit and share rally photos and videos.

The coordinated effort worked. Philadelphia newspapers, news radio stations, and news outlets reported on every protest, which they could now easily find because of the information available on Loke. TV news stations used the photos and videos shared on Loke and even began covering the protests live. The Philadelphia Times ran a series of news features. Bloggers wrote about it. Social media users posted, shared, and organized "not-in-my-neighborhood" rallies. A local talk radio show held several programs focusing on residents' opinions of the state's proposal. The hashtag began trending daily, and soon, national media outlets picked up the #PhillyPAIN message. People in other cities nationwide began to fear that if a safe site was established in Philadelphia, their own neighborhood could be next. Hashtags like #NashvillePAIN, #PhoenixPAIN, and #OmahaPAIN surfaced. In addition to her local involvement, Kendra spent significant amounts of time messaging and emailing activists in these other locations. She shared tips for gaining media coverage, templates for letters to politicians, and information on how their group used Loke.

Meanwhile Gianna Johnson felt increasingly discouraged. Several of her neighbors had PhillyPAIN signs posted in their yard or on bumper stickers. Gianna had been publicly criticized on social media after a newspaper article quoted her as speaking in favor of Refuge at a recent school board meeting. And last month's city council meeting was flooded with public comments against Refuge, with critics yelling that "importing addicts" from other neighborhoods would make their children vulnerable and destroy the community. Several argued that their community "shouldn't be ruined just to prevent 'druggies' from overdosing." The comments on social media were even worse with posts about addicts being shameful and "too lazy to get real treatment." Despite her belief and family's firsthand experience with opioid addiction, Gianna no longer felt comfortable speaking up in these public forums. Instead, she sought confirmation in anonymous support groups such as Nar-Anon, where she could share her story without judgment. Meanwhile, as the tide had clearly turned, Refuge abandoned their safe site plan altogether.

Questions for Consideration

1. Use channel expansion theory to explain how PhillyPAIN was successfully able to leverage characteristically "leaner" media (websites, social media sites, and smartphone applications) to organize their efforts.

2. In what ways might the three phases of social information processing be at work? How does Kendra engage in warranting? While not explicitly addressed, how might the hyperpersonal model exist with the online relationships Kendra has developed with other activists?

3. How does the MAIN model of media affordances help to explain the success of Loke for coordinating the protesters and generating media awareness of PhillyPAIN's activities? Use the affordances framework to predict whether other activist groups such as the Nashville, Omaha, or Phoenix PAIN groups will successfully implement Loke or any of the other channels that Kendra and her core activists have found successful.

4. In what ways does Gianna use her quasi-statistical sense? How does she experience isolation pressure and self-censorship? Do you think Gianna will remain silenced, or do you think her personal experience and strength of her convictions will turn her "hard core"? Explain your reasoning.

5. Do any of the mediated communication theories provide a better explanation than the others? Why do you believe this to be the case? What additional factors might have been included to make a different theory or combination of theories better at explaining the situation?

12 WHAT SHOULD A COMMUNICATOR DO?

LEARNING OBJECTIVES

After reading this chapter, you will be able to do the following:

1. Describe commonalities or points of convergence across the theories studied

2. Explain the influences and effects consistently associated with the theories studied

3. Articulate how understanding communication theory can aid in one's own communication competence

---

In Chapter 1, we asserted that the most competent communicators understand the underlying principles of communication. We proposed that scholarly theory provides a means to obtain that understanding. We then proceeded to inundate you with 36 distinct theories, each of which introduced several new concepts, and each of which illuminated a somewhat different aspect of the communication process. Chapter 12 helps you make sense of it all. In the following pages, we identify influences and effects consistently identified in research using the theories. In the end, we genuinely believe application of the individual theories, as well as a synthesis of commonalities across the theories, can assist professionals in enhancing their communication skill.

Before drawing any conclusions, recall that **communication competence** includes being both effective, which means achieving your goals, and appropriate, which means following social expectations for communication (Spitzberg & Cupach, 1989). Research indicates communication competence has profound effects on professional success. It is not surprising that the more communicatively competent a manager is, the more satisfied employees are with that manager (Berman & Hellweg, 1989; Steele & Plenty, 2015). More interesting is that strong relationships exist between a supervisor's communication competence and employee job satisfaction (Madlock, 2008; Mikkelson et al., 2015; Steele & Plenty, 2015) and organizational identification (Myers & Kassing, 1998). In fact, communication competence is a better predictor of job satisfaction than is leadership style (Madlock, 2008). As Madlock concluded, developing professionals' levels of communication competence might be the best way to increase employee satisfaction and performance while reducing absenteeism and turnover.

The theories discussed in this book provide clues about achieving communication competence in the professional setting. In this chapter, we highlight some conclusions we can come to about communication and the influences on communication drawn from intrapersonal/cognitive approaches; interpersonal, intercultural, group, organizational, persuasion, and mediated communication; and mass communication theory. We encourage you to pay attention to what the theories say about being both effective and appropriate in your professional communications.

CONCLUSIONS ABOUT COMMUNICATION

As abstractions, theories don't often provide specific templates with stock phrases for those individuals seeking communication advice. They are not topographical maps that can be followed mindlessly from point A to point B. Instead, theories tend to provide general sorts of directions, relying on practitioners to fill in the details. As an analogy, think of a theory as a compass, not as a GPS. Unlike a GPS, a theory will not tell you to follow Bethlehem Pike for four lights, make a left on Dager Road at the BMW dealership, and then take the first left onto Houston Road. Rather, a theory will tell you that you should be traveling north; it is up to the driver to use their own creativity in figuring out the best way to go north. Nevertheless, in reviewing Chapters 3 through 11, you will note the theories seem to converge on two general decision points that commonly face communicators: whether communication should be direct or indirect (or some point in between) and whether the communication should be like or different from previous communication.

Direct or Indirect

The first decision point is whether communicators ought to assert directly what they are thinking or what they need. Certainly, being direct is likely to be an effective choice because there is less room for misunderstanding (e.g., going "bald on record"). The communication theories discussed in this book suggest, however, numerous influences on whether a direct strategy is also appropriate.

First, as should be clear after reading Chapter 5, diverse cultures hold different values about clarity and openness. This is true not only for international cultures, but also for microcultures such as ethnic and gender cultures. For instance, communicators with a more masculine or agentic approach, prefer crisp, direct communication more so than those with a feminine communication style. To maximize communication competence, you should recognize and adapt to these cultural preferences for directness.

Second, there are situational influences on the appropriateness of directness. Politeness theory, for example, suggests those in power are more likely to be direct, and those with less power tend to use more indirect strategies. There is also a time and place for directness; expectancy violations theory suggests context plays a role in our expectations for communication. Thus, you might expect a coworker to give a direct answer to a straightforward question during decision-making (e.g., "Did the plant finish production last night?"). You might not expect a direct answer during labor negotiations (e.g., "What is the smallest salary increase you would accept?"). Likewise, in mediated communication, the need for clarity increases yet can be obscured due to the loss of nonverbal cues. Senders of mediated messages need to keep in mind that receivers may interpret the content differently in the absence of signals such as tone and facial expressions (see Chapter 11).

Finally, there are individual preferences for being direct. Recall our discussion of message design logics (MDL) in Chapter 3. Individuals using an expressive MDL will value direct communication, whereas those with a conventional MDL will hold stricter expectations for being appropriate. To be a competent communicator you need to consider not only whether you think being direct might be appropriate behavior but also what the culture would expect, what the situation demands, and what your conversational partner might prefer.

Reciprocate or Compensate

The second decision point that emerges from reviewing the theories presented in this book is whether a person should communicate in a similar fashion to previous messages or whether they ought to behave differently. This question is at the core of numerous theories. Systems theory makes the general point that patterns of communication can be symmetrical (the same) or complementary (different). Expectancy violations theory projects whether a person will reciprocate or compensate based on the reward valence of the communicator and the valence of the violation. Uncertainty reduction theory predicts people are more likely to reciprocate during times of high uncertainty. And communication accommodation theory suggests converging (behaving more like the other person) can lead to attraction, whereas diverging (behaving in a different fashion) can be a means of asserting power.

Certainly, these factors play a role in whether you choose to behave in a similar or different fashion. What if the issue isn't how you are going to act, however, but getting someone else to act in a particular manner? Beyond the specific advice offered by the theories described here, a wealth of research suggests a strong reciprocity effect (see Burgraff & Sillars, 1987; Cupach et al., 2009; Dindia, 2002; Salazar, 2015; Sillars, 1980). This means that, over time, people tend to mirror each other's behavior. Therefore, if you want someone to behave in a certain way, you should behave in the fashion you want the other person to behave. Eventually, the other person is likely to reciprocate.

CONCLUSIONS ABOUT INFLUENCES AND EFFECTS

In addition to specific questions that emerge about communication, a review of the theories presented in this book suggests many variables influence communication with numerous effects. Notably, the same variable can be both an influence and an effect. Consider your own values or beliefs. These values can influence how you choose to communicate; being a feminist, for example, might cause you to use gender-neutral language. At the same time, communication can inspire you to change your values or beliefs; someone might persuade you that using the generic *he* is exclusionary, thereby changing your beliefs about the power of language.

Throughout this book, 14 variables emerge as consistent explanations of areas that influence or are affected by the communication process. Table 12.1 provides an overview, but we briefly explain each concept and its importance, providing advice along the way.

Cohesion, Connection, and In-Groups

The degree to which individuals relate to others is a function of the communication experienced by those individuals. For example, symbolic convergence theory suggests communication practices, called fantasy chaining, create group cohesion. Organizational assimilation theory suggests communication practices socialize employees into becoming members of an in-group. Conversely, many theories focus on the reverse process, suggesting one's connection to an in-group will influence that individual's communication. Uncertainty reduction theory, for instance, suggests shared social networks decrease uncertainty, thereby decreasing uncertainty-reducing messages. Similarly, organizational assimilation asserts that when members feel connected to the organization, metamorphosis will occur, leading to greater satisfaction. In an unusual way, organizational identification and control theory suggests cohesion can function as a means of controlling employees. Connection is achieved through communication, but once achieved it can have both positive and negative results. With groupthink, too much cohesion and similarity can lead to poor decision-making due to overestimating the group's ability.

The practical implication of this recognition is an appreciation for when team-building activities are appropriate and when they are not. For example, some amount of team building is often important at the initial stages of group interaction. Team building might be avoided, however, if the group is facing a high-stress decision; such efforts might only lead to groupthink. Moreover, too much cohesion might exacerbate tensions between two groups in a workplace.

Context

A few theories identified contextual influences on communication. Expectancy violations theory, for example, states that context influences your expectations for how interactions will occur. Organizing theory proposes that the central challenge facing organizations is making sense of an equivocal information environment. Groupthink talks about the role of the situational context in the likelihood of making a poor decision. The context, then, can influence not only the nature of our communication but also our expectations for and understanding of communication. Accordingly, professionals should stop and think about the context in which communication occurs because the same message might be understood very differently in another context. For example, consider how often individuals argue that media stories present them in a negative light because their quotes were taken "out of context," or that a misunderstanding occurred because their text message was taken "out of context."

TABLE 12.1 ■ Concepts Appearing in Multiple Theories		
Influence or Effect	**Theories Identifying the Influence or Effect**	
Cohesion, connection, and in-groups	Cocultural theory (Ch. 5) Com accommodation (Ch. 5) Cultural dimensions (Ch. 5) Dialectics (Ch. 4) Groupthink (Ch. 8)	Organizational assimilation (Ch. 9) Organizational identification and control (Ch. 9) Symbolic convergence (Ch. 8) Spiral of silence (Ch. 11) Uncertainty reduction (Ch. 3)
Context	Adaptive structuration (Ch. 8) Attribution theory (Ch. 1) Channel expansion (Ch. 11) Cocultural theory (Ch. 5) Company privacy management (Ch. 4) Expectancy violations (Ch. 3)	Groupthink (Ch. 8) Organizing (Ch. 9) Situational crisis communication theory (Ch. 7) Social information processing (Ch. 11) The Rhetoric (Ch. 6)
Expectations	Attribution theory (Ch. 1) Cultural dimensions (Ch. 5) Expectancy violations (Ch. 3) Social exchange (Ch. 4)	Social roles (Ch. 5) Social information processing (Ch. 11) Theory of planned behavior (Ch. 7) Uncertainty reduction (Ch. 3)
Face or self, versus other orientation	Company privacy management (Ch. 4) Politeness (Ch. 4) The Rhetoric (Ch. 6)	Social information processing (Ch. 11) Spiral of silence (Ch. 11) Systems/interactional (Ch. 8)
Individual qualities	Attribution theory (Ch. 1) Company privacy management (Ch. 4) Expectancy violations (Ch. 3)	Extended parallel processing (Ch. 7) Narrative paradigm (Ch. 6)
Interest and involvement	Agenda setting (Ch. 9) Elaboration likelihood (Ch. 7) Social cognitive (Ch. 11)	Social judgment (Ch. 6) Spiral of silence (Ch. 11) The Rhetoric (Ch. 6)
Needs or Goals	Cocultural theory (Ch. 5) Functional groups (Ch. 8) Planning theory (Ch. 3) Politeness (Ch. 4)	Situational crisis communication theory (Ch. 7) Symbolic convergence (Ch. 8) Uses, gratifications, and media affordances (Ch. 11)

(Continued)

TABLE 12.1 ■ Concepts Appearing in Multiple Theories (continued)		
Influence or Effect	**Theories Identifying the Influence or Effect**	
Power and control	Adaptive structuration (Ch. 8)	Politeness (Ch. 4)
	Cocultural theory (Ch. 5)	Org identification & control (Ch. 9)
	Company accommodation (Ch. 5)	Theory of planned behaviour (Ch. 7)
	Cultivation (Ch. 10)	Systems/interactional (Ch. 8)
	Cultural dimensions (Ch. 5)	Spiral of silence (Ch. 11)
	Encoding/decoding (Ch. 10)	
Relationships	Adaptive structuration (Ch. 8)	Social information processing (Ch. 11)
	Expectancy violations (Ch. 3)	Systems/interactional (Ch. 8)
Rewards	Cocultural theory (Ch. 5)	Social exchange (Ch. 4)
	Company privacy management (Ch. 4)	Social cognitive (Ch. 11)
	Expectancy violations (Ch. 3)	Uncertainty reduction (Ch. 3)
	Elaboration likelihood (Ch. 6)	
Rules	Adaptive structuration (Ch. 8)	Message design logics (Ch. 3)
	Company accommodation (Ch. 5)	Organizational identification and control (Ch. 9)
	Company privacy management (Ch. 4)	Organizing (Ch. 9)
	Dialectics (Ch. 4)	
Social networks	Agenda-setting (Ch. 10)	Social cognitive (Ch. 10)
	Channel expansion (Ch. 11)	Spiral of silence (Ch. 11)
	Dialectics (Ch. 4)	Theory of planned behavior (Ch. 7)
Uncertainty and ambiguity	Agenda-setting (Ch. 10)	Organizational assimilation (Ch. 9)
	Cultural dimensions (Ch. 5)	Planning theory (Ch. 3)
	Channel expansion (Ch. 11)	Social information processing (Ch. 11)
	Dialectics (Ch. 4)	Uncertainty reduction (Ch. 3)
	Extended parallel processing (Ch. 7)	

(Continued)

TABLE 12.1 ■ Concepts Appearing in Multiple Theories (continued)		
Influence or Effect	**Theories Identifying the Influence or Effect**	
Values and beliefs	Cocultural theory (Ch. 5)	Organizational culture (Ch. 9)
	Cultivation theory (Ch. 10)	Social judgment (Ch. 6)
	Cultural dimensions (Ch. 5)	Social roles (Ch. 5)
	Encoding/decoding (Ch. 10)	Symbolic convergence (Ch. 8)
	Extended parallel processing (Ch. 7)	Systems/interactional (Ch. 8)
	Message design logics (Ch. 3)	The Rhetoric (Ch. 6)
	Narrative paradigm (Ch. 7)	Theory of planned behavior (Ch. 7)
	Organizational identification and control (Ch. 9)	

Expectations

A few theories make special note of individuals' expectations, suggesting these expectations play a role in your evaluation of communication events. To illustrate, both Hofstede's theory of cultural dimensions and social role theory suggest one's biological sex is associated with expectations for appropriate behavior. Attribution theory indicates our expectations for others influence our attributions—say, for example, when a man behaves in a manner not socially prescribed (and therefore expected). Both expectancy violations theory and social exchange theory suggest your expectations determine how you evaluate your interactions with others. The practical advice for the professional communicator is to challenge one's own expectations. Knowing why you have certain expectations and making sure to maintain realistic expectations can enhance perceptions of relational and interactional satisfaction. On the other hand, the professional communicator must also make sure the recipients of messages have appropriate expectations. As inoculation theory would suggest, if you want to prevent a potentially damaging counter-persuasive effort, the best thing you can do is to forewarn receivers to expect the persuasive effort. Within mediated contexts, the social information processing model offers that we have somewhat different expectations for purely onscreen interactions than for relationships that are or will be multimodal (e.g., online and face-to-face). Again, managing expectations across various mediums is important, while recognizing that individuals' digital representations of themselves may very well be exaggerated.

Face and Self Versus Other Orientation

Several theories implicitly recognize the importance of sustaining individuals' desired images. Not only is protecting one's own self-needs warranted, but theories such as politeness theory and communication privacy management propose communicators ought to consider others' face needs in interaction. In a slightly separate way, the Rhetoric also asserts that persuaders be cognizant of their audiences' needs. Such efforts are likely to lead to organizational success; transformational leaders, after all, are those skilled at understanding both themselves and others. Accordingly, the advice taken from these theories is to recognize others' needs to protect their image.

Individual Qualities

As indicated earlier, understanding oneself and others is important for effective communication. Several theories explicitly address how qualities of the individual might affect the communication process. For example, expectancy violations theory suggests that communicator characteristics (age, sex, and the like) influence your expectations for communication. Attribution theory proposes that one of the ways you answer the question "why?" is by looking for stable internal dispositions of the communicator. Somewhat differently, communication privacy management theory suggests that one's own individual values and beliefs will determine the privacy rules that they create. Finally, the narrative paradigm asserts that individuals' character, history, values, and experience determine what they will view as persuasive. The conclusion drawn here is that you cannot presume everyone will respond in the same way to the same message or situation; you need to tailor your communication to match the qualities of the interactants.

Interest and Involvement

Regarding persuasion, the elaboration likelihood model maintains the central route is used by people who are motivated—in other words, interested and involved. Similarly, social judgment theory specifies that a persuader consider audience members' ego-involvement to determine how open they might be to alternate ideas. Turning to mass media theories, agenda-setting theory states a person's need for orientation and the information's relevance determine whether news media set an agenda for that individual. Social cognitive theory suggests the media must gain our attention to influence us to model what we see. Successful communicators cannot presume interactional partners or audience members will naturally be engaged in each topic.

Needs

One way to engage communication partners is to recognize and seek to meet their needs. Noted earlier, politeness theory suggests everyone has both positive face needs (e.g., the desire to be liked and appreciated) and negative face needs (e.g., the desire to be free from imposition). A different view of needs is proposed by uses, gratifications, and media affordances, which states people select media forms to meet needs. Symbolic convergence posits that fantasy themes and fantasy chains meet psychological needs of the group. Finally, functional group decision-making argues communication in groups must meet four functions (or achieve four needs) to make effective decisions. Professional communicators, then, ought to match messages to the needs of those with whom they are communicating. Note that this is receiver focused; certainly, meeting one's own needs is important, but competent communication also recognizes the needs of the receiver.

Power and Control

A recurring theme among the theories discussed in this book is that communication is a central means for exerting power; power influences the type of communication used. The link between communication and power can take a macroscopic (big picture) or microscopic focus (individual interactions). On a large scale, Hofstede's cultural dimensions recognize that some cultures accept large differentials in power, whereas others don't. The extent to which a culture tolerates a high-power distance influences the perceived appropriateness of communication strategies. Also taking a macroscopic perspective, encoding/decoding theory suggests the media's use of the dominant ideology in encoding messages socializes us into adopting that ideology. Similarly, the spiral of silence maintains that individuals will self-censor if they perceive their opinions or beliefs are in the minority, particularly on divisive topics. A slightly different macroscopic view of communication and power is taken by organizational identification and control theory, which centers on the hidden forms of control in organizations, such as the role of unobtrusive (shared values) and concretive control (peer pressure) in organizational life. Adaptive structuration theory recognizes that structures created by organizational members also subtly constrain behavior, thereby serving as a form of control. Meanwhile, cultivation theory suggests that the medium of television in particular effects a form of social control; with a handful of media conglomerates repeating the same plots (often violent) and types of characters (often stereotypical), audiences come to view these archetypes as more realistic than the world right outside their door.

Other theories focus on the role of power in more microscopic settings. Both politeness and communication accommodation theories suggest people are more likely to adjust their behavior if they have less power than their interactional partner. Accordingly, you will likely engage in more politeness or will converge to your partner if you perceive this person as having more power than you. Finally, the theory of planned behavior suggests a person's perceived power over the situation determines whether they will be persuaded to act in a particular fashion.

At the beginning of this section, we stated that several the theories presented in this book suggest communication is how power is exerted. By now you should recognize that *who* gets to say things, *what* is said, and *how* it is said (or what is *not* said and *why* it is not said) are important questions for uncovering how power is understood and being carried out in any interaction. Competent communicators recognize not only obvious examples of power enactment but also less obvious examples.

Relationships

Just as different contexts call for differing types of communication, diverse relationships call for varied types of communication. To illustrate, expectancy violations theory asserts the relationship you have with interactional partners forms your expectations for how an interaction should proceed. Moreover, outside observers may be just as likely to understand a given relationship as are the relational partners; the systems/interactional perspective suggests all communication includes a relationship level that provides clues as to the nature of the relationship between communicators. As practical advice, communication professionals should be mindful of existing relationships (whether agreeable or poor) and monitor the relationship levels of messages to gauge how an interaction is proceeding. Within the context of mediated communication, the social information processing models offers that online relationship development can be both slower (e.g., asynchronous) and more intense (e.g., hyperpersonal). In online formats, this relationship monitoring may take different forms and competent communicators may do well to engage in warranting behaviors to determine congruence between a virtual partner's online presence and real-life characteristics.

Rewards

One way to understand individualistic cultures using Hofstede's cultural dimensions is to recognize that members of individualistic cultures ask, "What's in it for me?" Many theories discussed in this text explicitly recognize the power of rewards in making sense of communication interactions. Uncertainty reduction theory, for example, says the incentive value of an interactional partner can increase your uncertainty about them; the more rewarding the person is, the more likely you are to seek to reduce uncertainty. Several other predictions are associated with rewards. Expectancy violations theory suggests the reward value of the violator determines in part whether a person will reciprocate or compensate. Communication privacy management theory posits individuals will reveal or conceal risky behavior based on the potential rewards for doing so. Social exchange theory predicts people seek to maximize rewards and minimize costs in relationships; thus, lack of rewards can lead to dissatisfaction or relational termination. Elaboration likelihood proposes that rewards can provide peripheral motivation to comply, such as offering something in return (reciprocity). Meanwhile, social cognitive theory asserts that individuals need motivation to replicate observed behaviors. That is, even if we notice, remember, and can do a behavior, we likely won't be quick to replicate it unless there is some reward (whether direct, vicarious, or self-produced). All to say, people make choices based on perceived reward power. Those who have reward power will be subject to more uncertainty reduction, will have others compensate for perceived negative behaviors, will be privy to more confidential information, will be perceived as more attractive to relational partners, and will be emulated more often.

Rules

Several of the theories discussed in this book refer to the rules used to guide communication practices. Communication privacy management, for example, explicitly discusses the development of rules for sharing information. MDL talks about varying perspectives on rules. Individuals using a conventional logic tend to be rule governed, individuals using an expressive logic tend to eschew politeness rules, and individuals with a rhetorical logic learn to renegotiate the rules to meet their own goals.

Taking a distinct perspective on rules, two theories of organizational communication focus on how contemporary organizations might rethink reliance on rules. Organizational identification and control theory discusses how more sophisticated forms of control rely on more implicit, subtle rules than bureaucratic forms of control. Organizing theory also disdains formal rules, suggesting relying on rules rather than creative solutions might serve as the death knell of an organization.

Social Networks

Many theories focus not only on specific relationships we have with others but on the patterns of relationships in which our lives are embedded. For instance, social cognitive theory suggests the media can have an indirect path of effects on viewers through a socially mediated process, and agenda setting theory is now investigating the ways in which horizontal media via social networks influence the agenda setting function of news media. Channel expansion theory proposes that certain mediums become favored channels because that is what those around us use, not necessarily because of their effectiveness. Meanwhile both spiral of silence and the theory of planned behavior look at how individuals' perceptions of what they *think* their social network believes influence their own behavior.

Uncertainty and Ambiguity

The notion of uncertainty is frequently proposed as a central motivator for human communication. URT proposes that uncertainty is uncomfortable, so we use communication to reduce it. Indeed, this notion is used within a specific context in organizational assimilation theory. Agenda-setting theory says a person's need for orientation, which includes their uncertainty about an issue, determines the extent of the agenda-setting effect. Channel expansion theory suggests richer media forms are required when the message is ambiguous.

On the other hand, several theories propose a more complex relationship between uncertainty and communication; dialectics argues individuals have conflicting desires for certainty and uncertainty (in the form of the predictability and novelty dialectic). Hofstede's cultural dimensions suggest cultures vary on uncertainty avoidance, with some cultures more tolerant of uncertainty than others. Nevertheless, it seems clear that uncertainty is often perceived as problematic and can drive a person to send or seek specific messages.

Values and Beliefs

Finally, a theme that emerges consistently throughout our presentation of theories is yet another cognitive variable: people's values and beliefs. Suggested earlier in this chapter, values and beliefs have a complex relationship with communication. On one hand, a person's values and beliefs lead that individual to communicate in a particular fashion. On the other hand, communication might be how you reinforce, modify, or change your values and beliefs. More than a dozen theories discussed in this book address values and beliefs. The theories range from those focusing on individualistic approaches (MDL posits that people's beliefs about communication influence how they communicate); to persuasive settings (the narrative paradigm suggests an individual's values determine in part which stories they find reasonable); to group settings (symbolic convergence states that group members construct a rhetorical vision, which is a system of values or beliefs about how the world works); to organizational settings (Schein's model of organizational culture identifies values and assumptions as abstract ways of understanding how to operate within an organization); to mass-mediated settings (cultivation theory says heavy television viewers are "mainstreamed" into believing television reality); to cultural contexts (members of different cultures hold different values and beliefs that influence how people should communicate with members of that culture). In all cases, the advice to communication professionals is to understand others' values and beliefs and to recognize the difficulty in asking people to change them.

RETURNING TO COMMUNICATION COMPETENCE

At the beginning of this chapter, we asserted that competent communication requires one to be both effective and appropriate. After reviewing the 14 common concepts we have identified, it should be clear that achieving your goals often means considering what the receiver might view as appropriate. If we were to summarize the single biggest piece of advice culled from all the theories discussed in this book, it would be that competent communicators are those who take a receiver orientation to communication; in the pursuit of their own goals, they consider what others need to hear (and how they might hear it) so they might accomplish those goals.

According to Spitzberg and Cupach (1984, 1989), the development of communication competence requires three elements: knowledge, motivation, and skill. **Knowledge** refers to the cognitive content and understanding the procedures of how to act. Hoping you're doing the right thing is insufficient. Understanding what to do and how to it is required for consistently effective and appropriate in communication. We hope the theories discussed in this book have increased your knowledge in this area. **Motivation** references your reasons for doing things; it involves your interest in and willingness to approach rather than avoid communication. Wanting to develop your aptitude is another part of developing communicator competence. That you have taken this class and have read this book provides some indication of motivation for improving your communication skill.

The final component of competence is skill. **Skill** is the actual behavior. Despite the best of intentions and a wealth of knowledge, we don't always behave competently. As with any skill, however, communication skill can be developed and enhanced. Skill development requires practice, feedback (and being open to such constructive criticism), and adjustment after evaluation. The challenge you will face as a professional communicator is to use your knowledge and motivation as a foundation for increased skill.

CHAPTER SUMMARY

This chapter provided a synthesis of the theories presented throughout the text. First, we identified two decision points communicators face: whether to be direct or indirect and whether to behave in a similar or different manner compared with other communicators. These decisions were framed in the balance of the effectiveness and appropriateness needed to be a competent communicator. Then we turned our attention to 14 important variables that influence the communication process: cohesion, connection, and in-group's context; expectations; face and self-versus-other orientation; individual qualities; interest and involvement; needs; power and control; relationships; rewards; rules; social networks; uncertainty and ambiguity; and values and beliefs. Specific advice for the professional communicator was interspersed throughout the discussion of these variables.

DISCUSSION QUESTIONS

1. Create several examples for when a communicator might need to choose between being direct or indirect and between reciprocating or compensating. Compare your situations with another student's. What similarities do you see in your examples?

2. Review Table 12.1. Can you add any other influences or theories to the list?

3. Based on your own professional or personal goals, which theory do you believe is most central to realizing communication competence? What about pairs of theories?

KEY TERMS

Communication competence (p. 233)

Knowledge (p. 244)

Motivation (p. 244)

Skill (p. 244)

CASE STUDY 12
Arguments at Amazing Adventures

Selena Framingham is a 24-year-old woman from the South. She was the first in her family to attend college, and she was very proud of the fact that she paid for her entire education by earning scholarships and working summers at a theme park, Amazing Adventures. The hours were long at the theme park, but she and the other workers had a good time despite the oppressively hot weather, cranky children, and obnoxious parents. Besides, she made good money, and she had graduated debt free thanks to numerous scholarships and grants.

After receiving her undergraduate degree, Selena worked full-time doing public relations for a nonprofit company. She quickly became disillusioned with the job, and after doing this work for a little over a year, she decided that neither public relations nor the nonprofit world was a good fit for her. She decided to pursue a graduate degree and was excited to be accepted into a prestigious program. However, attending graduate school full-time was even more expensive than funding her undergraduate degree. She received a grant, which paid for part of her tuition, but she found she had to work both part-time during the semester and full-time during the summer to pay for both school and her living expenses.

Selena contacted Bonnie, one of her old friends at Amazing Adventures, and asked if she might be able to get a job at a senior level for the summer. "Gee Selena, I don't think there are any management-level jobs open, and even if there were, I don't think they would be seasonal. But let me check around and see what I can do," Bonnie replied.

Bonnie had moved up the ladder at Amazing Adventures, starting with Selena at a concession stand at the age of 18 before they were both promoted to ride operators. Bonnie had stayed with the company when Selena took the public relations job, and now she worked in the accounts payable department of the business office.

The next day, Bonnie called Selena. "Hey, would you mind working in the ticket office this summer? I know it isn't management, but I can make sure your seniority is used to calculate your pay grade. Plus, the ticket booth is air-conditioned, and best of all, there's no cleaning up involved!" Selena thought it was a good option to make a decent salary for the summer and decided to go for it.

On her first day back at work, she found a lot of the original management had left, including supervisors who had been there for a long time. Fortunately, Selena was told she would be working for Sam, whom she had known as a ride operator back in the good old days in the park. Sam had always been easy going, and she figured he would be the same laid-back guy she had hung out with in the past. While at work, Selena did everything she could to be what she considered a good employee. She typically did whatever her supervisors told her to do because she respected authority. And, if she were completely honest, she knew there were bonuses at the end of the summer if a supervisor thought you had been an exemplary employee.

Selena and Sam quickly fell into a habit. Each time he walked by her ticket booth, he would give her a different task to do, which was mainly tedious busywork. One day, he commanded, "Straighten up the maps and distribute some of them to the other ticket counters." Being the good employee she was, Selena hastily agreed and did it immediately.

On another day, Sam demanded, "The glass on these booths has fingerprints all over it. Get the glass cleaner, and clean it up." He didn't even stop to deliver his orders; he just yelled at her as he was walking by. Again, she quickly responded to his request.

This pattern continued for over a week, and Selena began to silently fume about his behavior. "Just who the heck does he think he is?" she silently contemplated. "I've known him for over 5 years, and I'm the one with a college degree and working on my master's degree. I deserve a little more respect!" she thought. But she didn't say anything; she just did what she was told to do.

During her third week on the job, she called Sam over to her booth because she needed more change. He came over to her register with the change, as requested. When he did so, he saw several promotional cards piled to the side of the register. The promotional cards were given by local companies, and they worked as discounts to the park.

Sam challenged Selena, "What are these doing here?" Selena was confused by the question. "Sometimes people want them back after they buy their tickets. I keep a few of them in a pile and throw them out later," she responded.

Sam rolled his eyes and sighed deeply. "Selena, throw these cards out so you don't get them confused with new ones." Selena was taken aback by his request. "I have never once confused an old card with a new card," she protested.

He rebutted, "Throw them out anyway."

Without thought, Selena argued, "I would have thrown them out *eventually*, and I was going to throw them out soon anyway. I just keep them because some people want them back."

Sam responded sarcastically, "You shouldn't wait until they pile up like that, and obviously you haven't given anyone back their cards because they are sitting there in a pile."

For Selena, it was the straw that broke the camel's back. She couldn't believe Sam was not picking about something so trivial! "Don't tell me how to do my job, Sam. I know what I'm doing. I've been here longer than you," she screamed, her temper rising.

Sam looked at her, laughed, and threw the cards in the bin underneath the register. Walking away, he didn't acknowledge Selena in any way. Selena stood there and sputtered, thinking she would complain to Sam's supervisor. However, before she could do so, a human resources representative approached her and told her she was being reassigned to a concession stand.

Questions for Consideration

1. This chapter suggests two decisions each communicator should make: whether to be direct or indirect and whether to compensate or reciprocate. Discuss both Selena's and Sam's behavior in terms of these two decisions, articulating what in each case leads you to the conclusions you draw.

2. Do you believe Selena and Sam are competent communicators? Why, or why not? What recommendations could you give to improve their communication competence?

3. Discuss how each of the following influenced Selena's and Sam's behavior:
   a. cohesion/connection/in-groups
   b. expectations
   c. face
   d. power/control
   e. relationships
   f. rewards
   g. uncertainty

GLOSSARY

Ability: a person's skill or aptitude.

Able: degree to which a person is capable of understanding logical arguments presented in an elaborated message.

Accidental cluster: a type of crisis, when an organization's actions associated with the crisis were unintentional.

Accommodating: cooperating with others but demonstrating little assertiveness—typically conceding to the partner's requests.

Accommodation: adjusting one's speech and/or conversational patterns.

Accuracy: in evaluating theory, the extent to which systematic research supports the explanations provided by the theory.

Active strategy: a moderately direct approach to reduce uncertainty whereby one goes to a third-party source to gather information.

Acuity: in evaluating theory, the ability of a theory to provide insight into an otherwise intricate issue.

Agency: a belief in free will.

Agenda: coverage by mass media, which provides an indication of what events the public "should" consider as important.

Agentic qualities: stereotypically male qualities, for example, being assertive, controlling, confident, ambitious, and forceful.

Aggregate: a set number of individuals—for example, the people standing at a bus stop or the people on an elevator.

Aggressive: an approach for cocultural communication that centers on achieving one's own goals without consideration of the other person's goals.

Allocative resources: material forms of assistance, such as time and money.

Ambiguity: the possibility of multiple interpretations.

Analogic code: a message that resembles what it means. Often nonverbal.

Anchor: a person's stance or position on a particular topic, issue, or message

Antecedent conditions: factors associated with group decision-making that might lead to groupthink.

Anticipatory socialization: the stage of organizational assimilation during which the individual gathers information about a specific vocation, position, and/or organization.

Articulation: the process whereby our cultural ideologies are reinforced.

Artifacts: observable evidence of an organization's culture.

Assertive: an approach for cocultural communication that seeks to achieve the individual's goal without imposing on the other person's goals.

Assimilation effect: when a persuasive message falls within a receiver's latitude of acceptance, the receiver minimizes the difference between the message's position and one's own position, thereby accepting the message.

Assimilation: an effort to become more similar to the dominant group.

Assumptions: part of organizational culture, when beliefs, values, and behaviors become so ingrained, and organizational members can no longer imagine an alternative.

Attention process: determined by both the observer's characteristics and the arrangement of intended behaviors. In other words, the observer needs to be attentive, and the actions in question need to be worthy of notice.

Attitude: a relatively enduring predisposition to respond favorably or unfavorably toward something.

Attribute agenda setting: also known as second-level agenda setting; the manner in which stories are framed influences audiences' attitudes and how to think about the issues covered.

Authoritative resources: interpersonal characteristics of group members, such as cohesion, experience, and status.

Authority: use of the perception of power or expertise to convince the audience to accept the beliefs or behaviors presented.

Autonomy–connection: the internal dialectical tension focusing on the desire to be alone versus the desire to be in a relationship.

Avoidance: refusing to enact a behavior that might be considered face threatening.

Axiom: a fundamental truth.

Bald-on-record: making no effort to be polite.

Behavioral intention: a plan to act a particular way.

Behavioral uncertainty: uncertainty as to how someone should behave in a given situation.

Behaviorism: in psychology, a narrow focus on cause and effect.

Bolstering: a crisis response strategy which involves presenting new, positive information about the organization, or reminding stakeholders about previous good works.

Boundaries: a metaphor for divisions between who has access to private information and who does not.

Boundary coordination: the ways collective boundaries are maintained.

Boundary linkages: alliances between owners of the information.

Boundary ownership: the rights and responsibilities borne by owners of the information.

Boundary permeability: how much information is easily passed through a privacy boundary.

Boundary turbulence: when privacy rules are unclear, making boundary coordination challenging.

Brainstorming: a specific technique used in decision-making to generate potential solutions.

Bridge exit: a hybrid type of organizational separation in which the member is given feedback on how to improve or transition to another role

Bridge: a member of more than one group.

Bureaucratic control: exerting control over employees by rules and procedures.

Central route: an elaborated route for persuasion. Succeed in long-term attitude change if the audience is motivated and able to process the message.

Change: in a dialectical approach, the assumption that a steady state is impossible to achieve.

Channel characteristics: part of media richness that includes speed of feedback, the user's ability to personalize a message, the availability of multiple nonverbal cues, and language variety.

Characterological coherence: part of narrative fidelity where the credibility or believability of the story's "characters" is assessed.

Closed-ended questions: in a survey, questions that require the respondent to use selected possible responses.

Closed-mindedness: viewing the world in extremes. For example, things are viewed either as purely good or purely evil.

Cocultural Groups: nondominant social groups embedded in a larger culture.

Cognition: the processes of reducing, elaborating, transforming, and storing stimuli.

Cognitive uncertainty: uncertainty about how someone should think or feel about a given situation.

Cognitive: in psychology, the focus on the internal processes that occur between cause and effect.

Cohesion: the connection between group members.

Collectivism: a belief that the views, needs, and goals of the group are more important than any individual views, needs, or goals. Focuses on obligation, connection, and cooperation.

Commitment: reliance on a person's dedication to a product, social cause, group affiliation, or political party to craft a persuasive effort.

Commonsense theory: theory in use. Typically created by an individual's own personal experiences or developed from helpful hints passed on from family members, friends, or colleagues.

Communal qualities: stereotypical female attributes, for example, the expression of affection and exhibiting sympathy, helpfulness, sensitivity, nurturance, and gentility.

Communal-face concern: managing in-group identity needs when challenged by an out-group.

Communibiological approach: an approach that assumes that neurobiological temperaments and traits cause variations in the communication process.

Communication competence: achieving a successful balance between effectiveness and appropriateness.

Communication: a complex process associated with sending, receiving, and interpreting messages. Scholars disagree as to the scope of the process, whether a source or receiver orientation should be taken or whether message exchange needs to be successful to count as communication.

Communicator reward valence: an evaluation about the person who has violated expectations; the extent to which the violator is perceived as attractive or rewarding.

Comparison level of alternatives: the alternatives to staying in the relationship.

Comparison level: rewards a person expects to receive in a particular relationship.

Compatibility: the extent to which an innovation is consistent with a potential adopter's values, life-style, or experience.

Compensate: making up for someone else's behavior, for example stepping backward if someone steps forward.

Competing: in conflict, a highly assertive style that lacks cooperation. Seeking a win-lose solution.

Complementary pattern: a pattern of communication in which the sender and the receiver use differing styles of communication.

Complete observer: in an ethnography, when the researcher does not interact with the members of the culture or context.

Complete participant: in an ethnography, when the researcher is fully involved in the social setting, and the participants do not know the researcher is studying them.

Complex-cyclic path: when group members cycle through the types of activities identified by functional group decision-making but do so in a circular fashion.

Complexity: the level of difficulty in understanding or using the innovation.

Compromising: in conflict, moderate concern for self and others.

Concept: an agreed-upon aspect of reality.

Concertive control: when coworkers develop mechanisms to reward and control behavior that influences the team.

Confirmation stage: part of the innovation decision process whereby the user evaluates and reconsiders whether or not the technology is worth adopting.

Connotative: associated or subjective meanings of a symbol.

Consensus: the extent to which an individual believes most people would behave in a given fashion.

Consistency: the extent to which an individual believes a target other typically behaves in a particular fashion.

Consonance: when two stimuli or pieces of information are in balance or achieve congruence.

Content analysis: a research method that involves creating categories for communication content and counting the number of times each category appears.

Content level: the actual symbols used in a message.

Content: information published by a medium, such as a television show, newspaper article, or video.

Contextual criteria: situations that encourage or dissuade one from sharing private information.

Contingencies: if/then elements of a plan such that "if" option A is occurs, "then" action B will be put into effect.

Contradictions: the essential but opposing needs experienced by relational partners.

Contrast: the use of uneven points of comparison in a persuasive effort.

Controllability: the extent to which a given action is within the actor's control.

Conventional message design logic: the belief that communication is rule governed and that communicators should follow those rules.

Conventionality–uniqueness: an external tension that focuses the desire to behave in ways considered normative versus wanting to emphasize their relationship's distinctiveness by doing something differently.

Convergence: altering speech and behavior so it matches that of the conversational partner.

Corrective facework: messages an individual can use to restore one's own face or to help another restore face after a face-threatening act has occurred.

Costs: lost resources.

Counteractive communication: in functional group decision-making, communication that returns discussion toward one of the requisite functions.

Crisis: a sudden and unexpected event that jeopardizes an organization's operations and poses both financial and reputational threats.

Critical mass: if a sufficient number of people adopt the innovation, additional adoption of the innovation becomes self-sustaining, assuring future growth.

Cross-cultural communication: the comparison of two or more cultural communities.

Cultural criteria: the degree to which a person's values, beliefs, and ways of communicating influence privacy decisions.

Cultural network: informal communication processes within an organization, including stories, jokes, and gossip.

Cultural studies: the study of the role of the mass media in producing and reproducing cultural beliefs. The media are simply one mechanism for the development and dissemination of cultural ideologies.

Culture: one's identification with and acceptance into a group that shares symbols, meanings, experiences, and behavior.

Cumulation: refers to the fact that news media repeat views and stories across and between outlets over time

Cyclic alteration: (spiraling alteration): managing a dialectical tension by fulfilling one pole or need at one time and then shifting to fulfill the other pole at a later time.

Danger control: a strategy that asks individuals to take protective action in order to avoid or reduce the threat.

Data analytics: activities related to gathering and analyzing social media data, as well as sharing the findings so as to support business activities.

Data mining: advanced form of data analysis that used to determine previously unidentified patterns or relationships in large data sets.

Decision stage: part of the innovation decision process whereby the users weighs pros and cons of an innovation and decides whether or not to adopt it.

Decoding: the interpretation of a message.

Deductive theory: developed by starting with a theory—or hypothesis—then gathering data to support, reject, or refine the theory.

Denotative: the dictionary-type definition of a symbol.

Density: the number of interconnections among network members.

Deny: a crisis response strategy that attempts to distance the organization from the crisis

Dependent variable: the presumed effect.

Descriptive prejudice: stereotype that women have less leadership potential than men because they lack agentic qualities.

Determine minimal standards: criteria for or characteristics of an acceptable solution.

Determinism: the belief that causes and effects can be uncovered when studying human communication.

Deviance: behavior that is counter to expectations for typical behavior.

Dialectical tension: opposing forces within relationships that must be managed.

Digital communication: a message that has no direct link between the symbol and its meaning. Often verbal.

Digital-native media: media outlets that originated online and distribute content primarily (or solely) via the Internet. Also known as web-native media.

Diminish: a crisis response strategy that attempts to minimize the crisis or the organization's role in the crisis.

Direct motivation: when you perceive you will be rewarded as a consequence of modeling an observed behavior.

Direct path of influence: the media influences viewers directly, from creating attention-getting messages, to enabling behavior and providing incentives, to replicating actions so the viewer changes her or his behavior.

Direction: the extent to which the link is reciprocal between network members.

Discipline: a sense of responsibility to the work group that fosters particular behaviors.

Disenchantment rejection: when individuals stop using an innovation altogether.

Disruptive communication: in functional group decision-making, communication not geared toward one of the requisite functions.

Divergence: differentiating from a partner by seeking to engage in speech and behavioral patterns different from that of the partner.

Dominant code: a preferred reading; interpreting a message using the dominant ideology.

Dominant group: social group in which members have a more privileged position within the larger culture.

Dominant ideology: a view of the world that supports the status quo.

Double bind: the dilemma women face in leadership. If they behave in a stereotypically female manner they are viewed as ineffective. If they behave in a stereotypically male manner they are viewed as inappropriate.

Double interact: an act, response, and adjustment.

Dramatizing message: a joke, pun, figure of speech, anecdote, double entendre, or metaphor, among other things, that meets emotional needs.

Duality of structure: the idea that group members' actions both create and constrain interaction.

Effective communication: communication that assists the communicator in achieving his or her goals.

Ego involvement: how personally significant an issue is.

Elaborated argument: argument designed to be processed in the central route.

Elaboration: in agenda-setting theory, the elements selected to accompany or build on a news story.

Emotionally expressive: an affective response to conflict as opposed to a cognitive response.

Emphasis: the particular slant taken by a news story.

Enactment: noticing and attending to particular information in the information environment.

Encoding: the process of putting an idea into symbolic form.

Encounter: the stage of organizational assimilation during which the individual begins to learn the norms of the organization.

Enthymeme: a type of syllogism that emphasizes probabilities, signs, and examples, while omitting either a premise or the conclusion.

Equifinality: the idea that there is more than one way to achieve the same goal.

Equivocality: ambiguity of information.

Ethnography: a research method that requires the researcher to immerse himself or herself into a particular context or culture in order to understand communication rules and meanings.

Ethos: the persuader's character.

Evaluate and select: in decision-making, comparing each solution to the preestablished criteria to ascertain the best solution.

Exclusion: which stories are not covered or which elements of a story are not included.

Expectancy: what an individual anticipates will happen in a given situation.

Experiment: a research method that involves control and manipulation of variables. The only method that allows for a determination of cause and effect.

Expressive message design logic: the belief that the purpose of communication is to express one's thoughts, feelings, or beliefs.

Extension: when new concepts or ideas are added to a theory.

External consistency: when evaluating a theory, the extent to which the theory is coherent with other widely held theories.

External dialectic: a tension between a dyad and a larger group, including social norms.

Face: desired public image.

Face-threatening act: behaving in a way that challenges another person's face needs.

Facework: specific messages that thwart or minimize face-threatening acts.

Fantasy chain: a fantasy theme that is developed and embellished through group interaction and enters group consciousness

Fantasy theme: emerges when group members respond to a dramatizing message.

Fantasy: a creative understanding of events that fulfils a psychological or rhetorical need.

Fantasy chain: when dramatizing messages are developed further by the group, creating an extended fantasy.

Fear appeal: a persuasive message that emphasizes danger or harm that will occur if the receiver does not adopt the persuader's recommendations.

Fear control: a strategy that focuses on educating the audience about their abilities to enact solutions.

Feminine culture: the cultural belief that norms for behavior should not be determined by biological sex.

Field experiment: an experiment that takes place in a location where people would normally engage in particular communication.

Field of experience: part of cocultural theory where individuals consider their own standpoint or point of reference with what has and hasn't worked in the past.

First-level agenda setting: also called primary agenda setting; news media tell audiences what "news" to consider as important.

First-order change: changing the behaviors of individuals in a system.

Focus group: a survey method that involves questioning a small group of people at the same time.

Foot-in-the-door tactic: a commitment principle tactic when a persuader convinces the target to agree to a small request first, then it becomes harder to refuse larger requests because of the threat of appearing inconsistent with your commitment.

Framing: mass media's ability to highlight aspects of news stories by selecting, emphasizing, elaborating on, and even excluding news stories or parts of news stories to create a certain effect for the audience.

Frequency: how often members of a network communicate with each other.

Function: what communication does. For example, an apology serves the function of relationship repair.

Gatekeepers: in agenda-setting theory, news editors who select which stories run.

Gender criteria: sex role norms that encourage or dissuade one from sharing private information.

Gender: cultural expectations for men and women. Genders are masculine, feminine, androgynous, and undifferentiated.

Generalization: a pattern that holds true across groups, time, and place.

Goals: desired end states.

Good reasons: in the narrative paradigm, that which influence us to accept a narrative. Good reasons are based on an individual's culture, character, history, values, and experience.

Gratification: what an individual seeks to gain from the use of a particular media form

Group role: a pattern of communicative behaviors performed by one individual in light of expectations held by other group members.

Group: a system of three or more individuals focused on achieving a common purpose who influence and are influenced by each other.

Groupthink: a type of decision-making that leads to poor decisions.

Hedonic relevance: the degree to which an individual believes an actor's behavior directly affects him or her.

Heroes: organizational members who best represent or personify the organization's values.

Hierarchy principle: when modifying plans, we are more likely to adjust specific levels of the plan as opposed to abstract levels.

Hierarchy: systems existing within other systems that are ranked with one above the other

High power distance: cultural beliefs that accept power as a scarce resource; power differences are viewed as natural and inevitable.

High-context communication: messages that privilege relational harmony over clarity or directness.

Homeostasis: the natural balance in a system.

Humanistic approach: the philosophical approach to that study of communication that involves pragmatism, as well as specific theoretical and methodological commitments.

Hyperpersonal phase: part of social information processing model; this phase encourages users to present an edited or filtered version of themselves to create a more desirable image.

Idealized influence: serving as a role model for employees.

Identification: the sense of oneness with or belongingness to an organization.

Identify alternatives: in decision-making, the process of generating possible solutions.

Ideology: a mental framework used to understand the world; it includes language, concepts, categories, and images used to make sense of experiences.

Impersonal phase: part of social information processing model; this phase is task-oriented whereby CMC users communicate simply to accomplish a task.

Incentive: the extent to which an individual can provide rewards or punishments.

Inclusion–seclusion: an external tension that focuses on the desire for the dyad to be alone versus spending time with others in their network.

Independent variable: the presumed cause.

Index of channel experience: four categories of media experience that shape our perceptions of a medium's richness: the media channel, the message topic, the organizational context, and one's communication partner.

Individualism: the belief that the individual is the essential unit of society. Focuses on independence, achievement, and uniqueness.

Individualization: organizational newcomers' desire to have an impact on his or her role and work environment.

Individualized consideration: considering each individual's needs and abilities while supporting development and mentoring efforts.

Inductive theory: a theory developed by gathering data first, then drawing conclusions.

Indulgence: part of Hofstede's indulgence—restraint continuum; indulgent cultures value individuals' ability to satisfy their own desires and needs

Influence: the capacity to affect others indirectly

Information environment: internal and external information within which an organization exists.

In-groups: social affiliations to which an individual feels he or she belongs.

Inoculation: a method of preventing persuasion.

Inspirational motivation: presenting employees with a clear vision and a desirable future.

Integration: managing a dialectical tension by incorporating aspects of both poles so as to create a more fulfilling experience.

Intellectual stimulation: challenging assumptions and encouraging new approaches.

Intension: a deeper or more nuanced understanding of theoretical concepts.

Intentional cluster: a type of crisis, when the organization knowingly engaged in actions that sparked the predicament.

Intentionality: the extent to which a definition of communication focuses on source intent or receiver interpretation.

Interaction analysis/conversation analysis: a research method that focuses on the nature or structure of interaction.

Interactive strategy: a direct means by which to reduce uncertainty whereby one goes directly to the source who has the most information.

Intercultural communication: interaction between members of different cultures.

Interdependence: the notion that all system members are dependent on all other system members.

Interior locus of control: the belief that an individual has control over his or her own behaviors.

Internal consistency: when evaluating a theory, the extent to which the ideas of the theory are logically built on one another.

Internal dialectic: tensions within a dyad.

Interpersonal communication: messages between two interdependent persons, with a particular focus on how these messages are offered to initiate, define, maintain, or further a relationship.

Interpersonal media: channels that provide individuals with direct and one-to-one interaction, such as texting, telephone, or video calls.

Interpersonal phase: part of social information processing model; this phase mirrors relationally oriented qualities of traditional interpersonal communication, including information exchange, impression management, and exchange of values.

Interpretation: the understanding someone derives from a message.

Interview: an oral survey method.

Involuntary exit: the forced removal of an organizational member, such as being fired or laid off.

Isolation pressure: part of spiral of silence, people will exclude or ridicule individuals who don't seem aligned with social norms or public opinion.

Knowledge: refers to the cognitive content and understanding the procedures of how to act; a requirement for communication competence.

Laboratory experiment: an experiment that takes place in a location other than where people would normally engage in particular communication.

Latitude of acceptance: part of social judgment theory and includes all of the ideas that a person finds acceptable.

Latitude of noncommitment: part of social judgment theory and includes all of the ideas for which a person has no opinion.

Latitude of rejection: part of social judgment theory and includes all of the ideas that a person finds unacceptable.

Legacy media: media forms originally distributed via a pre-Internet medium (print, radio, television), and media companies whose original business was pre-Internet. Also known as traditional media.

Legitimate power: a person's ability to influence another based on their positional authority or expertise.

Length: how long a news story is; this could be measured in minutes or seconds (broadcast TV), column length (print), or percentage of screen used (online).

Level of observation: the focus of a definition of communication. The level of observation might be narrow, limiting the focus of what "counts" as communication, or broad, accepting a wide range of activities as communication.

Liking: persuasive messages that stress affinity toward a person, place, or object.

Logos: the Aristotelian focus on logic as the foundation for persuasion.

Long-term orientation: a cultural approach that is associated with thrift, savings, perseverance, and the willingness to subordinate one's self to achieve a goal.

Low power distance: a cultural belief that values the minimization of power differences.

Low-context communication: a cultural approach to communication that values direct, explicit communication.

MAIN model: proposes four categories of affordances in digital media: modality, agency, interactivity, and navigability.

Mainstreaming: a common view of social reality based on frequent exposure to the repetitive and dominating images, stories, and messages depicted on TV.

Manipulation: in establishing causality, research participants are exposed to varying levels of the independent variable.

Masculine culture: a cultural belief that the appropriate roles for men and women are distinct.

Mass communication: a process in which professional communicators use technology to share messages over great distances to influence large audiences.

Mass media: the organizations responsible for using technology to send mass messages to the public.

Masspersonal media: blends aspects of interpersonal media with mass communication; provides users with direct and large audience interaction

Material coherence: the extent to which a narrative is consistent with other stories already accepted by the receiver.

Mean-world syndrome: heavy television viewers significantly overestimate real-life danger.

Media affordances: a user's perceptions of a given technology's action possibilities.

Media richness: the information-carrying capacity of a medium.

Media: a generic term that broadly encompasses messages augmented with technology

Mediated communication: communication in which there is something in between the sender and receiver. Most often the mediation is a technology.

Meme: ideas, behaviors, or practices that spread from one person to another in a network.

Message design logic: a belief about how communication should work.

Metamorphosis: the stage of organizational assimilation during which the individual is fully socialized into the organization.

Minimax principle: the assumption that people want to make the most of benefits while lessening costs.

Mission: a formal statement of the organization's purpose.

Model: either a synonym to the term theory, a precursor to a theory, a physical representation of a theory, or a specific—often mathematical—application of predication.

Modeling: by observing others one forms an idea of how new behaviors are performed, and on later occasions, this coded information serves as a guide for action.

Motivation process: the desire to use a learned action; part of the modeling process.

Motivation: refers to your interest in and willingness to approach rather than avoid communication; a requirement for communication competence.

Motivational criteria: individual variations that encourage or dissuade one from sharing private information.

Motivational process: to go from observation to action requires the motivation to use the learned action. Motivation is inspired by three types of incentives: direct, vicarious, and self-produced.

Multiplexity: the extent to which two network members are linked together by more than one relationship or type of communication.

Multiplicative: an assumption of extended parallel processing model that the threat variables and efficacy variables have the power to multiply in strength.

Muted group theory: suggests that people who do not have power are muted groups; their membership in a nondominant group influences what they talk about, how much they talk, the channels they use, the words and concepts that are used.

Mythos: a collection of stories expressing ideas that cannot be verified or proved in any absolute way.

Narrative coherence: a narrative that appears to flow smoothly, make sense, and be believable.

Narrative fidelity: a narrative that appears truthful and congruent with our own experiences.

Narrative rationality: a logical method of reasoning by which a person can determine how believable another's narrative is.

Narrative: the symbolic words and actions people use to assign meaning.

Need for orientation: relevance of a news story, as well as uncertainty.

Negative face: a person's desire to act freely, without constraints or imposition from others.

Negative politeness: when a speaker makes an effort to recognize another person's negative face needs.

Negotiated code: when decoding a message, the receiver accepts the dominant ideology implicit in the message but engages in selective interpretation so that the message betters first his or her worldview.

Nonaccommodation: failure to converge or diverge.

Nonassertive: an approach for cocultural communication where an individual puts others' goals above their own.

Nondominant group: social group in which members have a disadvantaged position within the larger culture.

Nonrandom sample: a sampling technique in which all members of the population do not have an equal chance of being included.

Nonsummativity: the notion that the system is more than simply a sum of its parts.

Normative beliefs: perceptions about what others in your social network expect you to do.

Normative judgment: whether a definition of communication requires success or accuracy in order for an activity to be considered communication.

Objectivity: the belief that researchers should be value free when conducting research.

Off-record: subtle hints or indirect mentions of a face-threatening topic.

Open-ended questions: in a survey, questions that allow a respondent to use his or her own words to respond.

Openness–closedness: an internal tension that centers on the desire to share information versus the desire to keep some information private.

Oppositional code: in decoding a message, the individual recognizes the ideological bias in the message. Individuals who use the oppositional code identify the preferred reading but deconstruct the message and reconstruct it from a different point of view.

Organization: an entity that systematically and consciously coordinates people and/or activities so as to accomplish a broader goal.

Organizational assimilation: the process of being socialized into an organization.

Organizational communication: the meaning created between individuals in an organizational setting, between individuals and organizations, and between organizations and societies.

Organizational culture: the lived experience of organizational members that consists of values, beliefs, and ways of behaving and communicating.

Organizing: the process of communication that creates an organization.

Other-face concern: demonstrating an awareness of the other person's positive and negative face needs.

Outcome value: in social exchange theory, what an individual receives from the relationship (i.e., rewards minus costs).

Out-groups: social affiliations to which a person feels he or she does not belong.

Overestimation of the group: when group members have an inflated view of the group's abilities.

Participant–observer: in an ethnography, when a researcher becomes fully involved with the culture or context but admits his or her research agenda before entering the environment.

Participatory media: media formats and entities where audience engagement or contribution is significant to the platform.

Particularism: approach of social science whereby narrowly defined areas are incrementally studied with the belief that the whole picture will be uncovered eventually.

Passive strategy: an unassertive approach to reducing uncertainty whereby one observes the situation so as to gather information rather than directly seeking information from another person.

Pathos: Aristotelian focus on emotion as a means of persuasion.

Perceived behavioral control: an inability to behave consistently with one's attitudes. Two components: self-efficacy and controllability.

Perceived rewards and costs: one's view of the best and worst outcomes.

Perceived severity: refers to an individual's belief about how serious the consequences of a behavior might be.

Perceived susceptibility: refers to an individual's belief in the likelihood of experiencing negative consequences.

Peripheral route: a route for processing persuasive messages when motivation or ability is missing. Results in short-term persuasion at best.

Person–job fit: how well an individual's skill set and personality align with the demands of a specific role.

Person–organization fit: how well an individual's values and beliefs align with the organization's values and beliefs, and vice versa.

Persuasion stage: part of the innovation decision process whereby a potential adopter goes beyond awareness of an innovation and actively seeks information about it.

Persuasion: human communication designed to influence others by modifying their beliefs, values, or attitudes.

Persuasion: human communication meant to influence others by altering beliefs, values, or attitudes.

Plan complexity: how complicated or sophisticated a plan is; includes having contingencies and specificity and increases communication effectiveness.

Planning: process of assessing a situation, determining the goals to be pursued, creating or, retrieving a plan, and then enacting it.

Plans: cognitive structures that allow us to develop a course of action.

Pluralistic ignorance: distortion in perception of the dominant view whereby we perceive public opinion to be either farther from or closer to our own opinion than it actually is.

Population: everyone or everything that demonstrates a particular characteristic.

Position: the location of a news story; this could be the order it appears (broadcast news), which page or section of a newspaper, or how far "down" on a digital screen.

Positive face: a person's need to be liked, appreciated, and admired.

Positive politeness: emphasizing the receiver's need to be liked or appreciated.

Power: the ability to influence others through rewards or punishments. Influences politeness.

Practicality: when evaluating a theory, the extent to which the theory can be used to solve real-world problems.

Pragmatism: the belief that scholars should focus on the communicative choices people make.

Praxis: the assumption that the development of a relationship is neither linear (always moving forward) nor repetitive (cycling through the same things again and again).

Predictability–novelty: an internal tension that centers on the desire to have new experiences versus the desire to manage uncertainty.

Preferred Outcome: part of co-cultural theory where individuals consider their goal—to assimilate, accommodate, or separate

Preferred reading: decoding a message using the dominant ideology.

Prescriptive prejudice: actual evaluations of women as less effective than men.

Pressure toward uniformity: Pressure placed on group members by other group members to reach a unanimous agreement.

Prestige: the social distance between communicators. Influences politeness.

Preventive facework: strategies used to help ourselves or others avoid or mitigate face-threatening acts.

Primary research: research reported by the person who conducted it.

Privacy rules: conventions that govern decisions about sharing private information.

Private information: information that is inaccessible to others.

Problem analysis: a realistic examination of the nature, extent, and likely causes of a problem.

Production: in adaptive structuration theory, the idea that the choices group members make create a structure.

Promotive communication: in functional group decision-making, communication geared toward one of the requisite functions.

Public opinion: the sum of beliefs about controversial issues that one feels comfortable expressing publicly, without fear of social ostracism or isolation.

Public–private: a tension between revealing and concealing private information.

Punctuation: the desire to understand the beginnings and endings and causes and effects of communication.

Qualitative: an approach to analyzing data that focuses on rich descriptions of what has been observed, interpreted, or critiqued.

Quantitative: an approach to analyzing data that focuses on numbers or statistics.

Quasi-statistical sense: individuals' sense or strong awareness of how their views align with what is perceived to be socially acceptable.

Questionnaire: a written survey method.

Random sample: technique in which all members of the population have an equal chance of being in the sample.

Rebuild: strategies are used to change the perception of the organization

Receiver orientation: the position in the intentionality debate proposing that anything a receiver considers a message should be considered communication.

Reciprocate: engaging in the same behavior as someone else.

Reciprocity: influence of efforts that emphasize a give-and-take relationship.

Refutational preemption: a counterpersuasive effort that involves raising specific challenges and then contesting them.

Relationship level: indicators in a message that suggest how to interpret the message and the nature of the relationship between the communicators.

Reproduction process: individuals' demonstration of a new behavior through modeling; beyond simply mimicry, individuals refine the action through self-corrective adjustments based on feedback and focused demonstrations of behavioral segments that have only been learned in part.

Reproduction: in adaptive structuration theory, the idea that the structures group members create constrain future actions, thus being reinforced.

Reputational threat: a challenge to the image that an organization has developed and has the potential to affect the organization's standing in the field.

Resonance: congruency between viewers' own violent experiences and that which they see on TV.

Response efficacy: the effectiveness of a proposed solution.

Restraint: part of Hofstede's indulgence—restraint continuum; cultures valuing restraint oppose the pursuit of personal pleasure and focus on conforming to social norms.

Retention process: visually and verbally storing mediated images.

Retention: The third step in sociocultural evolution. In this stage, the organization stores what was done and how it was done, either formally or informally, so that members can refer to it again.

Revelation–concealment: an external tension between keeping some information private within the dyad versus sharing information with the larger network.

Rewards: preferred resources (e.g., time, money, love).

Rhetoric: according to Aristotle, "the art of discovering the means of persuasion available for any subject."

Rhetorical criticism: a research method that involves describing, interpreting, and analyzing texts.

Rhetorical message design logic: the belief that communication is a cooperative game in which participants pursue multiple goals.

Rhetorical proofs: three types of rational arguments that can be used in various combinations—logos, ethos, and pathos.

Rhetorical situation: a specific type of persuasive event, for example, political, legal, or epideictic situation.

Rhetorical vision: a unified way of viewing the world.

Risk: the extent to which engaging in a face-threatening act will cause harm to another's face needs.

Risk–benefit criteria: an assessment of the rewards and costs for disclosing private information.

Rites and rituals: public performances that demonstrate organizational values.

Rules: how something should be done.

Sampling: studying only a small group of people or objects and assuming the results hold true of the entire population.

Scarcity: a peripheral persuasive message that preys on people's worry of missing out on something.

Schemata: cognitive structures for organizing new information.

Scholarly theory: one that has undergone systematic research.

Secondary research: research reported by someone other than the person who conducted it.

Second-level agenda setting: also known as attribute agenda setting; the manner in which stories are framed influences audiences' attitudes and how to think about the issues covered.

Second-order change: resolving underlying differences in perspective, most often through the process of reframing.

Segmentation: managing dialectical tensions by compartmentalizing the relationship such that certain issues coincide with one pole or need and other issues are appropriate for the opposite pole.

Selection: in the dialectical perspective, managing dialectical tensions by favoring one pole or need at the expense of the other. In organizing theory, an organization's decision to rely on either a rule or a double interact. In agenda-setting theory, news stories chosen to be printed or aired.

Selective attention: focusing solely on information that reaffirms beliefs.

Selective exposure: actively avoiding information inconsistent with previously established beliefs or behaviors.

Selective interpretation: deciphering ambiguous information so it is perceived to be consistent with established beliefs.

Selective retention: dismissing or forgetting information that creates dissonance.

Self-efficacy: an individual's belief that she or he can perform a behavior.

Self-face concern: being aware of one's own positive and negative face needs.

Self-produced motivation: when individuals rely on their own personal standards, engaging in observed activities they find personally worthwhile and refusing to participate in those activities of which they disapprove.

Separation: when the cocultural member avoids interactions with the dominant group.

Sex: the biological differentiation between males and females.

Short-term orientation: a cultural belief in immediate gratification.

Simple control: exerting direct authority through commands.

Situational characteristics: problems with the experiences of a group that might lead to groupthink.

Situational context: a consideration of the setting, circumstance, and characteristics of those involved

Situational factors: external causes for behavior that are relatively uncontrollable and determined by the environment or situation.

Skill: refers to the ability to perform a communication behavior; a requirement for communication competence.

Social desirability: consistent with social conventions.

Social influence: part of channel expansion theory, the perception of how others who are important to us refer to and/or use a medium.

Social media: digital technologies that allow people to connect, interact, produce, and share content.

Social power: a person's ability to influence based on perceived status, charisma, or prestige

Social proof: persuasive messages that focus on peer pressure.

Social scientific approach: the philosophical approach to a study of communication that involves determinism, as well as specific theoretical and methodological commitments.

Socialization: the process by which an organizational newcomer internalizes the values and behaviors in order to fulfill organizational expectations.

Socially mediated path of influence: media influences used to link participants to social networks and community settings. Through these social connections, individuals receive guidance, incentives, and social support, making behavioral change more likely.

Sociocultural evolution: the process of organizational information processing. Organizations that do not go through this process will cease to exist.

Socioemotional communication: communication focused on developing, maintaining, and repairing relationships between group members.

Solution-orientation path: group members make little or no effort to investigate the problem. Rather, group members assume they understand the problem and immediately seek a solution that will satisfy group members.

Source orientation: the position in the intentionality debate proposing the only messages that should be considered communication are those a source intends to send.

Specificity: the amount of detail presented in a plan.

Standpoint theory: suggests that people's position in society influences their experiences which in turn shapes their point of view(or standpoint).

Standpoint: a position from which an individual views and understands the world.

Strategic communication: refers to purposeful communication used by organizations to achieve organizational goals.

Strategy: a process of determining what should be done to achieve a goal.

Strength: the frequency, intimacy, or intensity of a network connection.

Structural coherence: the degree to which a narrative has a logical structure and flow.

Structural flaws: problems with the composition of a group that include homogeneity, biased leadership, and lack of decision-making norms.

Structure: patterns of relationships or interaction.

Subjectivity: the belief that meaning is unique to each person.

Subsystem: a smaller part of the group as a whole

Success bias: an inflated estimation of the likelihood that a plan will be effective

Succinctness: when evaluating theory, the extent to which a theory's explanation or description is sufficiently concise.

Suprasystem: is the larger system within which the system operates.

Survey research: a method for studying communication that centers on how people think, feel, or intend to behave. Specific types of survey research include interviews, focus groups, and questionnaires.

Syllogism: is a type of "if-—then" deductive reasoning that typically includes a major premise, a minor premise, and a conclusion.

Symbolic convergence: the transformation of a collection of individuals to an identifiable group with a group consciousness.

Symbolic double jeopardy: minority persons are significantly less visible on TV than in real life, and these minority TV characters are much more likely to be portrayed as victims of violence.

Symmetrical pattern: a pattern of communication in which the sender and receiver use similar styles of communication.

Synergy: the ability to achieve more through group effort than individual effort.

System: a group of people who interrelate to form a whole.

Task communication: communication focused on achieving an instrumental goal.

Team: an ongoing, coordinated group of people working together.

Technological control: exerting control over employees through the use of technology to manage what can and can't be done in the workplace.

Text/data mining: a research method that uses advanced data analysis techniques to uncover patterns in large amounts of information.

Textual analysis: a research method that studies the characteristics or patterns of a written or recorded message.

Theory: any systematic summary about the nature of the communication process.

Third-level agenda setting: how issue salience and attribute salience are, or may be, connected

Third-party help: asking a person outside of the relationship to help manage the conflict.

Threat: a forewarning of a potential persuasive attack on beliefs, making sure the target of the persuasive effort is aware of his or her susceptibility to the attack.

Totality: interdependence between relationship partners.

Traditional media: media forms originally distributed via a pre-Internet medium (print, radio, television), and media companies whose original business was pre-Internet. Also known as legacy media.

Typical Communication Approach: refers to how the cocultural group usually communicates, for example someone from an individualist culture is likely to prefer an assertive or aggressive approach as compared to someone from a collectivist culture who prefers a passive approach.

Ubiquity: part of spiral of silence; refers to the pervasiveness of mass media.

Uncertainty avoidance: cultural preferences for the extent to which ambiguity is tolerated.

Uncertainty: the inability to explain or predict one's own or others' behavior.

Unitary path: when a group uses the same process to generate solutions, regardless of the type of problem they are seeking to solve.

Unobtrusive control: exerting authority over employees by identification with an organizational mission.

Uses and gratifications approach: assumes media use is active and focuses on receivers' motivations for using various media forms.

Values: core beliefs.

Variable: any concept that has two or more values.

Vicarious motivation: when individuals are motivated by the successes of others similar to themselves.

Victim cluster: a type of crisis, when the organization itself is a victim of the crisis.

Violation valence: the positive or negative evaluation of an expectation.

Violence index: an objective research instrument that uses content analysis to measure the prevalence, frequency, and role of characters involved in TV violence.

Vision: a formal statement of what the organization wants to achieve

Vocational anticipatory socialization: the stage of organizational assimilation during which an individual learns what it means to work.

Voluntary exit: when an organizational member chooses to leave the organization.

Warranting: part of the hyperpersonal model in which online communicators seek to determine whether there is congruence between another's online presentation and that person's real-life attributes.

Web-native media: outlets that originated online and distribute content primarily (or solely) via the Internet. Also known as digital-native media.

Working theory: generalizations made in particular professions about the best techniques for doing something.

REFERENCES

Adler, N. J. (1997). *International dimensions of organizational behavior* (3rd ed.). South-Western College.

Afifi, W. A., & Weiner, J. L. (2004). Toward a theory of motivated information management. *Communication Theory*, *14*, 167–190. https://doi.org/10.1111/j.1468-2885.2004.tb00310.x

Ajzen, I. (1988). *Attitudes, personality, and behavior*. Dorsey Press.

Ajzen, I. (1991). The theory of planned behavior. *Organizational Behavior and Human Decision Processes*, *50*, 179–211.

Altabbaa, G., Kaba, A., & Beran, T. N. (2019). Moving on from structured communication to collaboration: a communication schema for interprofessional teams. *Journal of Communication in Healthcare*, *12*(3/4), 160–169. https://doi.org/10.1080/17538068.2019.1675427

Altman, D. (2020). Understanding the US failure on coronavirus—An essay by Drew Altman. *BMJ*, *370*, 1–3. https://doi.org/10.1136/bmj.m3417

Altman, I., & Taylor, D. (1973). *Social penetration: The development of interpersonal relationships*. Holt.

American Academy of Child and Adolescent Psychiatry. (2020, February). *Screen time and children*. *Facts for Families*, *54*. https://www.aacap.org/AACAP/Families_and_Youth/Facts_for_Families/FFF-Guide/Children-And-Watching-TV-054.aspx

American College of Pediatricians. (2016). The impact of media use and screen time on children, adolescents, and families. *Position Statement*. https://acpeds.org/position-statements/the-impact-of-media-use-and-screen-time-on-children-adolescents-and-families

An, C., & Pfau, M. (2004). The efficacy of inoculation in televised political debates. *Journal of Communication*, *54*, 421–436.

Anders, A. D., Coleman, J. T., & Castleberry, S. B. (2020). Communication preferences of business-to-business buyers for receiving initial sales messages: A comparison of media channel selection theories. *International Journal of Business Communication*, *57*, 370–400. https://doi.org/10.1177/2329488417702476

Anderson, K. (1998, February). Pop-psychology as science and infomerical as journalism: ABC News sponsors John Gray's interplanetary sexism. *Sojourner: The Women's Forum*, *23*, 1–14-2, 15, 44.

Ansari, A. (2015). *Modern romance*. Penguin Press.

Antheunis, M. L., Schouten, A. P., & Walther, J. B. (2020). The hyperpersonal effect in online dating: Effects of text-based CMC vs. videoconferencing before meeting face-to-face. *Media Psychology*, *23*, 820–839. https://doi.org/10.1080/15213269.2019.1648217

Ardener, E. (1975a). Belief and the problem of women. In S. Ardener (Ed.), *Perceiving women* (pp. 1–17). Malaby.

Ardener, E. (1975b). The "problem" revisited. In S. Ardener (Ed.), *Perceiving women* (pp. 19–27). Malaby.

Aristotle., Roberts, W. R, & Bywater, I. (1984). *Rhetoric*. New York Modern Library.

Armengol, X., Fernandez, V., Simo, P., & Sallan, J. M. (2017). An examination of the effects of self-regulatory focus on the perception of the media richness: The case of e-mail. International *Journal of Business Communication, 54*, 394–407. https://doi.org/10.1177/2329488415572780

Asch, S. E. (1956). Studies of independence and conformity: A minority of one against a unanimous majority. *Psychological Monographs: General and Applied, 70*, 1–70. https://doi.org/10.1037/h0093718

Ashby, W. R. (1962). Principles of the self-organizing system. In H. von Foerster & G. Zopf (Eds.), *Principles of self-organization* (pp. 255–278). Pergamon.

Atwell Seate, A., & Mastro, D. (2016). Media's influence on immigration attitudes: An intergroup threat theory approach. *Communication Monographs, 83*, 194–213. https://doi.org/10.1080/0363775 1.2015.1068433

Aubrey, A. (2017, April 5). Judge takes up big soda's suit to abolish Philadelphia's soda tax. *NPR*. http://www.npr.org/sections/thesalt/2017/04/05/522626223/judges-take-up-big-sodas-suit-to-abolish-philadelphias-sugar-tax

Aubrey, J., Behm-Morawitz, E., & Kim, K. (2014). Understanding the effects of MTV's 16 and Pregnant on adolescent girls' beliefs, attitudes, and behavioral intentions toward teen pregnancy. *Journal of Health Communication, 19*, 1145–1160. https://doi.org/10.1080/10810730.2013.872721

Avery, E., Lariscy, R., & Sweetser, K. D. (2010). Social media and shared—or divergent—uses? A coorientation analysis of public relations practitioners and journalists. *International Journal of Strategic Communication, 4*, 189–205.

Axley, S. R. (1984). Managerial and organizational communication in terms of the conduit metaphor. *Academy of Management Review, 9*, 428–437.

Aylor, B., & Dainton, M. (2001). Antecedents in romantic jealousy experience, expression, and goals. *Western Journal of Communication, 64*, 370–391.

Aylor, B., & Dainton, M. (2004). Biological sex and psychological gender as predictors of routine and strategic relational maintenance. *Sex Roles, 50*, 689–697.

Bailey, T. A. (2006, June 19–23). *Cultural studies and cultivation theory: Points of convergence* [Paper presentation]. The International Communication Association, Dresden, Germany.

Bales, R. F. (1970). *Personality and interpersonal behavior.* Holt, Rinehart & Winston.

Banas, J. A., & Miller, G. (2013). Inducing resistance to conspiracy theory propaganda: Testing inoculation and metainoculation strategies. *Human Communication Research, 39*(2), 184–207. https://doi-org.dbproxy.lasalle.edu/10.1111/hcre.12000

Banas, J., & Rains, S. (2008, November 21–24). *Testing inoculation theory: A meta-analysis* [Paper presented]. The Annual Meeting of the NCA 94th Annual Convention, San Diego, CA, United States. http://www.allacademic.com/meta/p261402_index.html

Bandura, A. (1977). *Social learning theory.* Prentice Hall.

Bandura, A. (1986). *Social foundations of thought and action: A social cognitive theory.* Prentice Hall.

Bandura, A. (1994). Social cognitive theory of mass communication. In J. Bryant & D. Zillmann (Eds.), *Media effects: Advances in theory and research,* (pp. 61–90). Lawrence Erlbaum.

Bandura, A. (2001). Social cognitive theory of mass communication. *Media Psychology, 3*, 265–299. https://doi.org/10.1207/S1532785XMEP0303_03

Bandura, A., Ross, D., & Ross, S. (1963). Imitations of aggressive film-mediated models. *Journal of Abnormal Psychology, 66*, 3–11.

Bar-On, R. (2006). The Bar-On model of emotional-social intelligence (ESI). *Psicothema*, *18*(Suppl), 13–25.

Baran, S. J., & Davins, D. K. (2020). *Mass communication theory* (8th ed.). Oxford University Press.

Barge, J. K. (1994). *Leadership*. St. Martin's Press.

Barker, J. R. (1999). *The discipline of teamwork: Participation and concertive control*, SAGE.

Barker, R., & Gower, K. (2010). Strategic application of storytelling in organizations: Toward effective communication in a diverse world. *Journal of Business Communication*, *47*, 295–312. https://doi.org/10.1177/0021943610369782

Barnett, E. (2011, November 22). Facebook cuts six degrees of separation to four. *Telegraph*. http://www.telegraph.co.uk/technology/facebook/8906693/Facebook-cuts-six-degrees-of-separation-to-four.html

Bass, B. M. (1985). *Leadership and performance beyond expectations*. Free Press.

Bass, B. M. (1997). Does the transactional–transformational leadership paradigm transcend organizational and national boundaries? *American Psychologist*, *52*, 130–139.

Bass, B. M. (1998). *Transformational leadership: Industrial, military, and educational impact*. Lawrence Erlbaum.

Baumgartner, R. J. (2009). Organizational culture and leadership: Preconditions for the development of a sustainable corporation. *Sustainable Development*, *17*, 102–113.

Baxter, L. A. (1988). A dialectical perspective on communication strategies in relationship development. In S. Duck (Ed.), *Handbook of personal relationships: Theory, research, and interventions* (pp. 257–273). Wiley.

Baxter, L. A., & Montgomery, B. M. (1996). *Relating: Dialogues and dialectics*. Guilford Press.

Beach, L. R. (1990). *Image theory: Decision making in personal and organizational contexts*. Wiley.

Beaton. (2017, January 6). Top employers say millennials need these four skills in 2017. *Forbes*. https://www.forbes.com/sites/carolinebeaton/2017/01/06/top-employers-say-millennials-need-these-4-skills-in-2017/#66eae9167fe4

Becker, S. L. (1984). Marxist approaches to media studies: The British experience. *Critical Studies in Mass Communication*, *1*(1), 66–80.

Behm-Morawitz, E., & Ta, D. (2014). Cultivating virtual stereotypes? The impact of video game play on racial/ethnic stereotypes. *Howard Journal of Communications*, *25*, 1–15. https://doi.org/10.1080/10646175.2013.835600

Bellware, K. (2021, September 17). Students are destroying bathrooms, swiping school supplies in latest TikTok challenge gone awry. *The Washington Post*. https://www.washingtonpost.com/technology/2021/09/17/devious-licks-tik-tok/

Benedict, B. C. (2020). Examining the experiences of remaining employees after a coworker dismissal: Initial message characteristics, information seeking, uncertainty, and perceived social costs. *Management Communication Quarterly*, *34*, 495–525. https://doi.org/10.1177/0893318920949327

Benoit, W. L. (2015). *Accounts, excuses, and apologies: Image repair theory and research* (2nd ed.). State University of New York Press.

Berger, C. R. (1979). Beyond initial interaction: Uncertainty, understanding, and the development of interpersonal relationships. In H. Giles & R. St. Clair (Eds.), *Language and social psychology* (pp. 122–144). Basil Blackwell.

Berger, C. R. (1995). Inscrutable goals, uncertain plans, and the production of communicative action. In C. R. Berger & M. Burgoon (Eds.), *Communication and social processes* (pp. 1–28). Michigan State University Press.

Berger, C. R. (1997). *Planning strategic interaction: Attaining goals through communicative action*. Lawrence Erlbaum.

Berger, C. R. (2015). Planning theory of communication: Goal attainment through communicative action. In D.O. Braithwaite & P. Schrodt (Eds.), *Engaging theories in interpersonal communication: Multiple perspectives* (2nd ed., pp. 89–102). Sage.

Berger, C. R., & Bradac, J. J. (1982). *Language and social knowledge: Uncertainty in interpersonal relations*. Arnold.

Berger, C. R., & Calabrese, R. J. (1975). Some explorations in initial interaction and beyond: Toward a developmental theory of interpersonal communication. *Human Communication Research, 1*, 99–112.

Berman, S. J., & Hellweg, S. A. (1989). Perceived supervisor communication competence and supervisor satisfaction as a function of quality circle participation. *Journal of Business Communication, 26*, 103–122.

Berr, J. (2016, November 8). Election 2016's price tag: $6.8 billion. *CBS Moneywatch*. http://www.cbs news.com/news/election-2016s-price-tag-6-8-billion

Bitzer, L. F. (1959). Aristotle's enthymeme revisited. *Quarterly Journal of Speech, 45*, 399–408. https://doi.org/10.1080/00335635909382374

Bitzer, L. F. (1992). The rhetorical situation. *Philosophy & Rhetoric, 25*, 1–14.

Bizzell, P., & Herzberg, B. (1990). *The rhetorical tradition: Readings from the classical times to the present*. Bedford Books.

Blossom, J. (2009). *Content nation: Surviving and thriving as social media changes our work, our lives, and our future*. Wiley.

Boeson, U. (2021, Feb 18). *Sugar taxes back on the menu*. Taxfoundation.org. https://taxfoundation.o rg/sugar-taxes/

Boguszewicz-Kreft, M., Kreft, J., & Żurek, P. (2019). Myth and storytelling: The case of the Walt Disney Company. In J. Kreft, S. Kuczamer-Kłopotowska & A. Kalinowska-Żeleźnik (Eds.), *Myth in Modern Media Management and Marketing*, (pp. 22–49). IGI Global. https://doi. org/10.4018/978-1-5225-9100-9

Bonito, J. A., & Wolski, S. L. (2002). The adaptation of complaints to participation frameworks. *Communication Studies, 53*, 252–268.

Bormann, E. G. (1982). The symbolic convergence theory of communication: Applications and implications for teachers and consultants. *Journal of Applied Communication Research, 10*, 50–61.

Bormann, E. G. (1996). Symbolic convergence theory and communication in group decision making. In R. Y. Hirokawa & M. S. Poole (Eds.), *Communication and group decision making* (2nd ed., pp. 81–113). Sage.

Bormann, E. G., Cragan, J. E., & Shields, D. C. (1994). In defense of symbolic convergence theory: A look at the theory and its criticisms after two decades. *Communication Theory, 4*, 259–294.

Brands, R. (2015, July 15). 'Think manager, think man' stops us seeing woman as leaders. *The Guardian (U.S. Edition)*. https://www.theguardian.com/women-in-leadership/2015/jul/15/ think-manager-think-man-women-leaders-biase-workplace

Brooks, R. (2018, August 2). 10 Companies with core values that actually reflect their culture. *Peakon Post*. https://peakon.com/us/blog/employee-success/best-company-core-values/

Brown, A., & Patton, E. (2017, April 3). The narrowing, but persistent, gender gap in pay. *Pew Research Center*. http://www.pewresearch.org/fact-tank/2017/04/03/gender-pay-gap-facts

Brown, P., & Levinson, S. (1978). Universals in language usage: Politeness phenomenon. In E. Goody (Ed.), *Questions and politeness* (pp. 56–89). Cambridge University Press.

Brown, P., & Levinson, S. (1987). *Politeness: Some universals in language use*. Cambridge University Press.

Bryant, S. E. (2003). The role of transformational and transactional leadership in creating, sharing and exploiting organizational knowledge. *Journal of Leadership and Organizational Studies*, *9*, 32–43.

Burgoon, J. K. (1978). A communication model of personal space violations: Explication and an initial test. *Human Communication Research*, *4*, 129–142.

Burgoon, J. K. (1994). Nonverbal signals. In M. L. Knapp & G. R. Miller (Eds.), *Handbook of interpersonal communication* (pp. 229–285). Sage.

Burgoon, M., Pfau, M., & Birk, T. S. (1995). An inoculation theory explanation for the effects of corporate issue/advocacy advertising campaigns. *Communication Research*, *22*, 485–505.

Burgraff, C. S., & Sillars, A. L. (1987). A critical examination of sex differences in marriage. *Communication Monographs*, *54*, 276–294.

Burns, M. E. (2015). Recruiting prospective students with stories: How personal stories influence the process of choosing a university. *Communication Quarterly*, *63*(1), 99–118. https://doi.org/10.1080/01463373.2014.965838

Buturoiu, D. R., & Gavrilescu, M. (2021). Key words associated with the COVID-19 pandemic. Comparing the media and the public agenda. *Journal of Media Research*, *14*, 5–25. https://doi.org/10.24193/jmr.40.1

Caldwell, D. F., & O'Reilly, C. A. (1990). Measuring person–job fit using a profile comparison process. *Journal of Applied Psychology*, *75*(6), 648–657. https://doi.org/10.1037/0021-9010.75.6.648

Calhoun, L. (2008, November 21–24). *One cannot not communicate (unless you are the US and Iran): An interactionist perspective on the foreign policy dilemmas between the US and Iran* [Paper presented]. Meeting of the National Communication Association, San Diego, CA, United States.

Calzo, J. P., & Ward, L. M. (2009). Media exposure and viewers' attitudes toward homosexuality: Evidence for mainstreaming or resonance? *Journal of Broadcasting & Electronic Media*, *53*, 280–299. https://doi.org/10.1080/08838150902908049

Camara, S., & Orbe, M. (2010). Analyzing strategic responses to discriminatory acts: A co-cultural communicative investigation. *Journal of International & Intercultural Communication*, *3*, 83–113. https://doi.org/10.1080/17513051003611602

Canary, D. J., Cody, M. J., & Manusov, V. L. (2008). *Interpersonal communication: A goals-based approach* (4th ed.). Bedford/St. Martin's.

Canary, D. J., Emmers-Sommer, T. M., & Faulkner, S. (1997). *Sex and gender differences in personal relationships*. Guilford Press.

Canary, D. J., & Hause, K. S. (1993). Is there any reason to research sex differences in communication? *Communication Quarterly*, *41*, 129–144.

Canary, D. J., & Zelley, E. D. (2000). Current research programs on relational maintenance behaviors. In M. E. Roloff (Ed.), *Communication Yearbook 23* (pp. 305–339). Sage.

Carlson, J. R. (1995). *Channel expansion theory: A dynamic view of media and information richness perceptions* [Doctoral dissertation, University of Michigan]. Available from ProQuest Dissertations (9526741).

Carlson, J. R., & Zmud, R. W. (1999). Channel expansion theory and the experiential nature of media richness perceptions. *The Academy of Management Journal, 42*(2), 153–170. https://doi.org/10.2307/257090

Carr, S. (2021, February 15). *How many ads do we see in a day in 2021?* PPC Protect. https://ppcprotect.com/blog/strategy/how-many-ads-do-we-see-a-day/

Caruso, D. R., Mayer, J. D., & Salovey, P. (2002). Relation of an ability measure of emotional intelligence to personality. *Journal of Personality Assessment, 79*(2), 306–320. https://doi.org/10.1207/S15327752JPA7902_12

Chaffey, D. (2021, June 21). *What happens online in 60 seconds in 2021?* Smart Insights.com. https://www.smartinsights.com/internet-marketing-statistics/happens-online-60-seconds/

Chaiken, S. (1980). Heuristic Versus systematic information processing and the use of source versus message cues in persuasion. *Journal of Personality & Social Psychology, 39*, 752–766.

Charoensap-Kelly, P., Mestayer, C. L., & Knight, G. B. (2020). To come out or not to come out: Minority religious identity self-disclosure in the United States workplace. *Management Communication Quarterly, 34*, 213–250. https://doi.org/10.1177/0893318919890072

Chatman, J. A. (1991). Matching people and organizations: Selection and socialization in public accounting firms. *Administrative Science Quarterly, 36*, 459–484. https://doi.org/10.2307/2393204

Chaudary, A. (2013, May 21). Boston Marathon Saudi "suspect" speaks out. *The Islamic Monthly.* http://www.theislamicmonthly.com/exclusive-interview-with-the-saudi-man-from-boston

Chefneux, G. (2015). Humour at work. *Language & Dialogue, 5*, 381–407. https://doi.org/10.1075/ld.5.3.02che

Chen, B. X. (2013, February 10). Samsung emerges as potent rival to Apple's cool. *New York Times.* http://www.nytimes.com/2013/02/11/technology/samsung-challenges-apples-cool-factor.html?pagewanted=all&_r=0

Chen, C. (2019, June 28). We asked 4 women to try Athleta's new sustainable swimsuits made from recycled nylon — here's what they thought. *Business Insider.* https://markets.businessinsider.com/news/stocks/athleta-swimsuit-review

Chia, S. C., & Sun, Y. (2020). Pluralistic ignorance. In J. Bulck (Ed.), *The international encyclopedia of media psychology.* https://doi.org/10.1002/9781119011071.iemp0073

Choi, M., & Choung, H. (2021). Mediated communication matters during the COVID-19 pandemic: The use of interpersonal and masspersonal media and psychological well-being. *Journal of Social & Personal Relationships, 38*(8), 2397–2418. https://doi-org.dbproxy.lasalle.edu/10.1177/02654075211029378

Choi, M., & Toma, C. L. (2014). Social sharing through interpersonal media: Patterns and effects on emotional well-being. *Computers in Human Behavior, 36*, 530–541. https://doi.org/10.1016/j.chb.2014.04.026

Choi, M., & Toma, C. L. (2017). Social sharing with friends and family after romantic break-ups: Patterns of media use and effects on psychological well-being. *Journal of Media Psychology: Theories, Methods, and Applications, 29*, 166–172. https://doi.org/10.1027/1864-1105/a000226

Chudzicka-Czupała, A., Grabowski, D., Mello, A. L., Kuntz, J., Zaharia, D. V., Hapon, N., Lupina-Wegener, A., & Börü, D. (2016). Application of the theory of planned behavior in academic cheating research–cross-cultural comparison. *Ethics & Behavior*, *26*(8), 638–659. https://doi.org/10.1080/10508422.2015.1112745

Chung, J. E. (2014). Medical dramas and viewer perception of health: Testing cultivation effects. *Human Communication Research*, *40*, 333–349. https://doi.org/10.1111/hcre.12026

Cialdini, R. B. (1993). *Influence: Science and practice* (3rd ed.). HarperCollins.

Cialdini, R. B. (1994). Interpersonal influence. In S. Shavitt & T. C. Brock (Eds.), *Persuasion: Psychological insights and perspectives* (pp. 195–218). Allyn & Bacon.

Cohen, B. C. (1963). *The press and foreign policy*. Princeton University Press.

Collier, M. J. (1989). Cultural and intercultural communication competence: Current approaches and directions for future research. *International Journal of Intercultural Relations*, *13*, 287–302.

Compton, J. A., & Pfau, M. (2004). Use of inoculation to foster resistance to credit card marketing targeting college students. *Journal of Applied Communication Research*, *32*(4), 343–364.

Condit, C. M. (2019). Public health experts, expertise, and Ebola: A relational theory of ethos. *Rhetoric & Public Affairs*, *22*, 177–216.

Coombs, W. T. (2007). Protecting organizational reputations during a crisis: The development and application of situational crisis communication theory. *Corporate Reputation Review*, *10*, 163–176. https://doi.org/10.1057/palgrave.crr.1550049

Coombs, W. T. (2014). *Applied crisis communication and crisis management*. SAGE.

Costanzo, L. A., & Di Domenico, M. (2015). A multi-level dialectical–paradox lens for top management team strategic decision-making in a corporate venture. *British Journal of Management*, *26*(3), 484–506. https://doi.org/10.1111/1467-8551.12073

Cowan, R. (2013). "**it rolls downhill" and other attributions for why adult bullying happens in organizations from the human resource professional's perspective. *Qualitative Research Reports in Communication*, *14*, 97–104. https://doi.org/10.1080/17459435.2013.835347

Craig, R. T. (1999). Communication theory as a field. *Communication Theory*, *9*, 119–161.

Craig, R. T., Tracy, K., & Spisak, F. (1993). The discourse of requests: Assessment of a politeness approach. In S. Petronio, J. K. Alberts, M. L. Hecht, & J. Buley (Eds.), *Contemporary perspectives on interpersonal communication* (pp. 264–283). Brown & Benchmark.

Craven, J. (2021, April 23). The media is finally addressing its police report problem. *Slate*. https://slate.com/business/2021/04/george-floyd-initial-police-report-false-journalism.html

Crawford, M. (2004). Mars and Venus collide: A discursive analysis of marital self-help psychology. *Feminism & Psychology*, *14*, 63–79. https://doi.org/10.1177/0959-353504040305

Cronin, B. (2021, February 16). *The Mandalorian: Gina Carano found out she was fired through social media*. Comic Book Resources. https://www.cbr.com/mandalorian-gina-carano-fired-social-media/

Cunningham, C. M. (2018). Unbeatable? Debates and divides in gender and video game research. *Communication Research Trends*, *37*, 4–29.

Cupach, W. R., Canary, D. J., & Spitzberg, B. H. (2009). *Competence in interpersonal conflict* (2nd ed.). Waveland Press.

Cupach, W. R., & Metts, S. (1994). *Facework*. SAGE.

Curran, E. (2021, April 22). Work from home to lift productivity by 5% in post-pandemic U.S. *Bloomberg.* https://www.bloomberg.com/news/articles/2021-04-22/yes-working-from-home-makes-you-more-productive-study-finds

Daft, R. L., & Lengel, R. H. (1984). Information richness: A new approach to managerial behavior and organizational design. In L. L. Cummings & B. M. Staw (Eds.), *Research in organizational behavior 6* (pp. 191–233). JAI Press.

Daft, R. L., & Lengel, R. H. (1986). Organizational information requirements, media richness and structural design. *Management Science, 32,* 554–571.

Dainton, M., Aylor, B., & Zelley, E. D. (2002, November 21–24). *General and relationship-specific social support, willingness to communicate, and loneliness in long-distance versus geographically close friendships* [Paper presented]. The National Communication Association Annual Conference, New Orleans, LA, United States.

Damstra, A., & Boukes, M. (2021). The economy, the news, and the public: a longitudinal study of the impact of economic news on economic evaluations and expectations. *Communication Research, 48,* 26–50. https://doi.org/10.1177/0093650217750971

Dance, F. E. X. (1970). The "concept" of communication. *Journal of Communication, 20,* 201–210.

Dance, F. E. X., & Larson, C. E. (1976). *The functions of communication: A theoretical approach.* Holt, Rinehart & Winston.

Dansereau, F., Graen, G., & Haga, W. J. (1975). A vertical dyad approach to leadership within formal organizations. *Organizational Behavior and Human Performance, 12,* 46–78.

Dawkins, R. (1989). *The selfish gene* (2nd ed.). Oxford University Press.

De Nooy, W., & Kleinnijenhuis, J. (2013). Polarization in the media during an election campaign: A dynamic network model predicting support and attack among political actors. *Political Communication, 30,* 117–138. https://doi.org/10.1080/10584609.2012.737417

Deal, T. E., & Kennedy, A. A. (1982). *Corporate cultures: The rites and rituals of corporate life.* Addison-Wesley.

Deal, T. E., & Kennedy, A. A. (2000). *Corporate cultures: The rites and rituals of corporate life* (2nd ed.). Basic Books.

Deetz, S. A. (1994). *Future of the discipline:* The challenges, the research, and the social contribution. In S. A. Deetz (Ed.), *Communication yearbook 17* (pp. 565–600). Sage.

Deetz, S. A., Tracy, S. J., & Simpson, J. L. (2000). *Leading organizations through transition.* Sage.

Dennis, A. R., Kinney, S. T., & Hung, Y.-T. C. (1999). Gender differences in the effects of media richness. *Small Group Research, 30*(4), 405–437. https://doi.org/10.1177/104649649903000402

Dennis, A. R., Valacich, J. S., & Fuller, R. M. (2008). Media, tasks, and communication processes: A theory of media synchronicity. *MIS Quarterly, 32,* 575–600. https://doi.org/10.2307/25148857

DePaulo, B. M., Stone, J. I., & Lassiter, G. D. (1985). Deceiving and detecting deceit. In B. Schlenker (Ed.), *The self and social life* (pp. 323–370). McGraw-Hill.

Dervin, B. (1993). Verbing communication: Mandate for disciplinary intervention. *Journal of Communication, 43,* 45–54.

Diel, S. (2017). New media, legacy media and misperceptions regarding sourcing. *KOME – An International Journal of Pure Communication Inquiry, 5,* 104–120. https://doi.org/10.17646/KOME.2017.17

Dillard, J. P., & Solomon, D. H. (2005). Measuring the relevance of relational frames: A relational framing theory perspective. In V. Manusov (Ed.), *The sourcebook of nonverbal measures: Going beyond words* (pp. 3250–334). Lawrence Earlbaum Associates.

Dillard, J.P. (2015). Goals-plans-action theory of message production: Making influence messages. In D. O. Braithwaite & P. Schrodt (Eds.), *Engaging theories in interpersonal communication: Multiple perspectives*, (2nd ed., pp. 63–74). SAGE.

Dillard, J.P., Anderson, J.W., & Knobloch, L.K. (2002). Interpersonal influence. In M. Knapp & J. Daly (Eds.), *The handbook of interpersonal communication* (3rd ed., pp. 423–474). SAGE.

Dimmock, J. A., Gagné, M., Proud, L., Howle, T. C., Rebar, A. L., & Jackson, B. (2016). An exercise in resistance: Inoculation messaging as a strategy for protecting motivation during a monotonous and controlling exercise class. *Journal of Sport & Exercise Psychology*, *38*, 567–578. https://doi.org/10.1123/jsep.2016-0146

Dindia, K. (2002). Self-disclosure Research: Knowledge through meta-analysis. In M. Allen, R. W. Preiss, B. M. Gayle, & N. Burrell (Eds.), *Interpersonal communication: Advances through meta-analysis* (pp. 169–185). Lawrence Erlbaum Associates.

Dingemans, E., & Henkens, K. (2014). Involuntary retirement, bridge employment, and satisfaction with life: A longitudinal investigation. *Journal of Organizational Behavior*, *35*, 575–591. Https://doi.org/10.1002/job.1914

Dion, K. K., & Dion, K. L. (1993). Individualistic and collectivistic perspectives on gender and the cultural context of love and intimacy. *Journal of Social Issues*, *49*, 53–59.

Dobosh, M. A., Poole, M. S., & Malik, R. (2019). Small group use of communication technologies: a comparison of modality on group outcomes. *Communication Research Reports*, *36*, 298–308. https://doi.org/10.1080/08824096.2019.1660869

Dockery, T. M., & Steiner, D. D. (1990). The role of initial interaction in leader–member exchange. *Group and Organizational Studies*, *15*, 395–413.

Dong, Z. (2015). How to persuade adolescents to use nutrition labels: Effects of health consciousness, argument quality, and source credibility. *Asian Journal of Communication*, *25*(1), 84–101. https://doi.org/10.1080/01292986.2014.989241

Doubek, J. (2021, September 17). Students are damaging school bathrooms for attention on TikTok. *NPR*. https://www.npr.org/2021/09/17/1038378816/students-are-damaging-school-bathrooms-for-attention-on-tiktok

Duarte, N. T., Goodson, J. R., & Klich, N. R. (1993). How do I like thee? Let me appraise the ways. *Journal of Organizational Behavior*, *14*, 239–249.

Duke, G. (n.d.). *The sophists (ancient Greek)*. Internet Encyclopedia of Philosophy. https://iep.utm.edu/sophists/

Dunegan, K. J., Uhl-Bien, M., & Duchon, D. (2002). LMX and subordinate performance: The moderating effects of task characteristics. *Journal of Business and Psychology*, *17*, 275–285. https://doi.org/10.1023/A:1019641700724

D'Urso, S. C., & Rains, S. A. (2008). Examining the scope of channel expansion: A test of channel expansion theory with new and traditional communication media. *Management Communication Quarterly*, *21*, 486–507. https://doi.org/10.1177/0893318907313712

Dutihl, D. (2012, November 29). *Divorce causes: Five communication habits that lead to divorce*. Huffington Post. http://www.huffingtonpost.com/2012/11/29/divorce-5-communication-h_n_2159531.html

Dyer, W. G. (1987). *Team building: Issues and alternatives* (2nd ed.). Addison-Wesley.

Eagly, A. H. (1987). *Sex differences in social behavior: A social-role interpretation*. Lawrence Erlbaum.

Eagly, A. H., & Karau, S. J. (2002). Role congruity theory of prejudice toward female leaders. *Psychological Review, 109*, 573–598. https://doi.org/10.1037/0033-295X.109.3.573

Eagly, A., & Wood, W. (2017). Gender identity: Nature and nurture working together. *Evolutionary Studies in Imaginative Culture, 1*, 59–62. https://doi.org/10.26613/esic.1.1.10

Edwards, R. (1981). The social relations of production at the point of production. In M. Zey-Ferrell & M. Aiken (Eds.), *Complex organizations: Critical perspectives*, (pp. 156–182). Scott, Foresman.

Elmore, K. C., Scull, T. M., Malik, C. V., & Kupersmidt, J. B. (2021). Rape myth acceptance reflects perceptions of media portrayals as similar to others, but not the self. *Violence Against Women, 27*, 529–551. https://doi.org/10.1177/1077801220908335

Elsesser, K. M., & Lever, J. (2011). Does gender bias against female leaders persist? Quantitative and qualitative data from a large-scale survey. *Human Relations, 64*, 1555–1578. https://doi.org/10.1177/0018726711424323

Entman, R. M. (1993). Framing: Toward clarification of a fractured paradigm. *Journal of Communication, 43*, 51–58. https://doi.org/10.1111/j.1460-2466.1993.tb01304.x

Erman, A., & Medeiros, M. (2021). Exploring the effect of collective cultural attributes on Covid-19-related public health outcomes. *Frontiers in Psychology*. https://doi.org/10.3389/fpsyg.2021.627669

Eshbaugh-Soha, M. (2013). Presidential influence of the news media: The case of the press conference. *Political Communication, 30*, 548–564. https://doi.org/10.1080/10584609.2012.737438

Evers-Hillstrom, K. (2020, February 11). *Most expensive ever: 2020 election cost $14.4 billion*. Center for Responsive Politics. https://www.opensecrets.org/news/2021/02/2020-cycle-cost-14p4-billion-doubling-16/

Ezzedeen, S. R., Budworth, M., & Baker, S. D. (2015). The glass ceiling and executive careers: Still an issue for pre-career women. *Journal of Career Development, 42*, 355–369. https://doi.org/10.1177/0894845314566943

Fahmy, S. S., & Ibrahim, O. (2021). No Memes No! Digital Persuasion in the #MeToo Era. *International Journal of Communication, 15*, 2942–2967. http://ijoc.org.

Fair, J. E. (1993). The women of South Africa weep: Explorations of gender and race in U.S. television news. *Howard Journal of Communications, 4*, 283–294. https://doi.org/10.1080/10646179309359784

Fan, C., & Jiang, Y. (2021). The role of local influential users in spread of situational crisis information. *Journal of Computer-Mediated Communication, 26*(2), 108–127. https://doi.org/10.1093/jcmc/zmaa020

Feldman, D. C. (1994). Who's socializing whom? The impact of socializing newcomers on insiders, work groups, and organizations. *Human Resource Management Review, 4*, 213–233. https://doi.org/10.1016/1053-4822(94)90013-2

Feldner, S., & D'Urso, S. C. (2010). Threads of intersection and distinction: Joining an ongoing conversation within organizational communication research. *Communication Research Trends, 29*, 4–28.

Feloni, R. (2016, January 28). Zappos Tony Hsieh reveals what it was like losing 18% of his employees in a radical management experiment—and why it was worth it. *Business Insider*. https://www.businessinsider.com/tony-hsieh-explains-how-zappos-rebounded-from-employee-exodus-2016-1

Felps, W., Mitchell, T. R., Herman, D. R., Lee, T. W., Holtom, B. C., & Harman, W. S. (2009). Turnover contagion: How coworkers' job embeddedness and job search behaviors influence quitting. *Academy of Management Journal, 52*, 545–561. https://doi.org/10.5465/amj.2009.41331075

Festinger, L. (1954). A theory of social comparison processes. *Human Relations*, *7*, 117–140. https://doi.org/10.1177/001872675400700202

Festinger, L. (1957). *A theory of cognitive dissonance*. Stanford University Press.

Fishbein, M., & Ajzen, I. (1975). *Belief, attitude, intention and behavior: An introduction to theory and research*. Addison-Wesley.

Fisher, B. A. (1978). *Perspectives on human communication*. Macmillan.

Fisher, W. R. (1984). Narration as a human communication paradigm: The case of public moral argument. *Communication Monographs*, *51*, 1–22.

Fisher, W. R. (1985). The narrative paradigm: An elaboration. *Communication Monographs*, *52*, 347–367.

Fisher, W. R. (1987). *Human communication as narration: Toward a philosophy of reason, value, and action*. University of South Carolina Press.

Fitzpatrick, M. A., & Ritchie, D. (1992). Communication theory. In P. Boss, W. Doherty & S. Steinmetz (Eds.), *Sourcebook of family theories*. Plenum.

Fleck, R. K., & Hanssen, F. A. (2013). How tyranny paved the way to democracy: The democratic transition in ancient Greece. *The Journal of Law & Economics*, 56, 389–416. https://www.jstor.org/stable/10.1086/670731

Folkenflik, D. (2018, April 2). Sinclair Broadcast Group forces nearly 200 station anchors to read same script. "All Things Considered." *NPR*. https://www.npr.org/2018/04/02/598916366/sinclair-broadcast-group-forces-nearly-200-station-anchors-to-read-same-script

Fombrun, C. J. (1996). *Reputation: Realizing value from the corporate image*. Harvard Business School Press.

Ford Motor Company. (2007, November). *Code of conduct handbook*. https://corporate.ford.com/microsites/integrated-sustainability-and-financial-report-2021/files/ir21-code-of-conduct-handbook.pdf

Fortenbaugh, W. W. (1986). Aristotle's platonic attitude toward delivery. *Philosophy & Rhetoric*, *19*, 242–254.

Foss, K. A., & Blake, K. (2019). 'It's natural and healthy, but I don't want to see it': Using entertainment-education to improve attitudes toward breastfeeding in public. *Health Communication*, *34*, 919–930. https://doi.org/10.1080/10410236.2018.1440506

Fox, J. D. (2019). *Understanding differences in expectations in the anticipatory socialization process between angel investors and entrepreneurs in extended due diligence* (Order No. 13917671). [Doctoral dissertation, Ohio University]. Available from ProQuest One Academic (2243745548)

Frey, L. R., Botan, C. H., & Kreps, G. L. (2002). *Investigating communication: An introduction to research methods* (2nd ed.). Allyn & Bacon.

Frey, T. K., & Lane, D. R. (2021). Nonaccommodation and communication effectiveness: an application to instructional communication. *Communication Research Reports*, *38*, 195–205. https://doi.org/10.1080/08824096.2021.1922372

Gabrenya, W. K., Jr. (2003). *Theories and models in psychology* [online]. http://my.fit.edu/~gabrenya/IntroMethods/eBook/theories.pdf

Gallois, C., Ogay, T., & Giles, H. (2005). Communication accommodation theory: A look back and a look ahead. In W. Gudykunst (Ed.), *Theorizing about intercultural communication* (pp. 121–148). SAGE.

Garcia-Retamero, R., & López-Zafra, E. (2006). Prejudice against women in male-congenial environments: Perceptions of gender role congruity in leadership. *Sex Roles*, *55*, 51–61. https://doi.org/10.1007/s11199-006-9068-1

Gardner, L., & Stough, C. (2002). Examining the relationship between leadership and emotional intelligence in senior level managers. *Leadership & Organization Development Journal*, *23*, 68–78.

Garrett, R. K., Weeks, B. E., & Neo, R. L. (2016). Driving a wedge between evidence and beliefs: How online ideological news exposure promotes political misperceptions. *Journal of Computer-Mediated Communication*, *21*(5), 331–348. https://doi.org/10.1111/jcc4.12164

Gender equality in Sweden. (2013). *Swedish Institute* [online]. http://sweden.se/society/gender-equality-in-sweden

Gerbner, G. (1998). Cultivation analysis: An overview. *Mass Communication & Society*, *1*, 175–194.

Gerbner, G. (2000, October-December). *Cultivation analysis: An overview. Communication*, pp. 3–12. https://web.asc.upenn.edu/gerbner/Asset.aspx?assetID=459

Gerbner, G., Gross, L., Morgan, M., & Signorelli, N. (1980). The "mainstreaming" of America: Violence profile no. 11. *Journal of Communication*, *30*, 10–29.

Ghanem, S. (1997). Filling in the tapestry: The second level of agenda setting. In M. McCombs, D. L. Shaw, & D. Weaver (Eds.), *Communication and democracy: Exploring the intellectual frontiers of agenda-setting theory* (pp. 3–14). Routledge.

Giannetti, L. (1982). *Understanding movies* (3rd ed.). Prentice Hall.

Giberson, T. R., Resick, C. J., & Dickson, M. W. (2005). Embedding leader characteristics: An examination of homogeneity of personality and values in organizations. *Journal of Applied Psychology*, *90*, 1002–1010. https://doi.org/10.1037/0021-9010.90.5.1002

Gibson, J. J. (1977). The theory of affordances, in perceiving, acting, and knowing: Toward an ecological psychology. In R. Shaw & J. Bransford (Eds.), *Perceiving, acting, and knowing*, (pp. 76–82). Lawrence Erlbaum.

Giles, H., & Coupland, N. (1991). *Language: Contexts and consequences*, Wadsworth.

Giles, H., & Gasiorek, J. (2014). Parameters of nonaccommodation: Refining and elaborating communication accommodation theory. In J. P. Forgas, O. Vincze, & J. László (Eds.), *Social Cognition and Communication* (pp. 155–172). Psychology Press.

Giles, H., Mulac, A., Bradac, J. J., & Johnson, P. (1987). Ethnolinguistic identity theory: A social psychological approach to language maintenance. *International Journal of the Sociology of Language*, *68*, 66–99.

Giles, H., Willemyn, M. Gallois, C, & Anderson, M. C. (2007). Accommodating a new frontier: The context of law enforcement. In K. Fiedler (Ed.), *Social Communication* (pp. 129–162). Psychology Press.

Gilpin, D. (2010). Organizational image construction in a fragmented online media environment. *Journal of Public Relations Research*, *22*, 265–287. https://doi.org/10.1080/10627261003614393

Glaser, B. G., & Strauss, A. L. (1967). *The discovery of grounded theory: Strategies for qualitative research*, Aldine.

Glazer, R. (2021, April 21). CVS lost $2 billion with 1 decision—Here's why they were right. *Forbes*. https://www.forbes.com/sites/robertglazer/2020/04/21/cvs-lost-2-billion-with-1-decision-heres-why-they-were-right/?sh=2379d140689c

Gloor, P. A., Fronzetti Colladon, A., Grippa, F., & Giacomelli, G. (2017). Forecasting managerial turnover through e-mail based social network analysis. *Computers in Human Behavior, 71*, 343–352. https://doi.org/10.1016/j.chb.2017.02.017

Glynn, C. J. (2018). *Public Opinion*. Taylor & Francis.

Godbold, L. C., & Pfau, M. (2000). Conferring resistance of peer pressure among adolescents: Using inoculation theory to discourage alcohol use. *Communication Research, 27*, 411–437.

Goffman, E. (1959). *The presentation of self in everyday life*. Doubleday.

Goffman, E. (1967). *Interaction ritual: Essays on face-to-face behavior*. Pantheon Books.

Goffman, E. (1974). *Frame analysis: An essay on the organization of experience*. Harper & Row.

Golden, J. C., & Jacoby, J. W. (2017). Playing princess: Preschool girls' interpretations of gender stereotypes in Disney princess media. *Sex Roles*. https://doi.org/10.1007/s11199-017-0773-8

Goldfarb, R. S., & Ratner, J. (2008). "Theories" and "models": Terminology through the looking glass. *Econ Journal Watch, 5*, 91–108.

Goleman, D. (1995). *Emotional intelligence*. Bantam Books.

Gordon, C. S., Howard, S. J., Jones, S. C., & Kervin, L. K. (2016). Evaluation of an Australian alcohol media literacy program. *Journal of Studies on Alcohol and Drugs, 77*, 950–957. https://doi.org/10.15288/jsad.2016.77.950

Gouran, D. S. (2010). Overcoming sources of irrationality that complicate working in decision-making groups. In S. Schuman (Ed.), *The handbook of working with difficult groups: How they are difficult, why they are difficult, and what you can do about it* (pp. 137–152). Jossey-Bass.

Gouran, D. S. (2011). *Leadership as reasoned argument in decision-making and problem-solving groups* [Conference Proceedings]. National Communication Association/American Forensic Association (Alta Conference on Argumentation) (pp. 104–112).

Gouran, D. S., & Hirokawa, R. Y. (1983). The role of communication in decision-making groups: A functional perspective. In M. Mander (Ed.), *Communications in transition* (pp. 168–185). Praeger.

Gouran, D. S., & Hirokawa, R. Y. (1986). Counteractive functions of communication in effective group decision-making. In R. Y. Hirokawa & M. S. Poole (Eds.), *Communication and group decision making* (pp. 81–92). SAGE.

Gouran, D. S., & Hirokawa, R. Y. (1996). Functional theory and communication in decision-making and problem-solving groups: An expanded view. In R. Y. Hirokawa & M. S. Poole (Eds.), *Communication and group decision making* (pp. 55–80). SAGE.

Grace, R., & Tham, J. C. K. (2021). Adapting uncertainty reduction theory for crisis communication: Guidelines for technical communicators. *Journal of Business & Technical Communication, 35*, 110–117. https://doi.org/10.1177/1050651920959188

Graen, G., & Uhl-Bien, M. (1995). Development of leader-member exchange theory of leadership over 25 years: Applying a multilevel perspective. *Leadership Quarterly, 6*, 219–247.

Gray, J. (1992). *Men are from Mars, women are from Venus: A practical guide to improving communication and getting what you want in your relationships*. Harper Collins.

Gray, J. (1997, 2005). *Mars and Venus on a date: A guide for navigating the 5 stages of dating to create a loving and lasting relationship*. Harper Collins.

Griffin, E. (2003). *A first look at communication theory* (5th ed.). McGraw-Hill.

Griffin, E., Ledbetter, A., & Sparks, G. (2015). *A first look at communication theory* (9th ed.). McGraw Hill.

Griffin, R. J., Dunwoody, S., & Neuwirth, K. (1999). Proposed model of the relationship of risk information seeking and processing to the development of preventive behaviors. *Environmental Research, 80*, S230–S245. https://doi.org/10.1006/enrs.1998.3940.

Guerrero, L. K., & Burgoon, J. K. (1996). Attachment styles and reactions to nonverbal involvement change in romantic dyads: Patterns of reciprocity and compensation. *Human Communication Research, 22*, 335–336.

Guerrero, L. K., Jones, S. M., & Burgoon, J. K. (2000). Responses to nonverbal intimacy change in romantic dyads: Effects of behavioral valence and degree of behavioral change on nonverbal and verbal reactions. *Communication Monographs, 67*, 325–346.

Guo, L. (2014). Toward the third level of agenda setting theory: A network agenda setting model. In T. Johnson (Ed.), *Agenda setting in a 2.0 world: New agendas in communication* (pp. 12–133). Routledge.

Guo, L., & McCombs, M. (2011, May 26-30). *Network agenda setting: A third level of media effects* [Paper presented]. The International Communication Association, Boston, MA, United States.

Haigh, M., & Pfau, M. (2006). Bolstering organizational identity, commitment, and citizenship behaviors through the process of inoculation. *International Journal of Organizational Analysis, 14*, 295–316.

Hall, A. D., & Fagen, R. E. (1968). Definition of a system. In W. Buckley (Ed.), *Modern systems research for the behavioral scientist*, (pp. 81–92). Aldine.

Hall, E. T. (1976). *Beyond culture*. Doubleday.

Hall, S. (1973). *Encoding and decoding in the television discourse*. Centre for Cultural Studies.

Hall, S. (1986). Gramsci's relevance for the study of race and ethnicity. *Journal of Communication Inquiry, 10*(2), 5–27.

Harkins, D. (2021). The Boy Scouts of America: How society's changing attitudes affect nonprofit culture. *Organization Development Journal, 39*, 83–96.

Heath, R., Brandt, D., & Nairn, A. (2006). Brand relationships: Strengthened by emotion, weakened by attention. *Journal of Advertising Research, 46*(4), 410–419.

Heath, R. L. (2013). Media fragmentation. *Encyclopedia of Public Relations, 1*, 553. https://doi.org/10.4135/9781452276236.n303

Hecht, M. L. (1993). 2002-a research odyssey: Toward the development of a communication theory of identity. *Communication Monographs, 60*, 76. https://doi.org/10.1080/03637759309376297

Hecht, M. L., Collier, M. J., & Ribeau, S. A. (1993). *African American communication: Ethnic identity and interpretation*. Sage.

Hefner, V., Galaviz, T., Morse, V., Firchau, R.-J. C., Basile, C., Todd, R., Naude, F., & Nitzkowski-Bautista, Z. (2015). Refusing to tolerate intolerance: An experiment testing the link between exposure to gay-related content and resulting attitudes and behaviors. *Sexuality & Culture: An Interdisciplinary Quarterly, 19*, 864–881. https://doi.org/10.1007/s12119-015-9297-y

Heider, F. (1958). *The psychology of interpersonal relations*. Wiley.

Heider, F., & Simmel, M. (1944). An experimental study of apparent behavior. *The American Journal of Psychology, 57*, 243–259. https://doi.org/10.2307/1416950

Hennessy-Fiske, M., Pearce, M., & Jarvie, J. (2018, May 19). Must reads: Texas school shooter killed girl who turned down his advances and embarrassed him in class, her mother says. *Los Angeles Times*. https://www.latimes.com/nation/la-na-texas-shooter-20180519-story.html

Hermann, E., Morgan, M., & Shanahan, J. (2021). Television, continuity, and change: A meta-analysis of five decades of cultivation research. *Journal of Communication, 71*(4), 515–544. https://doi-org.dbproxy.lasalle.edu/10.1093/joc/jqab014

Hirokawa, R. Y. (1994). Functional approaches to the study of group discussion: Even good notions have their problems. *Small Group Research, 25*, 542–550.

Hirokawa, R. Y., & Salazar, A. J. (1999). Task-group communication and decision-making performance. In L. R. Frey, D. S. Gouran, & M. S. Poole (Eds.), *The handbook of group communication theory and research* (pp. 167–191). Sage.

Hofstede, G. (1980). *Culture's consequences.* Sage.

Hofstede, G. (1986). Cultural differences in teaching and learning. *International Journal of Intercultural Relations, 10*, 301–319.

Hofstede, G. (1991). *Cultures and organizations: Software of the mind.* McGraw-Hill.

Hofstede, G. (2001). *Culture's consequences: International differences in work-related values* (2nd ed.). SAGE.

Hofstede, G., & Bond, M. H. (1984). Hofstede's culture dimensions: An independent validation using Rokeach's value survey. *Journal of Cross Cultural Psychology, 15*, 417–433.

Hofstede, G., Hofstede, G. J., & Minkov, M. (2010). *Cultures and organizations: Software of the mind* (3rd ed.). McGraw-Hill.

Hogan, S. J., & Coote, L. V. (2014). Organizational culture, innovation, and performance: A test of Schein's model. *Journal of Business Research, 67*, 1609–1621. https://doi.org/10.1016/j.jbusres.2013.09.007

Holody, K. J., & Daniel, E. S. (2017). Attributes and frames of the Aurora shootings. *Journalism Practice, 11*, 80–100. https://doi.org/10.1080/17512786.2015.1121786

Holsapple, C., Hsaio, S., & Pakath, R. (2014, August 7-9). *Business social media analytics: Definition, benefits, and challenges* [Paper presented]. The Twentieth Americas Conference on Information Systems, Savannah, GA, United States. https://pdfs.semanticscholar.org/d7d7/1ec49476e54a350e9091087345dcd3d7866c.pdf

Hopkins, A. E. (2015). Effects of the "Spiral of Silence" in digital media. *Inquiries Journal.* http://www.inquiriesjournal.com/articles/1104/effects-of-the-spiral-of-silence-in-digital-media

Hoppin, S. (2016). Applying the narrative paradigm to the vaccine debates. *American Communication Journal, 18*, 45–55.

Horowitz, J. M., Igielnik, R., & Kochnar, R. (2020, January 9). *Most Americans say there is too much economic inequality in the U.S., but fewer than half call it a top priority.* Pew Research Center. https://www.pewresearch.org/social-trends/2020/01/09/trends-in-income-and-wealth-inequality/

Houston, J. B., Spialek, M. L., & First, J. (2018). Disaster media effects: A systematic review and synthesis based on the differential susceptibility to media effects model. *Journal of Communication, 68*, 734–757. https://doi.org/10.1093/joc/jqy023

The H.R. Capitalist. (2019, June 5). *Bro-tastic vs. we care: A quick review of Uber's current and past corporate values.* https://www.hrcapitalist.com/2019/06/brotastic-vs-we-care-a-quick-review-of-ubers-current-and-past-corporate-values.html

Hubbard, K. (2021, July 22). Outside of sleeping, Americans spend most of their time watching television. *U.S. News & World Report.* https://www.usnews.com/news/best-states/articles/2021-07-22/americans-spent-more-time-watching-television-during-covid-19-than-working

Huckins, K. (1999). Interest-group influence on the media agenda: A case study. *Journalism and Mass Communication Quarterly, 76,* 76–86.

Huesmann, L. R., Moise-Titus, J., Podolski, C. L., & Eron, L. D. (2003). Longitudinal relations between children's exposure to TV violence and their aggressive and violent behavior in young adulthood 1977–1992. *Developmental Psychology, 39,* 201–221.

Humphreys, J. (2020). *Aristotle. Internet Encyclopedia of Philosophy.* https://iep.utm.edu/aristotl/

Hunter, T. (2021, September 24). Here are all the ways your boss can legally monitor you. *The Washington Post.* https://www.washingtonpost.com/technology/2021/08/20/work-from-home-computer-monitoring/

Irwin, R. E. (2020, August 3). Misleading media coverage of Sweden's response to covid-19. *BMJ, Letters, 370.* https://doi.org/10.1136/bmj.m3031

Iyengar, S., & Kinder, D. R. (1987). *News that matters: Television and American opinion.* University of Chicago Press.

Iyengar, S., Peters, M., & Kinder, D. (1982). Experimental demonstrations of the "not-so-minimal" consequences of television news programs. *American Political Science Review, 76,* 848–858.

Jablin, F. M. (1985). An exploratory study of vocational organizational communication socialization. *Southern Speech Communication Journal, 50*(3), 261–282. https://doi.org/10.1080/10417948509372635

Jablin, F. M. (1987). Organizational entry, assimilation, and exit. In F. M. Jablin, L. L. Putnam, K. H. Roberts, & L. W. Porter (Eds.), *Handbook of organizational communication: An interdisciplinary perspective* (pp. 679–740). SAGE.

Jablin, F. M. (2001). Organizational entry, assimilation, and disengagement/exit. In F. M. Jablin & L. L. Putnam (Eds.), *The new handbook of organizational communication* (pp. 732–818). SAGE.

Jackson, S. J. (2020, June 3). The headlines that are covering up police violence. *The Atlantic,* https://www.theatlantic.com/culture/archive/2020/06/george-floyd-protests-what-news-reports-dont-say/612571/

Jahn, J. L. S. (2019). Voice enactment: Linking voice with experience in high reliability organizing. *Journal of Applied Communication Research, 47*(3), 283–302. https://doi-org.dbproxy.lasalle.edu/10.1080/00909882.2019.1613555

Jandt, F. E. (2004). *An introduction to intercultural communication: Identities in a global community.* SAGE.

Janis, I. L. (1972). *Victims of groupthink: A psychological study of foreign-policy decisions and fiascoes.* Houghton Mifflin.

Janis, I. L. (1982). *Groupthink: Psychological studies of policy decisions and fiascoes.* Houghton Mifflin.

Jarvis, C. E. (2016). *The impact of communication style on organizational assimilation: A qualitative inquiry exploring generation Y employees during their first year of employment with an organization.* (Order No. 10108827). Available from ProQuest Dissertations & Theses Global. (1793669189)

Jax. (2020, June 19). The value of storytelling in marketing. *Jexan.* https://www.jexan.com/marketing/the-value-of-storytelling/

Jia, H., Zhong, R., & Xie, X. (2021). Helping others makes me fit better: effects of helping behavior by newcomers and coworker-attributed motives on newcomers' adjustment. *Journal of Business & Psychology, 36,* 401–416. https://doi.org/10.1007/s10869-020-09680-w

Jimenez, M. (2017). A quantitative study: The relationship between managers' emotional intelligence awareness and demographics and leadership styles. *Dissertation Abstracts International*, *77*, 8-A(E).

Jones, E. E., & Davis, K. E. (1965). From acts to dispositions: The attribution process in person perception. In L. Berkowitz (Ed.), *Advances in experimental social psychology* (Vol. 2, pp. 220–266). Academic Press.

Kapidzic, S., & Martins, N. (2015). Mirroring the media: The relationship between media consumption, media internalization, and profile picture characteristics on Facebook. *Journal of Broadcasting & Electronic Media*, *59*(2), 278–297. https://doi.org/10.1080/08838151.2015.1029127

Kaplan, A. (1964). *The conduct of inquiry*. Chandler.

Kashian, N., & Liu, Y. (2020). Posting exercise activity on social media for self-efficacy and well-being. *Southern Communication Journal*, *85*, 73–84. https://doi.org/10.1080/10417 94X.2019.1658801

Katz, E., Blumler, J. G., & Gurevitch, M. (1973). Uses and gratifications research. *Public Opinion Quarterly*, *37*, 509–523.

Katz, E., & Fialkoff, Y. (2017). Six concepts in search of retirement. *Annals of the International Communication Association*, *41*, 86–91. https://doi.org/10.1080/23808985.2017.1291280

Kearns, E.M., Betus, A., & Lemieux, A. (2017, March 13). Yes, the media do underreport some terrorist acts. Just not the ones most people think of. *Washington Post* [online]. https://www.washingtonpost.com/news/monkey-cage/wp/2017/03/13/yes-the-media-do-underreport-some-terrorist-attacks-just-not-the-ones-most-people-think-of/?utm_term=.88493239a8c9

Kelley, H. H. (1967). Attribution theory in social psychology. *Nebraska Symposium on Motivation*, *15*, 192–238.

Kelley, H. H. (1973). The processes of causal attribution. *American Psychologist*, *28*, 107–128.

Kelly, J. (2008). Mapping the blogosphere: Offering a guide to journalism's future. *Nieman Reports*, *62*(4), 37–39.

Kelly, J. (2020, May 13). Uber lays off 3,500 employees over a zoom call—The way in which a company downsizes its staff says a lot about the organization. *Forbes*. https://www.forbes.com/sites/jackkelly/2020/05/13/uber-lays-off-3500-employees-over-a-zoom-call-the-way-in-which-a-company-downsizes-its-staff-says-a-lot-about-the-organization/

Kelly, J. (2021, September 20). 'Turnover contagion' causes the best and brightest to leave their companies. *Forbes*. https://www.forbes.com/sites/jackkelly/2021/09/20/turnover-contagion-causes-the-best-and-brightest-to-leave-their-companies/

Kelly, L., Miller-Ott, A. E., & Duran, R. L. (2019). Phubbing friends: Understanding face threats from, and responses to, friends' cell phone usage through the lens of politeness theory. *Communication Quarterly*, *67*, 540–559. Https://doi.org/10.1080/01463373.2019.1668443

Kelman, S., Sanders, R., & Pandit, G. (2016). "I won't back down?" Complexity and courage in government executive decision making. *Public Administration Review*, *76*, 465–471. https://doi.org/10.1111/puar.12476

Kennedy, G. A. (1994). *A new history of classical rhetoric*. Princeton University Press.

Kim, E. A., Duffy, M., & Thorson, E. (2021). Under the influence: Social media influencers' impact on response to corporate reputation advertising. *Journal of Advertising*, *50*, 119–138. https://doi.org/10.1080/00913367.2020.1868026

Kim, E., Lee, J., Sung, Y., & Choi, S. M. (2016). Predicting selfie-posting behavior on social networking sites: An extension of theory of planned behavior. *Computers in Human Behavior*, *62*, 116–123. https://doi.org/10.1016/j.chb.2016.03.078

Kim, E. Y. (2001). *The yin and the yang of American culture: A paradox*. Intercultural Press.

Kim, J-N., & Grunig, J. E. (2011). Problem solving and communicative action: A situational theory of problem solving. *Journal of Communication*, *61*, 120–149. https://doi.org/10.1111/j.1460-2466.2010.01529.x.

Kim, S. (2013). Does corporate advertising work in a crisis? An examination of inoculation theory. *Journal of Marketing Communications*, *19*, 293–305. https://doi.org/10.1080/13527266.2011.634430

Kim, Y. Y. (2001). *Becoming intercultural: An integrative theory of communication and cross-cultural adaptation*. SAGE.

Kingsbury, K. (2008, June 18). *Pregnancy boom at Gloucester High. Time*. http://content.time.com/time/subscriber/article/0,33009,1816486,00.html

Kjeldsen, J., & Hess, A. (2021). Experiencing multimodal rhetoric and argumentation in political advertisements: A study of how people respond to the rhetoric of multimodal communication. *Visual Communication*, *20*, 327–352. https://doi.org/10.1177/14703572211013399

Kleinnijenhuis, J., Schultz, F., Utz, S., & Oegema, D. (2015). The mediating role of the news in the BP oil spill crisis 2010: How U.S. news is influenced by public relations and in turn influences public awareness, foreign news, and the share price. *Communication Research*, *42*, 408–428. https://doi.org/10.1177/0093650213510940

Klotz, A. C., & Bolino, M. C. (2016). Saying goodbye: The nature, causes, and consequences of employee resignation styles. *Journal of Applied Psychology*, *101*(10), 1386–1404. https://doi.org/10.1037/apl0000135

Kochigina, A. (2020). The parallel power in organizations' defense: Exploring faith-holders and their crisis communication. *Public Relations Review*, *46*(4). https://doi-org.dbproxy.lasalle.edu/10.1016/j.pubrev.2020.101950

Koenig, A. M., Eagly, A. H., Mitchell, A. A., & Ristikari, T. (2011). Are leader stereotypes masculine? A meta-analysis of three research paradigms. *Psychological Bulletin*, *137*, 616–642. https://doi.org/10.1037/a0023557

Kramer, M. (2010). *Organizational Socialization: Joining and Leaving Organizations*. Polity Press.

Kramer, M. W., & Bisel, R. S. (2017). *Organizational communication*. Oxford University Press.

Krongard, S., & Tsay-Vogel, M. (2020). Online original TV series: Examining portrayals of violence in popular binge-watched programs and social reality perceptions. *Psychology of Popular Media*, *9*(2), 155–164. https://doi-org.dbproxy.lasalle.edu/10.1037/ppm0000224

Labelle, S., & Waldeck, J. H. (2020). *Strategic communication for organizations*. University of California Press.

Lam, C., & O'Higgins, E. E. (2012). Enhancing employee outcomes: The interrelated influences of managers' emotional intelligence and leadership style. *Leadership & Organization Development Journal*, *33*(2), 149–174. https://doi.org/10.1108/01437731211203465

Lamke, L. K., Sollie, D. L., Durbin, R. G., & Fitzpatrick, J. A. (1994). Masculinity, femininity, and relationship satisfaction: The mediating role of interpersonal competence. *Journal of Social and Personal Relationships*, *11*, 535–554.

Langford, C. L., & Speight, M. (2015). #BlackLivesMatter: Epistemic positioning, challenges, and possibilities. *Journal of Contemporary Rhetoric*, *5*, 78–89.

Larkey, L. K. (1996). Toward a theory of communicative interactions in culturally diverse workgroups. *Academy of Management Review, 21*, 463–491.

Lea, M., & Spears, R. (1992). Paralanguage and social perception in computer-mediated communication. *Journal of Organizational Computing, 2*, 321–341. https://doi.org/10.1080/10919399209540190

Ledford, C. W., Saperstein, A. K., Cafferty, L. A., McClintick, S. H., & Bernstein, E. M. (2015). Any questions? An application of Weick's model of organizing to increase student involvement in the large-lecture classroom. *Communication Teacher, 29*, 116–128. https://doi.org/10.1080/17404622.2014.1003309

Lee, S.-Y., Chen, Y.-S., & Harmon, M. (2016). Reality TV, materialism, and associated consequences: An exploration of the influences of enjoyment and social comparison on reality TV's cultivation effects. *Atlantic Journal of Communication, 24*, 228–241. https://doi.org/10.1080/15456870.2016.1208659

Lee, T. (2011, February 4). *Know your enthymeme. The religiously sanctioned co-habitation chronicles.* https://cohabitationchronicles.wordpress.com/2011/02/04/know-your-enthymeme/

Lemay, E. J., O'Brien, K. M., Kearney, M. S., Sauber, E. W., & Venaglia, R. B. (2017). Using conformity to enhance willingness to intervene in dating violence: A theory of planned behavior analysis. *Psychology of Violence.* https://doi.org/10.1037/vio0000114

Lengel, R. H., & Daft, R. L. (1988). The selection of communication media as an executive skill. *Academy of Management Executive, 2*(3), 225–232.

Leung, F. F., Kim, S., & Tse, C. H. (2020). Highlighting effort versus talent in service employee performance: Customer attributions and responses. *Journal of Marketing, 84*, 106–121. https://doi.org/10.1177/0022242920902722

Leventhal, H. (1970). Findings and theory in the study of fear. In L. Berkowitz (Ed.), *Advances in Experimental Social Psychology* (Vol. 5, pp. 119–186). https://doi.org/10.1016/S0065-2601(08)60091-X.

Levine, M., & Harrison, K. (2009). Effects of media on eating disorders and body image. In J. Bryant & M. B. Oliver (Eds.), *Media effects: Advances in theory and research* (3rd ed., pp. 490–516). Routledge.

Levy, S., & Gvili, Y. (2020). Online shopper engagement in price negotiation: the roles of culture, involvement and eWOM. *International Journal of Advertising, 39*, 232–257. Https://doi.org/10.1080/02650487.2019.1612621

Lewallen, J., Miller, B., & Behm-Morawitz, E. (2016). Lifestyles of the rich and famous: Celebrity media diet and the cultivation of emerging adults' materialism. *Mass Communication & Society, 19*, 253–274. https://doi.org/10.1080/15205436.2015.1096945

Lewin, K. (1951). *Field theory in social science: Selected theoretical papers.* Harper & Row.

Lewis, B.K. (2010). Social media and strategic communication: Attitudes and perceptions among college students. *Public Relations Journal, 4*, 1–23.

Lewis, R. D. (2000). *When cultures collide: Managing successfully across cultures.* Nicholas Brealey.

Lewis, T., & Yoshimura, S. M. (2017). Politeness strategies in confrontations of prejudice. *Atlantic Journal of Communication, 25*, 1–16. https://doi.org/10.1080/15456870.2017.1251198

Likert, R. (1967). *The human organization: its management and values.* McGraw-Hill.

Lim, P. K., Koay, K. Y., & Chong, W. Y. (2021). The effects of abusive supervision, emotional exhaustion and organizational commitment on cyberloafing: A moderated-mediation examination. *Internet Research, 31*, 497–518. https://doi.org/10.1108/INTR-03-2020-0165

Lindzon, J. (2020, January 23). *Does blocking certain websites at work hurt employee productivity?* Fast Company, https://www.fastcompany.com/90453980/ does-blocking-certain-websites-at-work-hurt-employee-productivity

Litterst, J. K., & Eyo, B. (1982). Gauging the effectiveness of formal communication programs: The search for the communication-productivity link. *Journal of Business Communication, 19*(2), 15–26.

Littlejohn, S. W. (1989). *Theories of human communication* (3rd ed.). Wadsworth.

Littlejohn, S. W. (2002). *Theories of human communication* (7th ed.). Wadsworth.

Longobardi, E. (2009). How "subprime" killed "predatory." *Columbia Journalism Review, 48*(3), 45–49.

Lozano, E. (2015). The cultural experience of space and body: A reading of Latin American and Anglo-American comportment in public. In A. Gonzalez, M. Houston, & V. Chen (Eds.), *Our voices: Essays in culture, ethnicity, and communication* (5th ed., pp. 283–289). Oxford University Press.

Luo, Y., Burley, H., Moe, A., & Sui, M. (2019). A meta-analysis of news media's public agenda-setting effects, 1972-2015. *Journalism & Mass Communication Quarterly, 96*, 150–172. https://doi.org/10.1177/1077699018804500

Mackelden, A. (2020, September 3). Chrishell Stause and Justin Hartley's divorce: Everything we know so far. *Harper's Bazaar.* http://www.harpersbazaar.com/celebrity/latest/a33612707/chrishell-stause-justin-hartley-split-divorce-details/

Madlock, P. E. (2008). The link between leadership style, communicator competence, and employee satisfaction. *Journal of Business Communication, 45*(1), 61–78.

Mael, F., & Ashforth, B. E. (1992). Alumni and their alma mater: A partial test of the reformulated model of organizational identification. *Journal of Organizational Behavior, 13*, 103–123.

Malacane, M., & Martins, N. (2017). Sexual socialization messages in television programming produced for adolescents. *Mass Communication & Society, 20*, 23–46. https://doi.org/10.1080/15205436.2016.1203436

Malle, B. F. (2011). Attribution theories: How people make sense of behavior. In D. Chadee (Ed.), *Theories in social psychology* (pp. 72–95). Wiley.

Manfredi, R., Guazzini, A., Roos, C. A., Postmes, T., & Koudenburg, N. (2020). Private-public opinion discrepancy. *PLoS ONE, 15*(11). https://doi.org/10.1371/journal.pone.0242148

Mann, M. (2012). *The sources of social power: Globalizations,* 1945-2011 (Vol. 4). Cambridge University Press.

Manzoni, J. F., & Barsoux, J. L. (2002). *The set-up-to-fail syndrome: How good managers cause great people to fail.* Harvard Business School.

Marger, M. N. (2019). The mass media as a power institution. In M. E. Olsen, M. N. Marger & V. Fonseca (Eds.), *Power in Modern Societies* (pp. 238–249). Routledge.

Margolin, D., & Markowitz, D. M. (2018). A multitheoretical approach to big text data: Comparing expressive and rhetorical logics in Yelp reviews. *Communication Research, 45*, 688–718. https://doi.org/10.1177/0093650217719177

Markus, M. L. (1987). Toward a "critical mass" theory of interactive media: Universal access, interdependence and diffusion. *Communication Research, 14*, 491–511.

Marshall, R. (2015, September 10). How many ads do you see in one day? Red Crow Marketing. http://www.redcrowmarketing.com/2015/09/10/many-ads-see-one-day

Martins, N., & Riddle, K. (2021). Reassessing the risks: An updated content analysis of violence on US Children's primetime television. *Journal of Children and Media*. https://doi-org.dbproxy.lasalle.edu/10.1080/17482798.2021.1985548

Martins, N., & Wilson, B. J. (2012). Social aggression on television and its relationship to children's aggression in the classroom. *Human Communication Research*, *38*, 48–71. https://doi.org/10.1111/j.1468-2958.2011.01417.x

Masip, P., Suau, J., & Ruiz-Caballero, C. (2020). Incidental exposure to non-like-minded news through social media: Opposing voices in echo-chambers' news feeds. *Media & Communication*, *8*(4), 53–62. https://doi-org.dbproxy.lasalle.edu/10.17645/mac.v8i4.3146

Matthes, J., Knoll, J., & von Sikorski, C. (2018). The "spiral of silence" revisited: A meta-analysis on the relationship between perceptions of opinion support and political opinion expression. *Communication Research*, *45*, 3–33. https://doi.org/10.1177/0093650217745429

Mayer, J. D., Caruso, D. R., & Salovey, P. (1999). Emotional intelligence meets traditional standards for an intelligence. *Intelligence*, *27*(4), 267–298. https://doi.org/10.1016/S0160-2896(99)00016-1

Mayer, J. D., & Salovey, P. (1997). What is emotional intelligence? In P. Salovey & D. J. Sluyter (Eds.), *Emotional development and emotional intelligence: Educational implications* (pp. 3–34). Basic Books.

Mayer, J. D., Salovey, P., & Caruso, D. R. (2008). Emotional intelligence: New ability or eclectic traits? *American Psychologist*, *63*(6), 503–517. https://doi.org/10.1037/0003-066X.63.6.503

Mayfield, M., Mayfield, J., & Walker, R. (2021). Leader communication and follower identity: How leader motivating language shapes organizational identification through cultural knowledge and fit. *International Journal of Business Communication*, *58*, 221–253. https://doi.org/10.1177/2329488420979285

McCarthy, B. (2021, Apr 22). *What the first police statement about George Floyd got wrong*. Politifact: The Poynter Institute. https://www.politifact.com/article/2021/apr/22/what-first-police-statement-about-george-floyd-got/

McCombs, M., & Bell, T. (1974). The agenda-setting role of mass communication. In M. Salwen & D. Stacks (Eds.), *An integrated approach to communication theory and research*, (pp. 100). Lawrence Erlbaum.

McCombs, M. E., Shaw, D. L., & Weaver, D. H. (2014). New directions in agenda-setting theory and research. *Mass Communication & Society*, *17*, 781–802. https://doi.org/10.1080/15205436.2014.964871

McCombs, M., & Evatt, D. (1995). Issues and attributes: Exploring a new dimension in agenda setting. *Comunicación Y Sociedad*, *8*, 1–20.

McCombs, M., & Shaw, D. (1972). The agenda-setting function of the mass media. *Public Opinion Quarterly*, *36*, 176–187.

McCombs, M., & Weaver, D. H. (1973, April 25-28). *Voters' need for orientation and use of mass communication* [Paper presented]. The International Communication Association, Montreal, QC, Canada. https://api.semanticscholar.org/CorpusID:150526340

McCormack, K. C. (2014). Ethos, pathos, and logos: The benefits of Aristotelian rhetoric in the courtroom. *Washington University Jurisprudence Review*, *7*, 131–155.

McCown, N. D. (2008). The roles of internal public relations, leadership style, and workplace spirituality in building leader-employee relationships and facilitating relational outcomes [ProQuest Information & Learning]. In *Dissertation abstracts international section A: Humanities and social sciences* (Vol. 69, Issue 5-A, pp. 1585).

McDermott, K. C. P., & Lachlan, K. A. (2020). Polarizing organizations and image repair: The effects of extreme disposition and ego-involvement on ELM processing routes for organizational responses. *Communication Studies, 71*, 332–350. https://doi.org/10.1080/10510974.2020.1733039

McGuire, W. J. (1961). Resistance to persuasion conferred by active and passive prior refutation of the same and alternative counterarguments. *Journal of Abnormal and Social Psychology, 63*, 326–332.

McGuire, W. J. (1962). Persistence of the resistance to persuasion induced by various types of prior belief defenses. *Journal of Abnormal and Social Psychology, 64*, 241–248.

McGuire, W. J. (1964). Inducing resistance to persuasion: Some contemporary approaches. In L. Berkowitz (Ed.), *Advances in experimental social psychology* (Vol. 1, pp. 191–229). Academic Press.

McGuire, W. J., & Papageorgis, D. (1961). The relative efficacy of various types of prior belief-defense in producing immunity against persuasion. *Public Opinion Quarterly, 26*, 24–34.

McPhee, R. D., & Tompkins, P. K. (Eds.). (1985). *Organizational communication: Traditional themes and new directions*, SAGE.

McQuail, D. (1987). *Mass communication theory: An introduction* (2nd ed.). SAGE.

McQuail, D. (2010). *McQuail's mass communication theory* (6th ed.). SAGE.

Messaris, P. (1997). *Visual persuasion: The role of images in advertising*. SAGE.

Mieder, W. W. (1986). *Encyclopedia of world proverbs: A treasury of wit and wisdom through the ages*. Prentice Hall.

Miel, P., & Faris, R. (2008). News and information as digital media come of age. *Media Re:public*, Overview. Berkman Center for Internet and Society at Harvard University. https://cyber.harvard.edu/sites/cyber.law.harvard.edu/files/Overview_MR.pdf

Mikkelson, A. C., York, J. A., & Arritola, J. (2015). Communication competence, leadership behaviors, and employee outcomes in supervisor-employee relationships. *Business & Professional Communication Quarterly, 78*, 336–354. https://doi.org/10.1177/2329490615588542

Millar, F. E., & Rogers, L. E. (1976). A relational approach to interpersonal communication. In G. R. Miller (Ed.), *Explorations in interpersonal communication* (pp. 87–203). SAGE.

Miller, G. R. (1978). The current status of theory and research in interpersonal communication. *Human Communication Research, 4*, 164–178.

Miller, K. (2002). *Communication theories: Perspectives, processes, and contexts*. McGraw-Hill.

Miller, K. (2003). *Organizational communication: Approaches and processes* (3rd ed.). Wadsworth.

Mishel, L., & Davis, A. (2015, June 21). Top CEOs make 300 times more than typical workers. *Economic Policy Institute Report*. http://www.epi.org/files/2015/top-ceos-make-300-times-more-than-typical-workers.pdf

Mishel, L., & Kandra, J. (2020, August 18). CEO compensation surged 14% in 2019 to $21.3 million: CEOs now earn 320 times as much as a typical worker. *Economic Policy Institute Report*. https://www.epi.org/publication/ceo-compensation-surged-14-in-2019-to-21-3-million-ceos-now-earn-320-times-as-much-as-a-typical-worker/

Molina-Guzmán, I. (2016). #OscarsSoWhite: How Stuart Hall explains why nothing changes in Hollywood and everything is changing. *Critical Studies in Media Communication, 33*(5), 438–454. https://doi.org/10.1080/15295036.2016.1227864

Monge, P. R. (1973). Theory construction in the study of communication: The systemparadigm. *Journal of Communication, 23*, 5–16. https://doi.org/10.1111/j.1460-2466.1973.tb00928.x

Monge, P. R. (1977). The systems perspective as a theoretical basis for the study of human communication. *Communication Quarterly*, *25*(1), 19–29. https://doi-org.dbproxy.lasalle.edu/10.1080/01463 377709369244,

Monge, P. R., & Contractor, N.S. (2001). Emergence of communication networks. In F. M. Jablin & L. L. Putnam (Eds.), *Handbook of organizational communication: Advances in theory, research, and methods* (pp. 440–502). SAGE.

Montgomery, B. M. (1993). Relationship maintenance versus relationship change: Dialectical dilemma. *Journal of Social and Personal Relationships*, *10*, 205–224.

Moraru, M. (2015). Archetypes and myths: The hidden power of advertising storytelling. In S. J. Moenandar & N. K. Miller (Eds.), *Not ever absent: Storytelling in arts, culture and identity formation* (pp. 195–203). Brill.

Morley, D. D., & Shockley-Zalabak, P. (1991). Setting the rules: An examination of organizational founders' values. *Management Communication Quarterly*, *4*, 422–449.

Mornata, C., & Cassar, I. (2018). The role of insiders and organizational support in the learning process of newcomers during organizational socialization. *The Journal of Workplace Learning*, *30*, 562–575. https://doi.org/10.1108/JWL-06-2017-0045

Moy, P., & Hussain, M. M. (2014). Media and public opinion in a fragmented society. In W. Donsbach, C. T. Salmon, & Y. Tsfati (Eds.), *The spiral of silence: New perspectives on communication and public opinion* (pp. 92–100). Routledge.

Myers, S. A., & Kassing, J. W. (1998). The relationship between perceived supervisory communication behaviors and subordinate organizational identification. *Communication Research Reports*, *15*, 71–81.

Myrick, J. G. (2019). An Experimental Test of the roles of audience involvement and message frame in shaping public reactions to celebrity illness disclosures. *Health Communication*, *34*, 1060–1068. https://doi.org/10.1080/10410236.2018.1461170

Nabi, R. L. (2009). Cosmetic surgery makeover programs and intentions to undergo cosmetic enhancements: A consideration of three models of media effects. *Communication Research*, *35*(1), 1–27.

Neher, W. W., & Sandin, P. J. (2017). *Communicating ethically: Character, duties, consequences, and relationships* (2nd ed.). Routledge.

Neisser, U. (1967). *Cognitive psychology*. Appleton-Century-Crofts.

Neubaum, G., & Krämer, N. C. (2017). Monitoring the opinion of the crowd: Psychological mechanisms underlying public opinion perceptions on social media. *Media Psychology*, *20*, 502–531. https://doi.org/10.1080/15213269.2016.1211539

Nielsen. (2021, December 9). Being seen on screen 2021: The importance of quantity and quality representation on TV. *Neilsen*. https://www.nielsen.com/us/en/insights/report/2021/being-seen -on-screen/

Noelle-Neumann, E. (1974). The spiral of silence: A theory of public opinion. *Journal of Communication*, *24*, 43–51. https://doi.org/10.1111/j.1460-2466.1974.tb00367.x

Noelle-Neumann, E. (1977). Turbulences in the climate of opinion: Methodological applications of the spiral of silence theory. *Public Opinion Quarterly*, *41*, 143–158. https://doi.org/10.1086/268371

Noelle-Neumann, E. (1993). *The spiral of silence: Public opinion, our social skin* (2nd ed.). University of Chicago Press.

Nystrom, P. C. (1990). Vertical exchanges and organizational commitments of American business managers. *Group and Organizational Studies, 15,* 296–312.

Oeldorf-Hirsch, A., & Sundar, S. S. (2016). Social and technological motivations for online photo sharing. *Journal of Broadcasting & Electronic Media, 60,* 624–642. https://doi.org/10.1080/08838151.2016.1234478.

Offor, E. E. (2012). Analysis of sex stereotyping on women's positive evaluation and promotion to executive leadership roles. *Dissertation Abstracts International Section A, 73,* 260.

O'Hehir, A. (2014, March 22). *'Divergent" and "Hunger Games as capitalist agitprop.* http://www.salon.com/2014/03/22/divergent_and_hunger_games_as_capitalist_agitprop

O'Keefe, B. J. (1988). The logic of message design: Individual differences in reasoning about communication. *Communication Monographs, 55,* 80–103.

O'Keefe, B. J. (1997). Variation, adaptation, and functional explanation in the study of message design. In G. Philipsen & T. L. Albrecht (Eds.), *Developing communication theories* (pp. 85–118). State University of New York Press.

O'Keefe, B. J., & Delia, J. G. (1982). Impression formation and message production. In M. E. Roloff & C. R. Berger (Eds.), *Social cognition and communication* (pp. 33–72). SAGE.

O'Keefe, B. J., & Delia, J. G. (1988). Communicative tasks and communicative practices: The development of audience-centered message production. In B. Rafoth & D. Rubin (Eds.), *The social construction of written communication* (pp. 70–98). Ablex.

O'Keefe, B. J., Lambert, B. L., & Lambert, C. A. (1997). Conflict and communication in a research and development unit. In B. D. Sypher (Ed.), *Case studies in organizational communication 2* (pp. 31–52). Guilford Press.

O'Keefe, B. J., & Shepherd, G. J. (1987). The pursuit of multiple objectives in face-to-face persuasive interaction: Effects of construct differentiation on message organization. *Communication Monographs, 54,* 396–419. https://doi.org/10.1080/03637758709390241

O'Keefe, D. J. (1990). *Persuasion: Theory and research.* SAGE.

Oliveira, T., Thomas, M., Baptista, G., & Campos, F. (2016). Mobile payment: Understanding the determinants of customer adoption and intention to recommend the technology. *Computers in Human Behavior, 61,* 404–414. https://doi.org/10.1016/j.chb.2016.03.030

Orbe, M. (2021). The normative nature of racial microaggressions in the legal field: Exploring the communicative experiences of U.S. attorneys of colour. *Journal of Intercultural Communication Research, 50,* 207–224. https://doi.org/10.1080/17475759.2020.1866644

Orbe, M. P. (1998). *Constructing co-cultural theory: An explication of culture, power, and communication.* SAGE.

Orbe, M., & Roberts, T. (2012). Co-cultural theorizing: Foundations, applications & extensions. *Howard Journal of Communications, 23,* 293–311. https://doi.org/10.1080/10646175.2012.722838

O'Sullivan, P. B. (2005, May 26-30, May 26–30). *Masspersonal communication: Rethinking the mass interpersonal divide* [Paper presented]. The Annual Meeting of the International Communication Association, New York City, NY, United States.

Oyesomi, K., & Salawu, A. (2018). Influence of sexualisation of women in music videos on the body image of Nigerian female youths. *Gender & Behaviour, 16,* 12059–12072.

Palmer, B., Walls, M., Burgess, Z., & Stough, C. (2001). Emotional intelligence and effective leadership. *Leadership & Organization Development Journal, 22,* 5–11.

Park, J. S. (2008). The social reality of depression: DTC advertising of antidepressants and perceptions of the prevalence and lifetime risk of depression. *Journal of Business Ethics, 79*(4), 379–393.

Park, S.-Y., Cho, M., & Kim, S. (2021). The effect of CSR expectancy violation: value from expectancy violation theory and confirmation bias. *Journal of Marketing Communications, 27*, 365–388. https://doi.org/10.1080/13527266.2019.1671478

Parks, M. R., & Adelman, M. B. (1983). Communication networks and the development of romantic relationships: An expansion of uncertainty reduction theory. *Human Communication Research, 10*, 55–79.

Pattee, H. H (Ed.). (1973). *Hierarchy theory: The challenge of complex systems*. Braziller.

Paustian-Underdahl, S. C., Walker, L. S., & Woehr, D. J. (2014). Gender and perceptions of leadership effectiveness: A meta-analysis of contextual moderators. *Journal of Applied Psychology, 99*, 1129–1145. https://doi.org/10.1037/a0036751

Pazos, P., Chung, J. M., & Micari, M. (2013). Instant messaging as a task-support tool in information technology organizations. *Journal of Business Communication, 50*(1), 68–86. https://doi.org/10.1177/0021943612465181

Peake, J. S. (2001). Presidential agenda setting in foreign policy. *Political Research Quarterly, 54*, 69–86.

Pearce, W. B., & Cronen, V. (1980). *Communication, action, and meaning: The creation of social realities*. Praeger Books.

Pearson, J., Nelson, P., Titsworth, S., & Harter, L. (2008). *Human communication* (3rd ed.). McGraw-Hill.

Perks, L. (2012). Three satiric television decoding positions. *Communication Studies, 63*(3), 290–308. https://doi.org/10.1080/10510974.2012.678925

Peters, R. S. (1974). T. Mischel (Ed.), *Personal understanding and personal relationships. Understanding other persons*. Rowman & Littlefield.

Petronio, S. (2002). *Boundaries of privacy: Dialectics of disclosure*. SUNY Press.

Petronio, S., & Durham, W. T. (2008). Communication privacy management theory: Significance for interpersonal communication. In L. A. Baxter & D. O. Braithwaite (Eds.), *Engaging theories in interpersonal communication: Multiple perspectives* (pp. 309–322). SAGE.

Petty, R. E., & Cacioppo, J. T. (1986). *Communication and persuasion: Central and peripheral routes to attitude change*. Springer-Verlag.

Pfau, M. (1997). The inoculation model of resistance to influence. In F. J. Boster & G. Barnett (Eds.), *Progress in communication sciences* (Vol. 13, pp. 133–171). Ablex.

Philipsen, G. M. (2008). Speech codes theory: Traces of culture in interpersonal communication. In L.A. Baxter & D. O. Braithwaite (Eds.), *Engaging Theories of Interpersonal Communication* (pp. 269–280). Sage.

Pillai, P. (1992). Rereading Stuart Hall's encoding/decoding model. *Communication Theory, 2*(3), 221–233.

Platt, C. (2004, May 27-31). *A culture of thinness: Negotiated and oppositional decoding of eating disorder discourse by anorectics*. In *Paper presented at the meeting of the International Communication Association*. United States.

Ploeger, N. A., & Bisel, R. S. (2013). The role of identification in giving sense to unethical organizational behavior: Defending the organization. *Management Communication Quarterly, 27*(2), 155–183. https://doi.org/10.1177/0893318912469770

Poole, M. S. (1999). Group communication theory. In L. R. Frey, D. S. Gouran, & M. S. Poole (Eds.), *The handbook of group communication theory and research* (pp. 37–70). SAGE.

Poole, M. S. (2014). Systems theory. In L. L. Putnam & D.K. Mumby (Eds.), *The Sage handbook of organizational communication: Advances in theory, research, and methods, 3rd ed* (pp. 49–74). SAGE.

Poole, M. S., Seibold, D. R., & McPhee, R. D. (1985). Group decision-making as a structurational process. *Quarterly Journal of Speech, 71*, 74–102.

Poole, M. S., Seibold, D. R., & McPhee, R. D. (1986). A structurational approach to theory-building in group decision-making research. In R. Y. Hirokawa & M. S. Poole (Eds.), *Communication and group decision-making* (pp. 237–264). SAGE.

Powell, G. N. (1998). Reinforcing and extending today's organizations: The simultaneous pursuit of Person-organization fit and diversity. *Organizational Dynamics, 26*, 50–61. https://doi.org/10.1016/S0090-2616(98)90014-6

Procter, J. (2004). *Stuart Hall*. Routledge.

Putnam, V. L., & Paulus, P. B. (2009). Brainstorming, brainstorming rules and decision making. *The Journal of Creative Behavior, 43*(1), 23–39.

Rand, M. A. (1967). An empirical comparison of Sherif's social judgment approach and Festinger's dissonance theory at their points of contrast: Ego involvement and discrepancy of communication [ProQuest Information & Learning]. In *Dissertation abstracts international section A: Humanities and social sciences* (Vol. 28, Issue 3-A, pp. 1128–1129).

Randazzo, S. (2006). Subaru: The emotional myths behind the brand's growth. *Journal of Advertising Research, 46*(1), 11–17. https://doi.org/10.2501/S002184990606003X

Rapoport, A. (1968). The promises and pitfalls of information theory. In W. Buckley (Ed.), *Modern systems research for the behavioral scientist* (pp. 137–142). Aldine.

Rapp, C. (2010, Spring). Aristotle's Rhetoric. In E. N. Zalta (Ed.), *Stanford Encyclopedia of Philosophy*. Stanford Metaphysics Research Lab. https://plato.stanford.edu/archives/spr2010/entries/aristotle-rhetoric/

Rathnayake, C., & Winter, J. S. (2018). Carrying forward the uses and grats 2.0 agenda: An affordance-driven measure of social media uses and gratifications. *Journal of Broadcasting & Electronic Media, 62*, 371–389. https://doi.org/10.1080/08838151.2018.1451861

Ray, C. D., Floyd, K., Mongeau, P. A., Mark, L., Shufford, K. N., & Niess, L. (2019). Planning improves vocal fluency and the appearance of concern when communicating emotional support. *Communication Research Reports, 36*, 57–66. https://doi.org/10.1080/08824096.2018.1560251

Ray, R., Brown, M., Fraistat, N., & Summers, E. (2017). Ferguson and the death of Michael Brown on Twitter: #BlackLivesMatter, #TCOT, and the evolution of collective identities. *Ethnic and Racial Studies, 40*, 1797–1813. https://doi.org/10.1080/01419870.2017.1335422

Reinard, J. (1998). *Introduction to communication research* (2nd ed.). McGraw-Hill.

Reyes, A. (2020). I, Trump: The cult of personality, anti-intellectualism and the Post-Truth era. *Journal of Language & Politics, 19*, 869–892. https://doi.org/10.1075/jlp.20002.rey

Reynolds, P. D. (1971). *A primer on theory construction*. Bobbs Merrill.

Ritter, B. A., & Yoder, J. D. (2004). Gender differences in leader emergence persist even for dominant women: An updated confirmation of role congruity theory. *Psychology of Women Quarterly, 28*(3), 187–193. https://doi.org/10.1111/j.1471-6402.2004.00135.x

Rivera, L. A. (2012). Hiring as cultural matching: The case of elite professional service firms. *American Sociological Review, 77*, 999–1022. https://doi.org/10.1177/0003122412463213

Roberto, A. J., Zhou, X., & Lu, A. H. (2021). The Effects of perceived threat and efficacy on college students' social distancing behavior during the COVID-19 pandemic. *Journal of Health Communication*, *26*, 264–271. https://doi.org/10.1080/10810730.2021.1903628

Roberts, K. G. (2004). Texturing the Narrative Paradigm: Folklore and Communication. *Communication Quarterly*, *52*(2), 129–142. https://doi-org.dbproxy.lasalle.edu/10.1080/0146337040 9370186,

Roberts, L., Stevens Aubrey, J., Terán, L., Dajches, L., & Ward, L. M. (2021). The super man: Examining associations between childhood superhero imaginative play and wishful identification and emerging adult men's body image and gender beliefs. *Psychology of Men & Masculinities*, *22*(2), 391–400. https://doi.org/10.1037/men0000335

Robidoux, H., Ellington, E., & Lauerer, J. (2019). Screen time: The impact of digital technology on children and strategies in care. *Journal of Psychosocial Nursing & Mental Health Services*, *57*, 15–20. https://doi.org/10.3928/02793695-20191016-04

Rogers, E. M. (2003). *Diffusion of innovations* (5th ed.). Free Press.

Rogers, R. W. (1975). A protection motivation theory of fear appeals and attitude change. *Journal of Psychology*, *91*, 93–114. https://doi.org/10.1080/00223980.1975.9915803

Rogers, R. W. (1985). Attitude change and information integration in fear appeals. *Psychological Reports*, *56*, 179–182. https://doi.org/.2466/pr0.1985.56.1.179

Rosen, J. (2011, May 25). The people formerly known as the audience. *The HuffPost*. https://www.huffpost.com/entry/the-people-formerly-known_1_b_24113

Rothwell, J. D. (1998). *In mixed company: Small group communication* (3rd ed.). Harcourt Brace.

Ruggiero, T. E. (2000). Uses and gratifications theory in the 21st century. *Mass Communication and Society*, *3*(1), 3–37.

Rui, J. R., & Wang, H. (2015). Social network sites and international students' cross-cultural adaptation. *Computers in Human Behavior*, *49*, 400–411. https://doi.org/10.1016/j.chb.2015.03.041

Runes, D. D (Ed.). (1984). *Dictionary of philosophy*. Rowman & Allanheld.

Rusbult, C. E. (1980). Commitment and satisfaction in romantic associations: A test of the investment model. *Journal of Experimental Social Psychology*, *16*, 172–186.

Russ, G. S., Daft, R. L., & Lengel, R. H. (1990). Media selection and managerial characteristics in organizational communications. *Management Communication Quarterly*, *4*, 151–175. https://doi.org/10.1177/0893318990004002002

Ruth, T. K., & Rumble, J. N. (2019). Consumers' evaluations of genetically modified food messages. *Journal of Applied Communications*, *103*, 1–18. https://doi.org/10.4148/1051-0834.2193

Ryckman, M. L. (n.d.). How to strengthen organizational identification. *Small Business Chronicle*. https://smallbusiness.chron.com/strengthen-organizational-identification-31398.html

Salant, P., & Dillman, D. A. (1994). *How to conduct your own survey*. Wiley.

Salazar, A. J. (1995). Understanding the synergistic effects of communication in small groups: Making the most out of group member abilities. *Small Group Research*, *26*, 169–199.

Salazar, L. R. (2015). The negative reciprocity process in marital relationships: A literature review. *Aggression and Violent Behavior*, *24*, 113–119. http://dx.doi.org/10.1016/j.avb.2015.05.008

Salmon, S., & Joiner, T. A. (2005). Toward an understanding of communication channel preferences for the receipt of management information. *Journal of American Academy of Business*, *7*, 56–62.

Salovey, P., Caruso, D., & Mayer, J. D. (2004). Emotional intelligence in practice. In P. Linley & S. Joseph (Eds.), *Positive psychology in practice* (pp. 447–463). John Wiley & Sons.

Salovey, P., & Mayer, J. D. (1989). Emotional intelligence. *Imagination, Cognition and Personality*, 9(3), 185–211.

Schein, E. (2010). *Organizational culture and leadership* (4th ed.). Jossey-Bass.

Schein, E. H. (1985). *Organizational culture and leadership*. Jossey-Bass.

Schein, E. H. (1990). Organizational culture. *American Psychologist*, 45(2), 109–119. https://doi.org/10.1037/0003-066X.45.2.109

Schein, E. H. (1992). *Organizational culture and leadership* (2nd ed.). Jossey-Bass.

Schein, E. H., & Schein, P. A. (2016). *Organizational culture and leadership*. John Wiley & Sons.

Schmitz, J., & Fulk, J. (1991). Organizational colleagues, media richness, and electronic mail: A test of the social influence model of technology use. *Communication Research*, 18, 487–523. https://doi.org/10.1177/009365091018004003

Schneider, B. (1987). The people make the place. *Personnel Psychology*, 40(3), 437–453. https://doi-org.dbproxy.lasalle.edu/10.1111/j.1744-6570.1987.tb00609.x

Scott, L. (2019, April 21). A history of the influencer, from Shakespeare to Instagram. *The New Yorker*. https://www.newyorker.com/culture/annals-of-inquiry/a-history-of-the-influencer-from-shakespeare-to-instagram

Seargeant, Philip. (2020). *The art of political storytelling: Why stories win votes in post-truth politics*. Bloomsbury.

Sedereviciute, K., & Valentini, C. (2011). Towards a more holistic stakeholder analysis approach. Mapping known and undiscovered stakeholders from social media. *International Journal of Strategic Communication*, 5(4), 221–239. https://doi.org/10.1080/1553118X.2011.592170

Seib, P. (2017, June 3). Mainstream media fails in terrorism coverage. *Newsweek*. http://www.newsweek.com/mainstream-media-fails-terrorism-coverage-619883

Seifert, J. W. (2007, January 18). *Data mining and homeland security: An overview. Congressional Research Service Report for Congress, order code RL31798*. http://www.fas.org/sgp/crs/intel/RL31798.pdf

Serrone, R. O., Weinberg, J. A., Goslar, P. W., Wilkinson, E. P., Thompson, T. M., Dameworth, J. L., Dempsey, S. R., & Petersen, S. R. (2018). Grey's Anatomy effect: Television portrayal of patients with trauma may cultivate unrealistic patient and family expectations after injury. *Trauma Surgery & Acute Care Open*, 3. https://doi.org/10.1136/tsaco-2

Shadel, W. G., Martino, S. C., Setodji, C. M., Dunbar, M., Scharf, D., & Creswell, K. G. (2019). Do graphic health warning labels on cigarette packages deter purchases at point-of-sale? An experiment with adult smokers. *Health Education Research*, 34, 321–331. https://doi.org/10.1093/her/cyz011

Shanahan, J., & Morgan, M. (1999). *Television and its viewers: Cultivation theory and research*. Cambridge University Press. https://doi.org/10.1017/CBO9780511488924

Shaw, A. (2017). Encoding and decoding affordances: Stuart Hall and interactive media technologies. *Media, Culture & Society*, 39, 592–602. https://doi.org/10.1177/0163443717692741

Shelton, K. (2017, October 30). The value of search results rankings. *Forbes*. https://www.forbes.com/sites/forbesagencycouncil/2017/10/30/the-value-of-search-results-rankings/?sh=156474c644d3

Shepherd, M. M., & Martz, W. B. (2006). Media richness theory and the distance education environment. *Journal of Computer Information Systems, 47*, 114–122.

Sherif, C. W., Sherif, M., & Nebergall, R. E. (1965). *Attitude and social change.* Saunders.

Sherif, M., & Hovland, C. I. (1961). *Social judgment.* Yale University Press.

Short, J., Williams, E., & Christie, B. (1976). *The social psychology of telecommunications.* John Wiley & Son.

Sias, P. M., & Duncan, K. L. (2020). Not just for customers anymore: Organization Facebook, employee social capital, and organizational identification. *International Journal of Business Communication, 57*(4), 431–451. https://doi.org/10.1177/2329488418765930

Signorelli, N., Gerbner, G., & Morgan, M. (1995). Violence on television: The cultural indicators project. *Journal of Broadcasting and Electronic Media, 39*, 278–283.

Signorielli, N. (2009). Race and sex in prime time: A look at occupations and occupational prestige. *Mass Communication & Society, 12*, 332–352. https://doi.org/10.1080/15205430802478693

Signorielli, N., & Morgan, M. (1990). Cultivation analysis: Conceptualization and methodology. In N. Signorielli & M. Morgan (Eds.), *Cultivation analysis: New directions in media effects research* (pp. 13–24). SAGE.

Sillars, A. L. (1980). Attributions and communication in roommate conflict. *Communication Monographs, 47*(3), 180–200. https://doi.org/10.1080/03637758009376031

Simons, H. W. (1976). *Persuasion: Understanding, practice, and analysis.* Addison-Wesley.

Sink, A., & Mastro, D. (2017). Depictions of Gender on Primetime Television: A Quantitative Content Analysis. *Mass Communication & Society, 20*, 3–22. Https://doi.org/10.1080/15205436.2016.1212243

Sivanathan, N., & Fekken, G. C. (2002). Emotional intelligence, moral reasoning, and transformational leadership. *Leadership & Organization Development Journal, 23*, 198–204.

Smircich, L. (1983). Concepts of culture and organizational analysis. *Administrative Science Quarterly, 28*, 339–358.

Smith, E. B., & Kuntz, P. (2013, April 30). CEO pay 1,795-to-1 multiple of wages skirts U.S. law. *Bloomberg.* http://www.bloomberg.com/news/2013-04-30/ceo-pay-1-795-to-1-multiple-of-workers-skirts-law-as-sec-delays

Solomon, D. H., Knobloch, L. K., Theiss, J. A., & McLaren, R. M. (2016). Relational turbulence theory: Explaining variation in subjective experiences and communication within romantic relationships. *Human Communication Research, 42*, 507–532. https://doi.org/10.1111/hcre.12091

Spiegelman, P. (2021, March 21). Is hiring for culture fit perpetuating bias? *Forbes.* https://www.forbes.com/sites/paulspiegelman/2021/03/01/is-hiring-for-culture-fit-perpetuating-bias/?sh=81ecf1755e8a

Spitzberg, B. H., & Cupach, W. R. (1984). *Interpersonal communication competence.* SAGE.

Spitzberg, B. H., & Cupach, W. R. (1989). *Handbook of interpersonal competence research.* Springer-Verlag.

Spitzberg, B. H., & Manusov, V. (2015). Attribution theory: Finding good cause in the search for theory. In D. O. Braithwaite & P. Schrodt (Eds.), *Engaging theories in interpersonal communication: Multiple perspectives* (2nd ed., pp. 37–49). SAGE.

Spoel, P., Goforth, D., Cheu, H., & Pearson, D. (2008). Public communication of climate change science: Engaging citizens through apocalyptic narrative explanation. *Technical Communication Quarterly, 18*, 49–81.

Stache, L. C. (2017). Fisher narrative paradigm. In M. Allen (Ed.), *The Sage encyclopedia of communication research methods* (Vol. 1-4). SAGE.

Staffbase. (2021). 7 meaningful internal communication examples for 2021. *Staffbase*. https://staffbase.com/blog/internal-communication-examples/

Staton, A. Q. (1999). An ecological perspective on college/university teaching: The teaching/learning environment and socialization. In A. L. Vangelisti, J. A. Daly & G. W. Friedrich (Eds.), *Teaching communication*, (2nd ed., pp. 31-47). Lawrence Erlbaum.

Steele, G. A., & Plenty, D. (2015). Supervisor–subordinate communication competence and job and communication satisfaction. *International Journal of Business Communication*, *52*, 294-318. https://doi.org/10.1177/2329488414525450

Stefanone, M. A., & Lackaff, D. (2009). Reality television as a model for online behavior: Blogging, photo, and video sharing. *Journal of Computer-Mediated Communication*, *14*(4), 964-987. https://doi-org.dbproxy.lasalle.edu/10.1111/j.1083-6101.2009.01477.x

Steiner, S., & Cox, K. (2014). Aligning organizational and individual culture and values. In R. A. Bean, S. D. Davis, M. P. Davey, R. A. Bean, S. D. Davis, & M. P. Davey (Eds.), *Clinical supervision activities for increasing competence and self-awareness* (pp. 127-133). John Wiley & Sons.

Steppat, D., Castro, L., & Esser, F. (2021). What news users perceive as 'alternative media' varies between countries: How media fragmentation and polarization matter. *Digital Journalism*, *9*, 1-21. https://doi.org/0.1080/21670811.2021.1939747

Stoll, J. (2021, October 22). SVOD service user shares in the U.S. 2015-2021. *Statistica*. https://www.statista.com/statistics/318778/subscription-based-video-streaming-services-usage-usa/

Stoycheff, E. (2016). Under surveillance: Examining Facebook's spiral of silence effects in the wake of NSA internet monitoring. *Journalism & Mass Communication Quarterly*, *93*, 296-311. https://doi.org/10.1177/1077699016630255

Stuglin, S. (2009, September 23). A brief timeline of classical rhetoric – From Corax to Quintilian. *GSU History of Rhetoric (wiki)*. http://8170.pbworks.com/w/page/1115535/A%20Brief%20Timeline%20of%20Classical%20Rhetoric%20%E2%80%93%20From%20Corax%20to%20Quintilian

Sundar, S., & Limperos, A. M. (2013). Uses and grats 2.0: New gratifications for new media. *Journal of Broadcasting and Electronic Media*, *57*(4), 504-525. https://doi.org/10.1080/08838151.2013.845827,

Sundar, S. S. (2008). The MAIN model: A heuristic approach to understanding technology effects on credibility. In M. J. Metzger & A. J. Flanagin (Eds.), *Digital Media, Youth, and Credibility* (pp. 72-100). MIT Press.

Tannen, D. (1990). *You just don't understand: Women and men in conversation*. Morrow.

Taylor, C. C. W., & Lee, M-K. (2020, Fall). The sophists. In E. N. Zalta (Ed.), *Stanford encyclopedia of philosophy*. Stanford Metaphysics Research Lab. https://plato.stanford.edu/archives/fall2020/entries/sophists/

Ter Hoeven, C. L., Miller, V. D., Peper, B., & Den Dulk, L. (2017). "The Work Must Go On": The role of employee and managerial communication in the use of work–life policies. *Management Communication Quarterly*, *31*, 194-229. https://doi.org/10.1177/0893318916684980

Thibaut, J. W., & Kelley, H. H. (1959). *The social psychology of groups*. Transaction Books.

Thomas, B. J., & Petrow, G. A. (2020). Gender-based evaluations of integrity failures: Women leaders judged worse. *Public Opinion Quarterly*, *84*, 936-957. https://doi.org/10.1093/poq/nfaa045

Thornhill, M. F. (2017). *Black and blue: Competing social constructions of police on Instagram and Twitter (314)* [Master's thesis, The University of Southern Mississippi]. The Aquila Digital Community. https://aquila.usm.edu/masters_theses/314

Thory, K. (2016). To reveal or conceal? Managers' disclosures of private information during emotional intelligence training. *Human Resource Development Quarterly*, *27*(1), 41–66. https://doi.org/10.1002/hrdq.21222

Ting-Toomey, S. (1988). Intercultural conflicts: A face-negotiation theory. In Y. Kim & W. Gudykunst (Eds.), *Theories in intercultural communication* (pp. 213–238). SAGE.

Ting-Toomey, S. (1991). Cross-cultural communication: An introduction. In S. Ting-Toomey & F. Korzenny (Eds.), *Cross-cultural interpersonal communication* (pp. 1–7). SAGE.

Ting-Toomey, S. (1992, April 15). *Cross-cultural face-negotiation: An analytical overview* [Paper presented]. The Meeting of the Pacific Region Forum on Business and Management Communication, Vancouver, BC, Canada.

Ting-Toomey, S. (2005). The matrix of face: An updated face-negotiation theory. In W. B. Gudykunst (Ed.), *Theorizing about intercultural communication* (pp. 71–92). SAGE.

Ting-Toomey, S. (2017). Conflict face negotiation theory: Tracking its evolutionary journey. In X. Dai & G. M. Chen (Eds.), *Conflict management and intercultural communication: The art of intercultural harmony* (pp. 123–143). Routledge.

Ting-Toomey, S., & Oetzel, J. (2002). Cross-cultural face concerns and conflict styles: Current status and future directions. In W. Gudykunst & B. Mody (Eds.), *Handbook of international and intercultural communication* (2nd ed., pp. 143–164). SAGE.

Ting-Toomey, S., Yee-Jung, K. K., Shapiro, R. B., Garcia, W., Wright, T. J., & Oetzel, J. G. (2000). Ethnic/cultural identity salience and conflict styles in four US ethnic groups. *International Journal of Intercultural Relations*, *24*, 47–81. https://doi.org/10.1016/S0147-1767(99)00023-1

Tompkins, P. K. (1989). Organizational communication: The central tradition. *Spectra*, *25*(5), 2–3.

Tompkins, P. K., & Cheney, G. E. (1985). Communication and unobtrusive control in contemporary organizations. In R. D. McPhee & P. K. Tompkins (Eds.), *Organizational communication: Traditional themes and new directions* (pp. 179–210). SAGE.

Tracy, M. (2019, November 19). Gannett, now largest U.S. newspaper chain, targets 'inefficiencies.' *The New York Times*. https://www.nytimes.com/2019/11/19/business/media/gannett-gatehouse-merger.html

Trevino, L. K., Lengel, R. H., & Daft, R. L. (1987). Media symbolism, media richness, and media choice in organizations. *Communication Research*, *14*(5), 553–574.

Triandis, H. C. (1995). *Individualism and collectivism*. Westview Press.

Trifiro, B., & Zhang, Y. (2021). Media vs. candidates and minorities vs. majorities: Who sets the public's agenda in the 2020 Democratic presidential primary? *Agenda Setting Journal: Theory, Practice, Critique*, *5*, 84–106. https://doi.org/10.1075/asj.20009.tri

Tukachinsky, R., Mastro, D., & Yarchi, M. (2015). Documenting portrayals of race/ethnicity on primetime television over a 20-year span and their association with national-level racial/ethnic attitudes." *Journal of Social Issues*, *71*, 17–38. https://doi.org/10.1111/josi.12094.

Tyrrell, I. (2016, October 21). What, exactly, is "American exceptionalism?" *Aeon* [online]. http://theweek.com/articles/654508/what-exactly-american-exceptionalism

United States Food and Drug Administration. (2021, June 14). Birth control chart. *U.S. FDA*. https://www.fda.gov/consumers/free-publications-women/birth-control-chart

U.S. Bureau of Labor Statistics. (2021, October 12). *Job openings and labor turnover—August 2021*. https://www.bls.gov/news.release/pdf/jolts.pdf

Valkenburg, P. M., & Peter, J. (2013). The differential susceptibility to media effects model. *Journal of Communication, 63*(2), 221–243. https://doi.org/10.1111/jcom.12024

Van Vonderen, K. E., & Kinnally, W. (2012). Media effects on body image: Examining media exposure in the broader context of internal and other social factors. *American Communication Journal, 14*(2), 41–57.

Vecchio, R. P., Griffeth, R. W., & Hom, P. W. (1986). The predictive utility of the vertical dyad linkage approach. *Journal of Social Psychology, 126,* 617–625.

Vergeer, M., Lubbers, M., & Scheepers, P. (2000). Exposure to newspapers and attitudes toward ethnic minorities: A longitudinal analysis. *Howard Journal of Communications, 11*(2), 127–143.

Verghese, A. K. (2019, March 26). *Building a storytelling culture in organizations with internal communications*. Institute for Public Relations. https://instituteforpr.org/building-a-storytelling-culture-in-organizations-with-internal-communications/

Victor, D. (2017, April 5). Pepsi pulls ad accused of trivializing Black Lives Matter. *New York Times*. https://www.nytimes.com/2017/04/05/business/kendall-jenner-pepsi-ad.html?mcubz=2

Vivero, V. N., & Jenkins, S. R. (1999). Existential hazards of the multicultural individual: Defining and understanding "cultural homelessness.". *Cultural Diversity and Ethnic Minority Psychology, 5,* 6–26.

von Bertalanffy, L. (1968). *General system theory: Foundations, development, applications* (Rev. ed.). Braziller.

Vorvoreanu, M. (2009). Perceptions of corporations on Facebook: An analysis of Facebook social norms. *Journal of New Communications Research, 4,* 67–86.

Wadsworth, A., Patterson, P., Kaid, L., Cullers, G., Malcomb, D., & Lamirand, L. (1987). "Masculine" vs. "feminine" strategies in political ads: Implications for female candidates. *Journal of Applied Communication Research, 15*(1/2), 77.

Waldron, V. R. (1997). Toward a theory of interactive conversational planning. In J. O. Greene (Ed.), *Message production: Advances in communication theory* (pp. 195–220). Lawrence Erlbaum Associates Publishers.

Walker, R. (2021). Communication perspectives on organizational culture and organizational identification. *International Journal of Business Communication, 58,* 147–151. https://doi.org/10.1177/2329488420957073

Wallen, A. S., Mor, S., & Devine, B. A. (2014). It's about respect: Gender–professional identity integration affects male nurses' job attitudes. *Psychology of Men & Masculinity, 15,* 305–312. https://doi.org/10.1037/a0033714

Walther, J. B. (1992). Interpersonal effects in computer-mediated interaction: A relational perspective. *Communication Research, 19,* 52–90. https://doi.org/10.1177/009365092019001003

Walther, J. B. (1996). Computer-mediated communication: Impersonal, interpersonal, and hyperpersonal interaction. *Communication Research, 23,* 3–43. Https://doi.org/10.1177/009365096023001001

Walther, J. B. (2015). Social information processing theory (CMC). In C. R. Berger (Ed.), *The International Encyclopedia of Interpersonal Communication* (pp. 1–13). John Wiley & Sons.

Walther, J. B., & Parks, M. (2002). Cues filtered out, cues filtered in: Computer-mediated communication and relationships. In M. L. Knapp, J. A. Daly, & R. Miller (Eds.), *Handbook of interpersonal communication* (3rd ed., pp. 529–563). SAGE.

Walther, J. B., Van Der Heide, B., Hamel, L. M., & Shulman, H. C. (2009). Self-generated versus other-generated statements and impressions in computer-mediated communication: A test of warranting theory using Facebook. *Communication Research*, *36*, 229–253. https://doi.org/10.1177/0093650208330251

Walther, J. B., & Whitty, M. T. (2021). Language, psychology, and new new media: The hyperpersonal model of mediated communication at twenty-five years. Journal of *Language and Social Psychology*, *40*, 120–135. https://doi.org/10.1177/0261927X20967703

Wang, H., & Parris, J. J. (2021). Popular media as a double-edged sword: An entertainment narrative analysis of the controversial Netflix series 13 Reasons Why. *PLoS One*, *16*(8). https://doi.org/10.1371/journal.pone.0255610

Wang, Y., & Huang, T. (2009). The relationship of transformational leadership with group cohesiveness and emotional intelligence. *Social Behavior and Personality*, *37*, 379–392.

Ward, M. (2020, March 4). C-suite leaders are making a big assumption about their workforce—and it's bleeding the economy of $1.05 trillion. *Business Insider*. https://www.businessinsider.com/accenture-report-perception-gap-shows-economic-cost-lack-of-diversity-inclusion

Watkins, M. D. (2007, September 10). Demystifying strategy: The what, who, why, and how. *Harvard Business Review*, H0005X-PDF-ENG.

Watzlawick, P., Bavelas, J. B., & Jackson, D. D. (1967). *Pragmatics of human communication: A study of interactional patterns, pathologies, and paradoxes*. Norton.

Weaver, D. H. (2007). Thoughts on agenda setting, framing, and priming. *Journal of Communication*, *57*, 142–147. https://doi.org/10.1111/j.1460-2466.2006.00333.x

Weick, K. E. (1969). *The social psychology of organizing*. Addison-Wesley.

Weinstein, N. D. (1984). Why it won't happen to me: Perceptions of risk factors and susceptibility. *Health Psychology*, *3*, 431–57. https://doi.org/10.1037//0278-6133.3.5.431. PMID: 6536498

West, R., & Turner, L.H. (2017). *Introducing communication theory: Analysis and application* (6th ed.). McGraw Hill.

Whole Foods Market. (n.d.). *Our core values*. https://www.wholefoodsmarket.com/mission-values/core-values

Wieland, S. M. B. (2020). Constituting resilience at work: maintaining dialectics and cultivating dignity throughout a worksite closure. *Management Communication Quarterly*, *34*(4), 463–494. https://doi.org/10.1177/0893318920949314

Williams, M. (2013, April 17). *FBI urges media to "exercise caution" after inaccurate arrest reports. The Guardian*. http://www.guardian.co.uk/world/2013/apr/17/fbi-media-exercise-caution-bombings

Willis, J. (2017). Moving toward extremism: Group polarization in the laboratory and the world. In S. C. Cloninger, S. A. Leibo, S. C. Cloninger, & S. A. Leibo (Eds.), *Understanding angry groups: Multidisciplinary perspectives on their motivations and effects on society* (pp. 53–76). Praeger/ABC-CLIO.

Wilson, L. E., & Ogden, J. (2004). *Strategic communications planning: For effective public relations and marketing* (4th ed.). Kendall Hunt Publishing.

Witte, K. (1992). Putting the fear back into fear appeals: The extended parallel process model. *Communication Monographs*, *59*, 329–349. https://doi.org/10.1080/03637759209376276

Witte, K. (1994). Fear control and danger control: A test of the extended parallel process model (EPPM). *Communication Monographs*, *61*, 113–134. https://doi.org/10.1080/0363775940937632810.1080/03637759409376328

Wong, N. H. (2016). "Vaccinations are safe and effective": Inoculating positive HPV vaccine attitudes against antivaccination attack messages. *Communication Reports*, *29*, 127–138. https://doi.org/10.10 80/08934215.2015.1083599

Wood, J. T. (1992). Gender and moral voice: Moving from woman's nature to standpoint epistemology. *Women's Studies in Communication*, *15*, 1–24. https://doi.org/10.1080/07491409.1992.11089757

Wood, J. T., & Dindia, K. (1998). What's the difference? A dialogue about differences and similarities between women and men. In D. J. Canary & K. Dindia (Eds.), *Sex differences and similarities in communication: Critical essays and empirical investigations of sex and gender in interaction* (pp. 19–39). Lawrence Erlbaum.

Xiang, D., Zhang, L., Tao, Q., Wang, Y., & Ma, S. (2019). Informational or emotional appeals in crowdfunding message strategy: An empirical investigation of backers' support decisions. *Journal of the Academy of Marketing Science*, *47*(6), 1046–1063. https://doi.org/10.1007/s11747-019-00638-w

Xu, Z., Ellis, L., & Laffidy, M. (2022). News frames and news exposure predicting flu vaccination uptake: Evidence from U.S. newspapers, 2011–2018 using computational methods. *Health Communication*, *37*, 74–82. https://doi.org/10.1080/10410236.2020.1818958

Zanin, A. C., Hoelscher, C. S., & Kramer, M. W. (2016). Extending symbolic convergence theory. *Small Group Research*, *47*, 438–472. https://doi.org/10.1177/1046496416658554

Zappos. (n.d.). *Holacracy and self-organization.* Zappos Insights, https://www.zapposinsights.com/about/holacracy

Zerback, T., & Fawzi, N. (2017). Can online exemplars trigger a spiral of silence? Examining the effects of exemplar opinions on perceptions of public opinion and speaking out. *New Media & Society*, *19*, 1034–1051. https://doi.org/10.1177/1461444815625942

Żerebecki, B. G., Opree, S. J., Hofhuis, J., & Janssen, S. (2021). Can TV shows promote acceptance of sexual and ethnic minorities? A literature review of television effects on diversity attitudes. *Sociology Compass*, *15*. https://doi.org/10.1111/soc4.12906

Zhang, R., & Fu, J. S. (2020). Privacy management and self-disclosure on social network sites: The moderating effects of stress and gender. *Journal of Computer-Mediated Communication*, *25*(3), 236–251. https://doi.org/10.1093/jcmc/zmaa004

Zillmann, D. (1991). Television viewing and physiological arousal. In J. Bryant & D. Zillmann (Eds.), *Responding to the screen: Reception and reaction responses* (Chap. 5). Lawrence Erlbaum.

INDEX

ABOUT THE AUTHORS

Marianne Dainton (PhD, The Ohio State University) is a Professor of Communication at La Salle University in Philadelphia. She teaches interpersonal communication, intercultural communication, and communication theory. Marianne's research focuses on relationship maintenance. She is the author of six books: *Maintaining Relationships through Communication* (coedited with Dan Canary, published by LEA), *Applying Communication Theory for Professional Life* (coauthored with Elaine Zelley, published by Sage), *Maintaining Black Marriages: Individual, Interactional, and Contextual Dynamics* (published by Lexington Books), *Communication and Relational Maintenance* (with Scott Myers, published by Cognella), *Strategic Communication Research Methods* (with Pamela Lannutti, published by Cognella), and *Advanced Interpersonal Communication: Managing Communication Goals* (with Katie Neary Dunleavy, forthcoming from Cognella). Her personal life is spent eating her way through the city of Philadelphia, hanging at the Jersey Shore, and trying to pass as a local while visiting foreign countries.

Elaine D. Zelley (MA, PhD, The Pennsylvania State University; BA, Ursinus College) is an Associate Professor of Communication at La Salle University in Philadelphia. She teaches communication theory; communication ethics; interpersonal communication; organizational communication; group communication; and sex, gender, and communication. Elaine's interests focus broadly on women's roles and relationships including in the workplace and friendships. She was recently a contributing researcher for a collaborative census report on *The Gender Gap in Nonprofit Boardrooms*. She has also developed pedagogical expertise in curriculum assessment and in understanding by design (UbD). She has published in *Communication Yearbook* and has also coauthored several book chapters dealing with the topics of relationship maintenance, friendship, and competition.